Power and the

Manchester University Press

Power and the people

A social history
of Central European politics, 1945–56

*edited by Eleonore Breuning,
Jill Lewis and Gareth Pritchard*

Manchester University Press

Manchester and New York

distributed exclusively in the USA by Palgrave

Published by Manchester University Press
Oxford Road, Manchester M13 9NR, UK
and Room 400, 175 Fifth Avenue, New York, NY 10010, USA
www.manchesteruniversitypress.co.uk

Distributed exclusively in the USA by
Palgrave, 175 Fifth Avenue, New York,
NY 10010, USA

Distributed exclusively in Canada by
UBC Press, University of British Columbia, 2029 West Mall,
Vancouver, BC, Canada V6T 1Z2

British Library Cataloguing-in-Publication Data
A catalogue record for this book is available from the British Library

Library of Congress Cataloging-in-Publication Data applied for

ISBN   0 7190 7068 6 *hardback*
EAN   978 0 7190 7068 6
ISBN   0 7190 7069 4 *paperback*
EAN   978 0 7190 7069 3

First published 2005

14 13 12 11 10 09 08 07 06 05   10 9 8 7 6 5 4 3 2 1

Contents

III Youth

IV Women

List of contributors

Peter Barker lectures in the Department of German Studies at the University of Reading. He has published widely on the history of the GDR and on contemporary East Germany, including *Slavs in Germany – The Sorbian Minority and the German State since 1945* (London, 2000).

Vanessa Beck is a lecturer in Employment Studies at the Centre for Labour Market Studies, University of Leicester. She wrote her doctoral thesis on post-unification unemployment amongst East and West German women and is currently working on labour market segregation.

Eleonore Breuning is senior lecturer emerita in the History Department at the University of Wales Swansea. For twenty years she worked on the German Documents Project, Foreign and Commonwealth Office, and from 1985 to 1995 was Participating Historical Adviser.

Mark Dimond is a teacher in the History Department at the University of Wales Swansea. He has recently completed a doctoral thesis on the history of the Czech gymnastics movement, Sokol. He also runs a business in political consultancy specialising in links with the new member states of the EU.

Mark Fenemore is a lecturer in German history. He has published on youth subcultures and opposition in the GDR and is currently completing a book on the clashes which occurred between Stalinism and rock 'n' roll in Leipzig in the 1950s.

Dick Geary is professor of modern history at the University of Nottingham, a Fellow of the Alexander von Humboldt Foundation and founding editor of *Contemporary European History*. He has written several books on European labour, as well as an intellectual biography of Karl Kautsky, and *Hitler and Nazism* (second revised edition, London, 2000). He currently directs a project on Brazilian slaves and European workers.

Eva Hahn was a research fellow at the Collegium Carolinum in Munich until 1999, since when she has worked as a freelance historian in Oldenburg. She is the author of numerous articles on the intellectual history of Central

Europe in the nineteenth and twentieth centuries, and on Czech–German relations in particular. In 1999 she published two articles in the journal *Osteuropa* on the state of Czech studies in Germany, which sparked heated debate. For her publications, see www.bohemistik.de/evahahn.

Hans Henning Hahn is professor of East European History at the Carl von Ossietzky University of Oldenburg/Germany. He has specialised in Polish and Czech history. Recently his main fields of interest are historical research on national stereotypes and German attitudes to East European nations. He has edited *Stereotyp, Identität und Geschichte. Die Funktion von Stereotypen in gesellschaftlichen Diskursen* (Frankfurt/M, 2002), and written, together with his wife Eva Hahn, *Sudetoněmecká vzpomínání a zapomínání* (Prague, 2002).

Robert Knight lectures in the Department of Politics and International Relations at Loughborough University. He has published extensively on post-war Austria, including a documentation of post-war Austrian Cabinet discussions of Jewish issues: *'Ich bin dafür, die Sache in die Länge zu ziehen': die Wortprotokolle der österreichischen Bundesregierung von 1945 bis 1952 über die Entschädigung der Juden* (second edition, Frankfurt/Main, 2000). He is currently writing a book on assimilation politics and the Carinthian Slovenes.

Dagmar Kusá teaches in the Department of Political Sciences at Boston University. She is currently working on her dissertation thesis, 'Coming to terms with the past: politicization of ethnic identity in Slovakia', which focuses on the historical trauma of the Hungarian minority in Slovakia. She also works at the Nieman Foundation for Journalism at Harvard University.

Jill Lewis lectures in the Department of History at the University of Wales Swansea. She has published on inter-war and post-war Austrian history and is currently completing a study of post-war Austria, with particular reference to the mass strikes of 1950.

Alan McDougall is assistant professor in modern European history and European studies at the University of Guelph in Canada. He has published *Youth Politics in East Germany: The Free German Youth Movement, 1946–1968* (Oxford, 2004). He is currently working on a project examining the transition of young people from the Hitler Youth into the Free German Youth in Soviet-occupied East Germany after the Second World War.

Maria Mesner is research director of the Kreisky Archives Foundation in Vienna and lecturer in the Institute of Contemporary History at Vienna University. She is an expert on Austrian gender history. Her many publications on this topic include *Frauensache? Zur Auseinandersetzung um den Schwangerschaftsabbruch in Österreich nach 1945* (Vienna, 1994).

Andrea Pető is an assistant professor at the Central European University, Department of Gender Studies, in Budapest. Her specialism is gender history and her most recent publications include *The History of Hungarian Women in Politics, 1945–51* (Budapest, 2003).

Mark Pittaway is a lecturer in European studies at the Open University. He is the author of *Eastern Europe, 1945–2000* (London, 2004), and has published widely on Hungarian labour history.

Gareth Pritchard is a lecturer in modern European history at the University of Canterbury, New Zealand. He is the author of *The Making of the GDR, 1945 to 1953* (Manchester, 2000).

Karin M. Schmidlechner is professor of contemporary history at the University of Graz. She is also international editor of *h-women*. Her published research focuses on gender, youth culture and oral history. Recent publications include (with James Miller), *Die Liebe war stärker als das Heimweh: US-Immigration nach dem 2. Weltkrieg* (Graz, 2003).

Toby Thacker is a lecturer in modern European history at the University of Wales Swansea. He has published articles on dance music in the early GDR, on the censorship of music in the GDR, on American music in post-war Germany and on music broadcasting on the BBC German Service. He is currently working on the reconstruction of Bach and Handel biography in the GDR.

Glossary

Abwehrkampf	Defence struggle (of the Austrians of Carinthia against the South Slavs in 1918–19)
Agitprop	(Communist) agitation and propaganda
Alldeutsche Partei	Georg von Schönerer's Pan-German Party (Habsburg Empire)
Alte Verband	The Old Association (German Social Democratic miners' union, founded in 1890)
Antifaschistenausschüsse	Anti-fascist committees (founded in Germany in 1945)
Antifaschistische Frauenausschüsse	Anti-fascist women's committees (founded in Germany in 1945)
Arbeitsgemeinschaft Deutscher Sozialdemokraten aus der Tschechoslowakei	Working Group of Social Democrats from Czechoslovakia
Arrow Cross	Hungarian fascist movement that was briefly in power in Budapest between October 1944 and April 1945
Aufgebot	'Challenge': term used in setting tasks for East German youth organisations
Beneš decrees	Series of decrees which expropriated the property of ethnic German and Hungarian Czechoslovakians, and established terms for the expulsion of ethnic Germans to Germany and Austria, and of Hungarians to Hungary
Berlin Wall	Wall built in 1961 dividing East and West Berlin
Betriebsrat	Works/factory council (in Germany or Austria)
Betriebsvereinbarungen	Works agreements (concluded between labour and management in the British zone of occupation in Germany)
'Bevan boys'	Men who worked in the mines in Britain instead of doing military service during the Second World War
Bezirk	District

Bizone	American and British occupation zones of Germany
Bund der heimattreuen Südkärntner	League of Loyal Southern Carinthians
Bund der Landwirte	Landowners' Association; a Sudeten German group
Bundesländer	see *Land*
Bundestag	Federal parliament
Bundesvertriebenengesetz	(West German) Federal Law on Expellees
Christlichsoziale Bewegung	(Austrian) Christian Social Movement
Cominform	Communist Information Bureau, an organisation established in 1948 (and dissolved in 1956), the purpose of which was to co-ordinate policy across the various Communist states
Csemadok	Hungarian cultural association of workers, founded in 1949 in Czechoslovakia
Currency reform (Germany)	Replacement in June 1948 of the *Reichsmark* by the *Deutschmark* in the three western zones of occupation; the currency reform is usually seen as a major landmark in the economic revival of post-war West Germany
Democraticna fronta delovnega ljudstva/ Demokratischer Front des werktätigen Volkes	Democratic Front of the Working People (name adopted in 1949 by the OF (q.v.))
Demontage	Dismantling and removal (by the Allies of industrial plant from Germany and Austria as reparations)
Deutsche Gewerbepartei	German Business Party
Deutscher Osten	The German East
Deutschtum	Germandom
Distriktleiter	District leader (in East Germany)
Domowina	Sorbian cultural organisation in East Germany
Eindeutschungsfähig	Capable of Germanisation (Slavs deemed capable of Germanisation by the Nazis)
Einheitsgewerkschaft	Unified trade union (in West Germany)
First Republic	The Austrian state, 1918–34
Freizeitgestaltung	The organisation of leisure time (in East Germany)
gesetzgebende Körperschaften	(Quasi-legal) law-making bodies (in Austria)
Godesberg Programme	Party Programme of 1959 in which the SPD (q.v.) abandoned Marxism
Grundrechte	Basic rights (West German)
Hausarbeitstage	Domestic days (days of leave given to allow German women to attend to domestic duties)
Haus- und Strassen- beauftragten	House and street deputies (in East Germany)
Heimat	(German) homeland
Heimatkultur	(German) homeland culture
Heimattreue	Fidelity to the (German) homeland

Herrenvolk	The master race (Nazi term)
Hitlerjugend	Hitler Youth (Nazi youth organisation)
Junák	Czechoslovak scouting organisation
Junge Gemeinden	Christian youth groups in East Germany
Kader der Zukunft	Cadres of the future (an East German system for rewarding FDJ (q.v.) functionaries)
Kolkhoz	(Soviet) collective farm
Komsomol	Communist youth organisation of the USSR
Košice Programme	Agreement concluded in Moscow in March 1945 by representatives of Czechoslovak political parties, which laid out the major political tasks awaiting Czechoslovakia
Kreis	(German) area/ward
Kulturkampf	Cultural struggle (of Hungarian religious organisations against the post-war government)
Kulturträger	Bearers of the (German) cultural mission
Land (pl. Länder)	A regional administrative unit in Germany or Austria (also called Bundesland in post-war West Germany and Austria)
Landesregierung	Land (q.v.) government
Landesverräter	Traitor
Landtag	Regional assembly in Germany or Austria
Lastenausgleichgesetz	Law on the Equalising of Burdens (West German)
Marshall Plan	US plan for the economic recovery of Europe (1948), in which the Soviet Union prevented its satellites from participating
Minderheitenreferent	Local government representative responsible for minorities (in Carinthia)
Mitbestimmung	'Co-determination', the participation of workers or workers' representatives in management decisions in German and Austrian workplaces
Moscow Declaration	A joint declaration by the American, British and Soviets in 1943 to the effect that Austria had been the first victim of Nazi aggression, and that the Anschluß of 1938 was to be regarded as void
Munich Settlement	The outcome of the conference held at Munich in 1938 to discuss the future borders of Czechoslovakia
Narodni Svet koroških Slovencev	National Council of Carinthian Slovenes
Neulehrer	New teachers (in East Germany)
Orel	Catholic youth athletic body linked to the Czech People's Party
Parität	Parity (between decision-making groups in Austria)
Pionýrské organizace	Pioneers' Organisation (Czechoslovak Communist youth organisation)
Politburo	Communist party executive
Potsdam agreement	Allied agreement concluded in summer of 1945
Prague coup	The Communist take-over of government in

	Czechoslovakia
Prague Spring	Czechoslovak reform movement of 1968 suppressed by Warsaw Pact forces
Pravda	(lit. Truth) Soviet Communist Party newspaper
Proporz	Proportionality (distribution of ministerial portfolios in Austrian coalition governments)
Reichsbahn	The German railway network
Reichsprotektor	German war-time governor of Czechoslovakia
Republikflucht	Flight from (the East to the West German) Republic
Revier	District
Second Republic	The Austrian state from 1945
Seliger Gemeinde	Seliger Community (a Sudeten German Social Democratic organisation)
Serbska młodžina	Sorbian youth organisation, incorporated into the FDJ (q.v.) in 1949
Slet	Sokol gymnastic festival
Slovenska Ljudska Stranka	Slovene People's Party
Slovensko Kulturno Društvo/Slowenischer Kulturverein	Slovene Cultural League
Social Partnership	Austrian system of shared policy-making
Soforthilfegesetz	Law on Immediate Assistance (West German)
Sokol	Czech gymnastics and athletics organisation
Sonderschichten	Extra shifts (West Germany)
Staatsvolk	Majority population (Austria)
Stakhanovism	Soviet system of increasing productivity through worker competition
Städtetag	Festival day of a town or city (German)
Ständestaat	Austrian corporate state, 1934–38
Stasi	Abbreviation of *Staatssicherheitsdienst* (State Security Service) in East Germany (also known as MfS)
Sudetendeutsche Landsmannschaft	Organisation of Sudeten German Compatriots
Sudetendeutsche Volksgruppe	Sudeten German ethnic group
Sudetendeutscher Volkstumskampf	Struggle of Sudeten Germandom
Sudetendeutschtum	Sudeten Germandom
Tag X	'D-Day', a term coined by the Communist regime in East Germany to imply that the uprising of 17 June 1953 was in fact a *Putsch* attempt that had long been prepared in West Germany
Tass	Soviet news agency
Third Reich	Name given to Nazi Germany
Vertreibung	Expulsion (here, the expulsion of Sudeten Germans from Czechoslovakia)
Vertriebenenorganisationen	Expellees' organisations (Sudeten German)
Völkisch	Folkish (Nazi German)

Volksaufstand	Popular uprising (German)
Volksfront	Popular Front (German)
Volksgemeinschaft	People's community (Nazi German)
Volksgruppen	Ethnic groups (Germany and Austria)
Volkskammer	People's Chamber (East German)
Volkspolizei	People's Police (East German)
Volkssolidarität	People's Solidarity (East German charitable organisation)
Wandervögel	Ramblers (pre-1939 German hiking movement)
Warsaw Pact	Collective security treaty concluded in 1955 between the Soviet Union and its European satellites
Weimar Republic	Name given to the German state, 1919–33
Wende	The change (the collapse of Communism in Germany)
Wirtschaftstag	Austrian equivalent of German *Hausarbeitstag* (q.v.)
Wirtschaftswunder	Economic miracle (West German)
Yalta Agreement	Concluded in February 1945 between the United States, Great Britain and the USSR

Biographical notes

Altenburger, Erwin	(1903–84) Austrian Catholic trade unionist, member of the ÖVP, and deputy leader of the ÖGB
Attlee, Clement	(1883–1967) British politician (Labour) and Prime Minister from 1945 to 1951
Beneš, Eduard	(1884–1948) President of Czechoslovakia from 1935 to 1938, and again from 1946 to 1948
Bevan, Aneurin	(1897–1960) British left-wing Labour politician
Bevin, Ernest	(1881–1951) British trade unionist and politician (Labour) and Foreign Secretary from 1945 to 1950
Böckler, Hans	(1875–1951) West German trade unionist and first chairman of the DGB
Böhm, Johann	Austrian socialist trade unionist and leader of the ÖGB
Cefarin, Rudolf	Successor to Tischler (q.v.) as Slovene Catholic leader
Drtina, Prokop	Senior Czechoslovak politician
Ebert, Friedrich	President of the Weimar Republic (q.v.) 1919–25
Esterházy, János Count	Right-wing Czechoslovak politician of Hungarian ethnic origin, sentenced to life imprisonment for treason in 1947
Fiala, Gottlieb	(1891–1970) Austrian Communist trade unionist and deputy leader of the ÖGB
Fierlinger, Zdeněk	Head of the Czechoslovak government, 1945–46
Figl, Leopold	(1902–65) Austrian conservative politician, leader of the ÖVP and, from November 1945 to 1953, Austria's second post-war Chancellor
Gajda, Radola	Czechoslovak general, active in right-wing politics before 1939
Gottwald, Klement	(1896–1953) Czechoslovak Communist leader and, from 1948, President of Czechoslovakia
Grotewohl, Otto	Leader of the Social Democratic Party in the Soviet zone of occupied Germany between 1945 and 1946 and, from 1946, co-chairman of the SED

Hácha, Emil	President of Czechoslovakia, 1938–39
Helmer, Oskar	Austrian Minister of the Interior
Henlein, Konrad	(1898–1945) Sudeten German politician and leader of the separatist and pro-Nazi Sudeten German Party (SdP)
Hodža, Milan	Czechoslovak Prime Minister, 1936–38
Honecker, Erich	Chairman of the East German Communist youth organisation (FDJ) (q.v.)
Horthy de Nagybánya, Miklós	Regent of Hungary, 1920–44
Jaksch, Wenzel	Czechoslovak Social Democratic leader, in exile during the Second World War
Kazianka, Johann	Communist member of the Carinthian Landtag (q.v.)
Kodicek, Egon	Central secretary of the Austrian shoe-workers' union
Koenen, Wilhelm	KPD (q.v.) leader in Saxony, East Germany
Kopecky, Václav	Communist Minister of Information, Czechoslovakia
Krjeńc, Kurt	Sorbian Communist who took over leadership of the Domowina in 1950
Liebknecht, Karl	Founder of the KPD (q.v.)
Lodgman von Auen, Rudolf	Sudeten German politician
Mantler, Karl	President of the Viennese Chamber of Labour and Secretary of State in the Austrian Ministry of Provisions and Economic Planning
Masaryk, Jan	(1886–1948) Czechoslovak diplomat and statesman, Foreign Minister of the Czechoslovak government-in-exile in London and of post-war Czechoslovakia from 1945 to his death (under suspicious circumstances) in 1948
Masaryk, Tomáš	(1850–1937) President of Czechoslovakia, 1918–37
Mielke, Erich	Secretary of State and acting Minister in the Ministry for State Security, East Germany
Mindszenty, József	Hungarian Cardinal arrested, tried and imprisoned in 1948 on charges of treason
Nedo, Pawoł	Sorbian politician and leader of the Domowina from 1945 to 1950
Oelssner, Fred	Sorbian representative on the East German Politburo
Olah, Franz	Leader of the Austrian building and woodworkers' union
Pieck, Wilhelm	(1876–1960) East German Communist politician, co-chairman of the SED from 1946, and President of the GDR from 1949
Piesch, Hans	Austrian–German nationalist, governor of Carinthia from 1945 to 1947
Rákosi, Mátyás	Leading figure within the Hungarian Communist Party and a hard-line Stalinist
Renner, Karl	(1870–1950) Austrian socialist politician and, from April to November 1945, the first Chancellor of post-war Austria

Reusch, Paul	West German steel magnate
Schärf, Adolf	(1890–1965) Austrian socialist politician and Vice-Chancellor from 1945 to 1957
Schmidt, August	Chairman of the West German mineworkers' union
Slánsky, Rudolf	Secretary-General of the Czechoslovak Communist Party, executed in 1952
Steinacher, Hans	Austrian–German nationalist
Szakasits, Árpád	Hungarian President, arrested 1948
Szalási, Ferenc	Successor to Horthy (q.v.) as Hungarian head of state
Tischler, Josef (Joško)	(1902–79) Slovene Catholic leader
Tiso, Josef	President of Nazi-controlled Slovakia
Turba, Kurt	Student member of the Central Council of the FDJ (q.v.)
Tyrš, Miroslav	Founder of the Czech gymnastic association Sokol (q.v.)
Ulbricht, Walter	(1893–1973) German Communist politician and the most powerful figure within the KPD/SED in the post-war period
Wedenig, Ferdinand	Successor to Piesch (q.v.) as governor of Carinthia
Zwitter, Franci	Slovene nationalist in Carinthia

List of abbreviations

BÖS – Bund der österreichtreuen Slowenen
League of Austrian Slovenes, also known by its Slovenian acronym ZAS (q.v.)

CDU – Christlich Demokratische Union
Christian Democratic Union (East and West Germany)

CFM
Council of Foreign Ministers

ČSM – Československý svaz mládeže
Communist-dominated youth organisation in Czechoslovakia, successor organisation to the SČM (q.v.)

CWHIP
Cold War International History Project, Woodrow Wilson International Center for Scholarship

DFD – Demokratischer Frauenbund Deutschlands
Democratic Women's Association of (East) Germany

DGB – Deutscher Gewerkschaftsbund
German Trade Union Federation, the main trade union organisation established in post-war West Germany

FDGB– Freier Deutscher Gewerkschaftsbund
Free German Trade Union Federation, the official, Communist-dominated trade union organisation in East Germany

FDJ – Freie Deutsche Jugend
Free German Youth, the official youth movement in East Germany, established in 1946

GDR
German Democratic Republic (Communist East Germany)

GNP
gross national product

GST – Gesellschaft für Sport und Technik
Society for Sport and Technology (East German paramilitary youth organisation established in August 1952)

HJ – Hitlerjugend
Hitler Youth

KGB – Komitet Gosudarstvennoi Bezopasnosti
Committee for State Security (the Soviet Secret Police)

KPD – Kommunistische Partei Deutschlands
Communist Party of Germany

KPÖ – *Kommunistische Partei Österreichs*   Communist Party of Austria

LDPD – *Liberal-Demokratische Partei Deutschlands*   Liberal Party of (East) Germany

LPG – *Landwirtschaftliche Produktionsgenossenschaft*   Agricultural Production Co-operative (East German term for a collective farm)

MDP – *Magyar Dolgozók Pártja*   Hungarian Workers' Party (the ruling party in Hungary between 1949 and 1956, formed from a merger of the Hungarian Communist and Social Democratic parties)

MfS – *Ministerium für Staatssicherheit*   Ministry for State Security (East Germany)

MKP – *Magyar Kommunista Párt*   Hungarian Communist Party

MNDSZ – *Magyar Nők Demokratikus Szövetsége*   Democratic Alliance of Hungarian Women

MSZDP – *Magyarországi Szociáldemokrata Párt*   Hungarian Social Democratic Party

MP – *Magyar Párt*   Hungarian Party

NKVD – *Narodnyi Kommissariat Vnutrennikh Del*   People's Commissariat for Interior Affairs (the political police organisation of the USSR)

NWDR – *Nordwest Deutscher Rundfunk*   Northwest German Radio

ODD – *Organisation 'Dienst für Deutschland'*   'Service for Germany' Organisation (East German youth labour organisation)

OF – *Osvobodilna Fronta*   Liberation Front (organisation of Slovenian separatists in Austria)

ÖGB – *Österreichischer Gewerkschaftsbund*   Austrian Trade Union Federation

ÖVP – *Österreichische Volkspartei*   Austrian People's Party

POW   prisoner of war

RIAS   Radio in the American Sector (of Germany)

ROH – *Revoluční odborové hnutí*   trade union organisation in post-war Czechoslovakia

SA – *Sturmabteilung*   Nazi paramilitary organisation

SBZ – *Sowjetische Besatzungszone*   Soviet zone of occupation of Germany

SČM – *Svaz české mládeže*   Czech Youth Organisation

SED – *Sozialistische Einheitspartei Deutschlands*   Socialist Unity Party (the ruling party in East Germany created from a merger of the Communist Party and Social Democrat Party in the Soviet zone of occupation in April 1946)

SMAD – *Sowjetische Militäradministration in Deutschland*   Soviet Military Administration of Germany (the official title of the military government in the Soviet zone of occupied Germany from 1945 to 1949)

SNV – *Studentsky narodní vybor*   Czechoslovak Students' National Council

SPD – *Sozialdemokratische Partei Deutschlands*   Social Democratic Party of Germany

SPÖ – *Sozialistische Partei Österreichs*   Socialist Party of Austria

SVS – *Svaz vysokoskolského studentstva*	Union of Czechoslovak students (known between May and June 1945 as the Students' National Council, SNV (q.v.))
SWF – *Südwestdeutscher (Rund)funk*	Southwest German Radio
UN	United Nations
ÚRO – *Ústřední Rada Odborů*	Central Council of Unions in post-war Czechoslovakia (an umbrella organisation comprising the ROH (q.v.), the SVS (q.v.) and the SČM (q.v.))
USSR	Union of Soviet Socialist Republics
VdU – *Verband der Unabhängigen*	Association of Independents (a right-wing Austrian political party founded in 1949)
VP – *Volkspolizei*	'People's Police' (East Germany)
ZAS – *Zvesa Avstrijsih Slovencev*	see BÖS
ZR – *Zentralrat*	Central Council of the FDJ (q.v.)

1 *International boundaries in Central Europe, 1949–56*

2 *The languages of Central Europe c. 1945 (before expulsions)*

Introduction

The collapse of Communism and the end of the Cold War marked a turning point, not only in the history of post-war Central Europe, but also in its historiography. Most obviously, the opening of the archives of the former Soviet bloc enabled scholars of Cold War diplomacy to revisit many of the controversial questions which they had been debating for decades. Historians such as John Gaddis and Wilfried Loth have advanced intriguing reinterpretations of Soviet foreign policy and of the causes of the division of Europe in the immediate post-war period,[1] whilst collective ventures, such as the Cold War International History Project (CWIHP), are providing a stream of new documents and commentaries on the outbreak of the Cold War.[2]

But the demise of the Soviet bloc did not merely shed fresh light on old questions; it also created the potential for the historiography to develop in new directions, particularly in the field of social history. This book is primarily concerned with these innovative approaches, rather than the set-piece debates of traditional historiography.

Fresh historiographical perspectives

Before 1989, lack of access to relevant archives made life difficult for scholars wishing to study the social history of the Soviet satellite states during the immediate post-war period. Historians had access to official Communist documents and statistics, and to the testimony of refugees and the occasional defector, but on the basis of such limited evidence it was very difficult to reconstruct developments 'on the ground' in any detail. Much more was known about the stated policies of Communist regimes in regard to various social groups than about popular responses to such policies. Next to nothing was to be found in the historiography about the ways in which social realities might have influenced the formation and implementation of official policy.

To cite just one example: it had long been known in the West that Social Democrats in the Soviet sphere of influence had come under increasing pressure from their Communist rivals, and that, starting in East Germany in April 1946, there had been a series of mergers between Socialist and Communist parties to produce new, 'united' workers' parties in which the Communists invariably held the whip hand. Western scholars knew a fair amount about what impact these processes had on 'high politics', and they debated the degree to which such mergers were in fact shotgun weddings, representing a major step towards 'Stalinisation' and 'totalitarianism'. But they knew very little about how ordinary Social Democrats and Communists felt about these developments and how they responded to them, or about the interaction between 'high politics' and 'popular politics' inside the labour movement.[3] In short, studies of this issue before 1989 tended to be 'top-down', one-sided and superficial. Exactly the same criticisms could be made of our pre-1989 understanding of other aspects of social policy and popular politics in those parts of Central Europe that fell under Soviet domination.

Since the opening of the archives, a small army of social historians has been busily at work plugging these holes in our knowledge, and a huge number of monographs and articles has been published, particularly on East Germany. As a result, we now know a great deal more about the social history of issues such as land reform,[4] denazification,[5] economic policy[6] and policies towards ethnic minorities,[7] women,[8] young people[9] and workers.[10] Historians such as Norman Naimark and Mark Allinson have provided detailed and sophisticated analyses exploring, amongst other things, the relationship between 'high politics' and social realities in the years following the Second World War.[11] Although Czechoslovakia and Hungary have received rather less attention, the post-war social history of these countries, too, is in process of revision.[12]

The period since 1989 has also seen increasing interest in the social history of those parts of Central Europe that did not fall under Russian domination, namely, Western Germany and Austria. Particular areas of scholarly concern have been gender history,[13] the history of youth culture and 'Americanisation'[14] and the social construction of identities.[15] There are many possible reasons for this historiographical trend, one of which is no doubt the current popularity of gender and cultural history. In part, the rise of interest in social history is also a consequence of the fact that the collapse of Communism has made possible new approaches to the post-war history of the region.

Before 1989, both Austria and the Federal Republic were frontier states in the Cold War. The perceived need for internal unity in the face of the Soviet threat generated a dominant paradigm of historical writing that emphasised both German and Austrian victimhood at the hands of the Russians, and gave rise to a post-war consensus that enabled both countries to transform themselves into successful and prosperous democracies and bulwarks against Communism. The removal of the Iron Curtain, the shadow of which had long coloured the perspectives of historians, has now made it possible to take a fresh look at the founding narratives of post-war Germany and Austria. As Vanessa Beck, Dick Geary, Jill Lewis and Maria Mesner all demonstrate in their contributions to this volume (Chapters 13, 1, 3, 15), neither society was as free of social conflict as the traditional historiography would have us believe.

The fifteen years since the fall of the Wall, therefore, have witnessed a quantitative and qualitative transformation of the social historiography of post-war Central Europe on both sides of the Iron Curtain. Much progress has been made, but much remains to be done. Certain social groups – for example, the middle classes and the peasantry – have not yet received the attention that they deserve. Most of the scholars active in the field of social history have confined their attentions to individual countries and, as a result, there are still relatively few comparative studies. This is a serious lacuna, for a comparative approach to the history of post-war Central Europe can reveal far more than a study of any individual country in isolation. The lure of American culture, for example, was felt on either side of the Iron Curtain, and it is highly instructive to examine how the same cultural phenomenon was dealt with in different ways by different governments and elites, and with differing consequences. Our understanding of developments in the Soviet zone of occupation in Germany can be greatly enriched by comparing them to developments in the Soviet zone of Austria, where the Russians pursued a very different range of policies. Anybody concerned with the history of Austrian women can hardly fail to be interested in the experiences of Czech and Hungarian women, who endured similar material problems, but in different political contexts. In short, there is a strong case for setting the social histories of the countries in question in their regional context, which is precisely what this volume attempts to do.

Purpose and structure of the volume

The sixteen short chapters of this book cover various aspects of the social history of politics on both sides of the Iron Curtain (i.e. in East and West Germany, Austria, Czechoslovakia and Hungary) in the period 1945 to 1956, and provide a cross-section of the type of work currently being undertaken by researchers in the field. The contributors come from a range of countries (Austria, Germany, Hungary, Slovakia and the United Kingdom) and comprise a mixture of established historians and younger scholars engaged in pioneering research. Although all the chapters focus on social history and, in particular, the social history of politics, they also display a range of methodological approaches and thematic concerns. The volume thus provides a valuable insight into the state of recent research across the region.

'Central Europe' is a problematic and contested concept, and considerable thought was given to the selection of countries to be included in this book. The main reason for the choice of West Germany, East Germany, Austria, Czechoslovakia and Hungary was a pragmatic one: these territories formed the historic core of Central Europe, and were bound together by very strong historic, cultural and economic ties. They were also the countries that fell immediately to the east and west of the 'Iron Curtain', and were hence, in geographical terms, the most immediately affected by its advent. This particular selection, however, is not in any way intended to imply that countries such as Poland, Romania or Slovenia are not regarded by the authors as belonging to 'Central Europe'.

The individual chapters are organised into four sections dealing with workers, ethnic and linguistic minorities, youth and women. This structure was purposely chosen in order to enhance the comparative character of the volume. Each section contains four chapters which consider the position of these social groups in, respectively, West Germany, East Germany, Austria, and either Czechoslovakia or Hungary. Although many other social groups could legitimately have been included (for example, the middle classes, peasants and farmers, Christians, refugees etc.), the volume does not seek to provide a comprehensive survey. Instead, it was decided to focus on those social groups that have received the most historiographical attention and where the possibilities for comparison are accordingly greater.

The editors made a conscious decision to avoid matters relating to Cold War diplomacy and 'high politics', except where issues of social history are involved. Similarly, since one of the main purposes of this volume is to invite comparison between developments on either side of the Iron Curtain, issues affecting merely one side, such as the Stalinist purges in East-Central Europe of 1948–53, are covered only in outline.

The chronological limits of the volume should not require too much justification. The significance of 1945 is self-evident. The nominal closing date of this study, 1956, has an obvious significance for Hungary, but is less important in relation to German, Austrian or Czechoslovakian history. In practice, the time-span of this survey fades out gradually, rather than terminating abruptly, in the mid-1950s, by which time the societies of Central Europe on either side of the Iron Curtain had completed their transitions to consumerism in the west and Communism in the east. The chronological focus of the book thus embraces the period of post-war reconstruction, during which new types of social formation in Central Europe were constructed on the rubble of the old.

A number of important themes can be traced throughout this book, reflecting some of the salient concerns of historians working in the field. Here, there is only sufficient space to mention three of the most important.

Social control in post-war Central Europe

One major theme with which many of the contributors to this volume deal is that of the reimposition of social control in the states of post-war Central Europe. Under the circumstances of that time, it is hardly surprising that governments and elites on both sides of the Iron Curtain were extremely concerned with issues of social order. The war had bequeathed a terrible legacy in material terms: food, fuel, clothing, decent housing and all the other necessities

of life remained in desperately short supply for many years after the end of hostilities. Illness and diseases that resulted from hunger and cold proliferated. In
the rubble of Central Europe's ruined cities, the black market flourished and
crime, especially juvenile crime, was endemic. Millions of refugees, expellees
and other 'displaced persons' roamed the countryside and flooded into cities,
placing even greater pressure on scarce resources.[16] With millions of husbands
and fathers either fallen in battle or languishing in prisoner-of-war (POW)
camps, there were widespread fears that women and young people would
escape the constraints of the traditional gender and generational order.[17]

On top of all this, from the later 1940s new impulses from both West and
East began to be felt in Central Europe, furnishing elites with yet more reasons
for anxiety about social control. In West Germany and Austria, an improvement in the economic situation coincided with the emergence of new youth
identities, strongly influenced by American culture, which social elites often
found threatening. In East Germany, Czechoslovakia and Hungary, by contrast,
the later 1940s witnessed the introduction of harsher, Soviet-style policies that
sought to impose Communist control on every aspect of social life. On both
sides of the Iron Curtain there were continual skirmishes and occasional set-
piece battles along the border separating the public and private spheres.

In West Germany and Austria, the campaigns of elites to re-impose traditional modes of organisation and behaviour met with varying fortunes. Karin
Schmidlechner, in Chapter 11 on Austrian youth, and Toby Thacker, in Chapter
9 on music in West Germany, both comment on the failure of the authorities to
lure young people away from the attractions of Americanised youth culture. In
other instances the efforts of elites to re-impose social order were rather more
successful. Both Dick Geary and Jill Lewis, for example (Chapters 1 and 3), show
how the trade union bureaucracies in West Germany and Austria, respectively,
were tied to the interests of the state, and how rank-and-file workers, albeit after
a certain degree of friction, became subordinated to the union hierarchy. Similarly, Vanessa Beck, Gareth Pritchard and Maria Mesner (Chapters 13, 14, 15)
all argue that models of the family involving clearly defined traditional gender
roles underpinned reconstruction in both East and West Germany and in Austria. Beck, in her discussion of women workers in West Germany, and Mesner,
in her study of abortion in Austria, explore the ways in which the traditional
constraints on women's lives were first of all relaxed in the immediate post-war
period, before being vigorously reimposed by elites determined to restore pre-
war gender relations. Pritchard, by contrast, describes how the attempts by the
authorities to transform the role and status of women in East German society
foundered on deeply rooted social prejudices.

In those parts of Central Europe that fell under Soviet domination, the Communist authorities often tried to use organisational methods to increase their
purchase on society. One of their favourite ploys was to establish mass organisations for women, youth, workers, etc., which were designed to serve as 'trans-
mission belts', the purpose of which was to take Communist policy and

ideology to the masses and to act as agents of social discipline. Although some of these mass movements initially enjoyed a measure of success, they all eventually failed miserably, as a number of the chapters in this volume clearly illustrate. By the later 1940s, the Communists were increasingly resorting to coercion to impose the control that they had so signally failed to establish through persuasion, thereby alienating their subject populations yet further. This process of mutual alienation between Communist elites and diverse social groups is exemplified in Peter Barker's account of Sorbs in East Germany (Chapter 6), Alan McDougall's, Mark Fenemore's and Mark Dimond's consideration of youth in East Germany and Czechoslovakia (Chapters 1, 10, 12), Mark Pittaway's contribution on Hungarian workers (Chapter 4) and Gareth Pritchard's and Andrea Pető's chapters on women in East Germany and Hungary, respectively (Chapters 14, 16). As both McDougall and Fenemore demonstrate, however, the iron bonds that were constraining all Communist societies by the early 1950s could also prove surprisingly brittle. When underlying social tensions burst bloodily to the surface in East Germany during the uprising of June 1953, it was only the intervention of Red Army tanks that saved the regime from ignominious collapse. The same thing would happen, with even more bloody consequences, in Hungary three years later.

The revolution that never happened and the failure of Communism

A second theme that is explored by a number of contributors to this volume is the absence of revolution in post-war Central Europe and, linked to this, the failure of Communism to become a genuine mass movement capable of maintaining itself without Soviet support. Given the appalling material conditions obtaining after 1945, the relative weakness of the forces of revolution might seem rather surprising. It is not, after all, unknown in modern history for war to act as the midwife of revolution. The Second World War wreaked incomparably more destruction on Central European society than any eighteenth- or nineteenth-century conflict, and dwarfed even the First World War in scale and intensity. In its wake there was a discernible, though temporary, shift to the left of the political spectrum, accompanied by isolated outbursts of social protest. But, with the exception of the Hungarian uprising in 1956 (which in any case was due more to misguided Communist policies during the 1950s than to the legacy of the Second World War), there was nothing in post-war Central Europe that even approximated to a revolution.

One possible reason for the failure of the Second World War to create a revolutionary situation is touched on in a number of the contributions to this volume. Lewis, in particular, demonstrates in Chapter 3 how, in the face of the Soviet threat, trade unionist leaders and Socialist politicians in Austria made common cause with conservative politicians and business interests. In stark contrast to the situation after the First World War, class compromise rather than class conflict was the order of the day, and the corporatist state that emerged from the three-way alliance between labour elites, capital and government proved able to contain social protest.[18] Although Geary, in his contribution on the strikes of 1947 and 1948 (Chapter 1), alludes to it only indirectly, a similar process took place in post-war West Germany. Crucially, there was a parallel development in the Soviet sphere of influence in Central Europe. With the creation of 'official' trade unions in East Germany, Czechoslovakia and Hungary, the merger of Communist and Social Democratic parties in the period 1946-48, and the subordination of youth movements to Communist control in the later 1940s, the elites of the labour movement were effectively absorbed, more or less willingly, into the structures of the state apparatus.[19]

As a result of these processes, a gap was opened, in *all* the countries of Central Europe, between ordinary workers on the one hand, and the trade union and party functionaries who were supposed to represent their interests on the other. Since the lot of ordinary workers remained fairly desperate for several years after the end of the war, and since the normal trade union and political channels through which workers could express their grievances had been closed to them by the co-option of their own leaders into the establishment, there was a rash of spontaneous and uncoordinated outbursts of working-class anger, including the 1947 strikes in West Germany (see Chapter 1), the 1950 'general' strike in Austria (see Chapter 3), and the uprising of June 1953 in East Germany (see Chapters 2 and 10). By the mid-1950s, however, the destabilising potential of the gap between labour leaders and ordinary workers had been neutralised – in Austria and West Germany by prosperity, and in East Germany and Czechoslovakia by brutal oppression. Only in Hungary, where, from 1953 onwards, there was a paralysing split *within* the state apparatus, did the friction between ordinary workers and their self-professed representatives continue to pose a challenge to the established order.

But perhaps the most important reason for the absence of revolution in Central Europe in the post-war period was the unpopularity of Communist parties. Historians are fond of discussing post-war East-Central Europe in terms of the 'rise of Communist regimes', but in many ways these years can be said to have witnessed a failure of Communism so profound that the movement never recovered from it.

Taking their cue from Moscow, the various Communist parties of Europe had, during the Second World War, eschewed revolutionary militancy, embracing instead the idea of 'national' roads to socialism based on parliamentary politics and the construction of broad 'popular fronts' against fascism. In 1945, Communists throughout the region were confident that their apparent conversion to the principles of democracy, coupled with their programme of radical social reform, would enable them to win mass support and come to power democratically and under their own steam. Given the circumstances of the time, this did not appear to be an unrealistic expectation. After all, the Communist parties of France and Italy were doing exceedingly well, and even British and American observers expected that the appalling material conditions of Central

Europe, when combined with the region's long traditions of Marxist politics, would enable Communism to flourish.[20]

It soon became apparent, however, that, with the partial exception of Czechoslovakia, Communist dreams of electoral glory had been hopelessly optimistic. Humiliated in the first general elections in Hungary and Austria in November 1945, the Communists were also disappointed by election results in the Soviet zone of Germany in the autumn of 1946 and in the western zones of occupation in 1947. After this unsatisfactory start, Communist fortunes continued to decline and by the later 1940s it was blindingly obvious that, wherever free elections were still allowed, Communist parties would attract only minimal support, even in those working-class areas that had once been Communist strongholds.

As Lewis, Pittaway, Pritchard and Mesner all demonstrate in Chapters 3, 4, 14 and 15, one reason for the dismal performance of Communist parties was their close association with the Soviets and, by implication, with the depredations of the Red Army. Brutal and rapacious Soviet occupation policies in eastern Germany, eastern Austria and Hungary were hardly likely to win over the hearts and minds of those who suffered under them, particularly given the contrast with the apparent American generosity in the shape of Marshall Aid. In those Central European territories that fell under Soviet sway, Communist parties soon found themselves in a vicious circle: the more unpopular they became, the more they were forced to rely on the Soviets and upon the use of coercion, which in turn made them yet more unpopular. This process is dealt with explicitly in Fenemore's discussion of youth in East Germany (Chapter 10), and is touched on in a number of other contributions. In the western parts of Central Europe, by contrast, the Communists were unable to rely on Red Army bayonets to staunch their electoral decline, and by the mid-1950s the Party had ceased to exist as an effective political force in either Austria or the Federal Republic of Germany.[21] Indeed, so loathed were the Communists by the majority of Austrians and West Germans that anti-Communism became the glue that held together the fragile alliance that emerged of socialists, trade unionists, liberals, conservatives and not a few former fascists.

In 1945, the Communists had set out to construct a broad popular front of democratic forces against the far right. By the late 1940s, they had merely succeeded in provoking the formation of an alliance against them that stretched from committed socialists to the murkier marches of German and Austrian nationalism – a kind of popular front in reverse. It is unlikely that many West German or Austrian Communists would have appreciated this irony.

Cold War politics and social conflict

The end of the war in 1945 failed to bring with it the resolution of many of the long-standing social conflicts in Central Europe. Even before the partition of the region into Soviet and Western spheres of influence, and long before the construction of the Iron Curtain, there was much unfinished business along the fault-lines and fissures of Central European society. As the countries immediately to the east and west of the Iron Curtain embarked on the transition to Stalinism and consumerism respectively, new social conflicts were added to the old ones. It was, perhaps, inevitable that these existing and newly generated conflicts should become entangled in the quarrel between the superpowers in the sphere of high politics and diplomacy. The dynamics of this interaction between Cold War politics and social conflict is a third major theme with which our contributors concern themselves.

In her contribution on the Austrian 'general strike' of 1950 (Chapter 3), Lewis explores in some detail how the long-standing social fracture between capital and labour, which in some ways was actually intensified by post-war circumstances, nonetheless became subsumed into the Cold War confrontation between East and West. As Lewis shows, the Cold War had the effect of polarising the trade union movement, with pro-Russian Communist elements seeking to exploit class antagonisms, and pro-West moderates doing their best, in alliance with capital and the state, to contain them. Social protest, she concludes, had an ambiguous role in the formation of the new Austrian polity. Mass protest was opposed by the moderate union leadership, who feared that it would be utilised by the Communists to turn Austria into a Russian satrapy. Yet, at the same time, it was precisely the threat of mass protest that persuaded government and business in Austria to allow unions to play an important part in policy-making.

Pittaway (Chapter 4), in similar vein, investigates the way in which conflict between skilled workers and their managers in a Hungarian factory became entangled with the Cold War perspectives of the Communist state. In vivid detail, he demonstrates how, by the early 1950s, the plant had been identified by the state as a stronghold of 'right-wing Social Democracy', a blanket term used to link any form of opposition to the labour policies of the state to the machinations of American imperialism. Though the phrase 'right-wing Social Democracy' was an ideological construct, it emerged, as Pittaway shows, from the interaction of Communist policies and the realities of shop-floor micropolitics, and demonstrates how industrial relations in Hungarian factories were politicised by the Stalinist state.

The authors of several other contributions to this volume display a similar interest in the relationship between Cold War politics and social conflict. Fenemore, in Chapter 10 on East German youth, discusses how the Communist authorities 'drew on a common store of libel and innuendo' to label both young Christians and working-class street gangs as 'alien and other'. In particular, the authorities framed their generational conflict with non-conformist youth in terms of the larger struggle against the American enemy. Mesner, in Chapter 15 on abortion in Austria, explains how Socialist women abandoned their long-standing campaign to secure more liberal abortion legislation out of fear of disrupting the fragile coalition with conservative and Catholic forces against the Soviet menace. The significance of a traditional point of gender conflict in Austria was thus reformulated because of Cold War circumstances.

Perhaps the most obvious examples of Cold War politics interacting with existing social tensions are to be found in the section on ethnic and linguistic minorities. The outbreak of the Cold War drew a line across the topography of Central Europe. This new political frontier overlay, but did not erase, the ethnic and linguistic borders which for centuries had played so important and contested a role in Central Europe. In particular, the new political geography of Central Europe was mapped on to the historic linguistic boundaries dividing Germans from Slavs and Slavs from Hungarians. Deeply rooted conflicts along these messy linguistic borders had not been resolved by the Second World War; indeed, the racial policies of the Nazis and their allies had greatly intensified ethnic hatreds. With the outbreak of the Cold War, competing ethnic and linguistic groups attempted to exploit post-war circumstances to further their own agendas.

For example, as Peter Barker demonstrates in his chapter on Sorbs in post-war East Germany, the proponents of Sorbian particularism attempted to exploit the presence of their Russian 'slavonic brothers' to achieve their demands for greater autonomy. Unfortunately for the Sorbs, the Soviets, though in some ways sympathetic to the Sorbian cause, did not consider any further border changes to be in their great-power interests. The East German Communists, meanwhile, were not in the least bit sympathetic to Sorbian separatism, seeing it as an obstacle to their assertion of full political control over Sorb-inhabited territories. The only two powers in the region which were prepared to give the Sorbs even partial support were the Czechoslovak nationalist regime of Beneš and Tito's Yugoslavia, but the twists and turns of Cold War politics soon deprived both these parties of their ability to influence the Sorb question. As Barker shows, the Sorb National Council in Prague was shut down after the Communist coup in Czechoslovakia in February 1948, while the quarrel between Stalin and Tito in the same year caused Sorb organisations to be viewed with great suspicion on account of their erstwhile ties with the Yugoslav 'heretics'.

If the Prague coup had a negative influence on Sorb aspirations, it had, as Dagmar Kusá explains in Chapter 8, a rather different impact on the Hungarian minority in southern Slovakia. Between 1945 and 1948, Beneš, in pursuit of his dream of creating a homogenous Czechoslovak nation, had conducted a ruthless policy of 'ethnic cleansing' and forced assimilation *vis-à-vis* the Hungarian minority. After 1948, given the evident need for reconciliation with the 'fraternal' Communist state to the south, the Communists slowly reversed this policy of discrimination. Though no attempt was made to reverse the injustices of the period 1945-48, for example through the return of confiscated property, Hungarians were allowed, from the early 1950s onwards, to form their own associations and publish their own newspapers.

Chapter 5 by Eva Hahn on the Sudeten German '*Volksgruppe*' in the Federal Republic of Germany, and Chapter 7 by Robert Knight on the Slovene minority in the Austrian province of Carinthia, will be of particular interest to students of the relationship between Cold War politics and ethnic conflict in post-war Central Europe. The Sudetenland and Carinthia had long been regarded by their German-speaking inhabitants as bulwarks of German civilisation against the encroaching slavonic hordes. In both territories, there had emerged during the first half of the twentieth century a brand of racial (*völkisch*) politics that incorporated aggressive German nationalism, a maudlin cult of the soil and a strong sense of victimhood. After the outbreak of the Cold War, conditions were such as to allow these *völkisch* traditions to reassert themselves in a modified form, despite their strong connections with Nazism. In both cases, the German supremacist discourse was quietly dropped, to be replaced by an anti-Communist discourse that once again stressed the importance of 'Germandom' as a bulwark against the enemy to the east. The major change wrought by the Cold War was that the eastern 'other' was now defined in political rather than racial terms, but the cult of the soil, the sense of German victimhood and the aggressive German nationalism all remained.

The importance to regimes on both sides of the Iron Curtain of imposing social control, the absence of revolution together with the abject failure of Communist attempts to construct a popular front, and the interaction of Cold War politics with existing and newly generated social conflicts, are but three of the themes apparent in the contributions which make up this volume. It is hoped that observant readers of the various chapters will discern yet others.

The most important point, however, and the reason why this volume was produced in the first place, is that the social history of Central European politics in the post-war era is a dynamic field of modern European historiography, partly because of the availability of a mass of new archival evidence, and partly because of the new conceptual approaches that the end of the Cold War has rendered feasible. This volume is intended to serve as a contribution to the initial process of revision and re-evaluation. There can be little doubt that further comparative studies will yield evermore illuminating insights into the socio-political history of Central Europe during the early phases of the Cold War.

Notes

1 John Gaddis, *We Now Know* (Oxford, 1997); Wilfried Loth, *Stalin's Unwanted Child* (Basingstoke, 1998).
2 http://cwihp.sci.edu.
3 See, for example: Henry Krisch, *German Politics under Soviet Occupation* (New York, 1974); Reiner Pommerin, 'Die Zwangsvereinigung von KPD und SPD zur SED', *Vierteljahrshefte für Zeitgeschichte*, 36:2 (1988); Gregory Sandford, *From Hitler to Ulbricht* (Princeton, NJ, 1983); Dietrich Staritz, *Die Gründung der DDR* (Munich, 1984).
4 Arnd Bauerkämper, 'Auf dem Wege zum "Sozialismus auf dem Lande": Die Politik der SED 1948/49 und die Reaktionen in dörflich-agrarischen Milieus', in Dierk

Hoffmann and Hermann Wentker (eds), *Das Letzte Jahr der SBZ* (Munich, 2000); Jonathan Osmond, 'From *Junker* estate to co-operative farm: East German agrarian society 1945–61', in Patrick Major and Jonathan Osmond, *The Workers' and Peasants' State* (Manchester, 2002); Corey Ross, *Constructing Socialism at the Grass Roots* (Manchester, 2000), Chapters 2, 5, 9.

5 Gareth Pritchard, *The Making of the GDR, 1945–53. From Antifascism to Stalinism* (Manchester, 2000), chapter 4; Timothy Voigt, *Denazification in Soviet-Occupied Germany: Brandenburg, 1945-1948* (Cambridge, MA, 2000).

6 André Steiner, *Die Deutsche Wirtschaftskommission – ein ordnungspolitisches Machtinstrument?* in Hoffmann and Wentker, *Das Letzte Jahr der SBZ*; Raymond Stokes, *Constructing Socialism: Technology and Change in East Germany, 1945-1990* (Baltimore, 2000), Chapters 1, 2.

7 Peter Schurmann, 'The Sorbian Movement in Lusatia, 1945-1949', in Robert Pynsent (ed.), *The Phoney Peace* (London, 2000).

8 Donna Harsch, 'Approach/Avoidance: Communists and Women in East Germany, 1945–49', *Social History*, 25:2 (2000), 156-8 and 'The dilemmas and evolution of women's policy', in Major and Osmond, *The Workers' and Peasants' State*.

9 Ross, *Constructing Socialism at the Grass Roots*, Chapters 6, 10; Gareth Pritchard, 'Young people and youth movements in the Soviet zone of occupied Germany' in Pynsent, *The Phoney Peace*.

10 Pritchard, *The Making of the GDR*; Ross, *Constructing Socialism at the Grass Roots*, Chapters 3, 4, 8.

11 Norman Naimark, *The Russians in Germany* (Cambridge, MA, 1995); Mark Allinson, *Politics and Popular Opinion in East Germany* (Manchester, 2000).

12 The historiography of Czechoslovakia for the period 1945-56 is still heavily biased towards 'high politics', including, most notably, Karol Kaplan's *Five Chapters in February* (Prague, 1997) and František Hanzlík and Jaroslav Pospíšil, *The Twilight of Democracy* (Vizovice, 2000). The social history is deficient, though a picture of social developments is slowly emerging. The Institute of Contemporary History in Prague, for example, has produced a number of booklets on the plight of ethnic minorities living in Czechoslovakia in the period 1945–54, including 'The Greek community in Czechoslovakia, 1948–54' and 'The resettlement of Germans from Slovakia, 1944–53'. Other examples of recent work include Eagle Glassheim, 'National or social revolution? liquidating the Latifundia in Czechoslovakia', in Pynsent, *The Phoney Peace* and Norbert Kmet, *The Position of the Church in Slovakia, 1948–51* (Bratislava, 2000). The historiography of post-war Hungary is in a similar state. Much work has been done on 'high politics' and the revolution, such as Gábor Bátonyi's *Hungary* (London, 2005) and János Rainer's 'Ungarn 1953–56' in András Hegedüs and Manfred Wilke, *Satelliten nach Stalins Tod* (Berlin, 2000). There are, however, signs of increasing interest in social history, such as Mark Pittaway, *Eastern Europe: States and Societies, 1945-2000* (London, 2004); Andrea Petö, *Hungarian Women in Politics, 1945-51* (Budapest, 2003); Institute for the History of the 1956 Hungarian Revolution (www.rev.hu/archivum/archivum.htm, Oral History Archive).

13 Claire Duchen and Irene Bandhauer-Schöffmann, *When the War was Over: Women, War and Peace in Europe 1940-1956* (Leicester, 2000); Karin Schmidlechner, *Frauen in Männerwelten: Kriegsende und Nachkriegszeit in der Steiermark* (Vienna, 1997); Maria Mesner, *Frauensache? Zur Auseinandersetzung um den Schwangerschaftsabbruch*

in *Österreich* (Vienna, 1994); Petra Goedde, *GIs and Germans: Culture, Gender and Foreign Relations* (New Haven, CN, 2002); Elizabeth Heineman, *What Difference does a Husband Make? Women and Marital Status in Nazi and Post-war Germany* (Berkeley, CA, 1999); Maria Höhn, *GIs and Frauleins* (Chapel Hill, NC, 2002); Robert Moeller, 'Reconstructing the family in reconstruction Germany', in Robert Moeller (ed.), *West Germany under Construction* (Ann Arbor, 1997).

14 Reinhold Wagnleitner, *Coca-Colonization and the Cold War: the Cultural Mission of the US in Austria after the Second World War* (Chapel Hill, 1994). Edward Larkey, 'Americanization, cultural change, and Austrian identity', in David Good and Ruth Wodak (eds), *From World War Two to Waldheim: Culture and Politics in Austria and the United States* (New York, 1999); Kaspar Maase, 'Establishing cultural democracy: youth, "Americanisation", and the irresistible rise of popular culture', in Hannah Schissler, *The Miracle Years: A Cultural History of West Germany, 1949–1968* (Princeton, NJ, 2001); Diethelm Prowe, 'The "miracle" of the political–cultural shift: democratisation between Americanisation and conservative reintegration', in Schissler, *The Miracle Years*.

15 Wolfgang Kos and Georg Rigele (eds), *Inventur 45/55. Österreich im ersten Jahrzehnt der Zweiten Republik* (Vienna, 1996); Peter Thaler, *The Ambivalence of Identity: The Austrian Experience of Nation-Building in a Modern Society* (Lafayette, 2001); Günter Bischof and Anton Pelinka (eds), *Austrian Historical Memory and National Identity* (New Brunswick, 1997); Uta Poiger, 'Rock 'n' roll, female sexuality, and the Cold War battle over German identies', in Moeller, *West Germany under Construction*; Frank Biess, 'Survivors of totalitarianism: returning POWs and the reconstruction of masculine citizenship in West Germany, 1945-1955', in Schissler, *The Miracle Years*.

16 Mark Mazower, *Dark Continent: Europe's Twentieth Century* (London, 1998), Chapter 7; Mark Wyman, *DPs: Europe's Displaced Persons, 1945–1951* (Cornell, 1998); Thomas Albrich and Ronald W. Zweig (eds), *Escape through Austria: Jewish Refugees and the Austrian Route to Palestine* (London, 2002); Pertti Ahonen, *After the Expulsion: West Germany and Eastern Europe 1945–1990* (Oxford, 2004).

17 Claire Duchen and Irene Bandhauer-Schöffmann, *When the War was Over*; Heineman, *What Difference does a Husband Make?*

18 Jill Lewis, 'Austria 1950: strikes, "putsch" and their political context', *European History Quarterly*, 30:4 (2000).

19 Andreas Malycha, *Partei von Stalins Gnaden?* (Berlin, 1996); Pritchard, *The Making of the GDR*.

20 Patrick Major, *The Death of the KPD: Communism and Anti-Communism in West Germany, 1945–1956* (Oxford, 1997).

21 Stefan Berger and Hugh Compston (eds), *Policy Concertation and Social Partnership in Western Europe: Lessons for the Twentieth Century* (New York, 2002); Major, *The Death of the KPD*.

I
Workers

1

Social protest in the Ruhr, 1945–49

Dick Geary

'Capitalism is in its last gasps.' (Hans Böckler at the first trade union conference in the British zone, Hanover, 1946)

In the immediate aftermath of the Second World War, many European countries witnessed an upsurge in labour militancy and notable electoral successes for both the Social Democratic and Communist parties. Clement Attlee's election victory in the United Kingdom and Communist participation in governments in France, Italy and Czechoslovakia suggested to some that a new society was in the making. Yet most general accounts of the development of the Western zones of occupation in Germany and the emergence of the Federal Republic (except those by historians of the former German Democratic Republic, GDR) have rarely been noted for their attention to social protest in the immediate post-war years. Rather, the dominant paradigm of historical writing has been that of a collective overcoming of the carnage and material destruction of war, a success story, which ended in a new democratic state and the *Wirtschaftswunder* (the 'Economic Miracle'). This is scarcely surprising, for the democratic, as well as economic, achievements of West Germany between 1945 and the mid-1960s were colossal.[1] The recreation of successful capitalism in West Germany and the almost total disappearance of extremist politics (on both the right and the left) in the post-war period have thus seemed testament to social harmony. However, the years which followed the end of the Second World War in Germany's Western zones of occupation were free of neither the social problems nor the class-based aspirations which characterised other European societies after 1945. Moreover, the co-operation of labour in West Germany's economic recovery along free-market lines has sometimes disguised the very real conflicts and alternatives of the immediate post-war years.[2] These conflicts also cast doubt on the claims of some historians that traditional solidarities amongst the German working class were destroyed by the Nazis between 1933 and 1945, as a consequence of new (individualised) payment systems, technological rationalisation, the delivery of welfare services at the individual factory, the destruction of the organisations of the independent labour movement and the racial restructuring of labour.[3] This chapter hopes to cast some light on the unrest and aspirations of at least some workers in the American and British zones of occupation in the mid- and late 1940s, especially in the heartland of German heavy industry, the Ruhr. For these aspirations testify to the existence of at least some radical continuities in the history of German labour. However, I do not follow those who have seen in these aspirations a universal working-class challenge to German capitalism.[4] Rather, this chapter argues that some German workers had more radical aspirations than others in 1946–47 and that there was a marked de-politicisation of protest from 1948 onwards.

It is well known that 'socialist' views were widespread in Germany after the Second World War. As Volker Berghahn writes, 'the mood in all four occupation zones was distinctly "socialist" in the early years after the war'.[5] In May 1947, the official trade unions demanded not only the restoration of German economic and political unity but also land reform, a planned economy, the immediate socialisation of key industries, the banks and insurance companies and the creation of self-management bodies with trade union participation. The Social Democratic Party (*Sozialdemokratische Partei Deutschlands* – SPD) and the Communist Party (*Kommunistische Partei Deutschlands* - KPD) emerged victorious from the first (and only) free elections in the Soviet zone in 1946. In Hessen (in the American zone) almost 70 per cent of voters supported a clause in the new state constitution which allowed for the extension of public owner-ship in various areas of the economy. (The American occupiers subsequently deleted this clause!) At the SPD's 1946 Congress the party proclaimed its 'steadfast commitment to freedom and socialism', wishing to create a 'planned socialist economy'. Two years later the Western powers blocked a Social Demo-cratic attempt to socialise the coal industry of North Rhine-Westphalia. Amongst workers in the Ruhr, demands for the socialisation of the coal pits in 1946–47 came not only from supporters of the SPD and KPD but even from Christian Democratic miners. Moreover, the SPD emerged as the largest single party in the Landtag elections of North Rhine-Westphalia in 1947. Signifi-cantly, the party understood its success as a mandate for the socialisation of economic life.[6] In this context, it is important to realise that the differences between Social Democrats and Communists on this issue were far from clear-cut before 1948 at the earliest. Indeed, as is well known, it was not until the Godesberg Programme of 1959 that the SPD finally ditched a Marxist dis-course of socialism and class. This political history of Social Democratic aspi-rations is reasonably familiar, even if it occupies a relatively small place in the totality of work on post-war Germany. Less appreciated has been the appear-ance of demands for sweeping social change at shop-floor level and in numer-ous strikes and demonstrations between 1945 and 1948. For example, the *Deutschland-Jahrbuch* for 1949 quite simply tells us that '*Streiks im grösseren Umfang haben nicht stattgefunden* [no major strikes have taken place]'.[7] Neither the official report of the German Trade Union Federation (*Deutscher Ge-werkschaftsbund* – DGB) nor the memoirs of the Chairman of the Mineworkers' Union (August Schmidt) makes any mention of the strikes of early 1947 and early 1948.[8] This silence, however, reflects a long-standing tension between cautious trade union bureaucrats and more impetuous shop-floor activists, a tension which had been a characteristic of the history of trade unionism in Germany over several decades.[9] It does not represent a neutral portrayal of workers' behaviour or attitudes in the immediate post-war years. Even those (outside the GDR) who have discussed the social protests of 1946–48 have, with isolated exceptions, tended to see them primarily as responses to the desperate food and fuel shortages of the 1940s, as nothing more than 'apolitical' hunger marches and demonstrations.

It is obviously true that we need to analyse the material problems confronting German workers in those years before we can understand the various instances of social protest. Some of these problems were the result of the policies of the occupying powers, in particular of *Demontage* (the dismantling and removal of industrial plant as reparations) and denazification. Many workers were incensed by their treatment at the hands of the denazification courts, which were set up by the victorious Allies. They not only felt that their self-righteous conquerors had little comprehension of the realities of daily life in a police state, but also complained vociferously that the courts established by the victors to root out former Nazis only ever punished the small fry like themselves. At the same time, they protested, the managers of German industry, who had openly colluded with the Nazi regime and had seen their profits rise in consequence, went scot-free. Indeed, one major industrial dispute of 1948 involved workers' opposition to an American and British proposal to appoint Paul Reusch to the committee in charge of steel production in the 'Bizone' (as the American and British zones of occupation had become). For Reusch, the Director of the *Gute Hoffnungshütte*, a large steel firm in the Ruhr, had been an advocate of Nazi war aims. The threat of a strike, on this occasion with full support from the executive of the German Trade Union Confederation, led the Americans and British to back down.[10]

The dismantling of industrial plant by the victorious Allies and its shipment to Britain, France, the Soviet Union and the United States constituted a further cause of unrest on the part of German workers after 1945. For they recognised quite rightly that *Demontage* would slow down any potential economic recovery in the occupied zones and thus perpetuate unemployment in defeated Germany, especially as industrial production in 1946 stood at only 33 per cent of that in 1936. Such resentment was difficult to contain, not least because the adoption of the Marshall Plan and changing attitudes to German economic recovery on the part of the Americans and the British did not lead to a sudden end to dismantling – contrary to expectations. Even in April 1949, when the Western allies shortened the list of plants to be dismantled, 700 German factories still remained on the list. *Demontage* at the Salzgitter steelworks, for example, was halted only in April 1951, in the wake of demonstrations by German workers and a world-wide public outcry. There were many other instances of sit-in strikes to prevent dismantling, as at the major steelworks of the *Bochumer Verein*, where dismantling only began after April 1948.[11]

The problems of denazification and *Demontage*, however, were of only secondary importance when compared to the much more pressing issue of physical survival. First of all there was a massive housing crisis in post-war Germany, caused by fighting on the ground as well as by British and American bombing during the war. In the Ruhr town of Bochum about 80 per cent of homes had been destroyed, whilst in the district (*Revier*) as a whole only 50 per cent of the pre-war housing stock survived in 1945. This involved the destruction of some 1,405,000 housing units. Hamburg also lost 50 per cent and Bremen 46 per cent of its housing capacity.[12] The shortage of accommodation was further compounded by a massive influx of German refugees from Eastern Europe (some 12 million in total), who had either fled from their former homes to avoid retribution from newly installed national governments (in Czechoslovakia, Poland and the Baltic States) or had been driven out of their homes by the area's new rulers. The British zone of occupation alone absorbed 2.2 million of these refugees (11.3 per cent of the zone's total population), whilst the American zone took in even more: 2.6 million.[13]

The second and most pressing material problem was that of food supply in a country whose agriculture had been denuded of manpower and whose transport system lay in ruins. Responsibility for feeding the population now fell upon the occupying authorities, who were not invariably sympathetic to the plight of the local population. In 1945 the British set the food ration in their zone of occupation at 1,500 calories a day. (At the same time British homeland rationing set a daily target of 2,900 calories and UN experts calculated 2,650 calories as the essential daily minimum.) However, in the first three years of occupation the average daily *per capita* intake in the British zone was no more than 1,300 calories. Moreover, in early 1947, after a vicious winter and a breakdown in the German transport system, the situation was considerably worse than these figures suggest, especially in the major cities of the Ruhr. In Dortmund in the second week of May 1947, for example, average consumption fell to only 630 calories a day. In neighbouring Hagen it was only 29 calories higher. At the same time around 10,000 people suffered from hunger-related diseases in the Northern city of Hamburg.[14] (This did not prevent John Hynd, the British Minister with responsibility for German affairs, claiming that the food situation had improved considerably!)[15] Under these circumstances, it is scarcely surprising that some Germans engaged in various forms of 'self-help', such as pillaging food from farms and supply trains.[16] Others demonstrated and went on strike to protest against what they saw as hunger rations. In the strike waves of both early 1947 and early 1948 it was the food crisis which provided the spur to action. On 3 February 1947, 15,000 workers from the Krupp steel plant protested in Essen. Three days later 20,000 German workers took to the streets of Oberhausen and Mühlheim/Ruhr. Thereafter the protests escalated. On 25 March 1947, 80,000 strikers downed tools and protested against the food rations in Wuppertal. They were followed on 27–28 March in the depths of the hunger crisis by another 80,000 in Düsseldorf and on 1–2 April by 30,000 in Dortmund, 100,000 in Duisburg and 40,000 in Gelsenkirchen. On 12 May 1947, 120,000 Hamburg workers participated in a similar action. If anything, the strikes and demonstrations of January 1948 involved even more workers in even more towns.[17]

It should be noted that these two strike waves, though triggered by a crisis in the supply of food, were not simply aimed at increasing food rations. Even in 1948, when the strike wave was less 'political', as we will see, demands for higher rations were accompanied by calls for the dismissal of certain officials in the administration. Demands for land reform and the creation of representative supervisory bodies to oversee rationing were also common, though such calls were again clearly related to the problems of food distribution. As distinct from the strikes of 1948, however, those in the early months of 1947 involved more sweeping demands for what might be described as 'socio-political' reform. For example, on 3 April 1947, 300,000 miners in the Ruhr coalfield downed tools for 24 hours. Their demands included the socialisation of the mines, the appointment of proven democrats and especially trade union representatives to public positions, the dismissal of incompetent officials in the food administration and tough measures against black-marketeers. Earlier, shortly after the demonstration of 3 February 1947, a shop-stewards' conference of all Essen industries had also demanded land reform, the socialisation of the mines and of other key industries without compensation and the replacement of certain officials in the administration by trade union nominees. It also called for fascists and reactionaries to be purged from both the public administration and private economic organisations. A demonstration of 7,000 workers in Leverkusen on 22 March 1947 further demanded the reorganisation of the German chemical industry along lines that would 'prevent a selfish striving for power at the expense of the people'.[18] In 1947, therefore, although food rations still formed a pivotal concern for strikers and demonstrators, there also existed a set of demands which involved a fundamental challenge to existing social relationships (land reform, socialisation), and a desire to see off 'fascists and reactionaries'. This was less true in 1948.

Some kind of 'de-politicisation' of protest seems to have taken place in the Ruhr between the middle of 1947 and the strikes of January 1948. Of fifty-two recorded strikes in North Rhine-Westphalia in 1947, only three were concerned with wages, whilst no fewer than thirty-one involved disputes over the powers of factory councils.[19] Significantly, the issue of managerial control had been central to miners' protests in the Ruhr in both the Imperial and Weimar periods, as it was also to the revolutionary upheavals of 1918–23. It was no accident that syndicalism put down roots among the miners of this region.[20] Furthermore, a concern with the issue of worker participation in management

21

had played an important role in the formation of various 'anti-fascist committees' (*Antifaschistenausschüsse*) which had sprung up at the end of the war, often under Communist leadership. These aimed at a democratisation of economic as well as political life. Such committees were subsequently controlled, emasculated and ultimately dissolved by the occupying military authorities, not least because of the pathological anti-Communism of the Americans. A similar story applies to the 'factory councils' (*Betriebsräte*), which had sprung up spontaneously in 1945 and attempted to arrogate considerable powers of management to themselves in several industrial enterprises. Again, these were viewed with suspicion by the occupying powers. As a result, the Factory Council Law of the Allied Control Commission of 10 April 1946 made some attempt to circumscribe their authority. However, this legislation was sufficiently vague to allow widely differing interpretations of its provisions. These different interpretations subsequently gave rise to several industrial disputes, one of the most important of which took place at the Bode–Panzer works in Hanover in 1946. Here a highly unionised labour force (of over 90 per cent) confronted their employer, who also happened to be head of the German Employers' Association, which had recently decided upon a strategy to limit the powers of the *Betriebsrat*. With the unusual but energetic support of the local trade union organisation, a point to which we will return, the workers won the dispute after twenty-three days of industrial action. This victory was followed by a further twenty-one works agreements (*Betriebsvereinbarungen*) in the British zone, though in most cases the concessions granted to the factory council by the employer were significantly less extensive than those at the Bode works. Subsequently the British authorities introduced 'parity co-determination' (*Mitbestimmung*) in the larger firms of the German iron and steel industry specifically to forestall demands from the workforce for more sweeping changes. Extensive demands for the democratisation of industrial management thus accompanied those for socialisation in 1947 and lay at the core of workers' demands.[21]

In 1948, the situation was radically different. Whereas thirty-one of the fifty-two strikes in North Rhine-Westphalia in 1947 had been concerned with issues of management, only seven of seventy-five strikes related to managerial prerogatives in 1948. It was now the wage issue which was dominant and characterised thirty-three of the industrial disputes of 1948. Similarly, the mass demonstrations of 1948 were concerned almost exclusively with hunger rations and eschewed the issues of public ownership and managerial control.[22] Significantly, the organisations of German employers had failed to anticipate this de-politicisation of labour protest. They had not only recognised the *political* nature of the industrial disputes of 1946–47 but had come to believe – wrongly, as it turned out – that the early post-war conflicts were but the prologue to a real and more general confrontation between capital and labour in Germany.[23] So what had changed?

One explanation of the de-radicalisation of the demands of German labour between 1947 and 1948 relates at least in part to the involvement of different sectors of the workforce in the two waves of strikes. In 1947, coal miners played a much more prominent role than they did in 1948, when steel workers, whose traditions were in the main not radical, predominated. The radical traditions of solidarity amongst Ruhr miners, on the other hand, seemed to have survived the Third Reich and Nazi persecution, as Tim Mason, Klaus Wisotzky and Detlev Peukert have shown.[24] Moreover, German miners found themselves in an especially strong position in the labour market in the immediate post-war years, for this was one industrial sector where the victorious Allies were not concerned to limit output. On the contrary, the German coal industry was meant to increase output to enable the North German Coal Control Agency to organise the compulsory export of coal to the victors at below world market prices. This created a demand for labour in the pits of Germany at precisely the same time that the huge numbers of foreign workers who had been imported by the Nazis as slave labour were returning home. In fact, some 300,000 foreign workers were repatriated from the coalmines of the Ruhr alone after the end of the war. There was in consequence a massive labour shortage, which was further compounded by a 20 per cent reduction of the number of German males aged between eighteen and 40 in the course of the Second World War. As a result, the occupying powers first of all adopted a strategy of conscription, in order to send young German males down the mines (the equivalent of the 'Bevan boys' in the United Kingdom). When it turned out that this strategy created as many problems as it solved, however, the authorities resorted to a system of incentives, primarily in the form of increased rations, to lure workers into the pits. In consequence German coal miners enjoyed an extremely powerful bargaining position in the labour market, despite the fact that the overall level of unemployment in the British zone of occupation in the second half of 1947 was around 30 per cent (though the official figure was much lower). This strength explains in part why miners were prepared to demand much more than immediate improvements in their food rations in 1946 and 1947.[25] However, another – historical – explanation becomes important in this context.

The grievances of miners in the Ruhr in both the Imperial and the Weimar periods had almost invariably involved issues of authority and complaints about authoritarian management. After 1900, some pitworkers in the Ruhr demonstrated syndicalist tendencies. In the revolutionary upheavals at the end of the First World War a massive socialisation campaign in the Ruhr, which embraced roughly 75 per cent of the pit workforce, was as much about control of daily life in the individual pits as it was about social ownership. Moreover, from its very inception in 1890 the Free (i.e. Social Democratic) Miners' Union, the *Alte Verband*, featured socialisation as an ambition in its rule book.[26] Hence it was perhaps not surprising that the struggles of miners in 1946–47 should possess a dimension that went beyond questions of the food ration. This 'political' dimension was reinforced by the strength of the KPD in some of the mining communities of the Ruhr. Towns such as Herne, Recklinghausen, Gelsenkirchen and Wanne-Eickel had registered high KPD votes in the Weimar

Republic. In fact the KPD was the largest single party in Herne from 1924 until the Nazi seizure of power in 1933. Although almost half of all Communist militants were imprisoned, thrown into concentration camps or murdered in the Third Reich, the Nazis did not succeed in extinguishing the appeal of the KPD to significant numbers of workers in the Ruhr. In fact, the KPD here enjoyed an enhanced moral authority in the aftermath of Nazi terror. Thus, although the KPD won only 9.4 per cent of the votes cast in the *Land* elections of 1947 (still, incidentally, higher than the liberals' 9.3 per cent), it won 14 per cent of the popular vote in North Rhine-Westphalia as a whole and over 20 per cent in the following towns: Duisburg, Oberhausen, Gelsenkirchen, Gladbeck, Reckling-hausen, Bochum, Castrop-Rauxel, Dortmund, Herne and Wattenscheid. In some places, such as Remscheid, Solingen, Bottrop and Wanne-Eickel, the Communists won the support of 28 per cent or more of the electorate.[27] These electoral successes in the growing climate of Cold War should not be underestimated, and stand comparison with levels of support in the Weimar Republic. We are certainly not talking about a 'lunatic fringe' of the German working class. Yet these relative successes were nothing like as impressive as the role and influence of Communists in pit and factory assemblies, where it was often they who led the campaign for socialisation and *Mitbestimmung* and who organised resistance to the working of extra shifts (*Sonderschichten*) in the pits. Their influence is attested above all by the results of the factory council elections. On 20 November 1945, eighty pits in the Ruhr gave KPD delegates 44 per cent of their votes (SPD 28 per cent). Two months later, ninety-six pits voted 44.2 per cent Communist (SPD 25 per cent). In March 1946, a further forty-four coalmines in the Ruhr gave 42.1 per cent of their votes to the KPD (SPD 25.8 per cent). In all the pits of the *Revier*, the Communists won 38.8 per cent of the votes cast in *Betriebsrat* elections (SPD 36 per cent) in 1946, 31 per cent (SPD 33 per cent) in 1947 and 33 per cent (SPD 36 per cent) in 1948. Only in 1949 did the KPD vote in pit council elections fall below 30 per cent (to 27 per cent), when that of the SPD rose to 43 per cent. In the first *Bundestag* elections of 1949, of course, the KPD received only 5.7 per cent of the popular vote.[28] These figures suggest strongly that it was not Nazi persecution that destroyed German Communism, but rather the Cold War.

It is therefore clear that the KPD retained a strong presence in some factories and mines after 1945 but that this presence declined significantly in 1948 and 1949, when the strength of both the SPD and the official trade unions grew. This partly explains the de-politicisation of industrial disputes in the same period, when the intensification of the Cold War and the KPD's unswerving support for the Soviet Union increased its difficulties and hardened the divisions between Communists and Social Democrats, and between Communists and the official trade union leadership. In fact, one of the major differences between 1947 and 1948 was the increasing strength and organisation of the DGB at both national and local level. Trade unions had been established in the British zone from 6 August 1945, when the occupying authority allowed their

– gradual – development. By 1948, 42 per cent of the labour force in the British zone (some 2.8 million employees) had joined these unions. (In the American zone, union density stood at 38 per cent and in the French 30 per cent at the same point in time.) The industrial disputes of 1946–47 had originated on the shop floor and combined economistic concerns with more sweeping challenges to managerial authority and property rights. Those of 1948 were increasingly under the control of moderate trade union bureaucracies which, encouraged by the dominant American voice of the Bizone authorities, were increasingly quick to denounce strikes led by Communists as 'political manipulation'. A virulent campaign was waged against Communist influence in the mines and factories. On occasion, the official unions colluded with management and the occupying authorities to remove Communist shop-stewards; and the unions were noticeably reticent in the face of the dismissal of two KPD Ministers in North Rhine-Westphalia in 1948. Centralised German unions had been suspicious of shop-floor militancy and spontaneity from the 1890s, in the revolutionary upheavals at the end of the First World War and in the Weimar Republic, as they were of the anti-fascist committees of 1945. That the old elite of trade union functionaries rapidly regained control of the movement after 1945 perpetuated such suspicions. The DGB also inherited the classic distinction between trade union work (economism) on the one hand and the world of politics (peopled by political parties) on the other. If anything, this position was reinforced by the advent of the *Einheitsgewerkschaft* (the unitary union – i.e., a union meant to be neutral in terms of religious confession and politics) after the Second World War.[29]

The period between 1945 and 1948 therefore demonstrated two kinds of continuity, as far as German labour was concerned: on the one hand, the survival of aspirations for radical social change before the Cold War really set in and before the success of the *Wirtschaftswunder* and, on the other, the persistence of tensions between the limited aspirations of central union leaderships and more radical shop-floor protest.

Notes

1 On West German economic growth, see Alan Kramer, *The West German Economy, 1945–55* (Oxford, 1991); Werner Abelhauser, *Wirtschaft in Westdeutschland 1945–1948* (Stuttgart, 1975) and *Wirtschaftsgeschichte der Bundesrepublik Deutschland 1945–1980* (Frankfurt/Main, 1983); Volker Berghahn, *The Americanisation of German Industry* (Leamington Spa, 1986); Helga Grebing *et al.* (eds), *Die Nachkriegsentwicklung in Westdeutschland 1945–1949: (a) Die wirtschaftlichen Grundlagen* (Stuttgart, 1983).

2 See Christoph Klessman and Peter Friedemann, *Streiks und Hungermärsche im Ruhrgebiet 1946–1948* (Frankfurt/Main, 1977).

3 T. W. Mason's seminal *Arbeiterklasse und Volksgemeinschaft* (Opladen, 1975) detected various forms of daily opposition amongst workers in Nazi Germany. His revised English version of the book, *Social Policy in the Third Reich* (Oxford, 1993) was

already more circumspect about working-class behaviour and identities, and this was even truer of his article 'The containment of the German working class in Nazi Germany', reprinted in *Nazism, Fascism and the Working Class* (Cambridge, 1995), 231–73, which portrayed a working class that was at least partially susceptible to Nazi rhetoric in the aftermath of the destruction of independent trade unions and the socialist parties. Many other historians have gone even further, believing that the period between 1933 and 1945 saw a substantial restructuring of the German labour force and significant changes in the mentalities of German workers. Tilla Siegel's *Leistung und Lohn in der nationalsozialistischen 'Ordnung der Arbeit'* (Opladen, 1989) concentrates on the new individualised wage systems, which militated against solidarity in the workplace. It has also been argued that industrial rationalisation weakened the power of skilled workers, who had traditionally formed the backbone of working-class organisation, as did the delivery of social welfare at the individual factory. See Tilla Siegel and Thomas von Freyberg, *Industrielle Rationalisierung unter dem Nationalsozialismus* (Frankfurt/Main, 1991); Carola Sachse, *Angst, Belohnung, Zucht und Ordnung* (Opladen, 1987); *Betriebliche Sozialpolitik als Familienpolitik in der Weimarer Republik und im Nationalsozialismus* (Hamburg, 1987) and *Siemens, der Nationalsozialismus und die moderne Familie* (Hamburg, 1990); Dagmar Reese *et al.* (eds), *Rationale Beziehungen* (Frankfurt/Main, 1993); Rüdiger Hachtmann, *Industriearbeit im 'Dritten Reich'* (Göttingen, 1989). On the significance of symbolic concessions by the Nazis to the German working class, see Alf Lüdtke, 'The "honour of labour": industrial workers and the power of symbols under National Socialism', in David Crew (ed.), *Nazism and German Society* (London, 1994), 67–109. For the racial restructuring of the German labour force, see Ulrich Herbert's *Hitler's Foreign Workers* (Cambridge, 1997). For perceptive general surveys, see Günter Morsch, *Arbeit und Brot* (Frankfurt/Main, 1993) and Tilla Siegel, 'Whatever was the attitude of German workers?', in Richard Bessel (ed.), *Fascist Italy and Nazi Germany* (Cambridge, 1996), 61–77. That this work makes many valid points is beyond dispute. However, even before the Nazis came to power, many German workers, especially those employed in agriculture, handicrafts and domestic industry, and those resident in the provinces, had never subscribed to a politics of class. Hence both the SPD and the KPD were much stronger, both absolutely and proportionally, in Germany's largest cities. The same point could be made about many female employees, who remained distant from the politics of the Left. Secondly, the experience of mass and long-term unemployment in the Depression had already served to fragment and demobilise significant sections of the German working class. See Richard J. Evans and Dick Geary (eds), *The German Unemployed* (London, 1987). Thirdly, it may be mistaken to imagine that pay systems and workplace experience generate solidarity. See Dick Geary, 'Working-class identities in Europe', *Australian Journal of Politics and History* 1 (1999), 20–34. In any case, most German workers were not employed by 'rationalised firms'. Indeed, increases in productivity in the Third Reich were not great, especially in international perspective, and the really massive modernisation of German industrial plant had to wait until after the Second World War. This is clear from the economic histories: Richard Overy, *The Nazi Economic Recovery* (London, 1982); Harold James, *The German Slump* (Oxford, 1986); Volker Berghahn, *The Americanisation of West German Industry* (Leamington Spa, 1986). Fourthly, post-war continuities, as demonstrated here, require at least some qualification of arguments of discontinuity.

4 Ute Schmidt and Tilman Fichter, *Der erzwungene Kapitalismus: Klassenkämpfe in den Westzonen 1945–1948* (West Berlin, 1971), 23–30 and Jeremy Leaman, *The Political Economy of West Germany: An Introduction* (London, 1988), 36ff. This interpretation is decisively rejected by Lutz Niethammer, 'Rekonstruktion und Desintegration: Zum Verständnis der deutschen Arbeiterbewegung zwischen Krieg und Kaltem Krieg', in Heinrich August Winkler (ed.), *Politische Weichenstellungen im Nachkriegsdeutschland 1945–1953* (Göttingen, 1979), 26–43.

5 Volker Berghahn, *Modern Germany* (Cambridge, 1982), 185.

6 Christoph Klessman and Peter Friedemann, *Streiks und Hungermärsche*, 21, 33; Volker Berghahn and Detlev Karsten, *Industrial Relations in West Germany* (Oxford, 1987); Ossip K. Flechtheim (ed.), *Dokumente zur parteipolitischen Entwicklung in Deutschland seit 1945* (Berlin, 1963), iii, 17–20; Michael Schneider, *A Brief History of German Trade Unions* (Bonn, 1989), 230.

7 Klessman and Friedemann, *Streiks und Hungermärsche*, 14.

8 *Geschäftsberichte des Deutschen Gewerkschaftsbundes (britische Besatzungszone) 1947–1949* (Cologne, 1949); August Schmidt, *Lang war der Weg* (Bochum, 1958).

9 See the following articles in Wolfgang J. Mommsen and Hans-Gerhard Husung (eds), *The Development of Trade Unionism in Great Britain and Germany, 1880–1914* (London, 1985): Michael Grüttner, 'The rank-and-file movements and the trade unions in the Hamburg docks', 114–32; Klaus Tenfelde, 'Conflict and organization in the early history of the German trade union movement', 201–18; Dirk Müller, 'Syndicalism and localism in the German trade union movement', 239–49. Also Klaus Tenfelde, 'Linksradikale Strömungen in der Ruhrbergarbeiterschaft', in Hans Mommsen and Ulrich Borsdorf (eds), *Glückauf Kameraden!* (Cologne, 1979), 202ff.; Dick Geary, 'Radicalism and the German worker', in Richard J. Evans (ed.), *Politics and Society in Wilhelmine Germany* (London, 1978), 267–86; Manfred Bock, *Syndikalismus und Linkskommunismus* (Meisenheim, 1969); Dick Geary, 'Rhein, Ruhr und Revolution', *Mitteilungsblatt des Instituts zur Geschichte der Arbeiterbewegung*, 7 (1984), 30–6.

10 Klessman and Friedemann, *Streiks und Hungermärsche*, 53ff.

11 *Ibid.*, 19; Karl Hardach, *The Political Economy of Germany in the Twentieth Century* (Berkeley, CA, 1980), 95. For other work on *Demontage* see Alan Kramer, *Die britische Demontagepolitik am Beispiel Hamburgs* (Hamburg, 1990) and *The West German Economy, 1945–1955* (Oxford, 1991), 59–61, 117–21.

12 G. W. Harmsen, *Reparationen, Sozialprodukt, Lebensstandard* (Bremen, 1948), 95; Kramer, *The West German Economy*, 71ff.

13 Abelshauser, *Wirtschaft*, 100; Kramer, *The West German Economy*, 10–11.

14 Hardach, *The Political Economy*, 98; Klessman and Friedemann, *Streiks und Hungermärsche* 23; Kramer, *The West German Economy*, 73–82.

15 *Der Spiegel* (3 April 1947).

16 Kramer, *The West German Economy*, 83–8.

17 Klessman and Friedemann, *Streiks und Hungermärsche*, 41–53.

18 *Ibid.*, 42–6.

19 *Bericht des Arbeitgeberausschusses NRW über die Jahre 1945–1948* (Düsseldorf, 1948), 76.

20 See n. 9.

21 Klessman and Friedemann, *Streiks und Hungermärsche*, 37ff. On the Anti-fascist Committees (*Antifa-Ausschüsse*), see Lutz Niethammer *et al.*, *Arbeiterinitiative 1945*

(Wuppertal, 1976); Günter Benser, *Die KPD im Jahre der Befreiung* (Berlin, 1985) and 'Antifa-Ausschüsse – Staatsorgane – Parteiorganisation', in *Zeitschrift für Geschichtswissenschaft*, 26 (1978), 791ff.

22 Klessman and Friedemann, *Streiks und Hungermärsche*, 40.

23 *Westdeutsche Wirtschaftskorrespondenz* (27 September 1947).

24 On the relatively pacific history of German steel workers, see David Crew, *Town in the Ruhr* (New York, 1979), which compares them with more strike-prone miners. See also Elisabeth Domansky-Davidsohn, 'Der Grossbetrieb als Organisationsproblem des DMVs', in Hans Mommsen (ed.), *Arbeiter-Bewegung und industrieller Wandel* (Wuppertal, 1980), 96ff. On miners under Nazism, see Mason, *Arbeiterklasse*; Detlev Peukert, *Ruhrarbeiter gegen den Faschismus* (Frankfurt/Main, 1976); Klaus Wisotzky, *Der Ruhrbergbau im Dritten Reich* (Wuppertal, 1982). John R. Gillingham's *Industry and Politics in the Third Reich* (London, 1985) is rather more sceptical of opposition amongst miners, though his claims are countered by Detlev Peukert and Frank Bajohr, *Spuren des Widerstands* (Munich, 1987).

25 On the revival of coal production, see Kramer, *The West German Economy*, 29–30, 81–2, 92–5; Mark Roseman, 'The uncontrolled economy', in Ian Turner (ed.), *Reconstruction in Post-War Germany* (Oxford, 1989), 93–124.

26 See n. 9. Also Klaus Tenfelde, *Sozialgeschichte der Bergarbeiterschaft an der Ruhr im 19. Jahrhundert* (Bonn, 1981) and Hans Mommsen, 'Soziale und politische Konflikte an der Ruhr 1905 bis 1925', in Mommsen (ed.), *Arbeiterbewegung*, 64.

27 *Jahrbuch Nordrheinwestfalen 1949* (Düsseldorf, 1950), 323ff.

28 G. Schädel, *Die KPD in Nordrheinwestfalen von 1945–1956* (Bochum, Phil Diss, 1974), 47; G. Mannschaft and J. Seider, *Der Kampf der KPD im Ruhrgebiet* (Berlin, 1962), 53, 208; *Rheinische Zeitung* (11 November 1949).

29 Michael Schneider, *A Brief History*, 237; Diethelm Prowe, '"Ordnungsmacht und Mitbestimmung": The post-war labour unions and the politics of reconstruction', in David E. Barclay and Eric D. Weitz (eds), *Between Reform and Revolution: German Socialism and Communism from 1840 to 1990* (Oxford, 1998), 397–420.

2

Young workers, the Free German Youth (FDJ) and the June 1953 uprising

Alan McDougall

On 17 June 1953, the *Freie Deutsche Jugend* (FDJ) leadership was hastily summoned to the youth organisation's headquarters on Unter den Linden in central Berlin to discuss the escalating popular unrest in the capital and across the GDR. As this emergency meeting went on, a crowd of demonstrators – including many young people – passed by on their way to the Brandenburg Gate and tore down the extra security barriers that had been erected during the night to protect the imposing structure of the *Haus der Jugend* (House of Youth). One of the functionaries inside FDJ headquarters on that day, the Central Council (*Zentralrat* – ZR) student secretary, Kurt Turba, later recalled the uncomfortable recognition that 'the leadership of an organisation that deeply represented the interests of the young' had been forced 'to protect itself from thousands of its own members with steel grilles and iron bars'.[1]

It had not always been like this. The FDJ of 1946–47 was very different from the deeply unpopular Communist 'mass youth organisation' that was forced so suddenly onto the defensive in June 1953. In the period immediately after its founding in March 1946 as a 'united, democratic and non-partisan' organisation for young people of all political and social backgrounds, the FDJ had not been simply, or even mainly, a school of Communist indoctrination. Its primary organisational stronghold had then consisted of residential groups in urban and – in particular – rural areas, whose main purpose was to organise leisure-time activities (including sports and dance events, concerts, hikes and trips to the cinema) for the many young people without the money or means to otherwise enjoy themselves.[2] Though less important, there was also a political side to the FDJ's early appeal. It provided educational and career opportunities to young people – especially those from working-class backgrounds – who were either genuinely enthused by, or at least able to accept, its relatively inclusive 'anti-fascist' political programme.[3] Yet, by the summer of 1953, young workers – prominent in the strikes and walkouts that briefly engulfed the GDR in mid-June – were tearing up their FDJ membership books and leaving the youth organisation in droves.

This chapter attempts to explain how and why such a sorry situation came to pass – how and why the FDJ became, in the words of one of its senior functionaries, little more than a 'leadership without an army'.[4] It firstly recounts the experiences of the FDJ and young East Germans during the June unrest, before going on to examine in detail the gulf that emerged between the FDJ leadership and the GDR's youth population during the twelve months that preceded the uprising: a gulf that is central to understanding the role of young people on 17 June 1953 and that also reveals the fragile hold exerted by the SED regime over East German society during the early 1950s. Such was the FDJ's unpopularity and ineffectiveness during this period that only the intervention of Soviet tanks saved it from disintegration and collapse. The lessons learned by the party and FDJ leadership in the wake of the uprising – as well as those that went unheeded – set the boundaries for future displays of youth dissent in Walter Ulbricht's East Germany. 17 June also provided a case study that was largely ignored by Communist youth organisations elsewhere in the Soviet bloc when faced with similar anti-Stalinist uprisings in the later 1950s and the 1960s.

The FDJ and the young on 17 June

The June 1953 uprising in East Germany was the first major anti-Stalinist revolt in the Soviet bloc after the Second World War, embracing more than 350 towns and villages and more than 500,000 protestors. Recently declassified Soviet sources suggest that as many as 209 people may have been killed during the bloodshed which followed the armed Soviet intervention on the afternoon of 17 June.[5] The FDJ's role in the unrest, however, is a subject that has been treated in detail by surprisingly few historians. Before 1989 the paucity of documentary evidence made it difficult to judge the speculative claim of the West German historian Hanns-Peter Herz that 'about 70 per cent' of FDJ members demonstrated against the SED regime on 17 June.[6] Since the collapse of the GDR and the opening of its archives, it has been possible to give a more comprehensive account of the youth organisation during the June unrest. Yet an in-depth study is still lacking. Most of the relevant articles and books are furnished with plentiful extracts from a small number of party and FDJ documents, but offer little detailed analysis.[7]

The behaviour of young people during the June 1953 uprising can be divided into three main groups. Firstly – and often forgotten, particularly in the West German literature that depicted 17 June as a *Volksaufstand* or 'popular uprising' – there was the minority of young people who defended the SED regime against what party propaganda quickly came to describe as *Tag X* ('D-Day'), an 'attempted fascist counter-revolutionary *Putsch*'. This took two main forms: continuing to work through the strikes that paralysed parts of the GDR economy on 16 and 17 June and defending targeted buildings such as factories and local FDJ headquarters against crowds of angry demonstrators.[8] Young SED loyalists were thin on the ground. But it would be erroneous to dismiss their influence entirely, or to suggest that they simply did not exist in June 1953.

Secondly, there was the larger minority of young East Germans who actively participated in the uprising. Despite the plentiful archival sources now available to historians, no precise figures are known here. More young people actively protested against the SED regime than defended it. But pre-*Wende* estimations in the West that the majority of young East Germans participated in the strikes, walkouts and demonstrations are exaggerated. Particularly in many rural areas and places of higher education, youth unrest was in fact minimal in June 1953.[9]

The involvement of young people in anti-regime protests at this time worked on two levels. On one level, it constituted an 'outburst of violence' on the part of a disillusioned and largely apolitical part of East German society.[10] Documentary sources such as the profiles of young offenders compiled by the East German secret police (*Stasi* or MfS) in Magdeburg reveal that young people were frequently culprits in cases involving aggressive misbehaviour during the June unrest. These included breaking into a variety of public buildings such as police stations, district FDJ headquarters and schools; destroying property such as furniture, banners and files; and even assaulting individuals such as an MfS official and a collective farm (LPG) brigade leader.[11]

On another level, however, the actions of at least some young protestors in June 1953 went beyond such chaotic and sporadic scenes of violence into more organised and politicised protest. It is an exaggeration to claim that the majority of young dissenters on 17 June were 'more interested in western radio, western fashion and dancing than in politics'.[12] Young factory workers were not just impressionable hotheads who unquestioningly followed their older colleagues into trouble. Indeed, they were sometimes themselves at the head of walkouts and strikes. One young worker at the rubber factory in the Berlin district of Lichtenberg, for example, incited his colleagues to strike with a 'Three Point Programme', which called for a wage increase, free elections in the GDR and the withdrawal of plans to dismiss workers in the factory's economy drive.[13] At the Schultheiß brewery in the neighbouring district of Prenzlauer Berg, thirty young workers attempted on 18 June to provoke a new strike under the slogans 'we are not working under the pressure of the tanks' and 'we demand the release of those arrested [on 17 June]'.[14] Particularly in the factories, though also to a lesser extent in certain schools and universities, some youth protest thus had a political edge.

The overwhelming majority of young East Germans, however, were neither active defenders nor active opponents of the SED regime. They took up a third position that was characterised by the 'neutral' attitude of keeping a low profile and staying out of trouble. Among those who refused to come to the rescue of the East German state in its hour of need were large numbers of FDJ members and functionaries – in theory the 'millions-strong' *avant-garde* of the Marxist–Leninist youth movement in Germany. The FDJ secretary in the southwestern region (*Bezirk*) of Gera at the time of the uprising later conceded that the FDJ leadership organs there were 'paralysed' and 'played absolutely no role' on

17 June. He was unable to recall one example from the whole *Bezirk* of an FDJ leadership 'decisively' standing up to the strikers and demonstrators.[15]

In contrast, examples of 'cowardly' conduct on the part of FDJ officials in June 1953 were numerous. One particularly striking instance of this 'capitulatory' behaviour concerned the FDJ leadership organisation in the district (*Kreis*) of Jena-Land. Functionaries there 'disguised' the local FDJ headquarters on 17 June by taking down all slogans and flags. They then vacated the building as soon as it was stormed by a crowd of demonstrators, leaving behind a notice announcing that they had decamped to the FDJ headquarters in the neighbouring district of Jena-Stadt. In discussions a day later, the district functionaries from Jena-Land all refused to do any work in local FDJ groups without some sort of armed protection – on the grounds that, as one of them argued, 'in the villages, people are already waiting to hang me'.[16]

This fear of popular reprisals and desire to stay out of trouble was even more prevalent among ordinary FDJ members. Common indicators of their uncommitted attitude included refusing to wear the FDJ's blue-shirted uniform in public; failing to speak in defence of the Soviet intervention at FDJ meetings called after 17 June (or even failing to attend such meetings); and leaving the youth organisation for good. Between late 1952 and late 1953, FDJ membership figures dropped by more than 40 per cent from just under 2 million to just over 1.1 million.[17] Much of this mass exodus took place during the weeks and months after the June uprising.

This general portrait illustrates the stark sense of disillusionment with SED rule that was common among young East Germans in June 1953. As even the party leadership conceded privately in the aftermath of the uprising, 'the idea of socialism' had been 'shaken' among many young people.[18] So what had gone so badly wrong? How had the FDJ, and the SED regime more generally, fallen into such disrepute among a section of society with which the Communist movement – in Germany and elsewhere – had always sought so strongly to identify itself?

The FDJ and the building of socialism, 1952–53

The youth revolt of 17 June was not born of anti-communism *per se*. Nor was it, as some Western historians have claimed, a plea for the establishment of a re-unified and 'democratic' (that is to say, liberal and capitalist) Germany. It is more appropriate to view the behaviour of young people in June 1953 as the inevitable result of the fall-out from the catastrophic policies adopted in the name of 'accelerated socialist construction' in the GDR from mid-1952 onwards. Of course, such 'short-term' factors did not exist in a vacuum. Broader geo-political and socio-economic realities – in particular the escalating tensions of the Cold War in Europe and the GDR's futile efforts to prevent the mass migration of its population to the more affluent West (*Republikflucht*)[19] – constantly undermined the SED regime's efforts to create a popular and prosperous East

German state. Nonetheless, it is hard to dispute the argument that the party's disastrous crash course in socialism provides the key to understanding *Tag X*.

We can discern three main areas in which the SED's programme of 'accelerated socialist construction' affected GDR youth and the FDJ: its devastating impact upon the youth organisation's cadre ranks; the impact on young people of key socialist policies (most notably, remilitarisation and the increased workload in heavy industry); and the decline of organised leisure-time activities within the framework of the FDJ. Taken together, they illustrate the administrative, political, and socio-economic problems that brought the FDJ to its knees in June 1953. Time and again in reports on the youth organisation's experiences on and around 17 June, one reads of FDJ groups – particularly in the factories – that either existed only notionally or that were understaffed and thus 'incapable of work' (*arbeitsunfähig*). Such groups were powerless to prevent large numbers of young workers from joining anti-regime strikes and demonstrations. This temporary paralysis of the youth organisation at grass-roots level can be only partially explained by the panic and fear that was created by the threat of mob violence. It was in fact largely the product of the constant requisitioning of the best FDJ cadres for posts elsewhere in the burgeoning GDR state apparatus during 1952 and early 1953 and the concomitant heavy workload that was heaped upon the shoulders of the remaining – often young, inexperienced and politically 'unreliable' – FDJ functionaries.

As the self-styled 'helper and fighting reserve of the party', the FDJ had served as a reservoir for future party and state cadres since the late 1940s. But it was only in the spring and summer of 1952 that this drain on its resources reached unmanageable proportions. In late May, at its 4th parliament in Leipzig, the FDJ took on 'sponsorship' of the campaign for remilitarisation in the GDR, a campaign that was centred upon mass youth recruitment for the forerunner to a national army, the People's Police (*Volkspolizei* – VP). Less than six weeks later, at the SED's 2nd party conference (9–12 July), Walter Ulbricht officially announced the beginning of the programme of 'accelerated socialist construction', in which 'state power' – with all of its accompanying bureaucracy – was to play the key role.[20]

This premature march towards socialism in the GDR quickly wrought havoc in the cadre ranks of the FDJ, which was naturally the first port of call for newly created or expanding institutions on the lookout for young and skilled administrators, activists and soldiers. An extensive party report into the youth organisation's work in November 1952 revealed that 'at least 10–15 per cent' of the leading cadres in local FDJ groups had departed for the VP. The upheavals were so extensive in some places – particularly in rural areas and in factories – that the FDJ existed 'on paper only'. When one also takes into account the skilled FDJ cadres who were lost at this time to other branches of the party and state apparatus, it is hardly surprising that – as the November 1952 report admitted – 'between 40 and 60 per cent' of local FDJ groups lacked leadership organisations, while twenty-eight of the GDR's districts were without FDJ secretaries.[21]

To make matters worse, the decimation of the FDJ's cadre apparatus coincided with an unsustainable increase in the workload of the average youth functionary. Under the prestige-seeking and overambitious leadership of Erich Honecker, the united youth organisation was stretched to breaking point. The tasks set in the 'challenge' (or *Aufgebot*) adopted in the name of the East German president, Wilhelm Pieck, at the 2nd ZR session in August 1952 aptly illustrate the FDJ chairman's 'delusions of grandeur'.[22] In addition to recruiting young people between the ages of eighteen and twenty-five for the VP, every FDJ group was also instructed to recruit sixteen- and seventeen-year-olds for the short-lived youth labour project, the '"Service for Germany" Organisation' (*Organisation 'Dienst für Deutschland'* – ODD);[23] to evaluate the 'historic' resolutions of the 2nd party conference in membership meetings; to mobilise FDJ members in industry and agriculture for participation in 'socialist competitions' to fulfil quotas for the Five-Year Plan; to develop a 'happy youth life' (i.e. a full leisure-time and sporting programme) according to the wishes of its members; to increase membership numbers; and to create teaching circles for the second half of the FDJ's 'school year', in which young people were taught the basic tenets of Marxism-Leninism.[24]

As the party report from November 1952 – like countless other archival sources – graphically reveals, the vast majority of FDJ leadership organisations were in no position to carry out such a broad and demanding range of tasks. Overburdened and understaffed, the FDJ apparatus was utterly unprepared for a serious crisis on the scale of 17 June 1953.

It would, however, be misleading to suggest that the FDJ's difficulties in 1952 and 1953 stemmed only from the personnel crisis created by the demands of 'accelerated socialist construction'. In fact, the problems lay not just with the messengers, but also with the message itself. In two areas in particular – the remilitarisation campaign and work in the factories – policies that were associated specifically with the more radical course adopted by the SED in 1952 triggered widespread discontent among the GDR's youth population.

With its call for the rapid expansion of heavy industry at the expense of consumer goods, the programme announced by Ulbricht in July 1952 immediately increased the pressure on the East German industrial working class. Many of its problems – in particular the issue of fulfilling ever-increasing production quotas – affected young and old workers alike. But there were also more youth-specific aspects to the growing discontent in the workplace. In many factories, for example, qualified and well-trained apprentices were not employed in positions worthy of their skills. In the headlong rush to fulfil unrealistic production targets, young workers frequently ended up working on unsafe or poor-quality machines or doing the dirty work that their more senior colleagues shunned.

The increased focus on production also widened the gulf between FDJ leadership organisations and FDJ members in the factories. Organising leisure-time activities and social gatherings dropped rapidly down the youth organisation's list of priorities. Its increasingly detached and bureaucratic working methods minimised direct contact with young workers. On the 'day of activists' at the Brandenburg steel and sheet-metal factory on 13 October 1952, for example, the FDJ group could not honour anyone with the FDJ medal for 'outstanding achievements in the Five-Year Plan' because its leadership did not know which young workers to propose.[25] Such incidents, which were hardly uncommon, reveal the extent to which FDJ factory leadership organisations had lost touch with their members during the early 1950s.

Of all the policies associated with the SED's increasingly militant path to socialism, none was more unpopular among young East Germans than the remilitarisation campaign that was inaugurated under Soviet instructions during the spring of 1952. Just seven years after the end of the Second World War, and with the FDJ's previously pacifist rhetoric fresh in many minds, youth opposition to the idea of an East German army was almost universal. Young East Germans walked out of meetings called to discuss VP recruitment. Even full-time FDJ functionaries refused to volunteer for the VP or to recruit others for it. Numerous individuals and even entire FDJ groups resigned from the youth organisation in protest against the new policy – witness the young student at the art college in Weißensee, who sent his torn up membership book to the district FDJ leadership by post, together with a letter of resignation in which he commented: 'Sad that our organisation, to which I have belonged since it was founded, should concern itself with military toughening up to such an extent that I have the feeling that I belong to the HJ [*Hitlerjugend* – Hitler Youth].'[26]

These widespread 'pacifist' notions were hardened variously by parents reluctant to lose more of their children to war; by the Church, which still exerted a powerful influence – particularly in rural areas – on East German society during the early 1950s; and by the Western media.[27] But they stemmed ultimately from a fundamental desire to avoid any sort of military service that was encapsulated in a remark attributed to young railway workers in Leipzig: 'we are fed up and don't want to play soldiers again'.[28] Even the use of coercive measures – such as threatening reluctant youths with the sack from their regular jobs if they failed to 'volunteer' for the VP – rarely had the desired effect. It thus transpired that only the 'best' FDJ members (i.e., the minority of committed Socialists who were invariably also the most active members of the youth organisation) departed for the armed forces.

Though the worst effects of the remilitarisation campaign had passed by the summer of 1953, it had a long-term negative impact on youth perceptions of the East German state and the FDJ. In comparison, the short-lived and abortive campaign of persecution against the youth groups of the Protestant Church (the *Junge Gemeinden*) during the first half of 1953 – which was largely confined to some schools and universities – was a relatively minor bugbear for the majority of the GDR's youth population.[29] Both the recruitment campaign for the VP and the stricter regime in the workplace represented the unattractive face of 'accelerated socialist construction' for the young: more onerous duties and fewer rights; increased levels of coercion and propaganda; and the FDJ's retreat from its wider role as a social organisation into a much narrower 'campaign-style' concept of political and economic mobilisation.

Reports from the late summer and autumn of 1953, when chastened FDJ workers were instructed to abandon their offices and paper work and 'go to the young', repeatedly showed that what young people wanted above all from the FDJ was more fun. They wanted the return of the so-called 'happy youth life' (*das frohe Jugendleben*) that had been so conspicuous by its absence from the FDJ's work since the late 1940s – and particularly since the 4th parliament in May 1952. Various factors shaped the youth organisation's shifting attitude to the leisure-time interests of its young constituents at this time.

Firstly, as indicated in the introduction to this chapter, it is important to recognise that the FDJ of 1952–53 was a very different organisation from the amalgamation of anti-fascist youth committees that had first emerged in March 1946. In the early years, life in the grass-roots organisations of the FDJ, the majority of which were situated in residential areas, was often 'relaxed'. Ideological issues were hardly discussed at all, while 'fun' events – from dancing to skiing – topped the agenda.[30] By the early 1950s, the situation had changed dramatically. With the SED's focus now firmly concentrated on production, the focal point of the FDJ's activity also switched to the factories. The youth organisation's previously strong presence in the GDR's residential areas fell away. In particular, its influence in the countryside waned, leaving the field open for the *Junge Gemeinden* to become the chief organiser of youth leisure-time activities in many villages.[31] The FDJ's declining status as the purveyor of a 'happy youth life' was further eroded by the creation in August 1952 of the Society for Sport and Technology (*Gesellschaft für Sport und Technik* – GST), a paramilitary youth organisation that relieved its senior partner of many of the responsibilities for organising sports events for young people. By 1953 the FDJ lacked any real points of attraction in its activities outside the struggle to realise the SED's generally unpopular political and economic campaigns. Other aspects of its work had fallen by the wayside.

A second important factor in the FDJ's declining interest in youth 'organisation of leisure time' (*Freizeitgestaltung*) was also related to the increased focus on fulfilling its role as the party's 'helper and fighting reserve'. From the late 1940s onwards, when the youth organisation had been re-structured along the hierarchical lines of 'democratic centralism', the SED leadership had encouraged a 'cadres of the future' (*Kader der Zukunft*) system, according to which loyal FDJ functionaries were eventually rewarded for their service with posts in the party apparatus. By 1953 the FDJ was a huge and unwieldy operation, with a large annual budget from the East German state and a sizeable central apparatus of career-minded youth cadres. Functionaries, particularly at district level and above, were increasingly preoccupied with doing the party's bidding at any cost rather than meeting genuine youth needs. Bureaucratisation had set in. The average FDJ functionary spent most of his or her working day writing reports and attending meetings. Little time was set aside for organising football matches or weekend hikes, or for developing lively youth club programmes. Youth leisure-time activities thus tended to take place outside the FDJ's sphere of influence, a development that – as one party investigation into the youth organisation's work in the autumn of 1953 concluded – encouraged the 'worship of American culture' among certain sections of the GDR's youth population.[32]

However, the FDJ's failure to provide the 'happy youth life' promised in its propaganda was not simply caused by its gradual metamorphosis into a bureaucratic, production-based organisation. A third factor beyond its control was also of great importance, namely, the ongoing material shortages in the GDR during the 1950s and, in particular, the economic crisis that was provoked by the SED's programme of 'accelerated socialist construction'. From the spring of 1952 onwards, already scant state resources were being lavished on expensive projects such as rebuilding the armed forces, developing heavy industry, and collectivisation.[33] The FDJ, like other constituent parts of the regime, was instructed to tighten its belt and to inaugurate a campaign for 'thrift' (*Sparsamkeit*). Funds for youth leisure-time activities disappeared. Youth club rooms in factories and residential areas fell into disuse or were 'commandeered for other purposes' (*zweckentfremdend*) by state and party officials. Local FDJ groups could no longer afford to buy tents for hiking, just as young people themselves could not afford the exorbitant prices that were being charged for hiking gear and sports clothing in the state shops. 'Official' youth life in the GDR at this time, where it existed at all, was thus generally a rather joyless affair: a dull combination of membership meetings, ideological indoctrination and the occasional stage-managed propaganda event such as the 1 May celebrations.

The aftermath

The above picture of the FDJ in the year preceding the June uprising – an understaffed and overstretched organisation, detached from the mass of young people that it claimed to represent – holds the key to understanding its role on *Tag X*. During this period, the youth organisation – like the SED regime more generally – was in a state of crisis that was blissfully ignored by its central leadership, whose tendencies towards 'glossing things over' (*Schönfärberei*) prevented open discussion of the many real problems that the 'proud millions-strong organisation' (*der stolze Millionenverband*) was facing. The FDJ was in far too weak a position, both organisationally and politically, to rally large numbers of young East Germans in defence of the SED regime in June 1953. Without the intervention of Soviet tanks, its temporary paralysis would have turned into a more permanent collapse.

At first sight, it seemed that the party leadership both recognised the extent of the FDJ's failure on 17 June and was prepared to do something about it. During the late summer and autumn of 1953, various party reports called for drastic changes in the working methods of the youth organisation.[34] In a move unprecedented in the history of relations between the Soviet bloc states, a delegation from the Soviet youth organisation itself, the Komsomol, was dispatched to Berlin (at Ulbricht's prompting) to examine the work of its 'fraternal' East German counterpart.[35] There was even an unrealised call for Erich Honecker to be sacked as FDJ chairman.[36]

Some lessons were indeed learned from the June uprising. Never again, for example, did the youth organisation participate in such a sustained and openly repressive campaign of persecution against the *Junge Gemeinden*. In purely organisational terms, FDJ leadership bodies were never again so helpless in the face of youth unrest as they had been on 17 June. Particularly during potential flashpoints in the 1960s – most notably the construction of the Berlin Wall in August 1961 and the crushing of the Prague Spring in August 1968 – there was far greater loyalty and commitment to the party line among FDJ cadres.[37]

However, much of the extensive criticism that was levelled at the FDJ during late 1953 was not acted upon at all. There was no concerted attack on the FDJ's bureaucratic cadre apparatus. The rhetoric about 'going to the young' and organising activities in which they wanted to participate – so prevalent in the immediate aftermath of the uprising – quickly fizzled out, leaving the FDJ as detached as ever from real 'youth life' in many East German factories, villages and residential areas. The old FDJ routine of political and economic campaigning, allied with large-scale propaganda events and dogmatic Marxist–Leninist instruction, had almost fully reasserted itself by 1954. It was thus hardly surprising that much of the same, unrealised, censure to which the FDJ had been subjected after June 1953 was resurrected in the autumn of 1955, when the party leadership again attempted to tackle the FDJ's continued unpopularity and ineffectiveness among large numbers of young East Germans.[38]

More generally, the FDJ remained a prisoner of the political system that had shaped its development and the bipolar world in which it existed. The issue of remilitarisation, for example, such a widespread cause of youth discontent in 1952, remained a thorn in the FDJ's side until conscription was finally introduced in January 1962. In both 1955 and 1961, issues of East German state and Soviet bloc security (i.e. the creation of the Warsaw Pact and the construction of the Berlin Wall respectively) forced the youth organisation to take the leading role in further unpopular campaigns of 'voluntary' recruitment for the armed forces. The FDJ continued to be a victim of the sacred Marxist–Leninist principle that 'the party is always right'. There was no recognition that it was SED policies, rather than just the way in which they were implemented by the FDJ, that were the root cause of the problems in youth work during 1952 and 1953.

Most significantly, the June uprising and its aftermath did nothing to bridge the ideological gulf that separated the FDJ from the vast majority of young East Germans – members and non-members of the youth organisation alike. The mood among young people after 17 June – apathetic indifference towards organised youth life, interspersed with a raft of more explicitly hostile 'enemy', opinions about the GDR – encapsulated the attitudes that the FDJ had to over-come throughout the Ulbricht era in order to win over 'all young people' (*die gesamte Jugend*) for socialism. Despite the SED regime's periodic attempts to adopt a more tolerant ideological approach to youth policy, the battle lines first drawn in 1953 between the FDJ and the young were never entirely erased.

Before the dramatic events of the autumn of 1989, the June 1953 uprising constituted by far the biggest youth protest in the GDR's history. During the intervening period, both domestic issues (such as the building of the Berlin Wall and the campaign against Western 'beat' music in late 1965) and international events (such as the invasion of Hungary in 1956 and of Czechoslovakia twelve years later) triggered significant levels of anti-regime sentiment among the young. However, the crushing of *Tag X* seems to have instilled in young protes-tors an understandable sense of fear and caution. The majority of them con-sciously limited their anti-state behaviour after June 1953. This meant that offences upon which the regime came down most heavily (such as forming underground political groups or, after 1961, attempting to flee illegally to the West) were rare. But less dangerously provocative and more frequently tolerated gestures – such as listening to Western radio stations or refusing to wear one's FDJ blue shirt in public – occurred with greater regularity.

As a final point, it is worth mentioning how little youth organisations else-where in the Soviet bloc learned from the FDJ's sobering experiences in 1952–53. In 1956, the united youth organisations in both Poland and Hun-gary were hurriedly dissolved in the face of widespread anti-Stalinist protests. In Czechoslovakia, barely a decade later, the united youth organisation, the (ČSM *Československý svaz mládeže*), endured a similar fate. In all of these cases, the manifest failure of the bureaucratic, dictatorial precepts of the 'united youth' principle – the *sine qua non* of the FDJ's existence – exposed a sense of flawed legitimacy that was common to all of the Soviet satellite regimes in East-ern Europe after the Second World War. In the GDR and elsewhere, capitalising upon Karl Liebknecht's dictum that 'whoever has the young has the army' proved to be beyond Communist capabilities.

Notes

1 Interview with Kurt Turba, 26 October 2000.
2 Ulrich Mählert and Gerd-Rüdiger Stephan, *Blaue Hemden – Rote Fahnen: Die Geschichte der Freien Deutschen Jugend* (Opladen, 1996), 45–7.
3 See the numerous cases of post-war upward mobility recounted in Lutz Nietham-mer, Alexander von Plato and Dorothee Wierling's pioneering oral history of East German workers, *Die Volkseigene Erfahrung: Eine Archäologie des Lebens in der Indus-trieprovinz der DDR* (Berlin, 1991).
4 Interview with Helmut Müller, 7 July 1999.
5 Christian Ostermann, '"This is not a politburo, but a madhouse!" The post-Stalin succession struggle, Soviet *Deutschlandpolitik* and the SED: new evidence from the

Russian, German and Hungarian archives', *Cold War International History Project (CWIHP)*, Issue 10, 3/98, 67, 91.

6 Michael Walter, *Die Freie Deutsche Jugend: Ihre Funktion im politischen System der DDR* (Freiburg, 1997), 46.

7 See, for example, Mählert and Stephan, *Blaue Hemden – Rote Fahnen*, 95–8; Gert Noack, 'Die FDJ und der 17. Juni 1953 – Neue Dokumente aus dem Archiv der FDJ', *Geschichte Erziehung Politik (GEP)*, 4/93, 379–88.

8 See Alan McDougall, *Youth Politics in East Germany: The Free German Youth Movement, 1946–1968* (Oxford, 2004), 55–6.

9 *Ibid.*, 52.

10 Gareth Pritchard, *The Making of the GDR, 1945–53: From Antifascism to Stalinism* (Manchester, 2000), 217.

11 Der Bundesbeauftragte für die Unterlagen des Staatssicherheitsdienstes der ehemaligen Deutschen Demokratischen Republik (BStU), Mgd. Abt. IX/Nr. 14 ('Angaben 1953/54', undated, 25, 69, 173, 251, 255, 406); BStU, Mgd. Abt. IX/Nr. 15 ('Angaben 1953/54', undated, 17, 141).

12 Pritchard, *The Making of the GDR*, 215.

13 Stiftung Archiv der Parteien und Massenorganisationen der DDR im Bundesarchiv (SAPMO-BArch), DY 24/3666, 'Beispielsammlung für die 6. Tagung des Zentralrates der Freien Deutschen Jugend', 11 July 1953.

14 SAPMO-BArch, DY 24/2301, 'Das Verhalten der Jugend bei den Ereignissen am 17. und 18. Juni 1953', 26 June 1953.

15 Interview with Helmut Müller, 7 July 1999.

16 SAPMO-BArch, DY 24/2301, 'Bericht über das Verhalten der Jugend und des Verbandes am 17. und 18. Juni und die gegenwärtige Situation', 24 June 1953.

17 SAPMO-BArch, DY 24/3833, 'Statistischer Abschlußbericht über den Umtausch der Mitgliedsbücher', undated.

18 SAPMO-BArch, NY 4090/516, 'Bericht der Kommission zur Überprüfung der Arbeit der Freien Deutschen Jugend', undated, 90.

19 According to Soviet sources in the GDR, more than 120,000 East German citizens fled to the West during the first four months of 1953 alone – including 2,610 members of the FDJ. See Ostermann, 'This is not a politburo, but a madhouse!', 79.

20 McDougall, *Youth Politics in East Germany*, 27–8, 37–8.

21 SAPMO-BArch, DY 30/IV 2/5/267, 'Wie wurden die Beschlüsse der II. Parteikonferenz in der Freien Deutschen Jugend ausgewertet, wie ist der politisch-ideologische Zustand des Verbandes', 15 November 1952, 235–6, 238.

22 Interview with Kurt Turba, 26 October 2000.

23 For more on the ODD, which was discontinued in January 1953 after less than six disastrous months in existence, see McDougall, *Youth Politics in East Germany*, 33–7.

24 SAPMO-BArch, DY 24/2151, minutes of the 2nd ZR session, 14–16 August 1952.

25 SAPMO-BArch, DY 24/2521, minutes of the ZR secretariat meeting, 29 October 1952: 'Bericht über die Arbeit der FDJ Organisation im SWB und die Beteiligung der Jugend am sozialistischen Wettbewerb.'

26 SAPMO-BArch, DY 30/IV 2/16/9, 'Informationsbericht Nr. 44', 2 July 1952, 106.

27 McDougall, *Youth Politics in East Germany*, 29–30.

28 SAPMO-BArch, DY 30/IV 2/16/9, 'Information Nr. 6', 31 May 1952, 40.

29 McDougall, *Youth Politics in East Germany*, 42–7. Despite the propaganda hysteria that surrounded the campaign against the *Junge Gemeinden*, just 832 young Chris-

tians were removed from the FDJ and expelled from their schools before the SED was forced by the Soviets to relax its anti-Church position in early June 1953.

30 Ulrich Mählert, *Die Freie Deutsche Jugend 1945–1949. Von den 'Antifaschistischen Jugendausschüssen' zur SED-Massenorganisation: Die Erfassung der Jugend in der Sowjetischen Besatzungszone* (Paderborn, 1995), 195–6.

31 McDougall, *Youth Politics in East Germany*, 44.

32 SAPMO-BArch, NY 4090/516, 'Über die Freie Deutsche Jugend', 27 October 1953, 52.

33 Remilitarisation alone initially cost the GDR approximately two billion marks, or 10 per cent of the state's annual income. See Wilfried Loth, *Stalins ungeliebtes Kind. Warum Moskau die DDR nicht wollte* (Berlin, 1994), 194.

34 The most important of these reports can be found in SAPMO-BArch, NY 4090/516: 'Über die Freie Deutsche Jugend', 27 October 1953, 49–56; this was written by Fred Stempel, an aide to the GDR Prime Minister, Otto Grotewohl; 'Bericht der Kommission zur Überprüfung der Arbeit der Freien Deutschen Jugend' (undated, 59–96) summarised the findings of an SED commission, under the unofficial direction of Politburo member Karl Schirdewan, that had investigated the FDJ's work during November 1953. Both Grotewohl and Schirdewan were known to be strong critics of Honecker's leadership of the FDJ.

35 McDougall, *Youth Politics in East Germany*, 63–4, 65.

36 SAPMO-BArch, NY 4090/516, 'Über die Freie Deutsche Jugend', 27 October 1953, 56.

37 McDougall, *Youth Politics in East Germany*, 134–6, 222–3.

38 *Ibid.*, 69–75.

3

Worker protest and the origins of the Austrian Social Partnership, 1945–51[1]

Jill Lewis

Studies of Austrian post-war reconstruction seldom mention popular protest, but concentrate almost exclusively on the country's precarious situation in the early Cold War and the unique political system of corporatism based on *Proporz* (proportionality), *Parität* (parity) and shared decision-making which was formalised in the 1950s and 1960s. Austrians, it is argued, adopted a new political culture after the Second World War, reinforced by the 'victim' status conferred on the country by the Allies in the Moscow Declaration of 1943, and a determination to avoid the class conflict which had destroyed the First Republic.[2] This new political culture, which was based on compromise and social harmony was, the present writer would argue, not significantly different from later developments in West Germany, with two major exceptions, namely, the speed with which consensus emerged in Austria, and the scale and success of the system, which, by 1960, had resulted in the institutionalisation of corporative decision-making in the shape of the Social Partnership, and which then led on to the prosperity of the 1960s to 1980s. The foundations of this corporatism were laid at the end of the Second World War, when leaders of the dominant political parties accepted the concept of *Proporz*, and the country's economic elites – the employers' organisations and trade union leaders – announced publicly that they shared a common set of goals, including full employment, a stable currency, low inflation and increased productivity.[3]

In the case of the labour leadership, this approach reflected a fundamental ideological shift from belief in the inevitability of conflicting class interests, which had dominated the First Republic, to social harmony and compromise. In return, these same labour leaders were invited to join the political elite and participate in the formation of national economic and social policy. In particular, they played a key role in persuading their members to accept an incomes policy which was both crucial to economic growth and highly unpopular.

The core of this incomes policy was a series of five Wages and Prices Agreements which the Austrian government promulgated between August 1947 and July 1951, and which were designed to stem strong inflationary tendencies in the economy. Although these agreements were formally ratified by the Cabinet, they were actually drawn up by an ad hoc advisory body, later to be known as the Economic Committee, which included, on the one side, representatives of the main employers' associations, and, on the other, leaders of the Trade Union Federation (the *Österreichische Gewerkschaftsbund* – ÖGB), and its sister body, the Chamber of Labour. For the first time in Austrian history, labour leaders were directly involved in formulating government policy. Moreover, the two sides (or economic partners) had equal status within the committee, a point which was confirmed in 1959 when, after several years of inactivity, the Economic Committee was renamed the Parity Commission and was given legal status. In this form, it became the hub of the Social Partnership.

It will be argued in this chapter that, whilst the political and economic elites emerged from the war with a belief in consensus, the pattern of popular protest in the early post-war years suggests that many workers did not. Working-class discontent was expressed, firstly, in hunger protests, secondly, in 'offensive' strikes to improve working conditions, and, thirdly, in 'defensive' strikes to prevent extensions of wage controls, and was increasingly opposed by Socialist political and trade union leaders. Paradoxically, however, these episodes of worker protest had the effect of strengthening the labour leadership's position, thus helping to lay the foundations of the Social Partnership.

The prospect of social consensus appeared remote in the first six months of peace. In May 1945 the population of Vienna faced starvation. During that month, the ration was a kilo of bread per person per week but, in reality, most people in the city were forced to depend for their survival on what they had managed to hide away, foraging, or worm-eaten dried peas which the Soviet Red Army, who had occupied the city on 13 April, released from their own stores.[4] The first regular normal daily ration was introduced in June 1945 and set at 833 calories per person per day but, without steady food deliveries from the countryside, it was often impossible to distribute even this meagre allowance.[5] After being raised to 1,550 calories in September, it continued to fluctuate nationally as harvests and food deliveries remained precarious. Over the next three years, Austria suffered from a chronic lack of food, as well as a shattered economic infrastructure and a severe shortage of labour. In the spring of 1946, following the bitterest winter in living memory, rations fell to 700 calories in some areas.[6] The food problem was compounded by the labour shortage. Agricultural and unskilled workers were particularly scarce, a consequence of war casualties and imprisonment and the fact that many soldiers had learned a trade in the armed services during the war. There were too many competing demands for labour immediately after the war – on the farms where there were crops to plant and later to harvest, and in the bombed towns and cities where rubble had to be cleared by hand and shovel. The situation was so acute that the provisional government resorted to limited conscription in June 1945.

Initially this was restricted to ex-Nazi Party members and covered the Eastern provinces only, for the Renner government, which had been set up and recognised by the Soviet authorities in April 1945, was shunned by the Western Allies until September, and its jurisdiction was confined to the territory under Soviet occupation. This changed after the national elections of November 1945, and in 1946 the new coalition government reintroduced the Nazi Law on Compulsory Labour as an emergency measure, compelling all men between the ages of eighteen and fifty-five and all single women under forty to work.[7] This law remained in force until 1948, when unemployment began to rise.

The situation in these first years of peace was thus highly volatile. Hunger, economic crises and labour shortages can lead to riots, rebellion and even revolution, as had been the case in 1918 and early 1919. But events after the Second World War were significantly different. Although confusion and mayhem followed the defeat, which was officially hailed as 'liberation', there is little evidence of concerted popular protest in the first six months of peace. The main preoccupation for most people was to earn, barter or steal the basic essentials for survival. In Vienna, looting became widespread in the first days of liberation, as local inhabitants broke into department stores and dragged away whatever they could find. Shortly afterwards, gangs of Soviet soldiers joined in, extending their pillaging to shops, homes, and anyone who was rash enough to wear a watch on the street.[8] Rape became a major problem in the Soviet sector.[9]

In the summer of 1945 there were also mounting concerns about the long-term fate of the country, fuelled by the increasingly hostile relations between the Allied Powers. By the middle of May the country was under four-power occupation, but the Soviet decision to support the setting up of the Renner government, within days of taking control of Vienna and without consulting the other Allies, provoked the Western Allies into a policy of procrastination. They not only ignored the existence of Renner and his government, but also prevaricated until the middle of July over negotiations about setting the boundaries of the specific zones of occupation and re-establishing internal trade.[10] Relations between Austrians and the Red Army in the Eastern sector were also deteriorating and, although conditions appeared to be better in the southern and western provinces than in Vienna, and there were fewer reports of assaults, the local population was treated with cold disdain – British and American troops were forbidden to fraternise with locals.[11]

The apparent stalemate between the Allies in the summer of 1945 and its temporary resolution in September 1945 greatly influenced political attitudes in Austria. After months of uncertainty, and in stark contrast to their policy in Germany, all four Allied Powers agreed to allow political life to resume throughout Austria in September 1945 and endorsed the call for national elections. These were held on 25 November 1945 and, whilst none of the three political parties achieved an absolute majority, the conservative People's Party (*Österreichische Volkspartei – ÖVP*) gained 49.8 per cent of the votes, and the Socialist Party (*Sozialistische Partei Österreichs* or *SPÖ*) 44.6 per cent. The fate of the

Communist Party (*Kommunistische Partei Österreichs* – KPÖ), which obtained a mere 5.4 per cent, far less than the 20 per cent it had predicted, will be discussed later. The ÖVP leader, Leopold Figl, became Chancellor, but he appointed a coalition government based on the system of *Proporz*, which had been introduced by the Renner government, and allocated portfolios to the political parties according to their electoral support (which, for Renner in April, had perforce been a matter of guesswork). Political unity had been crucial for Renner's coalition government in the face of the hostility of the Western Allies, and this continued to be the case for future Austrian governments for the next ten years of occupation, when the country remained only semi-independent, with its own government and laws, but subject to the approval of the Allied Control Council. It was during this time that what eventually became known as the 'Social Partnership' began to take root.

The culture of consensus was also adopted by trade union leaders, as we have seen. Trade union membership had been strong in Austria during the First Republic, reaching a peak of 1.2 million in 1923, and falling to just under 1 million by the end of 1929, despite high unemployment.[12] But the power of the labour movement had been weakened by a plurality of union federations, each representing a political party or faction. It became obvious as soon as the fighting ended in April 1945 that the lessons of this factionalism had been learned. Within days of the announcement of the Second Republic, former trade union activists set up a single highly centralised umbrella federation of sixteen industrial unions (the ÖGB), adopting the new principles of consensus and shared power. Its leader was Johann Böhm, a Social Democrat, but his two deputies were Erwin Altenburger, from the Catholic labour movement, and Gottlieb Fiala, a Communist. Despite fifteen years of repression, trade unionism was still strong – by December 1946 the ÖGB had recruited almost 1 million members and was the largest representative body in the country.[13] The work of the ÖGB was supported by the reintroduction of the Chambers of Labour.

It was soon clear that this structural transformation was to be accompanied by a radical change in the goals of the labour movement. The first sign that trade union leaders (with the exception of the Communists) were abandoning the traditional objectives of protecting their members' wage rates, standards of living, and working conditions, came in the summer of 1945, when the Federation supported an emergency measure holding wages to the level of May 1945.[14] Its argument, that higher wages would inevitably lead to higher prices in an economy which was beset by shortages, was economically sound, but it contrasted starkly with the position of labour leaders in 1919 who had fought for and won index-linked wages.[15] The fact that trade union priorities had changed was confirmed in 1946, when, despite both the deepening food crisis and the shortage of labour, ÖGB leaders continued to warn their members that large wage demands would fuel inflation rather than raise living standards. They were particularly worried about the possibility of wildcat strikes and protests – formal negotiations between themselves and the government would, they argued, achieve far more than any unauthorised protests.[16]

This warning, however, appeared to fall on deaf ears. Three months after the 1945 national elections a wave of workers' protests began over the food issue. On 5 February, miners at the Fohnsdorf pit in British-occupied Upper Styria went on strike to demand an increase in their rations. During March and April, similar protests broke out in Vienna, the largest on 19 March in the machine shops in the Floridsdorf district in the Soviet sector, but by now basic complaints about the size of the ration were beginning to develop political overtones – the Floridsdorf workers blamed the government for failing to improve the food situation. When workers in a variety of Viennese plants staged a joint protest strike on 9 April they called on the unions to ensure that immediate improvements were made.[17] Food protests continued through the summer of 1946, as printers, tram workers, metal workers and miners all held short protest strikes. Thousands of people, most of them women, signed petitions demanding better rations and stricter controls to curb hoarding and the black market.[18] The petitions had been organised by the Communist Party, but found support across the country in areas where Communist support was minimal. Protests escalated in Vienna in March and April, when supplies of potatoes failed to reach the city, and culminated in a violent demonstration in the city centre on 5 May 1947. Demonstrators forced their way into the Chancellery and demanded a meeting with the Chancellor. At a cabinet meeting held the next day, Chancellor Figl described the situation as dangerous, for it was the first time in the short life of the Second Republic that the protesters appeared to have a political as well as an economic agenda; he blamed the violence on Greek and Albanian Communists and on local women. Ministers also accused the Soviet authorities of deliberately intensifying the discontent by delaying the movement of food into the city. But, despite public attempts to underplay the seriousness of the situation, the government knew it could not ignore the food protests, which had involved working men and women as well as housewives, had crossed zones of occupation, and were often led by elected shop-stewards and local politicians.[19]

It has already been noted that the trade union leaders, with the exception of the Communists, opposed grass-roots protest. Nevertheless, their political position was strengthened by it. In December 1945 the first shop-stewards' conference, held in Vienna, had passed a series of radical proposals, including a call for a centralised ministry of economics led by a trade unionist. This aspiration was not realised but, as discontent grew, union leaders mediated between their members, the government and even the Western Allies over the food issue and, as a result, their influence increased. On 25 April 1946, at a meeting with trade union leaders, Chancellor Figl announced a new central food directory comprising government representatives and members of the employers' associations, as well as two trade unionists who were to monitor decisions.[20] Reporting this to a shop-stewards' conference four weeks later, Johann Böhm made it clear that the language of class conflict was not yet entirely dead, even within the ÖGB executive. The role of the trade union representatives was, he declared, to prevent employers' bodies from exercising autocratic leadership.[21] Nevertheless, the unions were now involved in policy decisions, although not yet on an equal footing with the employers. The next stage came at the local level, when, in October 1946, the government set up advisory bodies to assist in the collection and distribution of scarce goods, which included this time representatives of the respective Chambers of Trade, Agriculture and Labour. Significantly, the three Chambers were to have equal influence, in other words 'parity of representation'. [22] In addition, on 29 May 1947, following the hunger protests, union leaders held talks with the Allies about raising the daily ration to 1,200 calories immediately and to 1,800 in July.[23] Böhm was appointed chairman of the Parliamentary Committee on Social Administration and, most crucially of all, trade unionists sat on the Economic Committee, the voluntary ad hoc body which drew up the first Wages and Prices Agreement in July 1947. The ÖGB described its contribution to drawing up legislation as threefold – influencing policy directly, operating indirectly through the Chamber of Labour and playing a direct role in policy formation through membership of law-making bodies (*gesetzgebende Körperschaften*) such as the Wages and Prices Committee. By 1948, the ÖGB was already calling itself a 'Social Partner', but to many union members it was more a case of poacher turned gamekeeper, a view which was promoted by the KPÖ.[24]

By 1947, there was a clear divergence within the labour leadership. The KPÖ had always stood alone in refusing to accept the new consensus. Nevertheless, it remained a member of the coalition government until 1947, and Fiala continued to serve as deputy chairman of the ÖGB. However, despite – or more likely because of – the Soviet presence in Austria, the KPÖ's position remained weak. It had been unable in the inter-war years to break the hegemony of the Social Democratic Party within the working class and had fallen far short of its own expectations in the November 1945 elections. Its poor showing was extremely important for the fate of Austria: the Soviet authorities never recovered their faith in the Party, despite continuing to encourage it to build a base amongst industrial workers by exploiting economic grievances and, in particular, attacking the Marshall Plan.[25]

The weakness of Communism in Austria was also important for the labour movement. While, on the one hand, the policy of the KPÖ threatened to undermine political stability, on the other, it strengthened the bargaining power of the ÖGB, which was based on the very close relationship between its leaders and the governing elite, as well as the Federation's ability to contain dissent amongst its members. In 1946 and 1947, unrest over food had not led to serious trouble, despite the inability of the government to secure the ration. Union leaders had successfully argued against large-scale direct action and in favour of negotiations, and had, as a result, increased their influence within government circles. But there was mounting evidence that they had not carried their members with them. At the 1948 Trade Union Conference, the Minister for Social Administration, Karl Mantler, who was also the leader of the Food-Workers' Union and president of the Viennese Chamber of Labour, argued that wage rises were in fact unnecessary because the prices of many rationed goods were stable and others were actually falling.[26] Sustained long-term growth was what was now needed. This required short-term sacrifices by workers, but would eventually lead to a higher standard of living for all. The implication was that the sacrifice and the benefits would spread across all classes. One woman delegate's response to this argument was that there had been no mention of profits, and that Mantler did not understand the problems workers faced. Women workers in her industry, textiles, took home an average weekly wage of 75–80 schillings. Rations for one person cost between 18 and 22 schillings a week, so a single working mother with two children had 25–30 schillings left for the rent, electricity and gas. Current wages did not cover the cost of basic essentials, let alone anything bought on the black market, even though prices there were falling.[27]

As time was to show, workers had not yet abandoned the traditional forms of protest. When new industrial conflicts arose in 1947 and 1948, they returned to the strike weapon. The main grievances were over wages and conditions and the reluctance of employers to implement the new Law on Collective Contracts. This had been passed in September 1947 and gave legal status to such contracts, introducing common wage rates across industries and the four zones of occupation.[28] It enhanced the power of the ÖGB, conferring on it the sole right to negotiate on behalf of all workers, with the exception of those employed in agriculture and forestry. Agricultural and forestry workers were the first to strike, over their exclusion from the legislation, but the main difficulty for the trade unions was to persuade the employers to negotiate. In November, 6,000 paper workers walked out over delays in settling their collective contract.[29]

But the most important action was an eight-week official strike of shoe workers which broke out in March 1948 amid growing political tension. It was an all-out strike involving all 5,800 workers in the industry, 55 per cent of them women or youths, who were demanding a shorter working week, one paid free day a month for women workers who also ran households (the Domestic Day – *Wirtschaftstag*), and the right of shop-stewards to be consulted on issues of hiring and firing. These demands involved improvements in working conditions, particularly for women workers, but none was unique to the shoe industry, and the first two, the 44-hour working week and the Domestic Day, had already been included in collective contracts which had been agreed in other sections of the textile industry. The shoe workers suspected that the employers had a hidden agenda. For six months their union, the shoe workers' section of the textile and leather union, had been unsuccessfully negotiating a collective contract with the employers on the basis of the new law. The union accused the employers of bad faith, and argued that, on the advice of the Chamber of Trade, the dispute was being used to test the commitment of the ÖGB to collective contracts. If the unions were to give way in this case, more employers would refuse to conclude collective agreements. In a secret ballot held on 2 March, 2,829 members of the shoe workers' union voted in favour of strike action, with twenty against and twelve blank papers.[30]

The strike lasted for eight weeks and ended in a partial victory for the workers – the 44-hour working week was conceded, but the employers rejected the other two demands and the textile union leaders concurred in this. The result was a furious row within the ÖGB. The fact that the ÖGB had recognised the strike as official, despite its general condemnation of industrial action, indicates the importance it placed on the issue – collective contracts had to be defended. But there was also a political division within the textile and leather union – the leaders of the main union were predominantly SPÖ, whilst the shoe workers' section had a strong Communist element and was led by Gottlieb Fiala, the increasingly isolated Communist deputy-chairman of the ÖGB.[31] Throughout the strike, Fiala and his supporters condemned government policy on wages and prices, and attacked Socialist ministers and union leaders for capitulating to the employers by accepting 'coalition politics'.[32] They accused Böhm and the ÖGB of giving only half-hearted support. The ÖGB opposed the committee of shop-stewards which ran the strike, and the *Arbeiter-Zeitung*, the SPÖ newspaper, carried articles describing solidarity actions as unnecessary and unhelpful.[33] The paper also focused exclusively on the demand for a 44-hour working week, following a majority decision within the ÖGB not to support either the Domestic Day or the extension of shop-stewards' powers.[34] Böhm was also accused of issuing a press statement at a crucial stage in the negotiations in which he asked if the strike could have been avoided, and opposed calls to extend the demand for shorter working hours to other industries.[35] The Minister for Food, a member of the SPÖ, suspended the strikers' supplementary rations on 9 April.[36] The strike finally ended after Chancellor Figl intervened. On 28 April, 1,829 strikers, half the original number, voted in a second ballot, with 912 in favour in favour of the offered settlement, and 716 against.[37] Some weeks later, Böhm responded to his critics by arguing that the strike had been a success, because it had achieved the 44-hour working week. There was no mention of the other two demands, just as there had been no reference to them for many weeks in the Socialist newspaper.

The shoe workers' strike was the first large-scale direct conflict between labour and capital in the Second Republic. Böhm's claims that it had been a success were exaggerated – 80 per cent of workers in the textile industry had already been working a 44-hour week before the strike began. The employers had been testing the ÖGB's determination to defend collective contracts, and the Federation had fought back. But the strikers were also demanding improvements in working conditions for female workers and the enhancement of shop-stewards' powers. Neither demand was particularly radical, and throughout the strike workers in other industries staged short solidarity protests and organised shop-floor collections, indicating that the shoe workers had clear support amongst other rank-and-file workers. Nevertheless, non-Communist union leaders gave the strike no more than tepid support and refused to back more than the one key demand. They were torn by conflicting interests. On the one hand, as trade unionists, it was imperative that they defended their right to collective contracts. But, at the same time, they did not want to undermine the economic policies which they had helped to draw up, nor to encourage social instability for, although the strike had been triggered by domestic economic issues, it took place at a point when political tensions in the region as a whole were reaching dangerous levels. The Communists had taken power in Hungary and, more recently, in Czechoslovakia, and the situation over Berlin was deteriorating. On the first day of the strike, the front page of the *Arbeiter-Zeitung* was devoted to the latest food crisis – diminishing food supplies had prevented the government from issuing increased rations, as it had promised. Readers were urged to pay heed to the fate of their neighbours and to boycott Communist action committees.[38] On 9 March, ÖGB leaders attended the opening Marshall Plan talks in London, and, in common with other members of the Cominform, the KPÖ increased its attacks on the SPÖ for capitulating to Western capitalism and US imperialism.[39] The political polarisation within the labour movement was clear to see. At the end of the strike, the Socialist leader of the parent textile union dismissed opposition to its outcome as Communist-inspired. As the liberal *Wiener Zeitung* pointed out, however, many of the most outspoken critics of the result of the strike were in fact Socialists.[40]

The ÖGB, having been compelled to support the strike, had acted as a moderating influence upon it. Subsequently, the Federation's opposition to strikes and its involvement in economic policy-making both increased. The KPÖ abandoned attempts to establish a Popular Front with the left wing of the SPÖ and began openly to advocate a People's Democracy.[41] Its attacks on the SPÖ intensified, focusing on the Marshall Plan and the government's economic policy, for which it also condemned the ÖGB. Rising unemployment provided the Communists with yet more grounds for linking wage restraint with coalition politics in general, and the SPÖ and the ÖGB in particular. The shared goals of the economic elites had been low inflation, a stable currency, increased productivity and full employment, the first three of which also lay at the heart of the Marshall Plan. The fourth aim, full employment, was the reward that trade union members had been promised by ÖGB leaders in return for wage regulation. But annual average unemployment almost doubled between 1947 and 1949.[42] In October 1948, American pressure on the Austrian government to abolish food subsidies led to a second Wages and Prices Agreement and, seven months later, in the wake of a serious budget deficit, a third was announced.[43] Each agreement triggered industrial unrest and strikes. The governing parties increasingly attributed all forms of protest to the Communists – at least in public. So, too, did the ÖGB. Internal memoranda show that within the SPÖ there was grave and well-founded concern about the response of workers if a fourth Wages and Prices Agreement were to be announced.[44]

The third wave of popular protest, and the most significant to date in the history of the Second Republic, began to manifest itself in September 1950. After a summer of secret negotiations, speculation and denial, the Economic Committee concluded a fourth Wages and Prices Agreement. Plans to make the formal announcement on Tuesday 26 September, after union and SPÖ officials had had a chance to sell it to their members over the weekend, were scuttled on the previous Saturday, when the main Communist newspaper, the *Volksstimme*, printed the story. At this point the paper did not call for strike action, and the following Monday, when work resumed, politicians could have reassured themselves that their fears of a violent reaction were exaggerated: metal workers in the country's largest industrial plant, the steelworks at Linz in the US zone, did stage a one-hour protest strike, as did some railway workers, but the reaction appeared to be generally low-key. The custom of not publishing newspapers on Sundays and Mondays may have contributed to this, for the situation changed on Tuesday when the news spread. Over the following three days, localised strikes broke out in every province except Carinthia, involving between 120,000 and 200,000 people, or 6–10 per cent of the country's entire working population.[45] Demonstrations were held the length and breadth of the country with, according to police figures, 16,000 converging on the centre of Vienna on 26 September. The same day, 20,000 people demonstrated in the centre of Linz, smashing windows in the town hall.[46] Workers at plant and factory gates voted by a show of hands to stage walk-out protests. Some of these lasted for less than an hour and some for several days. By 27 September there were very few areas in the country where strikes had not taken place, with the mines and steel plants in Linz and Donawitz and the factories in Vienna itself seeing the largest protests. The strikes were both unplanned and unofficial, and as a result they were unsynchronised. They were plant-based, organised by shop-stewards or, where the shop-stewards opposed strike action, by hastily formed strike committees. They took place in different areas at different times or even on different days; miners and steel workers in Styria, for instance, came out on strike on the same day that their colleagues in Linz went back to work. The ÖGB refused to recognise the strikes. In fact, the Federation became the prime target of the protesters in some areas, and was condemned by many of its members for being a major collaborator in the formation of a government economic policy which relied on wage controls and had provoked the strikers to action in the first place. Although strike demands varied to some extent across the country, they invariably included the abandonment of wage controls and immediate wage increases across the board, and often denunciations of the ÖGB leaders.

The role of the KPÖ in the 1950 strikes is contentious. At the time, the Western Allies and the Austrian government publicly accused the KPÖ of orchestrating events, with Soviet backing, as part of a plan to destabilise Austria and create a People's Democracy. This accusation has become part of Austrian folk-lore –

the strikes are usually represented as a failed *putsch*. Although this is not the place to develop the argument against this interpretation,[47] the actions of the KPÖ are important when assessing the impact of the strikes on the development of consensus politics. It is necessary, however, to put the influence of the KPÖ into perspective – it had not been much more successful in its attempts to win support on the shop floor than it had been in the parliamentary elections – in the 1949 works council elections it secured just under 7 per cent of the votes.[48] Nevertheless, it did have influence in some key plants, including the steel plant at Donawitz in Upper Styria and a number of firms under Soviet control, from which it could have mounted an immediate attack on the Wages and Prices Agreement as soon as the *Volksstimme* story appeared. However, Soviet documents indicate that the KPÖ's executive committee had not expected an immediate reaction to the news and had planned for a strike to break out on 2 October.[49] The speed and extent of the response took it by surprise. Fiala hurried to Styria on the Saturday to urge local party activists to call an immediate strike, but he was told that they needed more time to prepare.[50] As we have seen, the first strike actually broke out on the Monday, not in a Communist stronghold, but in the steelworks in Linz, where a new political party of re-enfranchised ex-Nazis, the Electoral Party of Independents (*Verband der Unabhängigen*), had a majority on the works council and where only two of the twenty-eight shop-stewards were Communists. The Styrian protest started two days later. Thwarted in its attempts to gain control of the situation, or even to direct its own members, the KPÖ took the unusual decision of calling off the strike and organising a national meeting of shop-stewards from all parties to consolidate further action. The first strike wave thus ended five days after it had begun, on Friday 29 September. The next day, roughly 10 per cent of all Austria's shop-stewards met in Vienna and agreed to a unified set of demands, including the end of the Wages and Prices Agreements, a 20 per cent wage increase, a price freeze and strike pay from ÖGB funds.[51] These were published, along with an ultimatum to the government – if the terms were not met within five days, the strike would resume. The government refused to negotiate, arguing that the ÖGB was the only legitimate representative of the workers. The strike re-started on 4 October. It was largely confined to the Soviet zone and involved violent exchanges between strikers and the police. The '*putsch* myth' was based on this, the second phase of the 1950 strikes.[52]

The 1950 strikes were the culmination of years of rank-and-file dissatisfaction with the wages and prices policy, which could have had serious repercussions for both the ÖGB and the SPÖ; Adolf Schärf, the effective leader of the SPÖ, wrote a private memorandum in 1949 in which he noted ÖVP astonishment that the SPÖ had approved the third agreement in what was an election year. There was obvious conservative glee at the prospect that this would alienate Socialist voters and persuade them to abandon the SPÖ in favour of the KPÖ, which might have led to an overall ÖVP majority.[53] The ÖVP's hopes were not realised, but throughout the winter and early spring of 1949–50 there were more warnings of large-scale protests if a fourth agreement were to be introduced. Socialist leaders tried to stifle newspaper discussion of the issue during that summer and, together with the ÖGB, they planned to pre-empt organised opposition by coaching local leaders in the arguments in favour of the agreement.[54] Neither the SPÖ nor the union leadership could allow such opposition to succeed – were they to do so, the government's economic strategy would be in ruins and with it the political consensus on which their power and the security of the country appeared to depend.

But the real significance of the 1950 strikes lay in the fact that consensus politics was actually strengthened as a result, despite very obvious divisions within the labour movement. The size and number of strikes, and their spontaneity in the first phase, show clearly the depth of hostility to the wages policy. The KPÖ hoped to harness these energies in the second phase, exploiting them by channelling economic grievances into a wider political campaign against the government and the entire system of post-war politics. This backfired seriously when most workers outside the Soviet zone ignored the call to join the renewed strike. They had won no concessions and were unlikely to do so if the strike failed but, faced with the choice between pursuing their fight under Communist leadership or abandoning it altogether, they chose the latter alternative. The strike confirmed the weakness of Communism in Austria. The national elections had shown that the KPÖ could not win many votes, but the 1950 strikes also showed that it was incapable of building support even on the basis of solid economic issues. Conversely, Socialist labour leaders emerged from the crisis looking stronger – they had, it is true, been unable to prevent the dispute breaking out, but they took full credit for its defeat and used the opportunity to reduce Communist influence within the ÖGB.[55] Eighty-six Communist shop-stewards were expelled from the union movement, including Gottlieb Fiala, for leading an unofficial strike. The strike, which became known as the 'October strike', a phrase which neatly diminished the importance of the first, September, wave, was generally dismissed as a Soviet-inspired *putsch* which had been confined throughout to the Soviet zone.

As this chapter has sought to show, there were food protests and strikes in the early years of the Republic which initially followed a traditional pattern and had little to do with social harmony. These protests were increasingly opposed by trade union leaders, who feared they would strengthen Communism, destabilise the country, undermine economic reconstruction – and threaten the unions' increasing role in the formation of economic and social policy, since the power of the union leaders lay in their ability to contain popular protest. Conversely, it was the threat of such protest which encouraged the government – and, eventually, the employers – to accept the right of the unions to a permanent and equal role in decision-making – the right to parity.

Notes

1 Research for this chapter was generously supported by the British Academy and the Leverhulme Trust.

2 Günter Bischof, *Austria in the First Cold War* (London, 1999); Audrey Kurth Cronin, *Great Power Politics and the Struggle over Austria 1945–1955* (New York, 1986); Manfried Rauchensteiner, *Der Sonderfall: Die Besatzungszeit in Österreich 1945 bis 1955* (Graz, 1979). For details of the Moscow Declaration, see www.yale.edu /lawweb/avalon/wwii/moscow.htm. Official strike statistics for the period 1945 to 1950 are unavailable. Figures from the Österreichische Gewerkschaftsbund published in Fritz Klenner, *Die Österreichischen Gewerkschaften von 1928 bis 1953* (Vienna, 1953), 1586, are problematic and exclude the 1950 strikes. There are no figures for demonstrations and protests.

3 Emmerich Tálos and Bernhard Kittel, 'Roots of Austro-corporatism: institutional preconditions and co-operation before and after 1945', in Günter Bischof and Anton Pelinka (eds), *Austro-Corporatism: Past, Present and Future*, Contemporary Austrian Studies 4 (New Jersey, 1996), 43.

4 Irene Bandhauer-Schöffmann and Ela Hornung, 'Von der Erbswurst zum Hawaii-schnitzel: Geschlechtsspezifische Auswirkungen von Hungerkrise und Freßwelle', in Thomas Albrich, Klaus Eisterer, Michael Gehler and Rolf Steininger (eds), *Österreich in den fünfzigern* (Innsbruck, 1995), 15–19.

5 Irene Bandhauer-Schöffmann and Ela Hornung, 'Der Topos des Sowjetischen Soldaten in Lebensgeschichtlichen Interviews mit Frauen', *DÖW Jahrbuch* (Vienna, 1995), 36.

6 *Tätigkeitsbericht 1945–1947 und stenographisches Protokoll des ersten Kongresses des Österreichischen Gewerkschaftsbundes* (Vienna, 1948), 1/17.

7 *Ibid.*, 1/74.

8 Josef Schöner, *Wiener Tagebuch 1944/45* (Vienna, 1992), 137.

9 *Ibid.*, 148–80; Ernst Fischer, *Das Ende einer Illusion. Erinnerungen 1945–1955* (Vienna, 1973), 41; Marianne Baumgartner, 'Vergewaltigungen zwischen Mythos und Realität: Wien und Niederösterreich im Jahr 1945', in *Frauenleben 1945. Kriegsende in Wien*, Sonderausstellung des Historischen Museums der Stadt Wien (Vienna, 1995).

10 Schöner, *Wiener Tagebuch*, 208, 287, 360.

11 *Ibid.*, 283.

12 Jill Lewis, *Fascism and the Working Class in Austria* (Oxford, 1991), 212.

13 *Tätigkeitsbericht des ÖGB 1945–1947*, 1/77. The actual figure was 924,274, of whom 75.3 per cent were men and 24.7 per cent women.

14 Fritz Weber, *Der Kalte Krieg in der SPÖ: Koalitionswächter, Pragmatiker und Revolutionäre Sozialisten 1945–1950* (Vienna, 1986), 116.

15 Lewis, *Fascism*, 74.

16 *Tätigkeitsbericht des ÖGB 1945–1947*, 1/17.

17 *Ibid.*, 3/63.

18 Siegfried Mattl, 'Frauen in Österreich nach 1945', in Rudolf Ardelt, Wolfgang J.A. Huber and Anton Staudinger (eds), *Unterdrückung und Emanzipation: Festschrift für Erika Weinzierl* (Vienna, 1985), 115–16.

19 Österreichisches Staatsarchiv, Archiv der Republik (AdR), Bundeskanzleramt (BKA), Ministerratsprotokolle, Figl 1, Box 15, Austrian Cabinet Papers, sitting 67, 6 May 1947.

20 *Tätigkeitsbericht des ÖGB 1945–1947*, 1/18.
21 *Ibid.*
22 *Tätigkeitsbericht des ÖGB 1945–1947*, 1/20.
23 The Austrian Minister for Food authorised the July increase, but this was delayed when the US Congress refused to approve the necessary funds. The ration was raised in November 1947 to 1,700 calories. AdR, BKA, Auswärtige Angelegenheiten, W.Po. WiEur. Box 87, Marshall Plan, Letter from the Minister for Food to the Austrian Ambassador in Washington, 19 September 1947.
24 *Tätigkeitsbericht des ÖGB 1945–1947*, 1/76.
25 Russian State Archive of Socio-Political History (RGASPI), Fond 575, Op.1, Delo 8, Reports, Informatory Material on the Activities of the Austrian Communist Party. Submitted to A.A. Zhdanov by an official of the Central Committee of the All-Union Communist Party (Bolshevik), 12 September 1947.
26 *ÖGB Tätigkeitsbericht 1945–1947*, 4/113–17. Paradoxically, Mantler resigned from the SPÖ executive later in 1948 in protest at the first Wages and Prices Agreement. Weber, *Der Kalte Krieg in der SPÖ*, 137.
27 *Tätigkeitsbericht des ÖGB 1945–1947*, 4/146.
28 Different systems had applied in different zones. The first wages agreement in Vienna was published on 12 July 1945, but wage regulation was banned in the US zone until March 1946. *Ibid.*, 3/52.
29 *Tätigkeitsbericht des ÖGB 1945–1947*, 3/71. This was shortly after the only recorded strike over the employment of an ex-Nazi, which broke out in the Guggenbach paper factory in August 1947 and lasted for five weeks. *Die Arbeit* (4 April 1948).
30 *Der Abend* (2 April 1948).
31 Kodicek, the Central Secretary of the Union, was also a Communist. Support for the Communists was strongest amongst miners and leather workers. RGASPI, Fond 575, Op.1, Delo 8, 12 September 1947.
32 *Protokoll des Achten Arbeiterkammertages abgehalten am 18. und 19 März 1948* (Vienna, 1948), 32–5.
33 *Arbeiter-Zeitung* (13 April 1948).
34 *Der Abend* (14 May 1948).
35 The accusation was made by Kodicek in an article published in *Die Arbeit* (6 June 1948), 16. Böhm had responded to criticisms of the ÖGB's position in the strike during the 1st ÖGB congress, which was held in Vienna on 18–23 May 1948. He argued that the Federation's executive had been taken by surprise when the strike broke out and that it could not afford the 3 million schillings which the action had cost. Such 'fun' (*Spass*) could take place once, but no more. *Tätigkeitsbericht des ÖGB 1945–1947*, 4/263.
36 *Österreichische Zeitung* (9 April 1948).
37 *Wiener Zeitung* (29 April 1948).
38 *Arbeiter-Zeitung* (3 March 1948). The Communists seized power in Hungary in May 1947 and in Czechoslovakia in February 1948.
39 Klenner, *Die Österreichischen Gewerkschaften*, 1441–2. The KPÖ had originally supported the Marshall Plan and had been vigorously criticised by the Russian Communist Party for this 'incorrect approach'. RGASPI, Fond 575, Op.1, Delo 8, 12 September 1947.
40 *Wiener Zeitung* (29 April 1948).
41 Hans Hautmann, Winfried Garscha and Willi Weinert, *Die Kommunistische Partei Österreichs: Beiträge zu ihrer Geschichte und Politik* (Vienna, 1987), 359.

42 It rose from 52,839 in 1947 to 100,083 in 1949. *Jahrbuch der Arbeiterkammer in Wien 1950* (Vienna, 1950), 380.

43 Klenner, *Die Österreichischen Gewerkschaften*, 1447.

44 Some of these are in the SPÖ Documents, Probst Correspondence, 1950, Verein der Geschichte der Arbeiterbewegung. Police reports in the winter of 1949–50 also described increasing opposition throughout the country; copies of these are to be found in the Schärf papers held in the Verein der Geschichte der Arbeiterbewegung (VGA), Vienna. VGA, Schärf Nachlass, 1(14), Box 44, 4/287, Helmer Correspondence, 'Lageberichte der Sicherheitsdirektion', 31 January 1950.

45 Jill Lewis, 'Austria 1950: strikes, "putsch" and their political context', *European History Quarterly*, 30:4 (2000), 533.

46 Ronald Gruber, 'Der Massenstreik gegen das 4. Lohn-Preisabkommen im September/ Oktober 1950' (University of Vienna, PhD thesis, 1975), 144. The official police figure was 8,000.

47 This argument is explored further in Lewis, 'Austria 1950'.

48 Klenner, *Die Österreichischen Gewerkschaften*, 1716.

49 Foreign Policy Archive of the Russian Federation (AVP RF), Fond 066, Op. 32a, Papka 162, Delo 6 (Austrian Section), 1.

50 Gruber, 'Der Massenstreik', 147.

51 Lewis, 'Austria 1950', 541.

52 *Ibid.*

53 VGA, Schärf Nachlass, 43 4/283, undated. The proportion of the votes gained by the SPÖ fell from 44.6 per cent to 38.7 per cent, but this was also due to the participation of the new right-wing party, the *Verband der Unabhängigen*.

54 In August 1950, Böhm complained to the General Secretary of the SPÖ about an article, concerning the question of wages, which had appeared in an SPÖ paper in the Tyrol. He argued that it was dangerous for the party press to inflame the situation by discussing the issue. The editor was reprimanded. VGA, SPÖ Documents, Probst Correspondence, Böhm to Probst, 19 August 1950.

55 Lewis, 'Austria 1950', 542–8. Franz Olah, the leader of the building and woodworkers' union in 1950, was still being feted in the 1990s in much of the Austrian press for having defeated the 'Communist' strike. See, for example, *Neue Freie Presse* (18 October 1990).

4

Workers in Hungary

Mark Pittaway

In his memoirs, written during exile in the Soviet Union in the late 1960s, the former secretary of the Hungarian Workers' Party and the country's leading Stalinist during the early years of dictatorship, Mátyás Rákosi, recounted that in 1950 he 'started to look into what the right-wing Social Democrats were doing . . . [T]hey were destroying work discipline and manipulating opinion in the factories, so we raised it as a political issue'.[1] Prior to the institutionalisation of socialist dictatorship in the late 1940s Hungary had been ruled by a popular front coalition. Competition for the working-class vote in the country's industrial communities had been intense. The Hungarian Communist Party (*Magyar Kommunista Párt* – MKP) struggled with the Social Democrats (*Magyarországi Szociáldemokrata Párt* – MSZDP) for dominance on the political Left, a dominance eventually achieved through a mixture of mobilisation, electoral fraud and police intimidation that was then sealed with an enforced merger that created the Hungarian Workers' Party (*Magyar Dolgozók Pártja* – MDP) in 1948.[2] Rákosi thereupon turned his attention to 'right-wing Social Democrats'; two years after the merger of the two parties, senior figures within the MDP who had a past that connected them to the MSZDP, led by Hungary's President, Árpád Szakasits, were imprisoned pending a series of show trials.[3]

Campaigns against 'right-wing Social Democrats' in the political sphere combined with a drive against shop-floor protest by skilled workers in Hungary's factories during the late spring of 1950. The Stalinist state's revolution in production was well underway several months after the introduction of the Stakhanovite movement on the country's shop floors, along with the transformation of wage systems in industry.[4] As wages were tied to performance, and the campaign-style production methods that had permitted the introduction of Stakhanovism lost momentum, production was hit by a wave of sporadic working-class protest.[5] Party propaganda blamed 'the press of the reactionary bourgeoisie, and to a considerable extent right-wing Social Democrats within the working class' for attempting 'to undermine the credibility of the Stakhanovite

57

movement among the workers'.[6] The regime dovetailed this attack with one on the persistent survival of pre-socialist cultures of shop-floor representation within the Stalinised trade unions, as no less a figure than Mátyás Rákosi attacked 'syndicalist tendencies' that 'can be seen' in the work of the unions.[7] As the campaign against 'right-wing Social Democrats' on the shop floor took shape, it became clear that those whom the regime branded 'right-wing Social Democrats' were synonymous with those skilled workers who defended traditional working practices against the assaults of the Stalinist state. According to the party committee of Budapest's seventh district, 'in the printing industry, many of whose members belonged in the past to the aristocracy of labour, syndicalism is particularly pronounced together with the aggressive appearance of the voice of right-wing Social Democracy'.[8]

With the consolidation of Stakhanovism, the introduction of the piece-rate wage system and the reductions in workers' wages that stemmed from the 'revision of the norms', the events of 1950 were fundamental to shaping patterns of conflict in Hungarian industry during the first half of the 1950s. They also shaped regime responses to such patterns of protest. This could be seen in recurring concern about the influence of 'right-wing Social Democrats' in factories throughout the 1950s; in one textile factory in the capital it was used to explain the demands of skilled joiners for higher wages in March 1951.[9] The regime initiated further campaigns in 1952 when it became clear that, in elections to factory-level union organisations, those whom party secretaries on the ground regarded as 'right-wing Social Democrats' were conspicuously successful in being elected.[10] Despite this, there has been almost no exploration of the meaning of manifestations of supposed 'right-wing Social Democracy' in Hungarian factories. The work on the afterlife of the MSZDP that does exist tells a story of 'high politics' and repression. It deals mostly with the fate of former members of the MSZDP in Rákosi's jails and prison camps, but often fails to mention the factories from whence the party had drawn much of its support prior to 1948.[11] Where authors have touched on the phenomenon in the factories, they have assumed implicitly that the survival of Social Democratic opinions among the workers fed a culture of protest against the actions of the Stalinist state.[12] The situation, however, was much more complicated than this. In 1952 the personnel department of the United Lighting and Electrics Factory in Budapest compiled a statistical survey of those considered to be 'right-wing Social Democrats' in the factory. Of the 291 employees so identified, only 50.5 per cent had actually been members of the MSZDP prior to merger in 1948, while a staggering 26.5 per cent had belonged to the MKP.[13] As the officials of the Budapest Party Committee made clear in their accompanying report, while the designation 'right-wing Social Democrat' was influenced by an individual's previous party membership, it was defined in part by social position – whether a worker had been a 'member of the aristocracy of labour'. What was most important, however, was the attitude of the worker, namely whether he or she exhibited 'chauvinist' attitudes towards newer workers, or was undermining 'work discipline'.[14]

'Right-wing Social Democrat' was a political identity that was 'ascribed' to workers by Hungary's Stalinist state, rather than one that unproblematically reflected the persistence of a Social Democratic political culture in the country's factories.[15] It formed part of an attempt to attribute political identities in Hungarian society, explaining social conflict through the actions of chimerical political 'enemies' who sought to undermine 'socialism'.[16] It enabled the state, at least at the level of propaganda, to link particular kinds of dissent to broader international conflict in the early Cold War years. The press frequently railed at the 'treason' of western Social Democratic parties in bolstering US hegemony and bourgeois politics in the western half of the continent.[17] This area of international conflict was conflated with a particular kind of working-class opposition to the labour policies of the regime, namely, the discontent expressed by the urban, skilled elite in the face of the state's transformation of production. The regime argued in 1950 that the emergence of new forms of working associated with Stakhanovism pointed to the occurrence of 'basic changes in the structure of our society and our economy'.[18] This 'new attitude to production' heralded a transformation of the working class. 'In the Stakhanovite movement', proclaimed the party newspaper, 'a new kind of worker has appeared; the first signs of the new Communist working class have emerged'. This 'embryonic Communist working class' was born from a struggle fought against 'the damaging legacy of capitalism to the mentality of the working class'.[19] The notion of 'right-wing Social Democracy' as a political identity crystallised as the regime faced growing skilled working-class opposition to its drive to transform the shop floor during the first half of 1950.

Yet while 'right-wing Social Democracy' was a political identity ascribed by the regime to skilled workers who opposed its policies in the factories, and its meaning crystallised in 1950, it was not simply invented by the regime after the introduction of the Stakhanovite movement. It drew upon Communist experience of the struggle for hegemony among the industrial working class during the period of popular front rule that followed the end of the Second World War. It was fed by the marked opposition of many skilled workers to some of the policies advanced in the coalition years by the MKP in the factories in the interests of reconstruction. It was, furthermore, defined by the way in which some of these localised shop-floor conflicts had become politicised in the climate of intense competition between the MSZDP and MKP, and then as the dictatorship was built following the enforced merger of the two parties. As standardised forms of labour competition, wage systems and later the Stakhanovite movement were promoted by the state to prepare for the introduction of comprehensive economic planning, local officials shaped the campaigns in their factories so as to destroy the cultures defended by the skilled elites. For this reason those skilled elites, particularly in sectors such as heavy engineering, resisted Stakhanovism and 'payment-by-results' systems of remuneration ferociously. Communists at both national and local level applied their memory and explanation of shop-floor conflict in the mid- and late 1940s to the different tensions of 1950. It bears mention that even in the mid- and late 1940s their explanations had often misread the complex reality of discontent in the factories.

This argument will be developed with reference to one particular case study. The United Lighting and Electrics factory, which lay on the northern fringes of the Greater Budapest conurbation in the town of Újpest, had been a stronghold of the labour movement between the wars and then of the MSZDP during the mid-1940s.[20] During the Stalinist years it figured prominently in the official promotion of Hungary's Stakhanovite movement[21] and was simultaneously a focus of regime concern about the influence of 'right-wing Social Democrats' over the industrial working class.[22] During the 1956 Revolution it was at the centre of the workers' councils movement, something that many, including the socialist regime restored in November, attributed to the persistence of a 'Social Democratic' culture in the factory.[23] The present chapter looks firstly at the way in which the micro-politics of the factory overlapped with the macro-political struggle between the MKP and MSZDP for hegemony within the working class between 1945 and 1948. It then moves on to consider the institutionalisation of dictatorship and the conflicts that surrounded labour competition and the institutionalisation of Stakhanovism. It focuses on how shop-floor conflicts were interpreted and misinterpreted by the officials of firstly the MKP and later the Hungarian Workers' Party (MDP). It does this in ways that illuminate the afterlife of Hungarian Social Democracy in the factories, showing how, after the MSZDP had ceased to exist, 'Social Democrat' re-emerged as a political identity ascribed by the regime to the opponents of aspects of its labour policy.

The micro-politics of the shop floor, the macro-politics of the parties: conflict in the United Lighting and Electrics Factory, 1945–48

In 1952, the Budapest party committee conducted an investigation into what it regarded as the prevalence of 'right-wing Social Democracy' in the United Lighting and Electrics factory. It traced this back to the history of labour movement activity in the plant: 'Social Democracy had very considerable influence in the factory before the liberation. This manifested itself in close relations with the owners of the plant.' It linked 'Social Democracy' to both class collaboration and to the skilled elite within the workforce of the factory – 'many engineers, many members of the aristocracy of labour, but', it conceded, 'many honest workers joined the MSZDP' after 1945. Even then, the report argued, in areas of the factory like 'the machine shop, the tool-making shop, machine maintenance, the power plant', in other words where the skilled elite were concentrated, 'a marked majority were members of the Social Democratic Party'.[24] The United Lighting and Electrics factory had indeed been a stronghold of the MSZDP between 1945 and 1948, even when compared to neighbouring factories. The Communists themselves estimated in mid-1946 that, of a workforce of around 2,700, 1,300 were members of the MSZDP. Among the neighbouring factories in industrial Újpest, the MKP predominated in factories in light industrial sectors, while in plants in the heavy engineering sector workforces were evenly divided between the MKP and MSZDP.[25]

The explanation for the strength of the MSZDP in the United Lighting and Electrics factory does not lie in the strength of the Social Democratic labour movement in the plant prior to the Second World War. During the 1930s the local branch of the Metalworkers' Union, closely tied to the MSZDP, dominated the channels of interest representation in the factory, as it did in most other Újpest factories in the sector. This, however, was unsurprising; the Horthy regime, based as it was on the suppression of the Soviet Republic that briefly governed Hungary after the First World War, criminalised Communist political activity. The United Lighting and Electrics factory was a centre of underground Communist activity in Újpest throughout the inter-war years; immediately prior to the onset of the depression in the late 1920s the factory had been nick-named 'red Tungsram' as a result of the militancy of many of its workers. The leadership of the official labour movement was deeply anti-Communist, and towards the end of the 1930s developed a close relationship with the owners of the plant.[26] This, however, was closely linked to the growing influence of the radical Right over the working class in the Greater Budapest area and to increasing, often officially sanctioned, anti-Semitism. At the end of the 1930s the radical Right, particularly the Arrow Cross party, had seriously weakened the Social Democratic labour movement by successfully winning the support of large numbers of younger workers through linking anti-capitalist rhetoric to anti-Semitism and radical nationalism.[27] The predominantly Jewish owners were, in the face of radical right-wing mobilisation, keen to weaken the radical Right among the workforce by strengthening the Social Democratic labour movement.[28]

Thus the existence of a Social Democratic political culture in the factory during the inter-war years does not provide a convincing explanation for MSZDP predominance in the post-war years. The alleged predominance of rep-resentatives of the 'aristocracy of labour', namely the skilled unionised elite, does not provide an explanation, either. The factory was engaged in the produc-tion of a wide range of electrical goods in both the inter-war and early post-war years: light-bulbs, a wide range of lamps and radio components. This diverse production profile meant that the labour process was extremely uneven across the factory, but even so a majority of the total workforce were semi-skilled work-ers. In December 1933, of a total workforce of 2,332 workers, 1,760 were employed in semi-skilled jobs; an overwhelming majority of these semi-skilled positions were filled by women producing electrical lighting equipment and radio components. Only 331 workers belonged to the skilled elite, the Commu-nists' 'aristocracy of labour', and the absolute majority of these workers were concentrated in the factory's machine shop and were entirely male.[29] Factory employment statistics from December 1947, when the reconstruction of the factory after the Second World War had been completed, revealed that a similar pattern persisted into the post-war period. From a total manual workforce of

2,426, 793 belonged to the skilled elite, while 1,459 were classified as semi-skilled workers.[30] While only certain shops, and certainly not the whole factory, were strongholds of what the regime would later brand 'the aristocracy of labour', close attention to the history of labour movement activism in the factory in the inter-war years shows that both Social Democrat and illegal Communist activism was concentrated among that skilled elite.[31]

The circumstances of the immediate months that followed Újpest's 'liberation' by Soviet troops at the beginning of 1945 provide a much more convincing explanation of why the MSZDP was so predominant in factory politics during the post-war years. The German occupation, the deportation of Újpest's 14,000 Jews, the banning and suppression of the labour movement and then the encirclement of Budapest by Soviet troops in the second half of 1944 were deeply traumatic for the town's residents.[32] As Hungary's German occupiers rounded up labour movement activists in the town, many went into hiding and lived off the land on the fringes of the town. They were later to form one of the most active partisan groups in the country as the Red Army moved on Budapest.[33] Amid this political turmoil, workers left the United Lighting and Electrics factory as real incomes collapsed; in 1944 the real incomes of skilled workers stood at only 55 per cent of their 1914 level.[34] Those workers who remained were faced with the threat that the Arrow Cross regime and Hungary's German occupiers would strip the factory of its machinery to prevent it falling into Soviet hands. Factory management took the unusual step of illegally arming the factory's workers to resist any German attempts to remove machinery, and armed conflict was prevented only because German plans were insufficiently advanced for it to be possible to remove machinery before Budapest was surrounded.[35]

The German occupation was brought to an end with the arrival of Soviet troops in January 1945; this, however, did not end Újpest's agony, but merely marked a new phase of conflict for the inhabitants of the town as Hungary's new occupiers instituted a reign of terror of their own. As the front moved south and then west, there came a second wave of Soviet troops; thus began what one working-class resident described as 'the period of fear, . . . they stole, they raped'.[36] The Red Army troops engaged in mass rape, looting and murder in the town, and the widespread rounding up and deportation of able-bodied males by Soviet troops increased popular hostility.[37] This reign of terror, in which members of the newly constituted Hungarian police force actively participated, was believed by many of the politically aware in the town to herald the immediate imposition of a Soviet-type regime, along the lines of the Soviet Republic of 1919. Jenő Pál Nagy, later the chief shop-steward in the United Lighting and Electrics, was genuinely surprised to hear that the MSZDP would be allowed to operate legally. This was because 'we [the workers] all believed, before the liberation, that there would naturally be no other party allowed than the Communists'.[38]

The brutality of the Red Army, the rapes and the mass deportations, damaged the newly founded MKP in Újpest. It was, however, able to construct an appeal to working-class supporters that exploited their fear of a return to the aggressive anti-labour politics of the Horthy years, when they had been marginalised and had generally been poorly served by the moderate policies of the MSZDP. It did this through promoting an ideology of democratic, national reconstruction that allowed the MKP to distance itself from the actions of the Red Army, and exploit the desire of many workers for real change.[39] But the workforce of the United Lighting and Electrics factory proved largely immune to such appeals, because the Red Army dismantled the factory in early 1945 as part of its drive to extract reparation from Hungary for siding with Nazi Germany during the Second World War. The Soviet command effectively dismantled the factory between March and mid-May 1945. Management estimated that, when the Red Army departed, only 4 per cent of the machinery remained in place, while some 75 per cent of all raw materials were seized.[40] The employment consequences for those dependent on the plant were catastrophic: the factory had employed around 5,000 in late 1944; by May 1945, when the Red Army left, it could only guarantee work to around 400, a figure that had risen to only 1,569 by October.[41] While the factory committee attempted to organise the workers to defend the factory against the attempts of the Red Army to dismantle it, these efforts were less than successful. The workforce was faced with the task of reconstructing a factory damaged not only by war but by the policies of the new occupiers.[42]

A year after the dismantling of the factory, the local newspaper of the MSZDP in Újpest explained that the machinery of the factory was the price to be paid 'for the Ukraine, for the villainy of Horthy and Szálasi'. It described the 'pain' with which the workers 'said goodbye to their machines and their tools'.[43] The paper understated the reaction at the time; the news of the dismantling of the factory was greeted with an explosion of anti-Soviet hysteria among the workforce. Some workers argued that the 'Russians would take away everything' because of an alleged impending war with Britain.[44] Sections of the workforce, organised by MSZDP members of the factory committee, engaged in a futile attempt to sabotage the dismantling of the plant, but in the end they had to concede that they 'could not hinder it'.[45] As the factory was rebuilt, lingering bitterness among the workers over the actions of the Red Army created a climate hostile to the MKP. As the Social Democrats recruited in the factory during early 1946, Communists complained that they were aggressively deploying 'anti-Soviet propaganda' to mobilise the workforce.[46]

Following the dismantling of the factory and in the face of hyper-inflation and misery in much of the country, reconstruction proceeded quickly. It began in August 1945 with banners above the factory proclaiming that 'life is stronger' and with staff optimistically arguing that the factory could be re-built 'more modern than before'.[47] Within the year, the local press proclaimed the success of the plant's reconstruction, praising 'the worthwhile struggle' of the staff in the difficult circumstances of Hungary's first post-war year.[48] The reconstruction failed, however, to re-build a factory such as that which had existed in the inter-war years. In 1947 total production stood at only 30.6 per cent of its 1939 level, while the plant only employed 2,514 manual workers as opposed to 4,635 eight years previously. Furthermore, real wages in 1947 still lagged behind the relatively high real wages enjoyed by workers in the plant during the late 1930s; average real earnings for skilled workers were 32 per cent lower than in 1939, while for the semi-skilled majority they had fallen by 33.05 per cent.[49]

At the national level, hyper-inflation ended in 1946 with the stabilisation of the currency and the introduction of economic planning, which was in many ways a precursor of the transition to a socialist economy that would occur after 1948. Within the framework of reconstruction the state, driven to a considerable extent by the MKP, introduced sporadic labour competition, and sought to introduce wage systems based on the principle of 'payment-by-results', with 'scientifically determined norms' across industry.[50] In the United Lighting and Electrics factory such wage systems could be introduced relatively easily; scientific management had dictated work organisation and payment practices in the semi-skilled workplaces in lamp and radio component manufacture in the inter-war years.[51] These parts of the factory and the assembly shop were those where 'scientific' norms, which bore an uncanny resemblance to pre-war practices, were already in force in August 1946.[52] While statistical returns for the whole of the late 1940s suggest that around 60 per cent of all hours worked by both skilled and semi-skilled workers were paid through 'payment-by-results' wages in the factory,[53] this picture is misleading. The skilled minority in the maintenance and machine shops were able to exert far more on-the-job control than the semi-skilled, who were far more fully subordinate to managerial authority. As late as 1948, the shop-stewards among the skilled exercised considerable informal control over the performance of skilled workers, ensuring that they made no more than 135 per cent of their norm, in order to preserve union control over wage rates.[54] A shop-floor culture that stigmatised 'rate-busting' in the machine shop was recalled in the official biography of the future Stakhanovite József Kiszlinger. In the late 1940s he 'managed to overfulfil his norm. The older ones attacked him, "Are you insane? You're undermining us!"'[55]

Although Communists would become concerned at the persistence of on-the-job control in the machine shop after 1948, during the period of reconstruction they were far more concerned to smash the political hegemony of the MSZDP in the factory. From January 1946 onwards the local MSZDP organisers regarded the United Lighting and Electrics factory as their most important stronghold in Újpest, in view of their success in organising party members in the plant, winning a majority on the factory committee and taking its presidency.[56] The MKP were deeply worried and saw MSZDP hegemony as giving disproportionate power over affairs in the factory to 'the aristocracy of labour'.[57] Consensus between the two parties over issues such as reconstruction and the importance of combating right-wing resurgence was replaced by marked tension during 1946 and 1947. The MKP used its hegemony in national union organisations and its campaigning strength ruthlessly in order to marginalise the MSZDP. Local Social Democrats complained bitterly that the Communist union officials 'take party politics into the factories. They thus undermine work discipline and undermine the will to produce.'[58] Following the 1947 parliamentary elections, in which the MKP achieved the status of the largest party on the Left, in part through electoral fraud, it began to press for a merger of the two parties. Social Democrats who opposed this faced a campaign of intimidation from the MKP.[59] The seeming inevitability of a merger, the strong support among the MSZDP membership for some form of socialist transformation and the MKP's campaign of intimidation led to the implosion of the MSZDP in the factory prior to the formation of the MDP. By February 1948 some 60 per cent of the membership had defected to the Communists.[60] The way in which this implosion occurred would lead many officials of the new unified party to believe well into the 1950s that many 'right-wing Social Democrats' were hidden within the membership of the ruling party in the factory.[61]

Building the dictatorship in the factory

The plant's nationalisation signalled the end of the era of reconstruction and the beginning of the 'construction of socialism'. As one shop-steward noted, 'socialism is the future, and with this the issues of capitalist supply and demand will disappear. There has been no change over the years in the management of the factory . . . The workers do not trust the management as a whole . . . [W]e need a workers' director immediately.'[62] This was achieved with the appointment of the factory committee president, László Somlai, as the plant's managing director.[63] The formation of the MDP from the MKP and the ruins of the MSZDP likewise heralded a new era. The new party's leadership at national level justified the merger on the grounds 'that the right of the Social Democratic Party [has] tied itself to the re-organisation of Hungarian reactionary forces' and also to the 'imperialist line of Truman' at an international level.[64] The leaders of the new party in the factory were also suspicious of former members of the MSZDP, particularly in the shops where the skilled elite dominated. Here, they reported, workers were 'indifferent' to the programme of the new party.[65]

As the party consolidated its power in the factory, it seemed more concerned about the continuing influence of political Catholicism among the semi-skilled female workers, given the state's attacks on church schools and the arrest of Cardinal Mindszenty, than it was about 'former Social Democrats'.[66] It did, however, aim to re-shape the remnants of the pre-socialist labour movement in order to incorporate them into the institutional framework of dictatorship, reorganising the trade union in early 1949 to subordinate it to party policy.[67] Worried about the influx of former MSZDP members into the party, and of others, labelled 'opportunists', the party both nationally and in the factory purged its membership. The long-term effects of this, however, were unclear and seem to have led to a large-scale expulsion of white-collar staff from the party.[68]

The drive for political control was accompanied by a concerted attempt to transform production in the factory in order to prepare the plant for comprehensive economic planning. During 1948, the factory was incorporated into the national labour competitions, while the brigade movement – which entailed the reorganisation of the shop floor into a series of work groups committed to the improvement of productivity – was introduced into the factory.[69] Labour competition spread quickly, with the plant newspaper announcing that the first national labour competition campaign, which ended in June 1948, had allowed the factory to fulfil its plan ahead of time.[70] Over the summer labour competition 'forged ahead at full power'.[71] Brigades spread during the autumn, though rather than initiating a lasting re-shaping of work practices they were instead formed to complete certain narrowly defined short-term tasks.[72] The spread of labour competition was aided by incentives that were both moral and financial. Individuals in the factory were rewarded with the title of 'outstanding worker' in recognition of their performance in production.[73] Financial incentives were, however, far more important in underpinning support for labour competition; according to party activists, 'most people's opinion is that labour competition should have started a long time ago. It bears mention that this opinion derives not so much from political opinion, but that extra earnings seem to be the most important factor.'[74]

This conditional support for an uneven implementation of labour competition underlined the degree to which it was a flawed instrument for transforming attitudes to work. It was, furthermore, clear that, while it was relatively successful in semi-skilled workplaces, it had failed to erode traditional working practices among the skilled elite. In early 1949, despite the fact that the union had been stripped of its autonomy, the rates achieved by turners, and other skilled workers paid by piece rates, were closely controlled by the skilled workers themselves, in order to maintain the pre-socialist union's 'solidaristic wage policy' to protect wages and differentials in the machine shop.[75] Both the campaign-like nature of the competition and the highly instrumental attitudes of workers toward it were reflected in the fact that, when norms were raised in order to increase productivity, such attempts were met with protest. This in turn necessitated campaigns to encourage the workers to overfulfil the new norms.[76]

The state was painfully aware of the fragility of labour competition in industry nation-wide by late summer 1949. Consequently it launched a campaign both to increase productivity and tighten central control over the shop floor by exhorting enterprises to promote individual labour competition as the motor of the movement. Though it did not say so publicly, this was designed to prepare for the radical spread of individualised 'payment-by-results' wage systems in preparation for the first Five-Year Plan.[77] Local party organisations in the factories were required to respond to the new campaign, however, and it displayed features that varied from factory to factory. In the United Lighting and Electrics factory the party committee warned when planning the new campaign in the factory that, while 'the innovators and brigades have gained certain good results', some parts of the factory 'worked according to very old working practices'. While little concern was expressed over semi-skilled workplaces in the plant, shortages of labour and 'old working practices' in the machine shop were exacerbating the fact that the shop was 'absolutely overloaded'.[78] A growing shortage of skilled labour in the machine shop and in the maintenance section, visible in September 1949, led the local party to make this shop the focus of its campaign to spread individual labour competition across the plant.[79]

Despite claims in the national press about the 'spontaneity' of labour competition, in the United Lighting and Electrics factory the party organisation ran the campaign from above. Its networks of activists were mobilised right across the factory to persuade and coerce workers into making pledges to improve their individual performance, while party members were expected to take the lead in making pledges in order to set an example to their more reluctant workmates.[80] In this campaign of mobilisation they were aided by the local branch of the metalworkers' union – the only union allowed to operate in the plant. Stripped of many of its traditional functions, it had by late 1949 evolved into an organisation that relentlessly removed obstacles to the regime's drive to increase production.[81]

Among semi-skilled workers, individual labour competition was characterised by pledges to increase rates of norm-fulfilment and workers undertaking to supervise production on more than one machine at once. In the machine shop – the focus of the local factory party's campaign – it was initiated with the formation of a brigade, the so-called 'Produce More' brigade, that promised to blaze the trail for new production methods.[82] A glance at the leading members of the 'Produce More' brigade is revealing as to the challenge they posed to the dominant culture of on-the-job control in the machine shop. All the members of the brigade were largely excluded from the informal networks that shaped established relationships among workers on the shop floor. Their leader, József Kiszlinger, a twenty-five-year-old turner at the beginning of the campaign, was a party member with an unusual employment history. He had begun working in the United Lighting and Electrics factory in 1946 after returning from being held as a POW by the Germans.[83] He stayed in the factory for a little over a year; as a believer in reconstruction he consistently overfulfilled his norms and was consequently stigmatised by his fellow workers in the machine shop and driven out. He returned in August 1948 and found that little had changed; 'there was a consensus among the workers: "we won't go above this level".' Anyone who went over the informally agreed 120 or 130 per cent incurred disfavour because 'they were busting the rate'.[84] At the core of the brigade were like-minded young workers in their twenties, who had either trained outside the factory or had only recently arrived in their present jobs. Of those who would later become Stakhanovites were János Lutz, who had trained in the provinces and came to the capital in the post-war period, and his friend, Ferenc Szlovak, both young workers committed to breaking the established shop-floor culture in the interests of social change.[85]

These attempts to use labour competition to bust rates and smash established shop-floor culture were, unsurprisingly, unpopular; nor was this unpopularity reduced by the assertions of members of the brigade that they intended to teach their 'less developed' workmates new production methods.[86] In the machine shop, it was often those who had been decorated as 'outstanding workers' during the labour competitions of the previous year who were active in opposition. One party activist reported that 'the outstanding workers are threatening those who want to radically increase their production'.[87] The opposition of much of the shop floor was expressed through rumours of higher production norms and lower wages if the shop engaged in competition *en masse*.[88]

As autumn wore on, the authorities in the factory shifted from simply seeking to promote individual competition and sought instead to respond to regime calls to introduce the Stakhanovite movement in the factory, and especially in the machine shop. For them the new movement 'will sweep away the old system and put another in its place'. In order to do this, local officials recognised that they would have to identify and promote a small number of individual workers who 'would know beforehand the results they would achieve'.[89] Production on the shop floor was therefore to be reorganised around certain preselected individuals who would work closely with the foreman and factory administration, and who would be ensured a regular supply of materials. Ferenc Szlovak, a founder-member of the 'Produce More' brigade, was able to achieve high performance as a turner, enjoying the 'permanent attention of the foreman and wage calculator'. Not surprisingly, many workers dismissed his results as 'not based on any kind of reality'.[90]

The national authorities urged the factory party organisation to deal with this kind of opposition through careful 'political work'.[91] This 'political work' was rooted in a two-track strategy that the party pursued with workers in the machine shop. The first track involved ensuring that all workers, not just those selected as Stakhanovites, benefited materially from the reorganisation of the shop; the local party regarded it as important that 'those workers who only make 120 per cent don't lose heart, they can get better results too'.[92]

Another way was to select workers who opposed the regime to become Stakhanovites; this was achieved through a mixture of persuasion and coercion. This method is illustrated by the case of János Sztankovits, a Stakhanovite machine miller. Sztankovits was older than most of the workers of the 'Produce More' brigade; he was thirty-two in 1949. He had also been a member of the MSZDP in the inter-war years and distrusted the Communists. Following the 'liberation' of Újpest in 1945, he was detained by Soviet troops and deported to the Soviet Union. He worked in a Moscow machine factory until 1948 and was decorated as a Stakhanovite in view of his achievements as a trained skilled worker in the disorganised post-war Soviet economy. Upon his return home he went back to work in the United Lighting and Electrics factory. Urged to join individual labour competition by party agitators in 1949, he turned on them: 'I . . . told him that Stalin could stick his shift up his arse, I worked for him for three years for free, I wasn't even given proper clothes, I was freed and why should I work for him again?'[93] Sztankovits was threatened with punishment for his conduct both by the factory party organisation and the local agents of the state security services. Immediately after this incident he was advised by the head of the machine shop to 'try and make the best of it so that they can at least see that you're not part of the enemy. On that basis I decided to show them that I knew how to work.'[94] With assistance from the shop management and a work method learned coping with Soviet machinery in Moscow, Sztankovits began to bust rates on the milling machines.[95] He faced immediate attacks from his workmates, who told him to 'go back to the Soviet Union, if you like it so much there'.[96]

This process can also be illustrated by the case of Ignác Pióker, who was to become the United Lighting and Electrics factory's only nationally known Stakhanovite. Aged forty-two in 1949, he had come to Budapest in the 1920s as a refugee from his native Transylvania. He was employed in the plant as a planer, which was not regarded as a skilled position and was poorly paid relative to other positions.[97] In the post-war years Pióker was a sympathiser of the MSZDP, and managed to persuade shop management that he was worthy of skilled worker status. He gained a special fixed hourly rate – rather than one dependent on his production results – in the late 1940s, in recognition of the quality of his work. When the 'Produce More' brigade was started, pressure was exerted on the hourly-rate workers to agree to being paid according to performance and to join individual labour competition.[98] Pióker initially refused to join the competition, because 'the quality of my work will be lost'.[99] Economic pressure was brought to bear on the hourly-paid skilled workers through their wage packets; the twenty that remained at the beginning of the competition earned 3 per cent less monthly than the very weakest skilled workers paid according to 'payment-by-results'.[100] The party's eventual persuasion of Pióker to exchange his hourly wage rate for the status of Stakhanovite was clearly designed to undermine dominant patterns of shop-floor culture, and was typical of the 'political work' necessary to create the Stakhanovite movement.[101]

The campaign was to culminate in the so-called 'Stalin shift', when workers were mobilised to bust rates spectacularly on the afternoon of the Soviet leader's seventieth birthday on 21 December. As it approached, the local press argued that the news from the United Lighting and Electrics factory was a sign of the arrival of 'the spirit of socialist competition' in the plant.[102] The factory party committee's twin-track policy towards resistance did successfully mobilise workers behind labour competition.[103] This culminated in the Stalin shift, which was a resounding success for the party in the plant; according to the factory newspaper, the shift was marked by 'the good organisation of production' while 'the tool-room worked like never before'.[104]

While the state was keen to proclaim the success of its transformation of the shop floor along socialist lines, a glance at the local implementation of those changes reveals that the new 'socialist' methods of working rested on precarious foundations. This was because, quite as much as previous mobilisations, it had taken the form of a temporary campaign. Events in 1950 revealed this to be the case as the state pressed ahead with unpopular attempts to introduce piece-rate systems of wages that rewarded performance according to the goals set down in the plan and raised production norms, thus slashing wages, in order to raise productivity.[105] Wage cuts continued to be opposed absolutely, particularly in the machine shop, where workers complained that 'they always take from us and we will never gain anything'.[106] Alongside this absolute opposition, it rapidly became clear that on-the-job control had not been eliminated by Stakhanovism, but had instead adapted to it and other pressures, such as the growing shortages of raw materials and tools that emerged during 1950. Workers engaged in patterns of 'informal bargaining' with the lower management at shop level, to manipulate wage classifications and norms; this enabled small groups of elite skilled workers to maintain a degree of control over remuneration.[107] It was in the face of this lack of control on the shop floor that the Budapest party committee first used the notion of 'right-wing Social Democracy' to explain the problems in the United Lighting and Electrics factory. In July 1950 it warned that in the factory 'development is being hindered, right-wing Social Democrats are holding back production and trying to persuade them [the workers] to keep down their output'.[108]

Conclusion

By 1952, the United Lighting and Electrics factory had become identified as a stronghold of 'right-wing Social Democracy'. By now, the term meant more, however, than skilled worker opposition to regime attempts to strip them of any semblance of on-the-job control over either the labour process or remuneration. It was a phenomenon that, according to party officials, 'appears in a changeable way in many different forms in the factory'. It could consist of anything from criticism of the role of the party organisation or complaints about low wages, to opposition to the erosion of the status of the urban, skilled elite faced with an influx of the young, women and workers from rural areas.[109] In short, during the years of Rákosi's dictatorship, it came to be synonymous with working-class opposition to the labour policies of the state.

It was an ideological construct, but one which arose from and fed on the interactions between Communist party, and then regime, policies and the realities of shop-floor politics between the end of the Second World War and the consolidation of the dictatorship – a consolidation that had occurred by 1950. In the case of the United Lighting and Electrics factory it was formed as a result of the memory of the struggle of the MKP for power, when faced with considerable support for a different vision of socialism in the factory. This memory fused with shop-floor struggle over the new regime's transformation of production to meet the requirements of central planning. Because of the strength there of the MSZDP in the immediate post-war years and the factory's designation as a stronghold of 'right-wing Social Democracy' during the early 1950s, the United Lighting and Electrics factory affords an especially useful standpoint from which to view the issue of how shop-floor conflict became politicised by the Stalinist state in Hungary. Conflicts over skills and control, as well as over hierarchy, in consequence of regime policies towards the working class were widespread during the 1950s across manufacturing industry as well as construction and mining.[110] 'Social Democrat' was a political identity ascribed to forms of opposition among the working class by the regime until 1956, and reflected more the desire of regime propagandists to link worker recalcitrance to supposed Cold War 'enemies of socialism' than the survival of a Social Democratic culture on the shop-floor. That it was closely linked with the practice of Hungarian Stalinism is shown by the circumstances of its eventual disappearance from the ideological armoury of the regime. It disappeared as the Rákosi dictatorship fell from power in July 1956, and as the former Social Democrats jailed in 1950 were rehabilitated and the regime sought to rebuild its shattered links to the working class after the 1956 Revolution.

Notes

1 Mátyás Rákosi, *Visszaemlékezések, 1940–1956 II kötet* (Budapest, 1997), 827.
2 I describe this struggle in Mark Pittaway, 'The politics of legitimacy and Hungary's post-war transition', paper prepared for a meeting of Team 1, 'Legitimacy in Politics and Culture', of the ESF programme 'Occupation in Europe: The Impact of National Socialist and Fascist Rule', Ghent, 14 September 2002. A shortened and revised version of this paper appears in *Contemporary European History*, 13:4 (2004), 453–75.
3 Zsuzsanna Kádár, 'A szociáldemokraták üldözése és diszkriminálása', in Lajos Varga (ed.), *A Magyar Szociáldemokrácia Kézikönyve* (Budapest, 1999), 163–9.
4 For more on this, see Mark Pittaway, 'The reproduction of hierarchy: skill, working-class culture and the state in early Socialist Hungary', *Journal of Modern History*, 74:4 (2002), 746–7.
5 Magyar Országos Levéltár (Hungarian National Archive, hereafter MOL), MSZMP Budapesti Bizottság iratai (Archive of the Budapest Committee of the Hungarian Socialist Workers' Party, hereafter M-Bp.)-95f.2/296ö.e., 106-10.
6 *A Sztahanov-Mozgalom* (Budapest, 1950), 18.
7 Mátyás Rákosi, 'Erősítsük a Pártunk kapcsolatait a tömegekkel, fejlesszük a pártonbelüli demokráciát, a kritikát és önkritikát', *Szabad Nép* (12 February 1950), 3.
8 MOL M-Bp.-95f.2/168/bö.e., 31.
9 MOL M-Bp.-95f.3/345ö.e., 8.
10 Lajos Sz. Varga, *Szakszervezetek a Diktatúrában. A Magyar Dolgozók Pártja és a szakszervezetek (1948–1953)* (Pécs, 1995), 137-69.
11 Zsuzsanna Kádár, 'A magyarországi szociáldemokrata perek története', *Múltunk*, 41:2 (1996), 3-49; Erzsébet Strassenreiter, 'A szociáldemokrata emigráció 1945 utáni tevékenysége', *Múltunk*, 36:1 (1991), 58-93.
12 This assumption appears implicitly in, Gyula Belényi, 'Bevezetés', in Gyula Belényi and Lajos Sz. Varga (eds), *Munkások Magyarországon 1948-1956: Dokumentumok*

(Budapest, 2000), 29. The assumption is more explicit in Éva Beránné Nemes and Erzsébet Kajari, 'A szociáldemokrata kérdése a szakszervezetekben (1948–1956)', *Múltunk*, 35:3 (1990), 129-42.

13 MOL M-Bp.-176f.2/194/19ö.e., 6.

14 *Ibid.*, 12-20.

15 I have drawn on Sheila Fitzpatrick's work on the ascription of class in the Soviet Union during the 1930s to make this argument. See Sheila Fitzpatrick, 'Ascribing class: the construction of social identity in Soviet Russia', *The Journal of Modern History*, 65:4 (1993), 745-70.

16 There are clear parallels here with Soviet Stalinist practice. See Gábor Rittersporn, 'The omnipresent conspiracy: on Soviet imagery of politics and social relations in the 1930s', in J. Arch Getty and Roberta T. Manning (eds), *Stalinist Terror: New Perspectives* (New York, 1993), 99-115.

17 For an example of this kind of propaganda, see Irén Komját, 'Bomlás a Jobboldali Szociáldemokraták Taborában', *Szabad Nép* (12 January 1950), 2.

18 Ernő Gerő, 'Felszolás a Magyar Sztahánovisták I. Országos Tanácskozásán', in Ernő Gerő, *Harcban a Szocialista Népgazdaságért* (Budapest, 1950), 620.

19 'Új munkásosztály születik', *Szabad Nép* (5 March 1950), 1.

20 For the history of the factory to 1945, see Ferenc Gáspár, *A Tungsram Rt. Története II. Rész* (Budapest, 1987).

21 Sándor Horváth, György Majtényi and Eszter Zsófia Tóth, *Élmunkások és sztahanovisták* (Budapest, unpublished manuscript, 1998).

22 MOL M-Bp.-176f.2/194/19ö.e., 12-20.

23 On the role of the factory during the revolution, see Mark Pittaway, 'Industrial workers, socialist industrialisation and the state in Hungary, 1948–1958' (University of Liverpool, PhD thesis, 1998), 345-57; István Kemény and Bill Lomax (eds), *Magyar munkástanácsok 1956-ban* (Paris, 1986); on regime explanations of events in the factory after the Revolution, see MOL M-Bp.-9f.1957-alapszervezetek/15ö.e., 102–5.

24 MOL M-Bp.-176f.2/194/19ö.e., 12.

25 Politikatörténeti és Szakszervezeti Levéltár (Archive of Political History and Trade Unions, hereafter PtSzL), Politikatörténeti Intézet Levéltára (Archive of the Institute for the History of Politics, hereafter PIL), Magyar Kommunista Párt iratai (Papers of the Hungarian Communist Party, hereafter 274f.), 20/35ö.e., 192.

26 Gáspár, *A Tungsram Rt. Története*, 96-103.

27 Miklós Lackó, *Nyilasok, Nemzetiszocialisták 1935-1944* (Budapest, 1966), 184–91.

28 Gáspár, *A Tungsram Rt. Története*, 104–5.

29 *Ibid.*, 90–1.

30 MOL Egyesült Izzó és Villámossági Rt., Ügyvezető Igazgatóság iratai (Papers of the Managing Directorate of the United Lighting and Electrics Company, hereafter Z601)/9cs./82t., 5.

31 Gáspár, *A Tungsram Rt. Története*, 94–107.

32 On the national picture during 1944–45, see Pittaway, 'The politics of legitimacy', 18–45; for circumstances in Újpest itself, see András Berényi, Mária Palasik, Csaba Rigóczki, Balázs Sipos and Erika Varsányi, *Újpest IV. Kerület* (Budapest, 1998), 24-5; Ede Gerelyes, 'Újpest a két világháború között', in Ede Gerelyes (ed.), *Újpest Története* (Budapest, 1977), 203-8.

33 For a participant's account, see Mihály Földes, *Pillanatképek az Újpesti Partizánharcokról. Kollektiv Riport* (Újpest, 1946).

34 MOL Z601/10cs./93t., 2–3.

35 'Az Egyesült Izzólámpa és Villámossági Rt. ügyevezető igazgatóságának feljegyzése a vállalat vezetőinek és munkásságának ellenállási mozgalmáról, valamint a kitelepítés és üzembénítás részbeni megakadályozásáról', reprinted in Károly Jenei (ed.), *A Munkásság az Üzemekért, a Termelésért, 1944–1945: Dokumentumgyűjtemény* (Budapest, 1970), 86–96.

36 1956-os Intézet Oral History Archivium (1956 Institute Oral History archive, hereafter OHA) 181 – Péterffy Miklós, 55.

37 Pittaway, 'The politics of legitimacy', 28–32.

38 OHA 177 – Nagy Pál Jenő, 27.

39 Pittaway, 'The politics of legitimacy', 34–8.

40 MOL Z601/10cs./93t., 15-6.

41 PtSzL A Volt Szakszervezetek Központi Levéltár anyaga (The materials of the former Central Archive of Trade Unions, hereafter SZKL), Vas-és Fémmunkások Szakszervezet iratai (Papers of the Metalworkers' Union, hereafter Vasas)/28d./1945; 'Jegyzőkönyv felvétetett az EIV Rt. Üzemi Bizottságának 1945. május 7-én megtartott IB. ülésen', 1; MOL Egyesült Izzó és Villámossági Rt. Személyzeti Osztály iratai (Papers of the Personnel Department of the United Lighting and Electrics Company, hereafter Z606)/4cs/9t., 5.

42 OHA 177 – Nagy Pál Jenő, 40-4.

43 'Látogatás az Egyesült Izzóban', *Jövő*(13 May 1946), 6.

44 PtSzL PIL 274f.16/130ö.e., 89.

45 OHA 177 – Nagy Pál Jenő, 40-4.

46 PtSzL PIL 274f.16/130ö.e., 38.

47 Ernő Kovács, 'Az Élet Erősebb!', *Szabad Újpest* (18 August 1945), 4.

48 'Látogatás az Egyesült Izzóban', *Jövő*(13 May 1946), 6.

49 MOL Z601/10cs./93t., 9-11.

50 Pittaway, 'Industrial workers', 85-8.

51 Gáspár, *A Tungsram Rt. Története*, 89-92.

52 MOL Z606/12cs./42t.

53 MOL Z601/9cs./82t.

54 MOL M-Bp.-134f.4ö.e., 04.

55 Domokos Varga, *Kiszlinger József Esztergályos Élete és Munkamódszere* (Budapest, 1951), 20.

56 PtSzL PIL A Magyarországi Szociáldemokrata Párt iratai (Papers of the Social Democratic Party of Hungary, hereafter 283f.)17/85ö.e., 24.

57 See the documents in PtSzL PIL 274f.16/130ö.e.

58 PtSzL PIL 283f.17/85ö.e., 127.

59 *Ibid.*, 140.

60 *Ibid.*, 172.

61 MOL M-Bp.-176f.2/194/19ö.e., 12.

62 PtSzL SZKL Vasas/353d./1948; 'Egyesült Izzó gyárértekezlet 1948. február 26-án', 5.

63 'Somlai László', in Imre Cserhalmi (ed.), *Történelmi Kulcsátvétel: Interjúk államosító igazgatókkal* (Budapest, 1983), 140–51.

64 Mátyás Rákosi, 'A Magyar Kommunista Párt és a Szociáldemokrata Párt Egyesülése', in Mátyás Rákosi, *Építjük a Nép Országát* (Budapest, 1949), 192.

65 MOL M-Bp.-134f./3ö.e., 24.

66 *Tungsram Híradó* (15 December 1948), 2; MOL M-95f.3/70ö.e., 102–3.
67 Varga, *Szakszervezetek a Diktatúrában*, 13-94; MOL M-Bp.-95f.2/319ö.e.
68 *Tungsram Híradó* (15 December 1948), 3; MOL M-Bp.-134f./5/a ö.e., 203–4.
69 Mark Pittaway, 'The social limits of state control: time, the industrial wage relation and social identity in Stalinist Hungary, 1948–1953', *Journal of Historical Sociology*, 12:3 (1999), 276–8.
70 *Tungsram Híradó* (1 July 1948), 2.
71 PtSzL SZKL Vasas/1948/353d.; 'Egyesült Izzó üzemi jelentése 1948 jun. 1-től jun. 15-ig'.
72 MOL M-Bp.-134f./3ö.e., 4; *Tungsram Híradó* (15 October 1948), 5.
73 PtSzL SZKL Vasas/1948/353d.; 'Egyesült Izzó üzemi jelentése 1948. junius 15-t_l julius 1-ig'.
74 MOL M-Bp.-134f./3ö.e., 24.
75 MOL M-Bp.-134f./4ö.e., 104–7.
76 MOL M-Bp-95f.3/70ö.e., 102.
77 Pittaway, 'The social limits of state control', 278.
78 MOL M-Bp.-134f./5/aö.e., 94–5.
79 MOL M-Bp.-134f./8/aö.e., 60–1.
80 *Ibid.*, 10–13.
81 *Ibid.*, 96–9.
82 *Tungsram Híradó* (8 September 1949), 5–6.
83 Kiszlinger had been a worker in a protected occupation in the Danuvia factory in Budapest. His official biography is unclear about the details, but he was arrested by the Germans in 1944 in the western town of Győr for draft-dodging (he did not have his identification documents showing that he was a worker in a protected occupation with him at the time), and was thus held by the Germans as a POW (Varga, *Kiszlinger József Esztergályos Élete és Munkamódszere*, 19).
84 *Ibid.*, 24.
85 *Tungsram Híradó* (5 December 1949), 1.
86 *Tungsram Híradó* (8 September 1949), 6.
87 MOL M-Bp.-134f.5/aö.e., 55.
88 MOL M-Bp.-134f./8/aö.e., 6.
89 *Ibid.*, 4.
90 *Ibid.*, 19.
91 MOL M-Bp.-95f.4/147ö.e., 55.
92 MOL M-Bp.-134f./5/aö.e., 8.
93 János Sztankovits, personal interview.
94 *Ibid.*
95 Zoltán Halázs, *Sztankovits János sztahanovista marós élete és munkamódszere* (Budapest, 1951), 3.
96 MOL M-Bp.-95f.4/147ö.e., 55.
97 Vilmos Zolnay, *Pióker Ignác az Ország Legjobb Gyalusa* (Budapest, 1951), 9.
98 Magyar Nemzeti Múzeum Legújabbkori Győjteménye (Hungarian National Museum, Contemporary History Collection), Pióker Ignác vegyes iratai (Miscellaneous papers of Ignác Pióker).
99 Zolnay, *Pioker Ignác az Ország Legjobb Gyalusa*, 15.
100 MOL M-Bp.-134f.5/aö.e., 243.
101 MOL M-Bp.-95f.4/147ö.e., 55.

102 'Fellendült az egyéni verseny – nincs többé szűk keresztmetszet', *Észak Pestkörnyék* (3 December 1949), 5.

103 MOL M-Bp.-95f.4/77ö.e.

104 *Tungsram Híradó* (5 January 1950), 1.

105 Pittaway, 'The social limits of state control', 280–2.

106 MOL M-Bp.-95f.4/123ö.e., 32.

107 MOL M-Bp.-95f.4/126ö.e., 103.

108 MOL M-Bp.-95f.4/119ö.e., 46.

109 MOL M-Bp.-176f.2/194/19ö.e., 15.

110 Pittaway, 'The reproduction of hierarchy'.

II

Ethnic
and linguistic
minorities

5

Between '*Heimat*' and 'expulsion': the construction of the Sudeten German '*Volksgruppe*' in post-war Germany

Eva Hahn and Hans Henning Hahn

Minorities do not exist until they are constructed;[1] this statement broadly encapsulates the conclusions resulting from my investigation into the history of the Sudeten German minority – or, to be precise, *Volksgruppe* (ethnic group) – in post-war West Germany. This is not to say that we wish to deny the existence of a group among the German population which consists of individuals identifying themselves as 'Sudeten Germans', or to suggest that such a group has been construed only in our fantasy. Our assertion concerns the *legal status* of this group as well as the way in which the Sudeten Germans are generally perceived. Not every group of people is a minority; any group needs to have been constructed as a minority before it can be one.

In pre-modern Europe, various groups, such as the aristocracy, the priesthood, townspeople, guilds, the peasant population, etc. were all minorities endowed with special legal rights and institutions.[2] In fact, all societies could be looked upon as consisting of minorities, so that, before the modern concept of nationhood emerged as a term of self-identification for the majority population of a nation-state, awareness of the special status of minorities was stronger than during the last two centuries, even though the word itself was not in use. The concept 'minority' makes sense only in a society with a clear-cut majority, and, even then, the question of who considers himself or herself as a member of a minority has always been determined by the particular historical context. Only groups who articulate their identity as a minority do become minorities.

Most of the groups discussed in this volume, such as youth, women, workers, intellectuals or artists, are not usually conceived of as minorities, even in the currently common usage of the term. Similarly, the German population in the Bohemian Lands – about one-third of the total population there – had never considered themselves as belonging to a 'minority' before 1918. Indeed, the term 'Sudeten Germans' did not even exist then. And yet, as we know, there are people who consider themselves as Sudeten Germans in present-day Germany, and who are organised as a *Sudetendeutsche Volksgruppe* (Sudeten German ethnic group), so that obviously between then and now a Sudeten German minority has been constructed.[3]

The current usage of the term 'minority' corresponds to a set definition – for example the one upon which the well-known Minority Rights Group International bases its work, i.e., an organisation which has been established to secure the rights of ethnic, religious and linguistic minorities and which acts as an advocate of the rights of minorities. The Sudeten Germans should therefore belong to the large number of groups on which this organisation focuses. However, by legal standards, there are only two minorities in present-day Germany, the Danes in the north and the Sorbs in the east. The question then arises as to why the Sudeten Germans are not regarded as a minority in German society, but are instead considered as a *Volksgruppe*.

On the Internet homepage of an organisation called *Sudetendeutsche Landsmannschaft* (Organisation of Sudeten German Compatriots), there is a definition of whom this organisation regards as 'Sudeten Germans', namely, 'the group of about 3.5 million people expelled in 1945–46 from the Bohemian Lands, the area of today's Czech Republic'. Surprisingly, the group has grown since then: 'We estimate that about 3.8 million Sudeten Germans (people with a Sudeten German identity) are alive today; the increase is due to the general German population growth during the 50s and 60s . . . However, the number of people who have at least one Sudeten German ancestor might exceed seven million, because of mixed marriages.'[4] On the same website, there is also a map of the Czech Republic, showing the so-called homeland of this group, the Sudetenland, as well as an outline of the history of the Sudeten Germans, and a section entitled 'Our Goals'.

These goals are those of the *Sudetendeutsche Landsmannschaft*, an organisation of 'rather less than 100,000 members', which claims to represent the Sudeten Germans, and are as follows:

1. The CR [Czech Republic] should declare the expulsion of the Sudeten Germans to be an international crime;
2. The Sudeten Germans should be granted the right to their homeland, ethnic group rights (German schools, protection of the German language in public life) and compensation for the losses incurred during their transfer from the post-war Czechoslovak state;
3. The Beneš decrees and some other Czechoslovak post-war laws should be abolished;
4. Direct negotiations between Czech officials and the leadership of the *Landsmannschaft* should be started: 'During these negotiations all problems concerning the future coexistence of Czechs and Germans in the Bohemian Lands/Czech Republic should be discussed and settled. The agenda of such talks should include property questions, although material problems are not our central point. It should not include territorial questions, as we have no territorial claims.'[5]

To judge by the foregoing, we are confronted with a familiar 'minority issue': a group of people claims to be represented by an organisation, and this organisation has the task of representing them *vis-à-vis* a government in order to secure collective rights for the group. Certain Sudeten German organisations have indeed been demanding their rights for decades, for example in a Petition to the United Nations of 17 January 1975: 'The Sudeten Germans, expelled from their ancestral homes in Bohemia, Moravia and Silesia, together with their friends throughout the world, hereby appeal to the United Nations to give ear to the freely elected representatives of this ethnic group and to support their demand for restitution of the rights of the Sudeten German people and for reparation of the wrong inflicted upon them.'[6] The Sudeten German representatives have also worked out in draft their own concept of the rights of ethnic groups (4 March 1979), and have repeatedly 'renewed the pledge to our ancestral homeland'.[7]

And yet, if we look more closely at the issues raised by Sudeten German organisations, we will find that this 'minority problem' has several unusual aspects: (1) The group demands to be granted rights by the government of a state of which its members are not citizens (and not by a state whose citizenship they hold); (2) The group claims to represent only those Czechoslovak citizens who fled or were forcibly moved to Germany after the Second World War, but not those Germans who remained in Czechoslovakia and are now living in the Czech Republic as its German minority; (3) The Sudeten German organisations involved do not represent all parts of the political spectrum among the Germans from Czechoslovakia who have lived in West Germany since the war, but only those who consider themselves 'Sudeten Germans'. Those who claim to be 'Germans from Czechoslovakia' and not 'Sudeten Germans' have been ignored, indeed treated as hostile and as renegades; (4) The so-called 'Sudeten Question' has not been defined as concerning the expulsion and its aftermath, but rather as 'the refusal to allow the Sudeten Germans to exercise the right of self-determination in 1919'.[8]

Whilst Sudeten German organisations have claimed for decades that they seek 'to achieve the peaceful co-existence of all nations and a liberated Sudetenland in a free Europe',[9] they have not defined themselves as representatives of the interests of every German who was expelled from Czechoslovakia in 1945–46. Clearly, the reference to the expulsion constitutes only one aspect of the overall self-identification of the Sudeten German *Volksgruppe*.

Are the Sudeten Germans an 'ethnic minority' in the currently understood sense of the word or are they not? It is important to raise this question, for two main reasons. Firstly, in practical terms, the question is politically relevant because the Czech government needs to clarify whether the demands raised in Germany during negotiations with the Sudeten German *Landsmannschaft* are about redressing human suffering caused by the brutal post-war treatment of the Germans in Czechoslovakia and by the expulsion, or whether they should negotiate with the *Sudetendeutsche Landsmannschaft* as representing an ethnic minority in a neighbouring state.[10] Secondly, in the context of our discussion of the social history of Central European politics in the years following the end of the Second World War, the question of whether the Sudeten Germans do or do not constitute an ethnic minority is an interesting topic of inquiry.

It was during the years 1945–53 that the Sudeten Germans emerged as a group and constituted themselves as a *Volksgruppe*, and, as we shall see, the term *Volksgruppe* is the clue to the question of whether they are or are not a minority.

In terms of social history, the expellees from Eastern Europe undoubtedly constituted a special group within post-war German society. Some 10 million people arrived in Germany in 1945–46 from Eastern Europe; homeless and deprived of all their possessions, they required special attention and social care.[11] Among them, about 2.5 million came from Czechoslovakia; two-thirds of these settled in the Western zones of occupation. Both in Austria and in post-war East Germany, the history of the expellees has been shaped by the determination to integrate the new citizens and, as a result, no Sudeten German *Volksgruppe* has ever emerged there.[12] Thus, the remainder of this chapter will focus solely upon developments in West Germany.

Prior to the establishment of the two German states in 1949, the refugees, as the expellees were then called, received poor relief or unemployment assistance on the same scale as the native population, and the Allied authorities did not allow any of the refugees to form any sort of special organisation, the aim being that they should be swiftly integrated into German society. It is also noteworthy that a large proportion of the Germans arriving from Czechoslovakia did not receive German citizenship until 1955,[13] having been considered as stateless until then.

Clearly, this scenario suggests that the original thinking about how to integrate the expellees into post-war German society was ambivalent; on the one hand, they were not granted citizenship, yet, on the other hand, they were integrated by means of social and economic assistance, as were other Germans, into the newly emerging democratic political system. And, in fact, many of them did use the opportunities this offered and set up their new homes just like many other Germans whose lives had been disrupted by the Nazi regime and the war, as was reported by the British historian Elizabeth Wiskemann in her 1956 book, *Germany's Eastern Neighbours: Problems relating to the Oder–Neisse Line and the Czech Frontier Regions*,[14] which contains many details about the gradual social and economic integration of these refugees.

It also contains information on policies regarding the resettlement of refugees, who in the immediate post-war period were crowded into rural areas where they could never be genuinely absorbed, on their inclusion in the newly emerging economy under special schemes to secure employment, retraining and the building up of new industries like the glass industry in Neu-Gablonz etc., on the construction of housing, on emigration (about 270,000 Germans emigrated overseas from 1945 to the end of 1953) and on financial measures offered to the refugees in the form of the *Soforthilfegesetz* (Law on Immediate

Assistance) from 1949 onwards. This process was completed by an all-embracing code for these immigrants and was formalised in the *Lastenausgleichgesetz* (Law on the Equalising of Burdens) of 1952 and finally the *Bundesvertriebenengesetz* (Federal Law on Expellees) of 1953.

Yet the unresolved question of citizenship must have made everyone aware that the Germans newly arrived from Czechoslovakia were not ordinary 'Germans' like all the others. Indeed, these newly arrived Germans were not warmly received in Germany, and the Allied authorities had to struggle hard to make the native population and their politicians take care of these new refugees. Post-Nazi German society was not an overly compassionate one; as the famous humourist George Mikes observed in 1952, 'there is not much brotherly love wasted on the refugees', and he continued:

> it is probably a favourable turn of events that German race hatred, or animosity, is turned against other Germans. This animosity is not very dangerous, after all, and whenever it becomes dangerous it is controlled by reason and legislation. But the Germans seem to be in need of discharging a certain amount of race hatred just as a car must discharge poisonous gases. It is much better if they discharge these gases on the home market.[15]

Moreover, the new arrivals brought with them their own social, political and cultural networks as well as their own kind of cultural heritage, which included not only their own, much-discussed, local dialects but also their own forms of political rhetoric. In the case of the Germans arriving from Czechoslovakia, there were several streams of cultural and political traditions which had been discernible before the Second World War. Of these, undoubtedly the best known were the liberal traditions represented, for example, by the literature of German Prague and its cultural life in general (Franz Kafka, Max Brod); alongside these were the left-wing political traditions (the Social Democratic as well as Communist traditions), the traditions of so-called Social Catholicism (*Christlichsoziale Bewegung* – Christian Social Movement), political parties and organisational networks representing the farmers and small manufacturers (the *Bund der Landwirte* – Landowners' Association – and the *Deutsche Gewerbepartei* – German Business Party), the right-wing populist traditions of national chauvinism and anti-Semitism, recalling the infamous Georg von Schönerer and his *Alldeutsche Partei* (Pan-German Party) of the late nineteenth and early twentieth centuries and represented by Konrad Henlein's Sudeten German party in the late 1930s.

During the years preceding the expulsion, this wide spectrum of cultural and political traditions had been greatly reduced by the National Socialist regime, and only some portions of it were recreated in post-war Germany. Above all, the German–Jewish population had either fallen victim to the Holocaust, or had survived through emigration and stayed overseas, or returned to Czechoslovakia after the Second World War. In spite of the unjust treatment of German-speaking Jewish survivors in post-war Czechoslovakia,[16] hardly any Jews from Czechoslovakia moved to post-war Germany (only after 1968 did their number increase and did they become publicly visible once more). The persecution of the German Communists and Social Democrats under the Nazis had also been very intensive, so that the political networks which the refugees brought with them from Czechoslovakia to post-war Germany were only those that had survived the Nazi regime. Moreover, many of those Germans who had been actively involved in the underground resistance to the Nazi regime either remained in Czechoslovakia or went to the GDR.

The emergence of the Cold War and the ensuing changes in the landscape of international relations on the European continent had a profound impact on the further development of the integration of these refugees into German society. The Western Allied governments, who had agreed at Potsdam in the summer of 1945 that the German population should be moved out of Eastern Europe, became reluctant to abide by their views once they became involved in the Cold War. West Germany, once part of an enemy state, had now become a Western ally, while the previously allied state of Czechoslovakia had become an enemy state after the Communist take-over in February 1948. Consequently, the British and Americans changed their view of both the Potsdam agreement and the efforts to integrate the new German arrivals.[17]

This being the case, it is hardly surprising that in the Federal Republic of Germany a whole network of expellee institutions and organisations, financed by the state, was established during the 1950s by recruiting above all people from the right-wing end of the cultural and political spectrum.[18] In terms of culture, this meant the establishment of Sudeten German organisations within the context of the so-called *völkisch* (folkish) traditions. Moreover, post-war 'denazification' was not as thorough as most people believed, as German historians have been finding out during the last five years or so,[19] and it was even less so among the Germans arriving from Eastern Europe. Here, the representation of refugees as victims and the spectacle of the sufferings caused to Germans by their East European neighbours primarily served to support revisionist attitudes towards the Potsdam agreement in the tradition of the pre-war opposition to the Peace Treaties of 1919–20. This is where the origins of the so-called *Sudetendeutsche Volksgruppe* are to be found.

The 'other' cultural and political milieux to which Germans from Czechoslovakia belonged were thus not included in these new Sudeten German organisations which enjoyed political and financial support in the Federal Republic. The fact that the *völkisch* milieu had also embraced many German exiles in London during the Second World War, and in particular the Social Democratic organisation led by Wenzel Jaksch, was used to conceal the close connections between the traditions represented by the Sudeten German organisations and National Socialism. The criticisms levelled at Wenzel Jaksch whilst in exile during the war were suppressed in the Federal Republic, so that the question raised by another Social Democrat in London, Franz Kögler, in the title of his book *Oppressed Minority?* never became a topic for discussion after the Second World War.[20]

Kögler's analysis of the ideology of *'Sudetendeutschtum'* (Sudeten German-dom) resulted in his rejection of the concept of a *Sudetendeutsche Volksgruppe* as incompatible with democracy: 'Henlein cannot have been in any doubt about the fact that this [i.e. Henlein's political goals] meant the disruption of Czecho-slovakian democracy. He and his followers were well aware that a State cannot rest on two diametrically opposing principles – namely, on democracy and dic-tatorship – simultaneously; or, in other words, on the libertarian equality of all citizens of the State, and at the same time on the privileged position of a domi-nant race, the *Herrenvolk*, over inferior races.'[21] However, the *Arbeitsgemein-schaft Deutscher Sozialdemokraten aus der Tschechoslowakei* (Working Group of German Social Democrats from Czechoslovakia), of which Franz Kögler was a member after the Second World War, has never been acknowledged as a 'Sudeten German organisation' in the Federal Republic, and has had to strug-gle hard for survival without any financial or political support and against strong hostility from 'official' Sudeten German Social Democratic organisa-tions, such as the *Seliger Gemeinde* (Seliger Community).[22]

In the course of these developments, the *Vertreibung*, or expulsion of Germans from Eastern Europe, has been represented not so much by references to the indi-vidual sufferings of the people concerned, but rather by the collectively shared myth of the *Deutscher Osten* (the German East),[23] familiar from the pre-Nazi era, but above all from Nazi propaganda and the policies of *'Generalplan Ost'* ('Gen-eral Plan East'). Numerous Sudeten German politicians well known as active National Socialists and participants in designing the Nazi policies towards the so-called 'Czech Question' in the years 1938–45 became leading functionaries in the post-war Sudeten German organisations, even though some of them, for example Franz Karmasin, were on the list of war criminals in Czechoslovakia.[24] The traditions of the so-called *Sudetendeutschtum* to which these political circles adhered had been extremely anti-Czech and had had their own special agenda even before the Czechs drove the Germans out of the country in the aftermath of the Second World War.

In the representation of this 'cultural heritage' of the expelled Germans, new variations of the old traditions of the Germans as the *Kulturträger* – that is, bearers of the cultural mission to bring civilisation to Eastern Europe – have flourished.[25] The so-called *Vertriebenenorganisationen* (expellees' organisations), mainly financed under the slogan of 'preserving the cultural heritage of the expellees', have engraved their views on the post-war German collective memory by propagating the earlier Sudeten German historical literature and its kinds of particular rhetoric, myths and stereotypes about Eastern Europe.[26] This was made possible not only by the generous financial support given to the expellees' organisations and activities, but above all by the publication of vast numbers of books and pamphlets for the use of both schools and adult educa-tion. Similar traditions have penetrated deeply into German academic histori-ography under the slogan of *Ostforschung* (research into the East).[27] The hostility towards the Poles and the Czechs felt by members of *Vertriebenen-*

organisationen are not a 'natural' consequence of these people's personal experiences, but are rather the result of post-war policies in the Federal Republic.

In fact, many Germans today still hold some of the infamous traditional attitudes and interpretations, for example in relation to Czech history, without being aware that what nowadays appears as 'academic historiography' originated from the *Sudetendeutscher Volkstumskampf* (struggle of Sudeten Germandom).[28] Through this process, the so-called *Heimatkultur* (culture of the homeland) came to represent the *Vertreibung*, and the *Sudetendeutsche Volksgruppe* those Germans who had lived for centuries in the Bohemian Lands and were transferred to West Germany after the end of the Second World War.

Nor were the images and rhetoric representing the Sudeten Germans as victims of Czech persecution a new invention by the expelled Sudeten Germans. From 1918 down to the present day, the Czechoslovak diplomat and president Eduard Beneš has stood as the personification of Czech hostility to the Sudeten Germans. Not surprisingly, the recent Sudeten German campaign against the so-called Beneš decrees bears a striking resemblance to the Nazi anti-Beneš campaign of the late 1930s.[29] Even the political conflicts among the Sudeten German organisations (for example, that between the Catholic organisation, the Ackermann Community on the one hand, which looks toward Vienna and the Austrian tradition and, on the other, the Witiko Association, which prefers the Prussian heritage) tended to be about pre-war issues rather than a reflection of post-war life. The most obvious 'mixture' of this kind can be seen in Sudeten German complaints about the legal aspects of the Sudeten German question; often, it was not clear whether a speaker or author was referring to the 'broken laws' of 1918, meaning the unfulfilled claim for Sudeten German national self-determination, or whether he meant the 'broken laws' of Potsdam in 1945.[30] According to Sudeten German politicians, the allegedly still unresolved so-called 'Sudeten German Question' does not primarily concern the removal of the German population from Czechoslovakia in 1945–46, but rather 'the refusal to allow the Sudeten Germans to exercise the right of self-determination' in 1918.[31] Accordingly, the traditions and literary images used by the Sudeten German organisations when referring to the *Vertreibung* are adaptations of traditions dating from the pre-war *völkisch* Sudeten German movement as well as from the Nazi era.[32]

Many images which seemed to reflect the post-war experience of Sudeten Germans had a long back-history in the German literature from Bohemia about the *Volkstumskampf*; the key words in the poems included here and in the Appendix, such as *Mahnung* (warning), *Sturm des Verderbens* (whirlwind of destruction), *deutscher Ahnen Erbe* (inheritance from our German forebears), *deutsche Heimat* (the German homeland), *Einheit im Dienst der Heimat* (unity in the service of the homeland), etc. should indicate this. A few examples from the period between 1904 and 1958 have been selected to demonstrate this continuity. The most remarkable poem in the selection is '*Deutsches Leid in Böhmen*', dating from 1923, in which even the motif of *Vertreibung* and *Heimat-*

losigkeit (homelessness) is already being used in a manner reminiscent of postwar Sudeten German literature, and is hardly comprehensible in the year 1923, when it was written:

'Deutsches Leid in Böhmen' by Hilda Hadina-Königsreiter
From: Emil Hadina and Wilhelm Müller-Rüdersdorf, *Großböhmerland.*
Ein Heimatbuch für Deutschböhmen, Nordmähren und das südöstliche Schlesien
(Leipzig, 1923), 2.

Deutsches Leid in Böhmen	German sorrow in Bohemia
Es klingt ein Lied vom Leide,	A song, a song of sorrow,
Vom Leide durch den Wind:	Is singing in the storm:
Die Heimat ist verloren,	Lost, lost is the homeland,
Du heimatloses Kind!	O child without a home!
Es fällt wie lauter Tränen,	Its notes like purest teardrops
Wie Tränen durch den Schnee –	Fall where the snow-flakes fly –
Das Auge wird mir trübe,	The road grows dark before me,
Ich weiß nicht, wo ich geh'.	I cannot see my way.
Ich geh' als wie im Traume,	As in a trance I wander
Im Traume durch die Welt –	The wide world endlessly –
Sind alle ihre Freuden	The joys it has to offer
Vergiftet und vergällt.	Are grief and pain to me.
Ich wollt', ich könnte wandern,	I would that I might wander,
Wohl wandern durch den Wind,	Companioned by the storm,
Durch die verlorne Heimat,	About that loved, lost homeland,
Als heimatloses Kind.	A child without a home.

A second especially noteworthy example is the poem '*Heimat*', by Erwin Guido Kolbenheyer, one of the most prominent writers in the Third Reich.[33] Kolbenheyer himself was born in Budapest in 1887 (dying in 1962 in Bavaria); yet he enjoyed immense popularity among the expellees in general, and the Sudeten Germans in particular, as 'their' poet, so much so that in Geretsried, one of the new Bavarian towns built for the Germans from Eastern Europe and originally inhabited to a large extent by Sudeten Germans, the name Kolbenheyer was repeatedly used in street names, etc. (for example, Kolbenheyer Museum, Kolbenheyer Building, Kolbenheyer Street, Kolbenheyer Square).[34] The poem by Kolbenheyer shows that both the particular manner in which the 'expulsion' is represented in the post-war public record, and the so-called Sudeten German cultural heritage, which were fixed upon by the Federal Republic as worthy of extensive support, should be studied as an expression of one particular, deliberately selected, cultural milieu, and not as a kind of 'natural' tradition of the Germans who were expelled from Czechoslovakia; needless to say, there were no Franz Kafka or Max Brod Streets in Geretsried . . .

Kolbenheyer had been a prominent Nazi writer, yet the book from which the chosen poem is drawn was written by a Catholic priest who during the Third Reich lived as an émigré in the United States. The author, known as 'Father E. J. Reichenberger', was among the first and most ferocious critics of the expulsion of the Germans from Eastern Europe and published numerous books in the post-war era, attacking in particular the Allied responsibility for endorsing the expulsion in a style closely reminiscent of pre-1945 Nazi anti-Western rhetoric.[35] Obviously, the cultural milieu which emerged in the Federal Republic and dominated the construction of public memory embraced wider public circles than just former Nazis. To study the forms in which the 'expulsion' has been engraved upon the German collective memory, we therefore need to look at the wider cultural context, rather than confining our examination to the context of the expulsion itself, or to German cultural traditions in pre-war Czechoslovakia, or to the Nazi regime and its after-echoes in post-war Germany. It seems to us that the term *"völkisch traditions"* would be a suitable designation for the peculiar cultural phenomenon which we are addressing.[36]

The Sudeten German *Volksgruppe* is the product of a particular political and cultural alliance that emerged in post-war Germany and participated in the construction of the public memory of the *Vertreibung*. The term *'Volksgruppe'* itself originates from Konrad Henlein's movement of the 1930s, and draws its main inspiration from the so-called *Heimatkultur*.[37] The historical context in which it re-emerged in its present form in post-war Germany was the Cold War; public support for it came from the German population expelled in 1945–46 from Czechoslovakia and politically it was constructed by a new alliance within the wider range of traditional political and cultural German milieux.

It should be added, however, that, somewhat paradoxically, the first leader of the *Sudetendeutsche Landsmannschaft*, Rudolf Lodgman von Auen, in 1938 denounced the attempts to construct a *Sudetendeutsche Volksgruppe*; in a memorandum to Adolf Hitler of April 1938, he presented himself as a faithful adherent of National Socialism and therefore as a critic of *Sudetendeutschtum*. After the war, he presided over the constitution of the *Sudetendeutsche Landsmannschaft*. This particular contradiction affords us the more reason, in the context of the present volume, to pay close attention to detail. Like Lodgman von Auen, other Sudeten German politicians have continued to adjust their political strategies to suit specific circumstances throughout the twentieth century. Without a detailed understanding of the relevant historical changes and continuities, Sudeten German political life in the Federal Republic is misperceived as the product of the post-war era, and the source of the collective images of the *Vertreibung* is wrongly seen as being the victims themselves.

It should not be forgotten that 'other' kinds of memories of the *Vertreibung* were also articulated during the first two or three decades after the war.[38] These may be found in books by liberal writers such as Günther Grass, Peter Hätling, Siegfried Lenz or Horst Bienek, who themselves were among the expellees from Eastern Europe but who were critical of the attitudes summarised above.

Unfortunately, they have never had much impact on German politics. Nor were the outspoken critics of the Sudeten German organisation in the German media, such as *Der Spiegel*, more successful. Nor, indeed, has the traditional historiography of the German left, cultivated in the GDR during the Cold War only within certain permitted limits, offered much in the way of an intellectually attractive alternative, though it is worth mentioning and studying in this context with more interest than has been the case to date. Only in recent years have new developments begun to take shape, indicating that new bridges might be being built between various sections of the German public.[39]

The institutional framework which secured the development of this particular form of the collective memory of the 'expulsion' within the continuity of the German *Heimatkultur* as it developed in the Bohemian Lands during the latter decades of the nineteenth century is still in being. The Federal government continues to support it financially with over 20 million Euros a year (with additional funds from the *Länder*). Even though these organisations find it difficult to attract public attention, they do provide jobs for young historians, ethnologists, Slavists and Germanists, so there is much lobbying on their behalf and very little interest in looking critically at what they are actually doing.[40] Any attempt to cut down on financial support for these organisations encounters strong opposition; even the Schröder government had reluctantly in 1999 to abandon the attempt it made to reorganise this whole network, which is surely as outdated as are its views.[41]

In these cultural traditions, popularised as the German cultural heritage from the Bohemian Lands, only the *völkisch* traditions of *Sudetendeutschtum* have been revived and developed, and this is the reason why the 'Germans from Czechoslovakia' have come to be represented by the Sudeten German *Volksgruppe* in Germany. It is in the light of these traditions alone that the Sudeten German *Volksgruppe* has been created as a specific form of 'minority' in post-war Germany.[42] By contrast, those members of the German population (originally around 200,000) who were exempted from being transferred and were allowed to stay in Czechoslovakia in the post-war era, had opposed Nazism and had not been sympathetic to the Sudeten German cause either. Hence, the German-speaking population which now constitutes the German 'minority' in the Czech Republic does not regard itself as belonging to the Sudeten German *Volksgruppe*.[43]

As matters stand at present, the 'Sudeten German Question' is generally viewed as a kind of natural consequence of the expulsion, not as the result of the political construction of this 'Sudeten German Question' in Cold War Western Germany, and certainly not as deriving from pre-Second World War roots. Hence, it has been largely forgotten that only some sections of the Sudeten German population were represented in the institutions and organisations which were established after 1949 with the clear purpose of serving specific political aims (the revision of the Potsdam agreement of 1945).[44] This misperception is the main cause of the political tensions which still exist between Germany and the Czech Republic, and which only the study of the post-war history of Central European politics can help to resolve.

Appendix

'Mahnung' by Georg Vogel
From: *Festschrift zur XX. Hauptversammlung des Deutschen Böhmerwaldbundes in Budweis am 28. August 1904* (Budweis, 1904), 9.

Mahnung	*Warning*
Wenn der Heimat Tannen rauschen,	When our homeland's pine-trees whisper,
von der Schöpfung Hauch bewegt,	Echoing the universe,
Laßt uns ihrer Mahnung lauschen,	Let us hear their quiet warning
Die Gott selbst hineingelegt:	Spoken to us by God's voice:
'Was des Landes Sturm verderbe,	'Though the tempest scar our homeland,
Nichts darf diesen Wald entweih'n;	Nought this forest may profane;
Deutscher Ahnen heilig Erde	The sacred soil of German forebears
Soll der Treue Hochburg sein.' . . .	Our truth's stronghold shall remain.' . . .
Was die Ahnen uns erstritten,	Conquered for us by our forebears,
Was ihr Mut und Fleiß erhielt,	Their nerve and labour held this ground;
Sei belebt durch deutsche Hütten,	German steadings shall enliven
Sei von deutschem Geist umspielt;	And German spirit fill our land.
Glück und Frieden ewig kröne	May peace and happiness for ever
Diese Burg aus Felsenstein;	Crown this fortress built of stone;
Deutscher Heimat wack're Söhne	The German homeland's watchful scions
Sollen darin Hüter sein.	Shall be its dauntless garrison.
Wie, um deutsches Recht zu wahren,	As, bound together by the struggle
Uns ein Band umschlungen hält,	To protect our German right,
Wie wir uns seit zwanzig Jahren	In the service of our homeland
In der Heimat Dienst gestellt,	We for twenty years have fought,
Sich das Banner stolz entfalte,	Still proud shall fly our cherished banner,
Daß es braust von Mund zu Mund:	Each pass to each the watchword loud:
'Treu' und Einheit stets erhalte	'Faithful and united ever,
Uns'res deutschen Waldes Bund'.	Our Geman forests' brotherhood.'

'Sudetenland!' by Hans Albert
From: *Sudetenland*, ed. Landesverkehrsverband Sudetenland
(Reichenberg, 1939), 1.

Sudetenland!	*Sudetenland!*
Aus Deinem schönem, ernstem Angesichte	The hatred in which thou wert held by the other, the looming stranger
Schwand nun des Fremden Hasses unheilvoller Schatten.	No longer shadows thy beauty nor stirs thy grave stillness.

Befreite Arme breiten sich erlöst empor
zum Lichte.
Großdeutschlands Sonne leuchtet über
Berg und Wald und Matten.
Gott hat das tiefe Leid und schwere Not
von uns genommen.
An deutscher Bruderliebe ward der Trug
zuschanden.
Und Millionen froher Herzen jubeln auf:
Willkommen!
Wir grüßen Euch in unsern ewig
deutschen Heimatlanden!

Arms that have been set free stretch
joyfully up to the heavens.
Great Germany's sun shines over
mountain and field and forest.
God has taken away the deep pain and
the terror we suffered.
The lie has been set at naught through
the love that binds German brothers.
Millions of hearts rejoice and utter their
greeting: Welcome!
We welcome you here in our homelands,
which shall forever be German!

'Heimat' by Erwin Guido Kolbenheyer
From: Father Emmanuel J. Reichenberger, *Europa in Trümmern. Das Ergebnis des
Kreuzzuges der Alliierten* (Graz-Göttingen, 1952), 348.

Heimat

Die Welle weiß, wohin sie geht,
Der Sturm, wohin sein Atem weht,
Die Saat fühlt ihren Bodenstand,
Der Wald, die Flur, das Wurzelland,
Und alles Tier hat Rast und Statt
Und wird noch seines Friedens satt,

Uns aber ist der Heimat Recht
Geschändet und geraubt.
Wir lebten alle recht und schlecht
Und haben treu geglaubt,
Geglaubt, daß Heimat heilig sei
Und frei vor Raub, vor Schändung frei.

Gott sei's geklagt: die tiefste Not
War nicht der Krieg, war nicht der Brand.
Die Heimat war uns Wort im fremden
Land,
Und fremdes Brot ist hart und schwer.
Weit ist es von der Heimat her.

Nur eines wird der bösen Lust
Zu Raub nicht und zu Mord:
Wir trugen tief in unsrer Brust
Die Heimat mit uns fort;
So bettelarm und vogelfrei
Wir sind, die Heimat steht uns bei.

Homeland

Ebb and flow-tide know their path,
The tempest breathes a conscious breath,
Seeds sense the soil in which they stand,
Forest and plough and pastureland.
And all beasts have their home and ease,
And even weary of their peace.

But our right to home and hearth
Was smirched and stol'n away,
Though we lived in faith and truth
And trusted earnestly,
Trusted our homeland still would be
From smirch and spoliation free.

But, God knows well, the deepest woe
Was neither war nor leaping flame.
In foreign lands our only thought was
home.
Bitter's the bread from foreign soil,
Eaten where far from home we dwell.

But there's one thing that ill intent
Will never catch or kill:
For with us in our banishment
Our loved land travels still.
Poor and outcast though we be,
The homeland's yet our prop and stay.

Die Welle weiß, wohin sie geht,
Der Sturm, wohin sein Atem weht,
Die Saat fühlt ihren Bodenstand,
Der Wald, die Flur, das Wurzelland,
Und alles Tier hat Rast und Statt
Und wird noch seines Friedens satt.

Wir haben nur das Herzensgut,
In dem die alte Heimat ruht,
Aus ihm blüht Liebe uns und Rat,
Es hält uns hoch, ruft uns zur Tat.

Ebb and flow-tide know their path,
The tempest breathes a conscious breath,
Seeds sense the soil in which they stand,
Forest and plough and pastureland.
And all beasts have their home and ease,
And even weary of their peace.

We only have, in our heart's core,
Our land enshrined for ever more;
It flowers in love and council true,
Bidding us nerve our will to *do*.

'Die Vorfahren' by Hilda Bergmann
From: *Sudetenland*, Vierteljahresschrift für Kunst, Literatur, Wissenschaft und
Volkstum, Heft 1, 1958, 172.

Die Vorfahren

Meine Älterväter waren nordböhmische
  Bauern
mit schwieliger Faust und
  sonnengegerbter Haut . . .
Ich habe nicht Erdreich, nicht Scholle
  noch Ackerkrume
und keinen Boden, der meine Wurzeln
  hält.
So wird meinem Herzen jede blühende
  Blume,
wird Baum und Gesträuch zum
  Heiligtume
und die Natur mir Erbteil, Heimat,
  Welt.
So grab' ich und furche und werfe mit
  leiser Gebärde
ins Brachland der Seele die Samenkörner
  hin.
Und wachsen einmal die Saaten empor
  ohne Fährde,
so ist's meiner Väter uralte, geheiligte
  Erde,
der Ähren entsprießen und
  Sommersänge entblühen.

The Ancestors

My forebears were North Bohemian
  farming folk,
With work-hardened hands and skin
  which the sun had tanned . . .
But I have no holding, no plot, no patch
  even for planting,
No soil into which my roots may creep
  and curl.
So my heart holds holy each blossom
  unfurling its petals,
To me every coppice and copse enfolds an
  altar,
And nature for me is inheritance,
  homeland, world.
My ploughshare carves out the furrow,
  and lightly I scatter
Over the soul's fallow ground the fistfuls
  of corn.
If ever the seedlings rise out of the
  darkness and prosper,
Then it is from my forefathers' ancient
  and hallowed acres
That the ears of wheat and the
  summer's-day songs will be born.

Notes

1 Hans Dietrich Schultz, 'Räume sind nicht, Räume werden gemacht: zur Genese "Mitteleuropas" in der deutschen Geographie', *Europa Regional*, 5:1 (1997), 2–14.

2 Hans Henning Hahn, 'Nationale Minderheiten und Mehrheitsnationen im 19. Jahrhundert: Einige grundsätzliche Überlegungen zur kollektiven Identitätsbildung', in Hans Henning Hahn and Peter Kunze (eds), *Nationale Minderheiten und staatliche Minderheitenpolitik in Deutschland im 19. Jahrhundert* (Berlin, 1999), 205–10.

3 Eva Hahnová, *Sudetoněmecký problém: Obtížné louceni s minulosti*, second edition (Usti nad Labem, 1999). See, in particular, chapter 'Kdo jsou sudetsti Nemci a konci 20. stoleti?', 60–129, and the bibliography, 336–76.

4 www.sudeten.de/sitese/ae0.htm (26 March 2001).

5 This version of the goals differs from the German version at the same internet site, which cites the goals as defined in the official statute of the *Sudetendeutsche Landsmannschaft*. See www.sudeten.de/sites/a61.htm. The differences are significant, particularly in that the German version states as a goal: 'den Rechtsanspruch auf die Heimat, deren Wiedergewinnung und das damit verbundene Selbstbestimmungsrecht der Volksgruppe durchzusetzen' ('to assert a legal claim to the homeland and achieve its recovery and the resultant right of self-determination of the ethnic group').

6 *The Sudeten Question, Brief Exposition and Documentation* (Munich, 1984), 24.

7 *Ibid.*, 16.

8 *Ibid.*, 3.

9 *Ibid.*, 4.

10 'Do the expelled Sudeten Germans hold the key to the Czech future?', in L.B. Sorenson and L.C. Eliason (eds), *Forward to the Past? Continuity and Change in Political Development in Hungary, Austria, and the Czech and Slovak Republics* (Aarhus, 1997), 178–93.

11 Elizabeth Wiskemann, *Germany's Eastern Neighbours: Problems Relating to the Oder-Neisse Line and the Czech Frontier Regions* (London, 1956), 146.

12 Dierk Hoffmann and Michael Schwartz (eds), *Geglückte Integration? Spezifika und Vergleichbarkeiten der Vertriebenen-Eingliederung in der SBZ/DDR* (Munich, 1999).

13 Bundesgesetz zur Regelung von Fragen der Staatsangehörigkeit vom 22.2.1955.

14 Wiskemann, *Germany's Eastern Neighbours*.

15 George Mikes, *Über Alles: Germany Explored* (London, 1953), 68.

16 Eva Hahnová, *Sudetoněmecký problém*, and '"My" a "oni": hledání české národní identity na strankach Dneska z roku 1946', in Karel Jech (ed.), *Strankami soudobych dějin: Sborník statí k pětašedesátinám historika Karla Kaplana* (Prague, 1993), 93–109.

17 For an overall survey, see Sylvia Schraut and Thomas Grosser (eds), *Die Flüchtlingsfrage in der deutschen Nachkriegsgesellschaft* (Mannheim, 1995). For the British discussion on the change of policy, see Johannes-Dieter Steinert, *Vertriebenenverbände in Nordrhein-Westfalen 1945–1954* (Düsseldorf, 1986), 50–61. For the change in US policy, see Bořivoj Čelovský, *Politici bez moci: První léta exilové Rady svobodného Československa* (Šenov u Ostravy, 2000), 102–25.

18 For a survey of the history of these organisations, see Samuel Salzborn, *Grenzlose Heimat: Geschichte, Gegenwart und Zukunft der Vertriebenenverbände* (Berlin, 2000).

19 Michael Burleigh, *Germany Turns Eastward: A Study of Ostforschung in the Third Reich* (Cambridge, 1988); Winfried Schulze, *Deutsche Geschichtswissenschaft nach 1945*

(Munich, 1993); Hartmut Lehmann and James van Horn Melton (eds), *Paths of Continuity: Central European Historiography from the 1930s to the 1950s* (Cambridge, 1994); Winfried Schulze and Otto Gerhard Oexle (eds) in collaboration with Gerd Helm and Thomas Ott, *Deutsche Historiker im Nationalsozialismus* (Frankfurt/Main, 1999).

20 Franz Kögler, *Oppressed Minority?* (London, 1943). For insights into the 'other' cultural milieux among German exiles from Czechoslovakia who belonged to the pronounced critics of Jaksch and his policies, compare *Stimmen aus Böhmen: Eine Sammlung* (London, 1944).

21 Kögler, *Oppressed Minority?*, 82.

22 For information about the conflicts within the German Social Democratic Party of Czechoslovakia, see Hans-Werner Martin: '. . . *nicht spurlos aus der Geschichte verschwinden': Wenzel Jaksch und die Integration der sudetendeutschen Sozialdemokraten in die SPD nach dem II. Weltkrieg, 1945–1949* (Frankfurt/Main, 1996), and the journal *Neue Kommentare*, ed. Georg Herde (Frankfurt/Main), 1 (1958) – 2 (1980).

23 Eva Hahn and Hans Henning Hahn, 'Flucht und Vertreibung', in Etienne Françoise and Hagen Schulze (eds), *Deutsche Erinnerungsorte I* (Munich, 2001), 335–51.

24 Kurt Nelhiebel, *Die Henleins gestern und heute: Hintergründe und Ziele des Witikobundes* (Frankfurt/Main, 1962); Václav Král (ed.), *Die Deutschen in der Tschechoslowakei 1933–1947: Dokumentensammlung* (Prague, 1964).

25 'Das postvölkische Stereotyp "Osteuropa" im Kalten Krieg: Eugen Lembergs "Osteuropa und die Sowjetunion" und die historische Stereotypenforschung', in Hans Henning Hahn and Elena Mannová (eds), *Nationale Wahrnehmungen und die historische Stereotypenforschung* (forthcoming).

26 The organisations which have published most of the Sudeten German historical literature in the Federal Republic are the Collegium Carolinum, Adalbert Stifter Verein and Sudetendeutsches Archiv in Munich.

27 See n. 19.

28 Concerning the transfer in German collective memory, see n. 23.

29 For details, see 'Edvard Beneš: trauma nejen sudetonemecke', in Eva Hahnová and Hans Henning Hahn, *Sudetoněmecká vzpomínání a zapomínání* (Prague, 2002), 42–6.

30 See, for example, '"Kampf der Sudetendeutschen um das Heimatrecht", Sudetendeutsche Selbstbestimmung, von Bundesminister Dr Hans Christoph Seebohm', in *Der europäische Osten*, July–August 1960, Heft 69/70, 396–405.

31 *The Sudeten Question*, 3.

32 Tobias Weger, '"Tracht" und "Uniform", Fahne und Wappen: Konstruktion und Tradition sudetendeutscher Symbolik nach 1945', in Elisabeth Fendl, *Zur Ikonographie des Heimwehs: Erinnerungskultur von Heimatvertriebenen* (Freiburg, 2002), 101–25.

33 See Appendix. For an example of his standing, compare the recommendations for school teachers regarding Kolbenheyer, in Rudolf Murtfeld (ed.), *Handbuch für den Deutschunterricht* (Langensalza, 1937), 1, 277–80.

34 The name is only very slowly disappearing. See 'Kolbenheyerstraße ist in Geretsried bald Vergangenheit', *Münchner Merkur* (15 December 1999).

35 Father E.J. Reichenberger, *Ostdeutsche Passion* (Düsseldorf, 1948) and Reichenberger, *Europa in Trümmern: Das Ergebnis des Kreuzzugs der Alliierten* (Graz-Göttingen, 1952).

36 Eva Hahnova and Hans Henning Hahn, *Sudetoněmecká vzpomínání a zapomínání* (Prague, 2002).

37 Emil Hruška, *Sudetendeutsche Kapitel: Studien zu Ursprung und Entwicklung der sude-tendeutschen Anschlußbewegung* (München, 2003). See, in particular, the chapter 'Vom eigenen Namen zur Konzeption der "Volksgruppe"', 13–20.

38 Louis Ferdinand Helbig, Johannes Hoffmann and Doris Kraemer (eds), *Verlorene Heimaten–neue Fremden: Literarische Texte zu Krieg, Flucht, Vertreibung, Nachkriegszeit* (Dortmund, 1995).

39 Eva Hahn and Hans Henning Hahn, 'Eine zerklüftete Erinnerungslandschaft wird planiert: Die Deutschen, "ihre" Vertreibung und die sog. Benes-Dekrete', *Transit* 23 (Summer 2002), 103–16.

40 These subsidies can be traced only from fragments of information, as there has always been a policy of covering up the amount of taxpayers' money spent in this way. See Eva Hahnová, *Sudetoněmecký problém*, 115ff.

41 For a comprehensive insight into the discussions surrounding this issue, see *Beauf-tragter der Bundesregierung für Angelegenheiten der Kultur und Medien: Konzeption zur Kulturförderung nach § 96 BVFG* (Stand 20.5.99, Konzept), and Deutscher Bun-destag, Ausschuß für Kultur und Medien, *Stellungnahmen der Sachverständigen zur öffentlichen Anhörung zum Thema 'Kulturförderung nach §96 – Bundesvertriebenenge-setz (BVFG)'*, Berlin 25 October 1999.

42 Timothy Burcher summed up his analysis of the problems concerning the Sudeten German question and Czechoslovak–German relations since 1989 as follows: 'With such a degree of consensus not only between political parties within the two states but between the governments of the states themselves, it is hard to see what all the arguing has been about.' He did not discuss those aspects of the 'Sudeten German Question' which we raise in this chapter, and it may be that they would have been of some help even to such an authority as he in understanding 'what all the arguing is about'. See Timothy Burcher, *The Sudeten German Question and Czechoslovak–German Relations since 1989* (London, 1996), 46.

43 See, for example, *Landeszeitung* (Prague) (17 August 1999).

44 Samuel Salzborn, *Heimatrecht und Volkstumskampf: Außenpolitische Konzepte der Ver-triebenenverbände und ihre praktische Umsetzung* (dissertation, Hanover, 2001).

6

The Sorbs of Lusatia, the Socialist Unity Party and the Soviet Union, 1945–53

Peter Barker

The Sorbian Slav ethnic group in Lusatia emerged from the Second World War in 1945 depleted demographically and weakened in terms of ethnic identity. During the period of German military domination of Central Europe, the Lusatian Sorbs found themselves in a unique position: they were Slavs, and therefore had ethnic ties with other Slav nationalities who were being maltreated by the German state, but they were by nationality German. Most Sorbs had reacted submissively to the almost total ban on Sorbian cultural activity during the Nazi period; most remained loyal to the German state and a number even joined the Nazi party. During the Second World War many Sorbs found themselves serving in the German army, some on the eastern front. It was only a small minority, mostly intellectuals such as teachers and priests, who went into exile, either internal or external, or who ended up in concentration camps for acts of defiance or for working underground against the Nazis.[1] There is a strong contrast here with the behaviour of the Slovene minority in Austria; about 3,500 Austrian Slovenes volunteered to fight with Tito's partisans. The link to the Slovene majority in Slovenia was crucial in this respect, whereas the Sorbs had no motherland with which to identify. However, when in April 1945 Lusatia was overrun by Soviet, Polish and Ukrainian troops, many Sorbs, in stark contrast to the German population, greeted the occupation troops as liberating Slav brothers, although in some instances the Sorbian population was treated as badly as the German population by the occupying forces.[2] The problem for this Slav minority with no mother country to turn to for support had been its extreme weakness in the face of German political and economic subjugation since the tenth century. The arrival of the largest Slav power in Europe as the occupying force in Germany brought the prospect of improvement in its status as a minority.

The situation in 1945

Many of the last battles of the war were fought in Lusatia. The Sorbian population of the area had not, however, fled westwards, apart from those who were
living on the eastern side of the Oder-Neisse, but had remained in their villages.
Around 50 per cent of the Sorbian population were independent small farmers,
while about 20 per cent were workers, mostly on the land. They lived in eastern
Saxony and south-east Brandenburg, an area roughly conterminous with
Lusatia. Their proportion of the total population was about 15 per cent,
although there were sharp variations from area to area. Apart from the immediate changes brought about by the collapse of the Nazi regime and its replacement by Soviet-led occupying forces, and the general problems associated with
staying alive in the chaos of the aftermath of war, the most immediate influence on the situation of the Sorbian population was the influx of refugees,
mostly from former German areas in Silesia and the Sudetenland. After the re-
drawing of frontiers, Lusatia was one of the first areas in Germany west of the
Oder–Neisse line that these refugees came to and, although Saxony was not
designated an official reception state for German refugees and deportees until
March 1946, many had already found refuge in the Sorbian villages by this
time. The Domowina, the Sorbian cultural organisation, carried out its own
survey in 1946, which showed that the average proportion of German refugees
in the Sorbian-language area was over 20 per cent, but in some villages it could
be over 50 per cent.[3] Although some refugees accepted living in a predominantly Slav environment, even learning the Sorbian language, there were a
large number of recorded incidents of extreme hostility. Many Germans who
had been expelled from their homes by Slav administrations found it difficult to
accept the presence of a Slav minority within Germany.

The re-creation of Sorbian institutions and the desire for autonomy

The Domowina was re-created on 10 May 1945 as an 'anti-fascist-democratic'
organisation, and was the first, apart from the Communist Party (KPD), which
was given permission to operate officially in the Soviet zone, on 17 May. It
regarded itself as the successor to the original organisation founded in 1912
and banned by the Nazis in 1937.

On 9 May, another group, the Lusatian National Committee, which saw
itself as the successor to an organisation of the same name set up in 1918 to
push for an independent Sorbian state under Czech protection, was reconstituted in Prague. Both organisations saw the end of hostilities in May 1945 as
providing the Sorbian minority with its last chance to achieve political and cultural independence from German dominance, although the Domowina from
the start showed greater readiness to co-operate with Germans. The previous
twelve years had marked a clear deterioration in the Sorbs' situation; during
the Nazi period they had been confronted, both individually and collectively,
with a German state which was determined to destroy their separate ethnic

identity. When the leaders of the Sorbian intelligentsia returned from prison, concentration camp or exile in May 1945, the attempt made in 1919 to set up a separate Sorbian state was very much alive in their minds. On the surface, the situation was more favourable in 1945, since German state authority had suffered a complete collapse, and Lusatia was occupied predominantly by Slav troops. For the first time ever, Sorbs saw the possibility of their fate being determined by fellow Slavs at a time when the German political structures around them were at their weakest. This weakness was expressed particularly by the changes in national borders which had been imposed at the end of the war, and by the continuing discussion about frontier adjustments, especially concerning Poland's western and Czechoslovakia's northern borders. This uncertainty led a substantial number of Sorbs to believe that the most favourable time had arrived for the realisation of their dream of an independent Sorbian state. It soon became evident, however, that the realisation of such a dream was impossible; the size of the Sorbian population was by any estimation no higher than 100,000 at the end of the war, and was probably closer to 80,000, and its assimilation into the German population of Lusatia, whose towns were dominated by Germans, was far advanced. Also, the strategic interests of the Soviet Union meant that it opposed any further substantial border changes.

Nevertheless, between May 1945 and December 1947 the leaders of the two Sorbian organisations submitted a series of telegrams and memoranda to the wartime allies, including Czechoslovakia and Poland, and to the United Nations, demanding political and cultural autonomy from Germany. While the negative experiences of many Sorbs during the Nazi period had led to a feeling of greater national pessimism, some Sorbs, particularly amongst the intelligentsia, had reacted to persecution with a raised national consciousness which led them to the conclusion, as expressed in the memorandum sent to Stalin and President Beneš of Czechoslovakia by the Lusatian National Committee at the beginning of June 1945, that the Sorbs could expect nothing but further hostility from the Germans.

This episode of the immediate post-war period was largely ignored by historians in the GDR or written off as an example of petit-bourgeois nationalist aspirations. It is, however, now clear that the initial vehemence of the German Communists' reactions to these separatist demands hid uncertainty about how they would be received by their Soviet allies. But, despite the Soviet authorities' initially sympathetic attitude towards the Sorbs – for example, their early recognition of the Domowina – it soon became apparent that the Soviet Union, the most crucial ally in this context, was not going to support Sorbian separatism. In its view, Sorbian political autonomy would represent a clear breach of Stalin's nationalities policy based on the internationalist principles of Lenin. According to this policy, any solution which united the working and middle classes of a nation, while at the same time driving a wedge between the working classes of different countries, had to be opposed, because it meant that nationalist considerations were being advanced at the expense of social ones.

The Sorbian separatist movement was also undesirable because it was led by middle-class intellectuals, priests and independent farmers, with little working-class involvement. Also, the secession of all or part of Lusatia from the Soviet zone would have meant a serious loss of territory and natural resouces. For their part, the western Allies, to judge by the example of the British Foreign Office, took the constant lobbying from Sorbian organisations more seriously than might have been expected, because of uncertainty as to how the Soviet Union might react to such demands, and the realisation that, with the extension of Poland's western frontier to the Oder-Neisse and the re-settlement of Poles from eastern Poland in Silesia, Lusatia was now much closer to Slav frontiers than it had been in 1939. Although it was felt unlikely that the Soviet Union would support claims for independence, there were fears that it might request the provision of special rights for the Sorbs in a future peace treaty, a possibility to which the British government was opposed. There was therefore relief that the Soviet Union did not raise the Sorbian claims at any of the Foreign Ministers' conferences between 1945 and 1947.[4]

The attitude of the KPD – from April 1946 SED – together with the policy of the Soviet military administration towards Sorbian separatist demands, was the most important element in the development of the policy of limited cultural autonomy for the Sorbs. The KPD had a privileged position in relation to the occupying power. German Communists were moved quickly into key positions in the local administration, and an important part of their role in Lusatia was to monitor closely any moves towards separatism on the part of Sorbian organisations. These came in the second half of 1945 and the early part of 1946, in the form of memoranda initiated by the National Committee in Prague which, after July 1945, also had an office in Bautzen. In September this office became its headquarters, although it maintained a presence in Prague until February 1948. Officers of the Domowina also started from June 1945 to become involved in discussions on autonomy with the National Committee and signed a number of the memoranda. Both organisations rejected from the start one possible line of approach which had been suggested by the Czechs, namely that Sorbs should be given the opportunity of settling in the Sudetenland in those areas from which Germans had been, or were about to be, driven out. The memoranda of May and June 1945 made no mention of this point and demanded incorporation into Czechoslovakia.[5] The KPD was clearly alarmed by any revival of separatist sentiment amongst representatives of Sorbian opinion, which included Sorbs who were members of the Communist Party and who were in turn demanding a separate Sorbian section within the KPD.

The KPD's alarm had been intensified by the development of clear links between the National Committee in Prague, which was regarded by the KPD as a bourgeois, separatist group, and the Domowina, which contained a number of party members and which had previously shown a greater readiness to co-operate with Germans. The latter emphasised the establishment of equal status for Sorbian language and culture with German and the creation of an autonomous Lusatian *Land* within a democratic Germany. But in September 1945 there was a joint meeting between the National Committee and the Domowina which agreed to set up the Lusatian National Council as the executive arm of the two organisations. The nature of this cooperation became clear to the KPD in the campaign by the Domowina in January 1946 for the creation in the Sorbian villages of National Committees which were intended to provide grass-roots support for the National Council, and in the submission of memoranda signed in the name of the Council to the Polish government in November 1945 and to the United Nations in January 1946 which were no longer calling for incorporation into Czechoslovakia, but for the creation of an independent Lusatian state under international protection.[6]

The election campaign for the National Committees revealed the depth of hostility between some sections of the German and Sorbian populations. This hostility, as has been mentioned above, had been intensified by the large influx of refugees from the Sudetenland and Silesia into Lusatia. Many reports from 1946 reveal in particular the depth of hostility between Sorbs and Germans from the Sudetenland.[7] In this highly charged atmosphere the Communists in Saxony took the side of the Germans. They had received reports from the police of threats by Sorbian nationalists against Germans, in particular against KPD functionaries and mayors, and of a pamphleting campaign with slogans such as 'Strike the Germans dead'.[8] They had also received a number of reports of the meeting of the elected committees in Bautzen on 27 January 1946 which was addressed by officials from the Domowina and the National Committee, and at which a twenty-one-strong commission was set up 'for the creation of a completely independent Wendish state'.[9] The tone at this meeting was strongly anti-KPD.

The KPD's response was to show itself willing to support the cultural aspirations of the Sorbs as the major element in a stategy designed to isolate separatist tendencies in the Sorbian organisations. At the same time, it was trying to brand all attempts to achieve Sorbian political autonomy, and particularly to establish the Domowina as a political party, as the work of bourgeois nationalists who were tainted by involvement with the Nazis. By the end of February 1946, a KPD campaign was under way at local level to confront the political ambitions of the Domowina and to separate it from the National Committee by stressing the KPD's willingness to support Sorbian language and culture.

Since October 1945 the National Committee and the Domowina had been working together in the National Council despite wide-ranging differences in religious and political beliefs. The Committee had strong representation and support from Catholic, conservative Upper Sorbs, the section of the Sorbian population with the strongest ethnic identity, whilst the socialist and liberal elements were concentrated in the Domowina. But from March 1946 there was evidence both of a shift in the Domowina's position towards greater co-operation with the KPD in the formulation of a policy of support for Sorbian cultural interests and of a move away from the more strongly separatist National Committee. At the beginning of March an extraordinary meeting of the Domowina signalled this change in direction, which was reflected in a memorandum sent to all officers at the end of March. In it, the Domowina pointed out that the KPD had exhorted all its Sorbian members to work actively for the strengthening of Sorbian culture, and for its part the Domowina declared that it was prepared to co-operate with all progressive and socialist forces. It is extremely likely that this change in direction resulted from pressure from the Soviet authorities, but no direct evidence of this has yet emerged. Indirect evidence is provided by a statement from the Domowina at the end of April 'that they had no choice but to obey the orders of SMAD [the Soviet Military Administration of Germany]'.[10] This insistence on the necessity of obeying SMAD directives set the Domowina apart from the National Committee, which concentrated on the foreign policy arena; particularly those who were based in Prague had little understanding of the political pressure under which the Domowina was having to work.

Further evidence of the growing split between the two Sorbian national organisations was provided by the fact that the memorandum dated 7 January 1946 and sent by the National Council to the United Nations meeting in London was signed by leaders of the National Committee and the Domowina, whilst later memoranda and letters sent to the Foreign Ministers' conference in Paris in May and July 1946 were signed only by representatives of the National Committee. During this period the leaders of the Domowina were more concerned with the negotiations leading to the signing of an electoral agreement with the SED in July, which meant that the Domowina would not, as it had hoped, be allowed to operate as a separate party for the first elections in the Soviet zone, namely the local elections in Saxony on 1 September 1946. The agreement allowed Domowina candidates who were not members of the SED to be placed on the SED list. The immediate effect was to exclude those Sorbs who wished to stand as candidates for the Christian Democratic Union (CDU) from representing the Domowina and to ensure that any hope of being able to bring together Sorbian candidates under one banner had to be abandoned. This agreement was a direct result of the Soviet authorities' ruling in August that no further groups in Saxony beyond the existing parties and mass organisations were to be allowed to stand in the elections. In defence of this agreement the Domowina argued that the SED was the only party it could support because of the SED's 'anti-fascist and socialist outlook', and its willingness to allow religious freedom and the ownership of private property.[11] The agreement was extended to include the *Landtag* (provincial assembly) elections in October, in the face of strong opposition from the National Committee leaders.[12] Its implementation by the SED was extremely half-hearted, if not obstructive, and must have provided Domowina leaders with a pointer to the problematic nature of any co-operation with the SED. Co-operation between the SED and the Domowina proved difficult in both the local and the *Land* elections. In the local elections, Domowina candidates were struck from the lists without consultation, and in the *Land* elections none of the Domowina candidates was put high enough on the *Land* list to have any chance of winning a seat. The clear intention of the

SED was to use co-operation with the Domowina to drive a wedge between what it regarded as progressive and reactionary forces. This is in essence what happened, although the decision of the Domowina on 14 October 1946 to withdraw from the National Council was also a result of personal and tactical differences with the National Committee leadership in Prague, particularly in relation to constitutional guarantees for Sorbian rights.

The Domowina was becoming unhappy at the lack of any specific reference to the Sorbs in the draft constitution of Saxony. When a delegation of Sorbs went to Dresden in February they were told that the state constitution was already ready for presentation to the *Landtag*, and the Sorbs would have to wait for a special law to be formulated. The frustration of Sorbian leaders of all political colours at the delaying tactics of the Saxon government, and also at the disappointing results of the census of October 1946, in which only around 32,000 people overall declared their nationality to be Wendish and during the conduct of which it was alleged that German officials had put pressure on Sorbs to declare both their nationality and citizenship as German,[13] led to renewed activity on the international front. The two Sorbian organisations sent separate memoranda to the Foreign Ministers' conference of the war-time allies in Moscow in March 1947 demanding the political separation of Lusatia from Germany. The only support for these demands came from Yugoslavia.

The Domowina's experience of the difficulties of co-operating with the SED at local level over the previous year caused it to turn to the leadership of the party in the Soviet zone. Implicit in this was a recognition by the Domowina that it could not simply rely on appeals to the Soviet authorities. If it was to achieve any of its aims in relation to Sorbian rights, it had to establish a working relationship with the party, which was clearly going to play the central political role in the Soviet zone. In October 1947, it wrote to the Central Committee in Berlin requesting a meeting. The fact that a delegation from the Domowina was able to meet the top SED leadership on 21 November 1947, including Wilhelm Pieck and Otto Grotewohl, the two chairmen of the party, and Wilhelm Koenen and Friedrich Ebert, representing Saxony and Brandenburg, respectively, was evidence of the high priority the SED in Berlin gave to a resolution of the Sorbian question, largely as a result of pressure from the Soviet authorities. But it was clear right from the start of the meeting that any agreement was going to be on the SED's terms and not those of the Domowina. Grotewohl took the lead in countering the three major demands of the Domowina: the recognition of a Sorbian nation, the creation of a '*Land* Lausitz' and the formation of a Sorbian section of the SED. The SED leadership then laid out what it was prepared to offer, as long as the Domowina recognised that the interests of the Sorbian people were best served 'by working in close co-operation with the German people'.[14] On that basis, the SED was prepared to support the creation of cultural institutions to promote the development of Sorbian culture and language. In the case of Saxony this involved support for the introduction of an emergency motion by the anti-fascist, democratic bloc of parties, led by the SED, 'to support the cultural and political rights of the Sorbian people'.[15] The question of the introduction of similar provision in Brandenburg was left open, but it was envisaged that similar arrangements would be made. It took three years for this to happen.

It is difficult to avoid the conclusion that the leaders of the Domowina achieved very little of their original demands. It is true that they were taken seriously by the SED leadership in that they were recognised as the only Sorbian organisation with which the SED was prepared to deal. But the confines within which the SED was prepared to develop a policy of cultural support for the Sorbs already made it clear that Sorbian national interests had to be subordinated to the SED's plans for society as a whole. The meeting did, however, lead to the introduction of a Law on Sorbian Rights in Saxony in 1948, which for the first time gave the Sorbs guaranteed educational and cultural rights. The beginnings of a bilingual school system were in place by 1950, providing the first concrete results of the Domowina's policy of co-operation with the SED. But despite the legal basis furnished by the Saxon Law, the system was still a very arbitrary one, with no consistency over the Sorbian-speaking area in Saxony. In Lower Lusatia in Brandenburg, meanwhile, there were still no schools for speakers of Lower Sorbian. A similar law was not introduced in Brandenburg until two years later.

The major goals of the SED were to isolate the main Sorbian leadership in Bautzen from the more strongly separatist National Committee in Prague, and to bring the Domowina under SED influence. This was achieved by the granting of limited rights to the Sorbs in principle in 1947, and in practice from 1948 with the introduction of a Law in Saxony. The agreement of November 1947 and the Saxon Law of March 1948 had put the SED in a more positive light, even for those Sorbs who were more inclined to support the CDU.[16] The Domowina's claim to represent the Sorbs as a whole was strengthened by the fact that after the Communist take-over in Prague in February 1948 the National Committee closed its office, and the Domowina set up an office in Prague in its place. This claim was further underlined by the fact that its membership had increased substantially between 1945 and 1947. For example, in the Bautzen district it had over 12,000 members by 1947.[17] In Lower Lusatia, however, it had no official status until January 1949. But the Domowina was clearly the organisation with which the SED was going to deal, and ultimately the one it was going to put under its control. Kurt Krjeńc, the Sorbian Communist who was to take over the leadership of the Domowina in 1950, was already reporting in 1948 that 'our strong point is that we already have the leadership of the Domowina firmly in our hands'.[18] In December 1950 Krjeńc replaced the original chairman, Nedo, with a clear brief to restructure the Domowina along Stalinist lines and to remove nationalist elements from its ranks. The Domowina had therefore made a significant advance in terms of the recognition of Sorbian rights by German institutions in the Sorbian Law of 1948, which was then confirmed by the inclusion of a minorities article (Article 11) in the first GDR constitution of October 1949; but in doing so it had had to negotiate with a party with its own political agenda which was determined to destroy the independence of any other organisations. Further evidence of this came with the banning of the Sorbian youth organisation *Serbska młodžina* in 1949 and its incorporation into the SED-dominated Free German Youth (FDJ). The effects of this close relationship with the SED were seen in an increasing number of resignations in 1948 and 1949 from Domowina groups, especially on the part of Catholic Upper Sorbs.[19]

In the international context, the accusations of nationalism against Tito in Yugoslavia by the Soviet Union in 1948 had a particular effect on the position of the Sorbs. Sorbian organisations had cultivated close ties with Yugoslavia, which had been the only country to support their cause at an international level. When 'Titoism' turned into a slogan to be used against nationalist Communists throughout the Soviet bloc, many Sorbs found that any expression of support for their political rights as Sorbs could be classified as such, and a number found themselves in prison in the 1950s as a result. Ultimately the policy of the SED, under the direction of the Soviet authorities, was designed to subordinate Sorbian national interests to its political and social goals, and although on the surface the policy was presented by the SED as one of generous support for an endangered culture and language, in its practice, as the 1950s and 1960s were to show, it was one which, despite good intentions on the part of some SED functionaries, was bound to accelerate the Germanisation process, while at the same time strengthening the power of the SED over the Domowina.

The period from the creation of the GDR in October 1949 to the Second Party Conference of the SED in July 1952 was crucial for the next phase in the development of the struggle by Sorbs to obtain equal treatment for their language and culture. During this period, the SED established itself as a Communist party on the Soviet model, with an organisational structure based on the principles of 'democratic centralism'; it purged a large number of its members, especially those who had been in the SPD before April 1946; at the 2nd Party Conference the programme for the socialist transformation of the GDR economy was announced. All these developments were to have a crucial effect on policy towards the Sorbs. On the surface, the Sorbs had achieved significant progress with the 1948 Law in Saxony and Article 11. But the attitudes of the SED leadership towards their promises were by no means unanimous. Ebert, the SED leader in Brandenburg, initially rejected any idea of special treatment for Sorbian interests and put forward legislation only under extreme pressure from the SED centrally and from the Soviet Military Administration. In Saxony, voices were soon to be heard describing the new policy as premature. Ernst Lohagen, who had succeeded Wilhelm Koenen as the head of the SED in Saxony, at a meeting in Dresden in February 1950 accused Sorbian leaders of nationalist and chauvinistic attitudes, and maintained that the Sorbs would in any case be assimilated within fifty years.[20] Again, the leadership of the Domowina turned to SED leaders in Berlin in order to force SED officials at a lower level to co-operate, but the result of the meeting in June 1950 was inconclusive. The Domowina had complained in its preparatory paper that whenever it tried to act in the spirit of the November 1947 agreement, it was accused of 'Titoism' and nationalist deviation.[21] Despite the fact that the meeting was attended by Pieck, Grotewohl and Koenen, the only really concrete measures to emerge were the decision to introduce a decree in Brandenburg along the lines of the Saxon Law and the creation of a central office for Sorbian affairs in Berlin. This was the last high-level meeting to discuss Sorbian affairs, but shortly afterwards the long-awaited executive laws started to emerge, and the Sorbs were soon to acquire an influential representative of their interests in the Politbüro, Fred Oelssner. But, despite this support from a high level in the SED, differences between attitudes at local level in the SED and the leadership in Berlin continued; for example, at a meeting in October 1951 between the SED leadership in Saxony and the Domowina, Lohagen went so far as to call into question the need for the continued existence of the Domowina.[22]

The political subjugation of the Domowina

After the decision taken by the SED in the summer of 1948 to restructure itself according to the principles of 'democratic centralism', the pressure on other organisations in the Soviet zone to fall into line intensified. Crucial to the agreement of the leadership of the SED to the implementation of a policy of limited cultural autonomy for the Sorbs was the willingness of the leadership of the Domowina to reorganise itself along Marxist–Leninist lines. In return for the support of the SED leadership, the Domowina leadership ensured that its General Assembly in March 1950 formally allied itself with the bloc party system of the National Front and recognised the leading role of the SED, despite strong opposition from Christian Democrat and Liberal members. By the beginning of 1950 the Domowina had its own SED party group, and in October 1950 the executive committee was replaced by a secretariat. There were also a number of changes in personnel. The pre-war leader of the Domowina, Pawol Nedo, who had resumed the leadership on 2 June 1945, was an SED member, but from the beginning had been suspected of nationalist tendencies. He was accused of not having the necessary class background, i.e., of being an intellectual from a middle-class family. In reality, his father had been a railway stoker and his mother a dressmaker. He did not oppose the extension of Marxist–Leninist principles to the Domowina, but he was regarded by the SED as being too conciliatory towards its religious members. The replacement in December 1950 of Nedo by Krjeńc, a working-class SED member who had joined the KPD in 1923, was symbolic of the capitulation of the Domowina to political pressure from the SED. At other levels a number of younger SED members took over full-time posts within the organisation.[23] Krjeńc was formally elected chairman of the Domowina in March 1951 and was responsible for the preparation of the new statute of the Domowina, which was passed at its 2nd Federal Congress in April 1952. This statute made it clear that the Domowina was now organised along Marxist–Leninist lines in full alliance with the SED, with a secretariat as its highest body, and as such could be used by the SED in its reorganisation of the GDR economy and society. The political function of the Domowina as an intermediary which was to prepare Sorbs for the drastic political and economic changes to come after the 2nd SED Party Conference in 1952, such as the collectivisation of agriculture and the industrialisation of Lusatia, was now obvious to all its members, and it started to acquire the nickname, 'the red Domowina'. As a result there was a sharp drop in membership with, in particular, a high number of resignations by religious Sorbs and independent farmers.[24]

It is, however, symptomatic of the paranoid atmosphere within the SED at this time that, although it now had a trusted placeman at the head of the Domowina and most of the full-time officials were SED members, the organisation was still distrusted by the SED, and especially by the Ministry for State Security (Stasi or MfS). In December 1951 Erich Mielke, later head of the MfS, wrote a memorandum to the local MfS office in Dresden headed 'Nationalist and Titoist subversion among the Sorbs', in which he stated that Sorbian organisations had to be watched closely because of their suspected sympathies with President Tito of Yugoslavia. Sorbian groups, and particular individuals, had been suspected of having too close links with Yugoslavia in 1945–47, when Sorbian youth brigades went to Yugoslavia to help with reconstruction work. Mielke was particularly suspicious of the fact that the Sorbs had their own language, publications and national anthem, and he demanded monthly reports from Dresden on any suspicious activities.[25] During the period from the end of 1951 to 1953 the Domowina was under particular surveillance by the SED, which culminated in an investigation in 1953 by the Central Party Control Commission, responsible for party discipline. During an interrogation on 3 August 1953 by the Commission, Krjeńc was questioned about a number of his colleagues and about his own actions. The purpose of the investigation seemed to be to establish close links between certain members of the Domowina and Czechslovakia, in particular with the Slánsky group. Krjeńc was himself strongly criticised for his links with former SED members who had been recently purged and for his submission of a map to the Politbüro which suggested the creation of a Lusatian region (*Bezirk*) after the abolition of the *Länder* in 1952.[26] He was also accused of favouring the idea of a Sorbian Communist party with membership books in Sorbian, charges which Krjeńc vehemently denied.[27] It is therefore clear that at the very time when a whole set of measures were being put in place by the SED with the declared intention of putting Sorbian language and culture on an equal basis with German, some inner circles of the party were treating all Sorbs, whether Communists or not, as potential enemies. They suspected 'Sorbian nationalists' of maintaining close links with 'reactionary' circles in Czechoslovakia and Poland after the failure of moves towards a separate Sorbian state, and even after the change in the leadership of the Domowina the Stasi complained that the proletarian group on the executive committee was overshadowed by bourgeois, nationalist Sorbs.[28] Above all, the Stasi complained of its inability to maintain strict control of what was published in Sorbian. The central press censorship office in Berlin was not itself in a position to exercise this control, and as a result it depended on the Domowina, which it did not wholly trust.[29]

In fact, by 1953 the split between the SED-dominated leadership of the Domowina and ordinary Sorbs was complete, and it remained until 1989. The drop in membership of the Domowina reflected the ending of the hopes of ordinary Sorbs that Sorbian institutions could represent the full range of Sorbian opinion. The intense ideological pressure from the SED after the 2nd Party Conference in 1952 meant that there could be no reconciliation of divergent interests. The farmers and the Churches soon began to feel the increased ideological pressure emanating from the collectivisation policy and the campaign against the Churches. They saw the SED leadership in the Domowina forced to concentrate on helping the state carry through these policies, rather than concentrating on maintaining a Sorbian ethnic identity through support for the Sorbian language and cultural activities. Ultimately the cultural aspirations of the Sorbs were irreconcilable with the social and economic policies of the SED. This became even clearer with the development of the energy industry in Lusatia from the mid-1950s with the building of the energy complex, 'Schwarze Pumpe', outside Hoyerswerda. It is clear from the documents of the Domowina from this time that even the leadership recognised its dilemma, but it was forced by political realities to accept and support policies which ultimately resulted in an acceleration of the assimilation process, against the wishes of the majority of the Sorbian population.

The Sorbs were in a much weaker position than most other ethnic minorities in Central Europe; they had no mother country to plead their case with the host country or to put pressure on it by threatening to make life difficult for the reciprocal minority, as in the case of Czechoslovakia and Hungary. In many ways, their situation was similar to that of the Slovenes, but with one major difference. The Sorbs came under the direct influence of Soviet policy; in their case, this meant that they were subject to the principles of the nationalities policy, which were often summed up as follows: 'national in form, socialist in content.' Economic, political and social considerations took precedence over national considerations: the granting of limited cultural autonomy did mean that during this period the Sorbs received the cultural institutions, such as bilingual schools, cultural and academic institutions, which have survived into the post-unification period, but it also meant the suppression of the national aspirations of many ordinary Sorbs.

Notes

1 For a detailed discussion in English of Nazi policy towards the Sorbs, see Todd Huebner, 'Ethnicity denied: Nazi policy towards the Lusatian Sorbs', *German History*, 6:3 (1988), 250–77. See also Martin Kasper, *Zeitzeichen 1918–1933: Quellen zur sorbischen Geschichte* (Bautzen, 1995).

2 For an account of the Soviet occupation of Lusatia in April and May 1945 by a German Catholic priest who was transferred to a village in Upper Lusatia in 1941, see Lucius Teichmann, *Steinchen aus dem Strom* (Cologne, 1984), 185–216.

3 Statistics quoted from Edmund Pech, *Die Sorbenpolitik der DDR 1949–1970* (Bautzen, 1999), 27.

4 Briefing prepared by the British Foreign Office for the Foreign Ministers' Conference in Moscow in March 1947, entitled 'Claims of the Lusatian Serbs', Public Record Office, Kew (PRO), FO 371/64542, file No. C3347.

5 'We want the incorporation of our country into Czechoslovakia.' From the German version of the memorandum, dated 1 June 1945, in the Pieck papers, Stiftung Archiv der Parteien und Massenorganisationen der DDR (SAPMO-BArch), NY 4036/741, 14.

6 *1500 Years of Struggle for National Existence. Memorandum of the Lusatians, the Last European Nation Still Fighting for its Independence* (Budyšin, 1946), 6.

7 For example, the reports in French, dated 8 July 1946, in PRO, FO 371/65800, file No. N4432.

8 'Bericht über die Lostrennungsbestrebungen der Wenden.' Report on separatist activities from the KPD regional office in Dresden to Walter Ulbricht, dated 22 February 1946, SAPMO-BArch, NY 4036/741, 22.

9 Report of the meeting by a KPD member, Max Duschmann, SAPMO-BArch, NY 4036/741, 19.

10 *Ibid.*, 91.

11 'Erklärung der Domowina', *Lausitzer Rundschau* (27 July 1946).

12 On the question of the Domowina's attempts to be recognised as a political party, see Peter Schurmann, *Die sorbische Bewegung 1945–1948 zwischen Selbstbehauptung und Anerkennung* (Bautzen, 1998), 116–22.

13 The exact figure for Saxony was 25,213, according to the Saxon Statistical Office. SAPMO-BArch, NY 4074/150, 9. On 19 November 1946, the Domowina wrote to SMAD in Karlshorst outlining the different ways in which German officials had put pressure on Sorbs not to declare their nationality as Wendish, thus ignoring the guidelines laid down by the Soviet authorities for the conduct of the census. Sorbian Cultural Archive, Bautzen, SKA, D II.1.9.A, 200–2.

14 *Ibid.*

15 *Ibid.*, 73.

16 Krjeńc's letter to the executive committee of the SED in Dresden, dated 4 December 1947, SAPMO-BArch, NY 4074/150, 33–6, and his letter to the Central Committee, dated 12 February 1948, NY 4036/741, 77.

17 Figures given in Pech, *Die Sorbenpolitik*, 30.

18 SAPMO-BArch, NY 4074/150, 36.

19 Pech, *Die Sorbenpolitik*, 36.

20 Report of the meeting by Otto Buchwitz, President of the Saxon *Landtag*, in a letter to Wilhelm Koenen, dated 28 April 1950, in SAPMO-BArch, NY 4074/151, 36.

21 'Vorlage der Domowina für die Beratung mit dem Parteivorstand der SED am 5. Juni 1950 in Berlin', SAPMO-BArch, NY 4036/741.

22 Report of this meeting sent by Krjeńc to Oelssner on 16 January 1952, SAPMO-BArch, DY30 IV 2/13/378.

23 Letter from Krjeńc to the Central Committee of the SED, dated 19 September 1950, in which he writes of his success in isolating nationalist and petit-bourgeois ele-

ments in the leadership of the Domowina and securing their replacement by prole-tarian comrades, SAPMO-BArch, NY 4036/741, 151.

24 See Pech, *Die Sorbenpolitik*, 37. He estimates that the membership halved between 1947 and 1951.

25 Directive No. 4/51 of 13 December 1951, Der Bundesbeauftragte für die Unterlagen des Staatssicherheitsdienstes der DDR – Zentralstelle Berlin (BstU), MfS GVS (Geheime Verschlusssache) 42/51. This directive was probably a response to a report, dated 1 November 1951, from Domowina functionaries around Krjeńc which was sent to Oelssner in the Central Committee in Berlin. It referred not only to increased hostile activities amongst reactionary Sorbs which had resulted in two Sorbs, Jurij Rjenč and Bjarnat Rachel, being sentenced in 1951 to twenty-five years' imprisonment for their links with Yugoslavia, but also to continuing traditional atti-tudes amongst the main body of Domowina officers. 'Bericht', in SAPMO-BArch, DY30 IV 2/13/377. For personal accounts of Stalinist repression of Sorbs, see *Serbja pod stalinistiskim socializmom 1945–1960* (Bautzen, 1992).

26 Report from the First Secretary of the SED in Bautzen, Schmidt, dated 27 August 1953, Sächsisches Hauptstaatsarchiv, IV/4.01.059, 26.

27 See 'Zur Untersuchung in der Angelegenheit Genosse Kurt Krenz', SAPMO-BArch, DY30 IV 2/4/268, 1–33.

28 'Analyse über die Angelegenheit der Sorben – Domowina', dated 20 November 1956 and written by the *Stasi* district office in Bautzen, BStU, MfS BV Dresden, KD Bautzen 8007, 12.

29 *Ibid.*, 13.

7

The Carinthian Slovenes

Robert Knight

The Carinthian Slovenes had a bit part in the Cold War. They entered at the start of Act One in May 1945 with alarums: a stand-off between British and Yugoslav troops in southern Carinthia (and Trieste) led to urgent messages being exchanged between Washington, London and Moscow (and Belgrade); under pressure from Stalin, Tito withdrew his troops but continued to assert Yugoslavia's claim to an area totalling 2,470 km² (1,273 square miles) and inhabited by about 180,000 people.[1] The Slovenes returned to the wings in June 1949 after the Council of Foreign Ministers (CFM), meeting in Paris to discuss the Austrian Treaty, confirmed the existing (and pre-war) borders between Austria and Yugoslavia. In the four intervening years the minority's ethnic concerns (such as language education, language rights and census results) were discussed by diplomats and politicians at the highest level, reported in the international press – from *Tass* to the *Christian Science Monitor*,[2] and debated in both Houses of the British Parliament.[3]

If the Cold War is viewed simply as a confrontation of 'high politics', this shift from obscurity to prominence and back again is straightforward enough. The minority became important because an international actor (Tito's Yugoslavia) used it as a pretext to expand the Communist sphere at the expense of the West. It ceased to be so once the same actor (albeit now as a breakaway from the Soviet bloc rather than an integral part of it) had been persuaded by the West's stance that it could not succeed in its ambitions.

Though this view clearly contains some truth, it is a narrow one. It reduces politics to a statist interaction of 'high politics', and ideology to Communism versus (Western-style) democracy. As a result, it underplays national or ethnic (and confessional) differences, or at best sees them as mere instruments of the 'actual' struggle. Last but not least, it underplays the historical roots of the conflict.[4] The following discussion attempts, in line with some recent historiography,[5] to examine ethnic politics in the locality (province) and its 'contribution' to 'the pattern of politics'.[6]

What was the situation of the Carinthian Slovenes after seven years of Nazi rule and five years of war? First and foremost, they were still there. Nazi attempts to eliminate them as a national/ethnic group had intensified after the invasion of Yugoslavia in April 1941 and been backed by enormous coercive power.[7] Hand-in-hand with manifest violence, notably the mass deportation of nearly 1,000 Slovenes in April 1942, went a policy of forced assimilation, which built on older provincial practices: German-speaking farmers and officials were brought into the area; the minority was deprived of economic, social and cultural sustenance; Slovene children were sent to German-speaking kindergartens and schools, no Slovene was allowed to be used in public. Slovene reactions to this oppression varied from armed resistance in the Communist-dominated *Osvobodilna Fronta* (Liberation Front, hereafter OF)[8] to collaboration; in between the two poles were degrees of grudging conformity but also participation in the Nazi *Volksgemeinschaft* (People's Community) by those deemed '*eindeutschungsfähig*' (capable of Germanisation). Some of the resulting tensions culminated in a bloody climax in May 1945.[9]

Though the failure of the project to 'make Carinthia German' is clear, the ethnic composition of the disputed area after these turbulent events is difficult to ascertain exactly. The Yugoslav Foreign Ministry referred to 120,000 Slovenes, including those 'alienated' from their 'true' identity; the result of the 1934 census, just over 26,000, is generally accepted as an underestimate,[10] while the 1951 census suggests an upper ceiling of 42,095 Slovenes, the adults among whom, even if not always nationally conscious, were at any rate ready to declare their vernacular language (*Umgangssprache*) to be other than German.[11]

As for Carinthian society as a whole, it functioned smoothly enough under Nazi rule. There is little evidence that resistance grew steadily towards that rule's close and even less to suggest that Nazi treatment of the minority was a catalyst for it.[12] Though there had been mutterings, even protests, at the deportation of 1942,[13] the aim of Germanisation itself went largely unchallenged. The regime could build here on the traditions and self-identity of Carinthia as a 'marchland' of *Deutschtum* (Germandom) and the collective memories associated with it, above all the 1918–19 'defensive struggle' (*Abwehrkampf*) against the South Slav or Serbian enemy, and the result of the plebiscite which followed in October 1920; the latter had produced a surprisingly clear vote of 60:40 for Austria. The upshot was the affirmation of Carinthia's historically-based borders in preference to an ethnically-based division.[14]

The Nazi regime was not toppled by deep-rooted social discontent or a 'resistance movement'.[15] Power was transferred almost literally at one minute before midnight (on 7 May) after several days of good-tempered negotiation. The common aim of both sides was to put in place a government with which the approaching British forces could do business, and thus pre-empt actions by the Yugoslav partisans, who were also advancing over the border. The tactic proved successful. A Carinthian provisional government was confirmed – albeit downgraded to the status of an advisory committee – by the British military authorities. Apart from their concern to defend the territorial integrity of the province, its members' biographies varied from those who had had Nazi party membership to those who had suffered Nazi repression; two Communists were apparently co-opted for cosmetic reasons. Overall, it is therefore difficult to accept the contemporary claim that Carinthia had responded to the Allied call to resist the Nazi regime in a uniquely sucessful way.[16] On the other hand, the politicians probably could fairly claim to be broadly representative of (non-Slovene) Carinthian society.

Minority politics: secession or participation?

The OF's attempt to form an alternative administration in May 1945 failed; the British refused to recognise it and – after a flurry of telegrams – Yugoslav troops were withdrawn. Almost immediately, agitation for secession began. Its aim was both to win over hesitant or hostile Slovenes and to persuade international decision-makers that this aim had been achieved. The OF was claiming not so much that the 1920 plebiscite had been unfair as that it had been invalidated by the Germanisation and war which had taken place since. Their case was based on the demand less for the right of self-determination than for the fruits of victory, the so-called 'plebiscite of blood'.

The OF fought under the banner of anti-fascism and 'national liberation'. Though it is difficult to separate motives, Communist or Bolshevik ideology in the strict sense appears to have been less important than a mixture of Slovene (or South Slav) nationalism, adulation for Tito and exultation at the defeat of Germany.[17] It was a heady brew which left little or no room for critical reflection about the repression prevalent in the post-war Yugoslav state. Instead, an incessant activism began with the passing of resolutions, the holding of meetings, collecting of signatures, the sending of protest telegrams and petitions and so on. Traditional cultural activities such as dance and not least amateur theatricals (*igras/Spiele*) were used, and if necessary revised for the purposes of *agitprop*.[18]

Though there are no reliable figures for OF membership, age or social composition, its core support was probably no more than a few thousand, many of these being young, possibly under voting age. It is even more difficult to assess the overall support for secession in the disputed area. But it was almost certainly less than the 16,000 pro-Yugoslav votes of the 1920 plebiscite and probably well below the 10,000 who voted before 1932 for the pre-war Slovene People's Party (*Slovenska Ljudska Stranka*). In trying to alter this situation, the OF faced a triple hurdle. Firstly, the negative image held by many Slovenes of their own ethnic background which, despite some signs of a post-war revival,[19] probably persisted. Secondly, the Catholic milieu, where Slovene consciousness tended to be more resistant to assimilation, was also most likely to be hostile to the Yugoslav regime.[20] Thirdly, the working class in small towns like Ferlach or Feistritz, which until 1932 had supported the Social Democrats, had then generally accepted or supported Nazi rule.[21]

112

There was also a competing strategy on offer, that of participating in local government. Between June and November 1945 this was the line supported by Josef (Joško) Tischler, the Slovene Catholic leader in the First Republic, grammar school teacher and former head of the Slovene Cultural League (*Slovensko Kulturno Društvo/Slowenischer Kulturverein*). Tischler agreed to be co-opted into the local government as member with special responsibility for the minority (*Minderheitenreferent*). Though he was probably overoptimistic in his hopes for a new chapter in majority–minority relations, Tischler was able to exercise more real power than at any time in the Carinthian Slovenes' history. His pragmatic aim was to exploit the readiness, even eagerness, of the mainstream parties, above all the Social Democrats, to accommodate (some) minority demands. As well as overseeing (partial) restitution for the returning expelled farmers,[22] he proposed and pushed through a radical reform of primary education, a sector which had long been criticised by Slovene leaders as an instrument of Germanisation.[23]

Even if – or especially if – it worked, this kind of reform clearly ran counter to the OF's strategy. So did Tischler's intention to fight in the elections which were announced for November. Apart from legitimising the *status quo* in the disputed area, any Slovene vote which was much below the 1920 plebiscite result would clearly be a propaganda blow.[24] After some internal tussles and (perhaps) misunderstandings over a British demand that he promise not to make an election issue of the border, Tischler resigned from the local government early in November 1945. The OF then withdrew from the elections altogether, calling on its followers to either boycott the elections or to vote Communist.[25] Overall OF support could hardly have exceeded the total of around 9,000 abstentions and Communist votes and was probably lower.[26] Many Slovene voters must have voted for one or other of the two main parties, the more Catholic voters for the People's Party, the less nationally conscious for the Socialists.

Partly thanks to Slovene support, the Communists were able to put three representatives in the *Landtag*.[27] One of them, Johann Kazianka, was from a Slovene background and frequently voiced Slovene concerns (for example, about the failings of denazification, or in education). Yet Communism was not about to spread into southern Carinthia. Firstly, Communists disagreed with the OF about border revision and more broadly were mistrustful of its nationalism.[28] Secondly, the Communists were weakly rooted in the agrarian society of southern Carinthia. Thirdly, as the Cold War progressed, Communist support became more of a liability. In contrast to the anti-Communist fear of the power of world Communism, in the minority's perspective it was precisely the linkage of its grievances to Stalinist Russia that allowed them to be ignored or discredited.[29]

Mistrust of, or distaste for the new Yugoslav regime was clearly felt by many Slovenes. Though Tischler did not break with the OF publicly after being forced out of the government, the tension between his advocacy of participation and the OF's secessionism was evident.[30] Hostility between the OF and the Church hierarchy was more open. One major point of bitter dispute was the Church's stance under Nazi rule.[31] More broadly, the OF saw the church as representing a discredited tradition of deference and passivity.[32] The Church for its part saw the OF, in the words of the veteran Slovene clerical politician Valentin Podgorc, as a *'politischer Irrweg'* ('political blind alley').[33] Apart from ideological incompatibility, the Church was looking to rebuild itself after years of persecution and, in contrast with inter-war 'political Catholicism', adopted a cautious apolitical stance. The demands of the minority were not a high priority even in areas of church competence, such as the return of Slovene priests to the parishes or the use of Slovene in the pulpit.[34] Church support for secession was made even less likely with the growing repression of the church in Slovenia, which gathered pace at the end of 1945.[35]

On the other hand, there is some evidence of support for secession among the lower clergy. One widely publicised petition of 1947 was signed by fifty-one priests. Admittedly the Gurk diocesan authorities complained that many of these signatures had been obtained by pressure or trickery,[36] but this still left some significant support.

Without representation in the *Landtag*, the OF resumed its activities in a semi-legal limbo, being neither a legally recognised party nor actually banned.[37] One eye was cocked to the diplomatic arena, where it was expected – wrongly, as it turned out – that the border was about to be decided on; the OF and the Yugoslav foreign ministry bombarded the Allied Council in Vienna, Western governments and the press with a stream of protests and petitions, denouncing the continued strength of Nazism and the persecution of the minority.[38] Agitation was also linked to the politics of memory, with special emphasis on the partisan war and the deportations of April 1942.

Accommodation and loyalism, 1945–47

The policies developed by post-war power holders in Carinthia were not simply a reaction to the demand for secession. Like the demands themselves, they arose from a longer history of ethnic tension and conflict. Yet it may be possible to distinguish two approaches to the issue of the minority; one which sought to escape from the spiral of escalation by accommodating the minority in key areas, for example bilingual education or the restitution of expropriated property. The other, centred on loyalty to the Carinthian *Heimat*, was essentially a continuation of past escalation.

The case for accommodation was frequently made by both British and Austrians (Carinthians). As one of the former put it, 'genuine representation' of the minority 'could dispose conclusively of the Yugoslav pretensions'.[39] The Carinthian government, for its part, made a series of public statements promising redress for Nazi persecution almost from the outset. Determining whether the proposed accommodation was 'genuine' or merely 'tactical' is a difficult and probably pointless exercise, for the two were intertwined. On the other hand, it is clear that those who supported accommodation used 'prudential' arguments much more readily than the claim that the support of the minority culture was desirable in itself.

The second approach, which can be labelled 'loyalism', saw loyalty to the Carinthian homeland (*Heimattreue*) as the touchstone of political allegiance, and sought to mobilise around its re-affirmation. Most important, it more or less explicitly regarded assimilation of the minority as an essential expression of this loyalty. The powerful mythology of the *Abwehrkampf* stressed the role of those loyal Slovenes, often called '*Windisch*', who had stood shoulder-to-shoulder with German Carinthians in defence of the *Heimat*. In a loyalist perspective, accommodation was not merely ineffective in deterring secession but positively dangerous, since it would be construed as weakness by minority leaders and result in more extreme demands. For example, delimiting an area for bilingual primary education would strengthen Yugoslav claims to that area.[40] Kindness would only encourage secession.

Given the smoothness of the transition from the Third Reich, it is not surprising that the Nazi version of loyalism, in which Carinthia was seen as a bulwark of the Reich, survived into the post-war era.[41] But it was also adapted to the new context: the re-established Austrian State and its new multi-party democracy. And, at least in public discourse, the right of the individual to choose his or her ethnicity displaced the right of the superior German race to dominate.[42] In an important discussion within the provisional government in June 1945, post-Nazi loyalism and accommodation were both evident. The trigger was an OF memorandum to the British military government. While ostensibly demanding participation in the new structures being established, it was couched in roundly irredentist language which caused an uproar.[43] Hans Piesch called for a counter-offensive to 'enlighten' the population in the disputed area. He suggested that an organisation similar to the *Heimatdienst* (homeland service) which had organised the 'defence' of Carinthia after 1918 was needed, albeit 'in the positive sense of the word'. He also stressed the need to avoid any chauvinism.[44]

Once Tischler had left government, the counter-offensive could begin. It was mainly organised by the Carinthian Socialists after they emerged from the November elections as the largest single party (SPÖ). In Carinthia, the Socialists had a long history of being at the fringes of provincial power. Especially since the crisis years of 1918–20 they had shown that they were not immune to German nationalism. In part, this may have started as the classic Marxist dismissal of the 'national question' as a distraction, but it was also linked to a positive hostility towards what was considered a reactionary, backward, clerically led minority. In the post-war era German nationalism became a structural factor, in that the Socialist success, which far exceeded pre-1932 levels, was partly explicable by its success in winning over former supporters of German national parties, including Nazis. For some of these the clerical connections of the People's Party (ÖVP) were a greater stumbling-block than the Marxist traditions of the Socialists.

Yet at the same time the Socialists, as the strongest single party in the mixed-language area, could claim to speak for the minority. After November 1945 they gained control of many parish councils, which in the First Republic had been among the last remaining bastions of Slovene power.

The Socialist shift towards loyalism was shown by the establishment, under Tischler's successor, of the 'League of Slovenes loyal to Austria' (BÖS – *Bund der Österreichtreuen Slowenen*, or ZAS – *Zvesa Avstrijsih Slovencev*). The League claimed to be the 'real' voice of the minority. Local groups were formed in about thirty parishes.[45] Before long the BÖS was claiming as many as 30,000 members. It described its aim as resisting 'the unrestrained hate-propaganda' of the OF and seeking to represent the vast majority of Slovenes. Its members rejected the accusation that they were 'renegades', and 'declared their adherence to the Slovene people'.[46] Nevertheless it is clear that the BÖS was not rooted in any real ethnic consciousness. Indeed it was not really a Slovene organisation at all, and many of its activists were probably only 'tactically' Slovenes.[47] The BÖS began, like the OF, to collect signatures for petitions, telegrams and declarations in the villages of southern Carinthia. Last but not least, it sought the endorsement of both the occupation authorities and the Federal government.

The British authorities responded with reserve. Admittedly they saw the OF as 'a continual nuisance' and a fifth column reminiscent of Henlein's Sudeten Germans.[48] But they also wished to avoid precisely the kind of over-reaction which the OF was seeking to provoke. Early in February 1946, the British Senior Military Government Officer, Simson, warned 'both Slovene parties' (*sic*) that 'provocation and intimidation and unnecessary political activity generally must be kept under control'. If they were not, 'a conflagration might ensue which would have serious repercussions'.[49] And the British disputed the need for agitation to influence the decision-making in Paris, where the situation was already well known.[50]

The Federal Government in Vienna was more receptive to appeals from the province. At the end of January 1946 there was a clash between OF activists and counter-demonstrators (including Croatian and Hungarian displaced persons) and police at a performance of Chekhov's 'Three Sisters' in the village of St Kanzian, which led to OF protests to the Allied Council in Vienna and hostile reports in the Communist press, subsequently taken up by *Pravda*.[51] Rudolf Cefarin, Tischler's successor, reported that 'the terroristic pressure which is being exerted on the loyal population by the many Yugoslav emissaries has increased to a level which is beyond endurance'.[52] Further reports followed in similar vein.[53] In the Federal Cabinet the Minister of the Interior, Oskar Helmer, described the clash (*Zusammenstoss*) as a 'fair-ground story' ('*eine Kirchtagsgeschichte*') which had been blown up into a case of persecution. It was the 'old game' with reports circulating in which 'every detail is blown up' ('*jede Kleinigkeit wird aufgebauscht*'). However, he added, these were precisely the issues which could give rise to concern at the border.[54]

In response to Piesch's 'urgent wish',[55] politicians of both main parties travelled from Vienna to the border area. Vice-Chancellor Adolf Schärf told a thousand-strong meeting in the Socialist stronghold of Ferlach that it was only the Nazis who had had the idea of separating Slovenes and Germans, their cruelty having been directed against both Slovenes and German Carinthians. He closed with an appeal to the population to remain calm in order to ensure the unity of the province.[56] Helmer, too, stressed that, while the government was determined to maintain Carinthia's existing borders, it had no intention of hindering the minority in pursuing their 'habits and customs' (*'in der Übung ihrer Sitten und Gebräuche'*) so long as these did not run counter to the attitudes of the majority population (*Staatsvolk*).[57] The next day Helmer, his (Austrian People's Party) state secretary Ferdinand Graf and governor Piesch toured the small towns of the mixed-language area and – apart from some OF heckling – met with an enthusiastic reception.[58]

Reporting to the Cabinet on his return to Vienna, Helmer noted that the provincial government (*Landesregierung*) was 'anxious' to 'meet the wishes of the Slovene deportees to the highest degree'. His visit had been greeted as 'nothing less than [our] salvation' by the population, which was 'completely on the side of Austria'. The Foreign Minister, Karl Gruber, appealed to Helmer to make sure that the local police showed restraint, since otherwise problems might arise not just with the Yugoslavs but also with the occupation authorities. Helmer indignantly denied that any of the police had overstepped the bounds of legality.[59]

Despite Helmer's indignation, Gruber's comments do point to a basic tension, even contradiction, between the call for calm from politicians and the mobilising effect of their visits. Intentionally or not, the visits were pouring oil on the flames. For example, on the back of the ministerial visits, Piesch struck a loyalist note, recalling the 1920 plebiscite victory, reaffirming Carinthia's determination to maintain its unity and giving a robust warning to OF 'trouble-makers' that if they were unhappy they could always 'travel south' (*'südwärts abwandern'*).[60] Piesch's comment, printed in the Socialist newspaper, was duly picked up by the Slovene press and interpreted as blatant intimidation.[61]

The visits certainly did not silence OF agitation. At the end of March, 150 members of the OF youth movement marched into Klagenfurt singing Slovene songs, their route taking them near the seat of military and provincial government.[62] The latter now told the British that it was no longer prepared to accept such 'provocations' and would introduce tougher police checks and punishment of foreigners.[63] These were put into practice a fortnight later on the fourth anniversary of the 1942 deportation. Police road-blocks were set up beforehand, and after the meeting about 500 persons staged an unauthorised demonstration, walking through a police cordon. The police in the end doused the crowd with fire-hoses and arrested, but later released, forty-two people.[64] British reports put most of the blame on the 'irresponsible leaders' of the OF, but also criticised the Austrian police for showing 'excessive zeal' and inexperience.[65]

The international background to these events was the meeting in Paris of the CFM to negotiate the 'Satellite' Peace Treaties, including that with Italy which involved Yugoslav claims on Trieste and the *Kanaltal* (Canal Valley). The OF renewed its collection of signatures.[66] In reaction, a working committee for Southern Carinthia (*Arbeitsauschuss für Südkärnten*) was set up, including BÖS representatives, to organise an unofficial plebiscite. The British blocked it and shortly afterwards the plebiscite action was abandoned.[67] Without its rationale the BÖS went into decline. But the loyalist direction of local politics continued; Tischler's attempts to negotiate a return to the accommodation of 1945 had no effect.

Ethnic politics and Cold War politics, 1947–49

Even before the CFM began its meetings in London in January 1947, Western diplomats and policy-makers were clear that the Yugoslav claim to southern Carinthia was to be given 'short shrift'.[68] This rejection stemmed initially from the basic decision to re-establish Austria, coupled with the sense that economic difficulties and the weakness of Austrian national identity would not make this an easy task. The early Cold War further strengthened the case for maintaining the existing border, since it aligned Austria with the West (albeit with the complication that Eastern Austria was under Soviet occupation).[69] Geopolitics was decisive. By the same token, Western rejection of border revision did not stem from any particular regard for the ethnicity of the population, or for the assimilation of the minority which had taken place since the 1920 plebiscite. To international decision-makers, the ethnic politics were of interest only as a security issue in a potentially unstable area bordering on the Iron Curtain. Admittedly, Western support of the territorial *status quo* had also, where necessary, to be justified by the argument that the minority was being treated sympathetically and tolerantly. But the subtext, for many Western decision-makers, was that the continued assimilation or 'absorption' of the minority would in any case be no bad thing.

Soviet support for the Yugoslav claim was more indirect than Western support for Austria. Generally it was restricted to the argument that the Yugoslavs had a case and it should be heard. Two years after a confrontation which the Soviet leadership had not sought, and with Trieste 'disposed of', it saw the Yugoslav claim as little more than a bargaining chip, waiting for the best time to cash it in against concessions in other areas (notably the disposition of German external assets in Austria). Western officials recognised the Soviet lack of interest in the issue. So did the Austrians. The discussions and the periodic pleas of Austrian and Yugoslav foreign ministers which took place over the following two years therefore have something of a ritualistic element about them. There is even room for some doubt about how strong the Yugoslav commitment to its own revisionist case was.

Nevertheless, whether as ritual or not, the confrontations of 'high politics' deepened the provincial polarisation.[70] The activists of the OF clearly thought that their hour had come. One of their leaders, the former partisan major Franz

Primoschitz/Franc Primožić, issued a rallying-cry for a more combative affirmation of Slovene nationality. Amateur theatricals would now have to make room for more important tasks.[71] The decision-making in Moscow (where the CFM reconvened in March 1947) had to be influenced by reports from the spot. As was stressed at a meeting of young OF activists, any evidence of oppression should be immediately reported to Moscow.[72]

These tactics of calculated confrontation reached a climax at the town of Eisenkappel on 16 March 1947. In the course of a demonstration, about 200 OF activists, carrying Yugoslav flags and portraits of Tito and shouting slogans, were confronted by about a thousand loyalist opponents. A full-scale fight developed in which the outnumbered OF demonstrators were nearly lynched. The clash showed the strength of loyalist counter-forces. In contrast to the Austrian police report, which blamed the OF completely,[73] the OF claimed their treatment proved allegations of repression. British Field Security, while largely blaming the OF, also noted the 'bestiality' of the loyalist reaction. Four German-Carinthians and nine OF members were arrested and later tried in a British military court. The British authorities then banned the public display of all flags.[74]

Both the clash and the subsequent ban were duly taken up by the OF and the Yugoslav government in protest notes to the Moscow CFM.[75] But it is hard to see that they had much impact, if any, and certainly not that hoped for by the OF. Indeed, it was precisely at this point that the Soviet Foreign Minister asked the Yugoslavs to agree in principle to reduce or even abandon their territorial claim. The Yugoslav delegation agreed.[76] If no deal was done, and the Moscow meeting ended in deadlock, it was because the West, and in particular the Americans, did not trust the Soviet Union not to take unfair advantage of the terms of the economic settlement (the issue of German external assets). Given that the West knew of the Soviet lack of commitment to Yugoslav claims to southern Carinthia, it was difficult to see how these could be genuinely viewed, in line with the doctrine of containment, as part of a global Communist threat to the West which had to be resisted by all means. It became even more difficult when in the summer of 1947 the Yugoslavs signalled directly to the West their readiness to reduce their claim or drop it altogether. But by now, the hostility between East and West meant that, even if it was accepted that an agreement in this (relatively minor) arena was possible, it was still undesirable because of the wider signals it might send out. By the time of the crisis year of 1948–49 and the Berlin blockade, this consideration applied to Austria as a whole. In May 1948 the West manufactured a breakdown of the Treaty talks over the disputed border.[77]

Thus mistrust between East and West prolonged an international dispute, which – when viewed in isolation – might have been settled in April 1947. More important here is the way the prolongation of the dispute affected provincial politics. Precisely because the suspension of a decision was not recognised as a manoeuvre but interpreted as part of the province's struggle for survival, it sustained loyalist politics. In an atmosphere of fevered excitement and rumour the province was portrayed as suspended 'between hope and fear' ('*zwischen Hoffen und Bangen*') in the words of an often-used cliché. [78] At the same time the rhetoric which drew upon the constructed memories and myths of 1918–20 became overlaid with the rhetoric of containment. Both spoke of an imminent threat from a powerful and implacable enemy and called for strength and unity to counter it. Piesch's successor as governor, Ferdinand Wedenig, returned from the London CFM and to a mass demonstration in Klagenfurt recalled the 'fateful days of the years 1919 and 1920'. Carinthians were once again faced by a 'fateful decision', and once again they were responding by a demonstration of determination, unity and self-sacrifice for the sake of freedom and the home-land. If Wedenig expressed optimism, it was based on the belief that the loyalty of the Carinthians and the acceptance by the world of the justice of their claims ensured that their cause would prevail. The solidarity shown to Carinthia not just by the rest of Austria but by the whole of the Western world was decisive.[79] The Cold War was the Carinthian *Abwehrkampf* writ large.

It would be wrong to label Wedenig anti-Slovene. Yet, precisely because of his basic sympathy with minority grievances, his shifts from accommodation to loyalism are significant. In May 1948 he was still arguing (privately) to the Austrian Foreign Minister that the minority should be given more rights to avoid alienating them. And he saw the threat from the OF as less serious than that from the revival of the German national right in the border area. The latter was personified by Hans Steinacher, a veteran German national activist in the cause of *Deutschtum* who had returned to Carinthia after the war, joined the ÖVP as *Grenzlandreferent* (borderland expert) early in 1947 and founded a *Bund der Heimattreuen Südkärntner* (League of Loyal Southern Carinthians) soon afterwards.[80] By 1948 the League was extending its defence of the unity of the province to attacks on bilingual education, which it saw as an affront to the traditions of the *Abwehrkampf* and a move towards the 'Slovenisation' of southern Carinthia. The Socialists who had introduced the measure were attacked as traitors (*Landesverräter*).

The continued state of limbo in relation to the border allowed Steinacher and his associates to decant their old wine into new bottles. The basic founda-tion of their politics and world view remained *völkisch* (folkish), but explicit racism or German superiority now tended to be avoided. Anti-Slav and anti-Communist fears and resentments mingled. A proposal for Slovene autonomy on the model of South Tyrol, for example, was described by Steinacher as an instrument of the 'the Communist–Slav Eastern bloc'.[81]

In the run-up to the October 1949 elections, playing on anti-Slav resent-ment became a common currency of both political parties and was at the ideo-logical core of the newly founded extreme right *Verband der Unabhängigen* (Association of Independents – VdU).[82] All parties knew that the votes of former Nazis, previously disfranchised, could decisively swing the election result.[83] The Socialists now intensified their recruitment of this group. As for the minority, they dropped earlier suggestions of further concessions, for example an autonomy statute, and stressed the governor's role in defence of the *Heimat*. The ÖVP stressed the role of 'their' Foreign Minister in the same defence.[84] Once the borders had been settled, both sides claimed the credit. Shortly before the elections, Steinacher (moving into the public arena for the first time) and Wedenig competed for the mantle of the *Abwehrkampf*. Steinacher derided Wedenig's claim to have been involved in the *Abwehrkampf*; on the contrary, the Socialists had shown a *'Nichtverstehen völkischer Schutzaufgaben'* ('incomprehension of folkish self-defence tasks') throughout their history.[85] In the elections of October 1949 the VdU ended up with 20.9 per cent of the electoral roll and eight seats in the *Landtag*. The gains were made at roughly equal expense to both the main parties, though the Socialists continued to hold the office of governor. More importantly in terms of our analysis, the joint efforts of ÖVP and VdU placed the attack on bilingual education at the centre of their agitation. In response, the SPÖ sought increasingly to 'take the wind out of their sails' by moving down the loyalist path.

The prolonged border dispute also took the OF down the blind alley of secession. A core of activists, though steadily depleted, continued to agitate for secession, apparently unaware of how hopeless their cause was. Doubts about the wisdom of 'pursuing a campaign which might later be unsupported by Yugoslavia', which were apparently expressed after the failure of the Moscow CFM in April 1947, were swept aside by Franci Zwitter, who stated confidently that 'in time all his [Tito's] demands will be met'.[86]

By the start of 1948, the tensions between the OF leadership and Catholic leaders had become an open break. Tischler finally broke with the OF and put forward autonomy proposals as an alternative to secession. A bitter public slanging-match followed.[87] The rift deepened a year later when the Vatican condemned Communist activity, and even reading the Communist press became an excommunicable offence.[88] Tischler set up the National Council of Carinthian Slovenes (*Narodni Svet koroških Slovencev*) and entered the election campaign with exaggerated hopes. The 4,644 votes it won were too few to gain it a single seat in the *Landtag*.

The OF was also forced to abandon its pusuit of secession. A clear indication to even the most short-sighted that it was bound to fail was the public rift between Tito and Stalin of the summer of 1948. As one OF official complained, 'Now I have absolutely no idea what is going on'.[89] After disputes with the Austrian Communist Party and much wrangling with the authorities, the OF changed its programme and its name to the Democratic Front of Working People (*Demokratična fronta delovnega ljudstva/Demokratischer Front des werktätigen Volkes*) in July 1949, and began to work towards the forthcoming election. By implication, it recognised that it had travelled down a blind alley for the past four years.

The election results confirmed the primacy of ethnic or national motivations in the (dwindling) ranks of the OF, and showed how few Bolsheviks or Stalinists were to found among Slovene farmers or agricultural labourers.[90] The Communists received only a handful of votes in the mixed-language area.[91] However, the Democratic Front did little better, gaining a mere 2,095 votes and thus less than half those gained by its clerical rivals. Though it is true that, even when aggregated, the votes for the two Slovene parties (6,739) would not have produced a single representative in the *Landtag* (compared to the two elected under the First Republic), this arithmetic fails to take account of the greater momentum which a united candidacy and single programme might have created. As it was, both Slovene groups began a phase of petty bickering at the margins of provincial politics, unable to lobby effectively, much less forge effective alliances to withstand the advance of loyalism.

For international actors, these events were no more than faint Central European noises off. Yet only a few weeks before the elections, in August 1949, having reaffirmed the existing borders, the CFM agreed a measure of minority protection which on the face of it offered extensive protection to the Slovenes (and the Burgenland Croats). But the paradox was more apparent than real, for the basic lack of interest remained. Security concerns about Yugoslav interference led the West to oppose a minority statute implacably. Ernest Bevin told Aleš Bebler, the Yugoslav Foreign Minister, that 'it was easy to see through the Yugoslav game. If their claim were granted, they would try to foment trouble in the Slovene area'.[92] The further claim that British 'experience of over nearly four years' had satisfied them that 'no sort of autonomy was required by the Slovene population in Carinthia' is less credible, especially since immediately after the war autonomy had been accepted by a range of local actors.[93] When the Soviet Union presented its proposal for minority protection (without autonomy), the British sought at first to water it down.[94] But Soviet concern for the minority was not much greater. As Gruber reported from the Paris CFM, the Soviet Foreign Minister, Vyshinsky, 'didn't show any particular interest at all in this question'.[95] What evidently did matter to the Soviet Union was to avoid giving ammunition to the dissident Yugoslav government. In other words, it was the Cominform dispute (coupled with Austrian readiness to make concessions in the interest of a Treaty) which led to the minority protection article. Though the long-term repercussions, legal and political, of Article 7 should not be dismissed, and indeed continue to this day, they do not support the case for the influence of 'high politics' on the politics of the province. Even as international law, Article 7 of the Austrian State Treaty could do little to prevent assimilationist pressure on the minority.

Conclusion

In the four years between the partisan incursion into southern Carinthia in May 1945 and the confirmation of Austria's border with Yugoslavia four years later, ethnic politics shifted decisively. For a brief period, Slovene participation within the existing borders was tried, then abandoned in favour of a fruitless pursuit of secession. Treatment of the minority by the local authorities (generally backed up by the British occupation authorities) was initially based on a pragmatic accommodation, but increasingly this was superseded by the re-assertion of policies which placed loyalty to the province at their centre and saw, more or less explicitly, assimilation to German culture as a necessary aspect of this. The Cold War gave an international dimension to this provincial polarisation, and in particular the prolongation of the border dispute between 1947 and 1949 influenced it in two ways; it aggravated tensions between Catholic and Communist parts of the minority leadership until they became an unbridgeable fissure; and it allowed some of the most extreme forms of loyalism, barely distinguishable from that promoted by the Nazi regime, to regain a political role and political respectability and in the 1950s to set the agenda of ethnic politics. Yet influence should not be confused with dominance; the Cold War did not, for example, bring a re-alignment of politics or submerge existing ethnic cleavages; Catholic Slovenes and German nationalists were not about to unite in their shared dislike of Tito's Yugoslavia. Seen in the longer perspective, the assimilation of the Carinthian Slovene minority, which had already been observable a century earlier, having reached a low-point of brutality and coercion under National Socialism, continued in the changed conditions of post-war Austria.

Notes

1 *The Question of 200,000 Yugoslavs in Austria – The Slovene Carinthia and the Burgenland Croats* (Belgrade, 1947); for the diplomatic background, see Gerald Stourzh, *Um Einheit und Freiheit: Staatsvertrag, Neutralität und das Ende der Ost-West-Besetzung Österreichs 1945–1955* (Vienna, 1998), 63–70, 81–5; also Arnold Suppan, *Die österreichischen Volksgruppen. Tendenzen ihrer geschichtlichen Entwicklung im 20. Jahrhundert* (Munich, 1983), 175–87. In addition, the Yugoslav government claimed 130 km^2 of Styria and $150 million in reparations for war damage.

2 C. Sulzberger, 'Balkans again center of big-power rivalry', *New York Times* (29 December 1946); Ernest Pisko, 'Austria sees Yugoslav move to shift border', *Christian Science Monitor* (26 December 1946); 'Difficult situation for Slovenes in Carinthia', *Tass* (24 March 1946).

3 Hansard, *House of Commons Debates*, Fifth Series, 3 March 1947, vol. 434, cols 201–12; Hansard, *House of Lords Debates*, Fifth Series, 28 January 1947, vol.145, col. 231.

4 See, *inter alia*, Hanns Haas and Karl Stuhlpfarrer, *Österreich und seine Slowenen* (Vienna, 1977); Thomas Barker, *The Slovene Minority of Carinthia* (New York, 1984); Janko Pleterski, *Slowenisch oder deutsch? Nationale Differenzierungsprozesse in Kärnten (1848–1914)* (Klagenfurt, 1996).

5 For example, Odd Westad (ed.), *Reviewing the Cold War: Approaches, Interpretations, Theory* (London, 2000), 149–79. Tony Smith, 'New bottles for new wine: A pericentric framework for the study of the Cold War', *Diplomatic History*, 24:4 (2000), 567–91; on Trieste, see Glenda Sluga, *The Problem of Trieste and the Italo-Yugoslav Border: Difference, Identity and Sovereignty in Twentieth Century Europe* (New York, 2001); Arnold Offner, *Another Such Victory: President Truman and the Cold War*

1945–1955 (Stanford, 2002), 43; Gianpaolo Valdevit, 'Yugoslavia between the two emerging blocs 1943–1948: a reassessment', in Antonio Varsori and Elena Calandri (eds), *The Failure of Peace in Europe 1943–1948* (Basingstoke, 2002), 184–6; see also Robert Knight, 'Ethnicity and identity in the Cold War: the Carinthian border dispute, 1945–1949', *International History Review*, 22:2 (2000), 274–303.

6 George Schöpflin, 'Nationalism and ethnicity in Europe, East and West', in C.A. Kupchan (ed.), *Nationalism and Nationalities in the New Europe* (Ithaca, IL, 1995), 37–8.

7 Most recently, see Verband slowenischer Ausgesiedelter/Zveza slovenskih izseljencev (ed.), *Die Vertreibung der Kärntner Slowenen/Pregon Koroških Slovencev, 1942–2002* (Klagenfurt, 2002).

8 See Valdevit, 'Yugoslavia', 84–5; Sluga, *The Problem*, chapter 2.

9 Thomas Barker, *Social Revolutionaries and Secret Agents: The Carinthian Slovene Partisans and Britain's Special Operations Executive* (New York, 1990); Josef Rausch, *Der Partisanenkampf in Kärnten im Zweiten Weltkrieg*, Militärhistorische Schriftenreihe 39/40 (Vienna, 1979).

10 Suppan, *Die österreichischen Volksgruppen*, 48–51; Arnold Suppan, *Jugoslawien und Österreich 1918–1938: Bilaterale Aussenpolitik im europäischen Umfeld* (Vienna, 1996), 683–5.

11 Suppan, *Die österreichischen Volksgruppen*, 56–7; Janko Pleterski, *Avstrija in njeni Slovenci 1945–1976* (Ljubljana, 2000), 68–9, 117–25, 179–203. The figure includes those giving 'Windisch' as their language, whether alone or in permutations.

12 As argued by August Walzl, *Gegen den Nationalsozialismus: Widerstand gegen die NS-Herrschaft in Kärnten, Slowenien und Friaul* (Klagenfurt, 1994).

13 See, for example, Peter Troppe (ed.), *Kirche im Gau: Die Diozöse Gurk im Dritten Reich* (Klagenfurt, 1995); Alfred Ogris, 'Der kirchliche Protest aus Klagenfurt gegen die Aussiedlung von Kärntner Slowenen im Jahre 1942', *Carinthia*, I, 182 (1992), 441–53.

14 On this, see the magisterial account in, Suppan, *Jugoslawien und Österreich*, 602–42, and more recently Tom Gullberg, *State Sovereignty and Identity: The Principle of National Self-Determination, the Question of Territorial Sovereignty in Carinthia and other post-Habsburg Territories after the First World War* (Åbo, 2000).

15 Wilhelm Wadl, *Das Jahr 1945* (Klagenfurt, 1985), 30; August Walzl, *Kärnten 1945* (Klagenfurt, 1985), 130, 147.

16 See Wadl, *Das Jahr 1945*, 7, 29–30; Alfred Elste, 'Entwicklungslinien des Kärntner Parteiensystems nach 1945', in A. Elste and Dirk Hänisch (eds), *Kärnten von der ersten zur Zweiten Republik: Kontinuität oder Wandel?* (Klagenfurt, 1998), 46; Gertrude Enderle-Burcel and Rudolf Jeřábek (eds), *Protokolle des Kabinettsrates der Provisorischen Regierung Karl Renner 1945*, 2 (Vienna, 1999), 86–7.

17 See, for example, ÖStA, Archiv der Republik, Bundeskanzleramt, Auswärtige Angelegenheiten (hereafter BKA AA), pol-1945, 2.350, Amt der Kärntner Landesregierung, Minderheitenreferat Report, 21 November 1945 (on the Catholic Vinko Zwitter); also Teodor Domej, 'Der Konflikt nach dem Krieg', in Andreas Moritsch (ed.), *Austria Slovenica: Die Kärntner Slowenen und die Nation Österreich/Koroški Slovenci in avstrijska nacija* (Klagenfurt, 1996), 125; Dokumentationsarchiv des österreichischen Widerstandes (hereafter DÖW) (ed.), *Spurensuche: Erzählte Geschichte der Kärntner Slowenen* (Vienna, 1990), 379.

18 Consolidated Intelligence Report (hereafter CIR) 14, 24 October 1945, Public

Record Office, Kew (PRO), FO 1007/296; Peter Fantur, *Der Christliche Kulturverband bei den Kärntner Slowenen im Wandel der Zeit* (Innsbruck, 1992), 104–5; Maja Haderlap, *Med politiko in kulturo: Slovenska gledališče dejavnost na Koroškem 1946–1976* (Klagenfurt, 2001); Thomas Busch and Brigitte Windhab (eds), *Jelka, Aus dem Leben einer Kärntner Partisanin* (Basel, 1984), 111–16.

19 Augustin Malle, 'Die Position der Kärntner Slowenen im Nationalitätenkonflikt', in Helmut Rumpler (ed.), *Kärnten: Von der deutschen Grenzmark zum österreichischen Bundesland* (Vienna, 1998), 495.

20 Domej, 'Der Konflikt', 125–6.

21 See intercepted OF paper (von der Organisation), Milena Mohor (German translation), 'Sicherheitsdirektion Carinthia, Wochenbericht' (Weekly report) 41, 8 June 1946, ÖStA, Archiv der Republik, Bundesministerium für Inneres (hereafter BMI), 123, 260–2/46.

22 See Augustin Malle, Alfred Elste, Brigitte Entner, Boris Jesih, Valentin Sima and Heidi Wilscher, *Vermögensentzug, Rückstellung und Entschädigung am Beispiel von Angehörigen der slowenischen Minderheit und ihrer Verbände und Organisationen* (Vienna, 2004).

23 PRO, FO 371/46651/C6377, 'Joint Weekly Intelligence Summary 9', 31 August 1945; Josef Tischler, *Die Sprachenfrage heute und vor 100 Jahren* (Klagenfurt, 1957).

24 CIR 14, 24 October 1945, PRO, FO 1007/296.

25 See Domej, 'Der Konflikt', 116–21; also Malle, 'Die Position', 494–519, 498; Brigitte Entner, 'Zwischen Machtteilhabe und Ausgrenzung – Die slowenische Minderheit in Kärnten und die Novemberwahl von 1945', in Lisa Rettl and Karl Stuhlpfarrer (eds), *5. Österreichischer Zeitgeschichtetag. Demokratie – Zivilgesellschaft – Menschenrechte* (Innsbruck, 2003).

26 See estimates in PRO, FO 1007/297, CIR 20, 5 December 1945, and *Neue Zeit* estimate of 8,746 cited by Domej, 'Der Konflikt', 123, both of which assign abstentions to OF supporters; see also Suppan, *Die österreichischen Volksgruppen*, 180; Hänisch, *Kärnten*, 238 (Tabelle 8.6), estimates that 19 per cent of Slovene voters voted Communist, 22 per cent failed to vote, 10 per cent were excluded because of Nazi membership, 33 per cent voted SPÖ and 15 per cent ÖVP. These estimates are of course to be treated with caution, not least because of the problems of defining a 'Slovene voter'.

27 According to Dušan Nećak, 'Die Wahlen in Kärnten nach dem Zweiten Weltkrieg: eine Analyse der Wahlresultate', *Jahrbuch für Zeitgeschichte* (Vienna, 1978), 225, the Communists gained 5,062 or 11.8 per cent of the vote in the sixty-two parishes in the mixed-language area (the area of the 1945 Education Decree) compared to only 1,917 in 1949.

28 Domej, 'Der Konflikt', 102, 124–5.

29 See, for example, Kärntnerischer Landtag, 32nd session, 15 March 1949, 129–62.

30 ÖStA, Archiv der Republik, BKA AA, pol-46, Österreich, 3, 110 162–111.507. Amt der Kärntner Landesregierung, Minderheitenreferat (German translation of speeches on 15 April 1946); Narodni Svet koroških Slovencev (ed.), *Zvest Domu, Narodu in Bogu: 40 let Narodnega sveta koroških Slovencev 10 let smrti dr. Joška Tischlerja* (Klagenfurt, 1989), 152–4.

31 See 'Amtliche Darstellung der Haltung des Gurker Ordinarius und seines Ordinariates in der slowenischen Frage 1941–1946', 12 March 1947.

32 PRO, FO 1007/298, CIR 29, 4 February 1946 (Annex A).

33 PRO, FO 1007/297, CIR 21, 13 December 1945.
34 Karl Heinz Frankl, '1945 – Ein Jahr der Wende für die Katholische Kirche in Kärnten?', in Peter G. Tropper (ed.), *Kirche im Gau: Dokumente zur Situation der katholischen Kirche in Kärnten von 1938 bis 1945* (Klagenfurt, 1995), 228–9, 262–5, 270.
35 CIR 9, 19 September 1945, PRO, FO 1007/296; for the background, see Stella Alexander, *Church and State in Yugoslavia since 1945* (Cambridge, 1979), 84ff.
36 *Documents on the Carinthian Question* (hereafter DCQ) (Belgrade, 1948), doc. 59, 128–131; Frankl, '1945', 267; Stossier to BMI, 22 April 1947, Fürstbischof Köstner to Figl, 2 May 1947, ÖStA, Archiv der Republik, BKA AA/pol-47/Österreich 3/106.707–106.707; Suppan, *Die österreichischen Volksgruppen*, 182; Frankl, '1945', 267. See also Peter G. Tropper, 'Die Diözese Gurk. Neue Aufgaben in einer neuen Welt', in Rumpler (ed.), Kärnten, 694–718, here 710–11; Malle, 'Katholische Kirche und Kärntner Slowenen', in Rumpler (ed.), *Kärnten*, 748–73.
37 Suppan, *Die österreichischen Volksgruppen*, 180; PRO, FO 371/46682/C8529, Meeting, 14 November 1945.
38 For example, PRO, FO 1020/1077, OF Memorandum to Allied Council, 25 January 1946; published in DCQ, 93–6.
39 PRO, FO 371/46611/C5138, 'Joint Weekly Intelligence Summary 6', 10 August 1945.
40 For a recent exposition see Wilhelm Neumann, 'Das Nationale Problem aus Deutschkärntner Sicht', in Rumpler, Kärnten, 464.
41 See *Kärntner Zeitung* (8 May 1945); also Elste, 'Entwicklungslinien', 55, note 165.
42 See Robert Knight, 'Liberal values in post-Nazi society', in Sieglinde Rosenburger and Andrej Markovits (eds), *Demokratie: Modus und Telos: Beiträge für Anton Pelinka* (Vienna, 2001), 143–58.
43 Memorandum from Carinthian Slovenes to the British military government, 27 June 1945, DCQ, doc. 35, 81–3 (original in PRO, FO 1020/2821/64B).
44 Kärntner Landesarchiv, Konsultativer Landesausschuss, 7th Meeting, 27 June 1945.
45 PRO FO 1007/298, CIR 27, 23 January 1946; see Domej, 'Der Konflikt', 147–51.
46 PRO, FO 1007/297, CIR 19, 29 November 1945; CIR 21, 13 December 1945 (BÖS 'Declaration', Appendix B).
47 See criticism by Tischler in PRO, FO 1007/298, CIR 25, 9 January 1946.
48 See PRO, FO 371/55114/C4187, Peter Wilkinson, 'The Slovene Minority in Carinthia', 10 April 1946, 6; Robert Knight, 'Schule zwischen Zwang und Verantwortung: Britische Besatzungsmacht, Kärntner Politik und die slowenische Minderheit 1945–1959', in Alfred Ableitinger, Siegfried Beer and Eduard Staudinger (eds), *Österreich unter alliierter Besatzung 1945–1955* (Vienna, 1998), 531–58, here 537.
49 PRO, FO 1007/298, CIR 29, 4 February 1946.
50 ÖStA, Archiv der Republik, BKA AA/pol-46/Österreich 3/110.162–112.112 (Meeting of 13 May 1946).
51 PRO, FO 1007/305, 'Weekly Security and Intelligence Report 28', 18–24 January 1946; PRO, FO 1007/298, CIR 28, 30 January 1946; 'St Kanzian wie in der Nazizeit', *Volkswille* (26 January 1946).
52 PRO, FO 1020/2822, Cefarin Memorandum, 27 January 1946.
53 For example, ÖStA, Archiv der Republik, BKA AA/pol-46/Österreich 9/110.513-110.523, Amt der Kärntner Landesregierung, Minderheitenreferat, Bericht, 20 February 1946.

54 ÖStA, Archiv der Republik, Ministerratsprotokoll (Cabinet Minutes) Figl I, 5th session, 29 January 1946; see also police report, in Alfons Schilcher (ed.), *Österreich und die Großmächte, Dokumentation zur österreichischen Außenpolitik* (Vienna, 1980), Dokument 38, 73.

55 ÖStA, Archiv der Republik, Cabinet Minutes Figl I, 12th session, 12 March 1946.

56 PRO, FO 1007/298, WSPD 36, 23 March 1946; 'Kärnten frei und ungeteilt', *Die Neue Zeit* (19 March 1946).

57 'Kärntens Minderheit und Südgrenze', *Die Neue Zeit* (18 March 1946).

58 PRO, FO1007/298, WSPD 36, 23 March 1946. According to this report the ministers spoke to crowds of some 500 at Ebendorf and Eisenkappel and addressed 8–10,000 in all.

59 ÖStA, Archiv der Republik, Cabinet Minutes Figl I, 13th session, 19 March 1946.

60 'Kärnten frei und ungeteilt', *Neue Zeit* (19 March 1946); PRO, FO 1007/298, British reports WSPD 36, 23 March 1946.

61 'Piesch droht Kärntner Slowenen', *Vestnik* (Marburg) (5 April 1946) (German translation in Archiv der Republik, BMI, 123.260-2/46, Sicherheitsdirektion (SiDion) Wochenbericht (Weekly Report) 41, 8 June 1946).

62 PRO, FO 1007/298, WSPD 37, 30 March 1946.

63 Kärntner Landesarchiv, Kärntner Landesregierung 13th session, 28 March 1946; see also PRO, FO 1020/2822, Piesch to Senior Military Government Officer, 25 March 1946.

64 See reports in PRO, FO 1020/2890; 'Hinter den Kulissen des 15. April', *Koroška Kronika*, 26 April 1946 (German translation *Amt der Kärntner Landesregierung, Minderheitenreferat*, in ÖStA, Archiv der Republik, BKA AA/pol-46/Österreich 9/110.162-111.503); Busch and Windhab (eds), *Jelka*, 103–4.

65 PRO, FO 1007/298, CIR 40, 21 April 1946; PRO, FO 1020/1077, Sharp to Wilkinson, 19 May 1946; Cole to Bell, Bell to Nicholls, 7 June, Nicholls, 10 June 1946.

66 ÖStA, Archiv der Republik, BMI, 123.260-2/46, Sicherheitsdirektion, Lagebericht (Situation Report), 3 June 1946.

67 ÖStA, Archiv der Republik, BKA AA/pol-46/Österreich 3/110.162-112.112 (meeting, 13 May 1946); PRO, FO 1020/1214 Field Security Section Report, 7 January 1947.

68 PRO, FO 371/63945/C861, Patrick Dean (FO) to Samuel Hood, 4 January 1947.

69 See Günther Bischof, *Austria in the First Cold War (1945–55): The Leverage of the Weak* (Basingstoke, 1999).

70 Carinthian *Landtag*, Formal Session (Festsitzung), 28 January 1947 (illustrated brochure) (Klagenfurt, 1947).

71 ÖStA, Archiv der Republik, BKA AA/pol-47/Staatsvertrag/105.005 – 105.56. Report of Bundespolizeikommissariat Villach, Sicherheitsdirektion Carinthia/SiDion Kärnten, 31 January 1947 (German translation in original).

72 ÖStA, Archiv der Republik, Bundesministerium für Inneres, 26.125–2/47, SiDion Lagebericht, March 1947 (meeting of Jugendbund für Slow. Kärnten).

73 ÖStA, Archiv der Republik, BKA AA/pol-47/Staatsvertrag/105.005 – 106.602, BMI to BKA AA, 14 April 1947. For a one-sided eye-witness account from the Deputy Bezirkshauptmann of Eisenkappel and later People's Party politician Wolfgang Mayrhofer-Grüenbühl, see 'Sturm in Eisenkappel im Jahre 1947', *Carinthia*, I, 185 (1995), 263–7; see also DÖW (ed.), *Spurensuche*, 380–1; DCQ, docs 67–69; Busch and Windhab (eds), *Jelka*, 109–10.

74 PRO, FO 1020/1214, 'FSS Eisenkappel', 16 March 1947.

75 PRO, FO 371/64058/C5909 and C5977 (DCQ, 156–57), Yugoslav Government to CFM, Moscow, 15 April 1947.

76 See Knight, 'Ethnicity'.

77 PRO, FO 371/70434/C3679, Special Deputies, 110th meeting, 6 May 1948; Reber to Marshall, 6 May 1948, *Foreign Relations of the United States 1948*, II (Washington, 1973), 1502; Stourzh, *Um Einheit*, 136–8.

78 'Zwischen Hoffen und Bangen', *Unterkärntner Nachrichten* (7 May 1948).

79 'Kärnten bleibt frei und ungeteilt', *Neue Zeit* (6 May 1948). On the German Carinthian media's use of the language of threat, see Florian Menz, Johanna Lalouschek and Wolfgang Dressler, *'Der Kampf geht weiter': Der publizistische Abwehrkampf in Kärntner Zeitungen seit 1918* (Klagenfurt, 1989), 111–17.

80 ÖStA, AdR, BKA AA/pol-48/Österreich 3/115.805-115.840, Wedenig to Gruber, 10 July 1948.

81 'Juzna Tirolska-Juzna Koroška', *Koroška Kronika* (5 March 1948); Steinacher memorandum, undated (forwarded by Schumy to Gruber, 13 March. 1948), ÖStA, AdR, BKA AA/Österreichische Botschaft London/Karton 10/Varia.

82 Knut Lehmann-Horn, *Die Kärntner FPÖ 1955–1983: Vom Verband der Unabhängigen [VdU] bis zum Aufstieg von Jörg Haider zum Landesparteiobmann* (Klagenfurt, 1992); Lothar Höbelt, *Von der Vierten Partei zur Dritten Kraft: die Geschichte des VDU* (Graz-Stuttgart, 1999), overlooks the VdU's anti-Slovene animus.

83 Hänisch (*Kärnten*, 176–7) estimates that 18.6 per cent of the 1945 electorate (i.e. 44,268) had been excluded as 'incriminated' (*belastete*). His definition includes those defined in the Austrian denazification legislation as both incriminated and less incriminated (*Minderbelastete*). Dieter Stiefel, *Entnazifizierung in Österreich* (Vienna, 1981), 309, gives a figure of 39,180.

84 Michael Gehler (ed.), *Karl Gruber in Reden und Dokumente 1945–1953: Eine Auswahl* (Vienna, 1994), 291–3.

85 *Volkszeitung* (4 October 1949), 'Kärntens Grenze fordert Einigkeit'.

86 PRO, FO 371/63975/C9758, 'Joint Fortnightly Intelligence Summary 35', 15–30 June 1947; see also Malle, 'Die Position', 497.

87 Domej, 'Der Konflikt', 125. See also Fantur, *Der Christliche Kulturverband*, 99–102; Narodni Svet koroških Slovencev (ed.), *Zvest*, 154–8.

88 'Eine Tat von geschichtlicher Bedeutung. Klare Fronten: Hie Christus-Hie Antichrist', *Kärntner Kirchenblatt* (3 March 1949); *Erzählte Geschichte*, 368; Tropper, 'Die Diözese Gurk', 694–718, here 711–12; Malle, 'Katholische Kirche', 763–4; see also Owen Chadwick, *The Christian Church in the Cold War* (London, 1992), 62–7.

89 ÖStA, AdR, BKA AA/pol-48/Jugoslawien 9/110.061-116.806, SiDion, Lagebericht, August 1948.

90 ÖStA, AdR, BKA AA/pol-48/Österreich 3/110.061-116.806, Lagebericht, August 1948 (Carinthian Communist leaflet); ÖStA, AdR, BKA AA/pol-49/Jugoslawien 9/80.369-83.190, SiDion Report (Stossier), 2 March 1949.

91 Hänisch, *Kärnten*, 238, estimates that Slovene support for the Communists dropped from 19 per cent to 3 per cent (of Slovene-speaking voters) while the KPÖ share of the vote in Lower Carinthia (Unterkärnten) dropped from 8 per cent to 4.6 per cent of the vote.

92 PRO, FO 371/7636/C1520, Bevin–Bebler conversation, 18 February 1949; Acheson

to Reber, 23 February 1949, *Foreign Relations of the United States 1949*, III (Washington, 1974), 1075.

93 PRO, FO 371/76475/C1998, FO to Vienna, 127th meeting of Foreign Ministers' Deputies, 4 March 1949.

94 PRO, FO 371/76482/C6521, British draft article (7 bis), 16 August 1949; German translation of Soviet and British proposals and text of final version of article 7 bis and Article 7, in Stourzh, *Um Einheit*, 156–7, 689–90.

95 ÖStA, AdR, Cabinet Minutes 162a, 23 June 1949; see also Schmidt to BKA AA, 29 July 1949, AdR, BKA AA/pol-49/Staatsvertrag 1/80.019-85.871.

8

Historical trauma in ethnic identity: the years of homelessness of the Hungarian minority in post-war Slovakia

Dagmar Kusá

The ethnic identity of nations, minorities and ethnic groups is to a large extent built on the fragile puzzles of collective memory, and hinges especially upon significant historical turning-points – victorious and heroic events as well as the tragic losses that history brings. Ethnic communities operate skilfully with these memories by imprinting them on the minds of the largest possible number of community members or, when desirable, by wiping them out of the historical text-books and surrounding them with an aura of taboo. Often the negative events involve direct conflicts with another ethnic community, which serve to boost feelings of group solidarity and allegiance, yet sometimes such events might be perceived as so harmful or confusing that the community or its leadership attempts to push them into the darkness of forgetting, or at least misinterpretation.

Many historical instances show that it is necessary for nations to deal with their traumatic historical past in order to reconcile tensions within society and to be able to face the future. For this purpose, the Truth and Reconciliation Committee was set up in South Africa, the current German government has issued an official apology for atrocities committed against Jews in the Holocaust during the Second World War, and purification ('lustration') committees were set up in the Czech Republic, Germany and Poland after the breakdown of the Communist regimes there, to exact retribution for the crimes of the Communist establishment.

Slovakia and Hungary failed to undergo the purification process successfully. It will be argued that this is due to the legacy of older historical traumas that beset the Slovak–Hungarian relationship, especially those of the years 1945–48 connected with the transfers of members of the Hungarian minority in Slovakia. The present chapter will consider the domestic and international causes that led to the mistreatment of the Hungarian minority in Slovakia in that period, the social situation of the Hungarian minority in Slovakia prior to and after the 'exchange of populations' between Slovakia and Hungary in 1947 and 1948, and the impact of the advent of Communism in Czechoslovakia on the situation of the Hungarians in Southern Slovakia.

Historical traumas are a crucial part of the formation of ethnic identity, for most often they contribute to the definition of 'otherness', of what the ethnic community defines itself *against*. In the case of the Slovaks and Hungarians of Slovakia there was a number of such defining turning-points, from the Austro-Hungarian settlement of 1867 that marked the beginning of decades of 'Magyarisation', and the Trianon Peace Treaty of 1920 that placed one-third of all Hungarians outside the borders of the new Hungary, with almost 1 million of them becoming part of the Czechoslovak Republic. The Vienna Arbitral Award of 1938,[1] which transferred a large portion of Southern Slovakia back to Hungary, was perceived by Czechoslovakia as a betrayal by the Western powers. Czechoslovakia was forced into agreement by Germany, Italy and Hungary, and abandoned by the Western powers. The massive transfers to Germany in the later 1940s of populations from all over Eastern Europe on the basis of collective guilt remain among the region's most sensitive international issues. Yet the question of the transfer of Hungarians in the years 1946–48 is even more painful, for it remains taboo to this day. Hungarians avoid the risk of using the topic as leverage in political discussions, yet public opinion, when tested, reveals that this wound is still raw among the Hungarians of Slovakia.

A fascinating and unparalleled sociological and ethno-psychological piece of research was carried out in Southern Slovakia in 1994, which showed that the question of the southern border of Slovakia is still a sensitive one today: 71 per cent of Hungarians living in the ethnically mixed region of Southern Slovakia consider the partition of Hungary after the First World War as the origin of a major misfortune that has afflicted the Hungarians of Slovakia ever since. By contrast, 68 per cent of Slovaks living in that area tend to think that the Hungarians were always expanding their territory at the expense of someone else.[2] The boundary issue has the effect of reinforcing the myth of a 'national Calvary' on both sides. On the Slovak side, this myth is connected with the 'thousand years of suffering' of the Slovak nation under Hungarian supremacy, which is believed in by 78 per cent of the Slovaks living in the ethnically mixed region. The Hungarian side connects the suffering with the aftermath of the Trianon Treaty, which deprived Hungary of two-thirds of its historic territory. The transfers of Hungarian population in 1947 are thus viewed as the sequel of Trianon. 87 per cent of Hungarians in Southern Slovakia still consider the transfers unjust.[3]

Key concepts

Before we proceed to discuss the events leading to the transfers of ethnic Hungarians from southern Slovakia, a few of the main concepts relevant to the subject need to be reviewed. Firstly, the concept of 'ethnic community' and the reasons for using this term, together with the related concept of 'ethnic identity', will be discussed. Secondly, we shall define the concept of 'territoriality', which should serve to clarify some of the intentions and consequences of the transfers, their place in the collective memory and their effect upon the relationship between the two ethnic communities.

As the reader will already have observed, the term 'ethnic community' is here being used in preference to more common terms such as 'nation', 'minority' and 'ethnic group'. The term is used to denote all those communities that identify themselves on the basis of their possessing in common a history, culture, moral and social norms, language and territory, without distinguishing between communities on the basis of their position within the state. Since it includes the categories of nation, minority and ethnic group, this term allows us to disregard the notion of power which the other three terms carry, and to compare ethnic communities more freely by placing them on an equal footing. It is therefore a wider term than the other three, although these latter will be used where the aspect of power does play a significant part.

When referring to the nation, I will use the definition so well formulated by Benedict Anderson, namely, of the nation as an imagined political community that is limited by, albeit elastic, boundaries (Frederick Barth would add, by physical as well as imagined boundaries), and is sovereign, for this concept was born in the era when the legitimacy of the hierarchical and dynastic rule of emperors and of the Pope was being questioned.[4] An important classification, useful for the purposes of this study, was propounded by George Brunner, who distinguishes between the 'state nation' and the 'cultural nation'. The state nation is characteristic for the countries of Western Europe and signifies the idea of a spatial entity which includes ethnic differences and also allows of regional and personal differentiation.[5] The modern concept of the state nation (which is not to be confused with the concept of the nation-state) dates from the time of the French Revolution and relates to a specific state with a civic constitution.

A nation of this kind is held together most of all by a common history. Central and Eastern Europe operate largely with an understanding of the nation as a 'cultural nation', which emphasises certain common criteria such as language, culture, roots and history – where territory and state did not originally play such a significant role, but were nevertheless included from the end of the nineteenth century.[6] The importance of establishing these categories will become apparent when we consider the differences between the Czech and Slovak perception of the nation in the inter-war period, when the former was equated with the idea of the state nation, the latter with the idea of the cultural nation.

The legal understanding of the term 'national minority' (e.g. Recommendation 1201 of the Council of Europe or the Framework Convention on National Minorities of the Council of Europe) defines it basically as a group of people living in a territory which they have long inhabited, and possessing specific ethnic, cultural, religious or linguistic traits in common. Such a minority is smaller in number than the rest of the population, but is still sufficiently numerous, and motivated, to maintain its collective identity, culture and language.[7]

Definitions of 'ethnic identity' are as broad and abstract as are definitions of the nation or the state, and may mean different things to different groups of people. While in some situations ethnic identity is equated with race, in other instances it may concern the rights of indigenous populations, carrying a notion of oppression or discrimination within itself. For present purposes, the term will be used only in relation to the concept of ethnic community as defined above.

First of all, ethnic identity denotes *self-definition* and a subjective perception of who an individual is: it embraces his or her own authenticity, uniqueness, belonging in time and space, as an individual or as a member of a human group or community.[8] This aspect of ethnic identity is especially important in the context of Slovak-Hungarian relations, for the official statistics may not in fact reflect the reality of someone's underlying self-identification. A brief look at the numbers of Hungarians in Slovakia appearing in the censuses throughout the twentieth century (see Appendix 1) will show that the drastic fluctuations in the size of this minority were probably due not to any process of change in ethnic identification, but rather to the effect of changing external conditions upon the position of this ethnic community in relation to others.

Seen from this angle, a second aspect of ethnic identity that is rarely mentioned stands out as significant. This is the aspect of *strategic choice* when it comes to proclaiming ethnic identity. Barth and Bačová both assert that, if individuals are to represent themselves as members of a given ethnic community, it is necessary that they should perceive membership as offering some benefit. Individuals weigh the pros and cons of belonging to an ethnic community, and if it brings more disadvantages than benefits they will tend to claim an ethnicity other than that which they might perceive on a deeper level as being their own. It is therefore essential to keep this distinction in mind. Another related factor is the *will* of the community to maintain its identity through time. As Bačová asserts, of all the aspects of ethnic identity, the single most important for its survival is perhaps the knowledge that a significant number of members of the community identify themselves *ethnically* with that community. The cultural attributes, language, or territory of the ethnic community may vary over time, and many communities have even ceased to exist.[9] Yet, as the case of the Hungarians in Slovakia shows, there are numerous other communities that have kept their identity despite the obstacles posed by external conditions and even despite (or arguably partially also owing to) the overt attempts of other ethnic communities or state authorities to eliminate it.

The third aspect of ethnic identity that is important from the perspective of this study is that of *control*. In pre-modern times, ethnicity was 'untamed', but with the creation of the modern state it has become organised and controlled. It has become a tool for gaining access to decision-making, the distribution of resources, etc. This aspect brings us directly to the last of the concepts to be considered before proceeding to our case study of the Hungarians in Slovakia after the Second World War.

Every ethnic community, regardless of its position within society, has links with a particular territory (real or mythical) in which its identity is rooted. Territory, and control over it, are thus crucial to ethnic communities today, especially since political representation is one of the most important means of survival for communities within states. Territories are, however, not usually inhabited by one homogeneous ethnic group, and the struggle for power among different groups can take various forms.

Robert D. Sack defines territoriality as 'the attempt of individuals to influence, control people, phenomena and relations by establishing and implementing control over a certain geographic area'.[10] Territoriality in this sense may be seen as constituting a *continuum of political action*. At one end of this continuum are the attempts of ethnic communities to create nation-states while eliminating the rights of other ethnic communities over the territories to which they lay claim, or the attempts of minorities to secede from the state of which they are citizens. Yet territoriality may take more subtle forms than these 'ultimate solutions'. Territoriality can take the shape of regional, political or cultural autonomy granted to an ethnic community, or merely of political representation at all levels of society – from seats in municipal government to membership of parliament and government, or a combination of any of these. Such forms of territoriality would be located at the other end of the continuum.

Territoriality is closely linked with the control aspect of ethnic identity – it is a modern feature of ethnic relations, connected with the creation of the modern state with its specific boundaries which have for the first time been precisely defined on the map. Anderson recognises two important features of what I here label 'territoriality': the *map* and the *census*. Both of these represent the 'totalizing classification [which has] led their bureaucratic producers and consumers towards revolutionary consequences . . . [T]he entire planet's surface had been subjected to a geometrical grid which squared off empty seas and unexplored regions in measured boxes.'[11] Ernest Gellner famously compares the pre-modern and the modern map with the paintings of Kokoschka and Modigliani, respectively. While the one map is a mixture of coloured points and areas that flow into one another, the other, that reminiscent of Modigliani, is a jigsaw puzzle of well-defined variously coloured pieces strictly separated by lines, on which it is clear at first sight where one piece begins and another ends.

The concept of territoriality aptly illustrates the motivations behind the Czechoslovak political leadership's specific actions and plans in regard to the Hungarian minority, and it also illuminates the sensitivity of certain issues which have been a factor in developments. The southern border of Slovakia remained Kokoschka-like until the Trianon Peace Treaty, when it was arbitrarily defined by the representatives of the Allied Powers, who ignored ethnic and historical boundaries (regional and district). Thus it remains a sensitive issue to this day, even though the Hungarian government has officially given up the goal of border revision and concentrates solely on the issue of political representation within the ethnically mixed regions, aiming for some level of political and cultural autonomy, for the sake of which any claim to territorial autonomy is strictly avoided.

When we glance at the censuses (Appendix 2) enumerating the population of Slovakia in the modern period, we notice the steady increase in the size of the Slovak population (except for the period of most vigorous 'Magyarisation' around 1910, which introduced Hungarian as the only official language and was reflected in the census of 1910), as opposed to the fluctuations in the population trends of Hungarians and Ruthenes. The first census following the First World War, that of 1921, was already marked by the attempts of the Czechoslovak leadership to create a less ethnically diverse state by means of statistics. The accounts of the 1921 census reveal that the directions given to the census-takers were aimed at achieving the highest possible number of 'Czechoslovaks' – in other words, at creating a politically constructed nation, and hence the illusion of a dominant nation within this extremely diverse state. Thus many people who merely demonstrated some knowledge of Czech or Slovak (especially in the Southern Slovakian and Silesian regions) were recorded as 'Czechoslovaks', which caused a decline in the numbers of the other ethnic communities.[12] The Vienna Award, which redrew the Southern Slovak border and awarded a large portion of Slovak territory to Hungary, resulted in a dramatic increase in people claiming Hungarian identity.

The greatest fluctuation is visible in the early post-war years, which saw a major decline in both the official and the actual numbers of the Hungarian ethnic community in Slovakia because of the causes described in detail below. Yet, as we know, the official tactics aimed at eliminating this minority largely failed, for the numbers of those claiming Hungarian identity have risen steadily ever since the 1950s, and the membership of this community is today well established and secured through the organised political and cultural representation of this group, and also as a consequence of the significant markers of history that serve as a glue which holds this community together and allows it to define itself over against other ethnic communities and especially the Slovaks.

Key issues determining the transfer processes after the war

Turning to our actual case study to demonstrate some of these aspects in practice, it is necessary to consider the causes that led to the expulsion of Hungarians from their homes after the Second World War and the denial of their citizenship rights for a period of three years. We shall look first at the different concepts of the nation which prevailed among the Czech and Slovak political representatives, respectively, and which led to their having different ideas about the internal organisation of the state. Next we shall consider the historical issues that were at play, and then turn to the international situation, which had a major impact on the actual process of the transfers as well as on their mere possibility. Lastly, the transfer process itself, and its consequences for the present relationship between the two ethnic communities, will be summarised.

During the war, the Western Allies recognised the Czechoslovak government-in-exile in London as the official government of Czechoslovakia. It was
made up of the political elite of Czechoslovakia, including the former president,
Eduard Beneš, and the former Minister of Foreign Affairs, Milan Hodža. The
National Council established in exile decided that the election of Emil Hácha
as president of the Czech Republic was invalid, instead recognising Eduard
Beneš as the president of Czechoslovakia despite his resignation in 1938.[13] The
government-in-exile was united only in appearance. There were serious differences, especially between Hodža and Beneš, concerning the internal organisation of the state and the position of the individual ethnic communities within
it. One needs to understand these differences as well as the specific situation
in which the exiled elite found itself in order to understand the origins of the
idea of transferring the German, Hungarian and Ruthene minorities of
Czechoslovakia.

There were two major opposing approaches to the question of the internal
organisation of Czechoslovakia with regard to its rich ethnic composition. One
was that of a truly multi-ethnic democracy based on representation, participation and a large degree of self-government for minorities, propounded most
prominently by the Slovak statesman Milan Hodža. In stark contrast was the
approach advocating the establishment of a new Czechoslovakia, after the
Second World War, as a nation-state, which called for the realisation of the idea
of the 'Czechoslovak nation' and demanded that Czechoslovak territory should
be 'cleansed' of the non-Slavic minorities. This approach at the far end of the
continuum of territoriality was advocated by the President, Eduard Beneš, who
was himself largely responsible for orchestrating the transfers.

Milan Hodža was an influential inter-war statesman who had been attempting to reform the public administration of the first Czechoslovak Republic in
order to allow for the multi-ethnic composition of the state. He recognised the
necessity for co-operation among the ethnic communities and the impossibility
of artificially creating a Czechoslovak nation. It was he who, in 1926, invited the
German and Hungarian minorities to participate in the government, and who
implemented a substantial administrative reform which created four self-governing regions, Bohemia, Moravia, Slovakia and Sub-Carpathian Ruthenia.
Hodža advocated his idea of 'regionalism', as opposed to the strengthening of
centralism sought by Prague and the extreme autonomism pursued by nationalists in Slovakia. Ethnic communities were to manage their own affairs at
regional level, which would lead to their satisfaction and increased co-operation.
This approach lay at the opposite pole of territoriality, seeking to exert control
through political representation and participation.

Shortly before the imposition of the Munich settlement, Hodža had managed,
after years of struggle with his colleagues in government, to get the Statute of
Minorities through the federal parliament; this granted equality and freedom
to choose one's nationality to all citizens of the state, and was later broadened
by the language law. These arrangements represented a comprehensive and

detailed guarantee of minority rights, but could not be implemented in practice, for Munich and the Second World War were around the corner.[14]

Hodža was also famous for his ideal of a Central European Federation. His view was that the small nations that made up Central Europe could implement their right to self-determination only within a larger political unit. This unit would include all Central European and most Slavic ethnic communities, each enjoying a large degree of self-government.

Eduard Beneš was the exact opposite of Milan Hodža. He believed that national homogeneity was necessary if the country was to be stable and democratic, and he had therefore been considering the transfer of the German, Hungarian (and Ruthene) population since the outbreak of the Second World War. Kálmán Janics writes: 'The thesis authored by President Beneš [was] that the war had been caused by the national minorities; the world press popularised the idea that the minorities must either be promptly liquidated by expulsion or left to their destiny and assimilation by the majority, with no protection of their minority rights as nationalities.'[15] Beneš was one of the advocates of the Czechoslovak nation, an idea which he had eventually to abandon. This construct was to be used as a tool for establishing the rule of the homogeneous dominant nation over the other ethnic communities, but it was not acceptable either to the Slovak leadership or to Czechs and Slovaks in general.

Beneš also advocated a confederation, but not in the 'Hodža style'. He was intent on fulfilling the wishes of the superpowers rather than on implementing ideals, and thus advocated a confederation with Poland. He admitted several times that he was considering this confederation solely because of the attitude of Britain and the United States towards Poland.[16] In the question of transfers, he largely relied on the help of the Soviet Union, and in negotiations with the United States, Great Britain and France, he manoeuvred skilfully to get them on his side.[17]

Beneš mostly made decisions alone, submitting them to the National Council for approval as a *fait accompli*. In relation to minorities in Slovakia, he first discussed his programme in detail with Moscow, which was much more receptive to his idea of transfers (for many similar processes were underway in the Soviet Union itself), and subsequently with the Western powers. Beneš and the rest of the émigré elite made a strict distinction between the Hungarian and the German question. The transfers of Sudeten Germans from Bohemia were based on the acknowledged principle of collective guilt, which justified the plan in the eyes of the Allies. Moscow and the Communists of Czechoslovakia did play a crucial role in the resettlement of the Hungarians; it was the latter who carried the programme out, but it could not have been realised without the initial support of Moscow.[18] Great Britain gave its approval to the transfer of the German population in 1942. At the same time, Beneš started to advocate the same treatment for the Hungarians in Slovakia, but this was never approved on the same terms by either Great Britain or the United States (where Milan Hodža and Jan Masaryk were greatly influential). Nor did Moscow initially agree to the unilateral transfer of Hungarians. 'Till the spring of 1944 the transfer of Hungarians was only Beneš's theory. There is no evidence in any literature that anyone has approved of Beneš's attempts in this sense.'[19]

Since Beneš was not finding support for his plan for the Hungarians, he began to consider how to simplify it. Instead of being transferred, the Hungarians of Slovakia were to be 'exchanged' for the Slovaks living in Hungary, which would have the same effect – the desired ethnic homogeneity. The Czechoslovak government-in-exile, the Slovak National Council and the Moscow leadership of the Czechoslovak Communists continued to differ on the Hungarian issue until 1944. Thereafter, the Slovaks and the Communists, too, adopted an anti-Hungarian stance and proceeded to put it into practice.

Prior to the enunciation of the Košice Programme,[20] the founding document of the post-war Czechoslovak government after its return from exile, domestic affairs were directed by presidential decree. Many of these were already replete with pronounced anti-Hungarian sentiment and were directed towards promoting the future plan for the 'exchange' of populations. The Hungarian Party (*Magyar Párt*) was dissolved, as were other Hungarian associations. The civil service was 'de-Hungarianised'. Hungarian representatives were not allowed to participate in municipal governments, even in towns with an overwhelming Hungarian majority. Despite these harsh measures, the question of the resettlement of the Hungarians was never discussed publicly in Czechoslovakia at the time. When the Slovak National Council returned to Slovakia from exile, the issue was not even mentioned in its Memorandum of February 1945. All it asked for was the return of supporters of the former Hungarian regime to Hungary.[21]

The peace agreement concluded between the Allies and Hungary on 20 January 1945 declared the provisions of the Vienna Arbitral Award to be invalid and recognised the pre-Munich Czechoslovak borders. It demanded that all Hungarian administrators and soldiers should leave the occupied territory of Southern Slovakia, that war-time costs should be reimbursed and all decisions made by the Hungarian administration of the territory rescinded, and that the property and valuables that had been seized should be returned.[22]

The Košice Programme was issued on 5 April 1945, immediately after the Czechoslovak government, led by Zdeněk Fierlinger, had taken power. Its eighth section (out of a total of sixteen) laid down that the Hungarians and Germans were to be deprived of their rights as citizens and that administrative posts in ethnically mixed regions were to be staffed by Slovaks. The ninth section concerned the confiscation of Hungarian land and the fourteenth the dissolution of minority schools throughout the entire territory of Czechoslovakia. The resultant discriminatory measures meant that Hungarian property came under the control of the state, Hungarian civil servants were dismissed and lost their entitlement to pensions, the use of the Hungarian language was forbidden in religious services, Hungarian priests were expelled from Slovak territory, Hungarian students were excluded from Slovak universities, Hungarian cultural and public associations were dissolved and their property was taken over by the state, etc.[23]

Hungarians were also much more severely punished for crimes of collaboration with the Tiso regime of 1939–45. Janics claims that the proportion of Hungarians facing criminal charges was ten times higher than that of Slovaks (0.8 per cent of Hungarians as opposed to 0.08 per cent of Slovaks), and the former generally received higher sentences for similar crimes.[24] This aspect is well illustrated by the fate of the leading figure in the Hungarian community in Slovakia, Count János Esterházy. While he was a member of the collaborationist Slovak parliament, Esterházy was the only representative who did not vote in favour when the parliament was voting on the issue of the deportation of the Jews.[25] He also came under constant attack by the German-language *Grenzbote* and the Slovak paper *Gardista*. Yet, after the war, he was accused of collaboration with the Nazi regime, taken to the Soviet Union by the KGB, later extradited to Czechoslovakia, and sentenced in 1947 on the charge of 'betrayal of the Republic' to death by hanging. This sentence was subsequently commuted by the President to life imprisonment. He died in prison in 1957.[26]

The transfers

Following the enactment of the Law on the Protection of the Republic, the deportations of 'unreliable' Hungarians began. Those from Bratislava were moved to a detention camp in Petržalka and those from the rest of Slovakia into a former concentration camp for Jews in Sered'. Presidential Decree No. 33/1945, signed on 2 August 1945, deprived all Hungarians and Germans living on Czechoslovak territory of their rights as citizens, and became the basis of all subsequent discriminatory policies and actions. The loss of citizenship was automatically followed by exclusion from state institutions and offices, from reimbursement for nationalisation of property and for war damage, etc. This decree was issued on the very same day that the Potsdam conference refused to include a paragraph on the deportation of 200,000 Hungarians in the peace treaty with Hungary.[27]

In consequence, the Czechoslovak government decided to resolve the situation by other means. Hungarians from Southern Slovakia were forcibly resettled in the distant parts of the Czech Republic vacated by the Germans deported to Germany. Other methods of eliminating the Hungarian community were 're-Slovakisation', and the 'exchange' of Hungarians for Slovaks living in Hungary on the basis of a bilateral agreement.

Czechoslovakia could afford to treat its minorities in this way because 'the fate of the Hungarian minority did not interest anyone after the Paris Peace Conference' of 1946.[28] The resultant peace treaty, signed on 10 February 1947, did not include any provision concerning the protection of minorities. After the advent of Communism, the Hungarians in Czechoslovakia lost all possibility of self-defence. Individuals could no longer rely on being able to own private property, independent small businesses shrank to nothing and there was no chance to form small, informal associations within the now-paralysed Church.

Resettlement in Bohemia was euphemistically labelled 'recruiting' of labour. The signs on the trains carrying the Hungarians from Slovakia said 'voluntary agricultural workers'. In reality, it was a deportation aimed at obtaining forced labour. The Czechoslovak administration began to carry out this programme in 1945 on the basis of Presidential Decree No. 88/1945 on universal labour service. 'It was on this basis that the compulsory labor service of the Hungarian population of South Slovakia was decreed (in November 1946), the intention being that, by the same token, the ethnic structure of South Slovakia's population would be altered.'[29] Decree No. 88/1945 empowered the government to draft men between the ages of sixteen and fifty-five and women between the ages of eighteen and forty-five into labour service for a period of one year. However, the deported Hungarians were of all ages and their property was confiscated, which was an illegal act and could not be justified under the Decree.[30] The Paris Peace Treaty declared that the matter of minorities was a question of domestic policy, and so not subject to outside interference, a provision which was widely used as an excuse for action against minorities in Czechoslovakia.[31] The Slovak and Hungarian churches protested publicly against this treatment, but theirs were among but few lonely voices amid the silence of the vast, and largely uninformed, majority.

The Czech historian Karel Kaplan has labelled these transfers 'internal colonisation', the political aim of which was to transfer a part of the Hungarian minority away from the Hungarian border and to destroy it as a compact territorial unit. This colonisation also had an immediate industrial goal – to provide the depopulated areas with a new workforce.[32]

The first stage of the resettlement involved the transfer of Hungarians from south-western Slovakia in exchange for the transfer of Slovaks from Hungary into that same region of Slovakia. The second stage took place in July and August 1946, under the slogan 'Slovak agricultural labour assisting the Czech lands'. The Hungarians who remained in southern Slovakia after the first wave of transfers were sent off to western Bohemia, a region vacated after a unilateral expulsion of the Sudeten Germans there.

The third and most large-scale phase of resettlement took place from November 1946 to February 1947, when 44,000 Hungarians were recorded as having been removed from 393 villages and seventeen South Slovak districts. The unofficial numbers given for Hungarians resettled in Bohemia between 1945 and 1948 are much higher.[33] According to Janics:

> The deportations of Hungarians from Southern Slovakia came to a sudden end on February 25 1947. The decision to stop the deportations had come, most likely as a result of the unfavorable publicity in the West and under pressure of the Great Powers, the United States in particular ... Thus, the Hungarians in the eastern counties of Southern Slovakia from Rožňava (Rozsnyó) to Vel'ké Kapušany (Nagykapos) were spared the experience of being deported to Bohemia. .... It was no secret that the deportations had a twofold objective. Its aim was to weaken the Hungarian ethnic element in Slovakia on the one hand and to force the execution

of the population exchange agreement with Hungary, on the other. In that sense, the action was successful on both counts.[34]

The policy of re-Slovakisation had already started with the decrees of the Slovak National Council issued immediately after the war. As already mentioned, the Hungarians along with the Germans were deprived of all rights of citizenship. Furthermore, a decree of May 1945 declared that Hungarians might no longer be members of Slovak political parties; thus, alongside the dissolution of all Hungarian political parties, all opportunities for legitimate self-defence were suppressed.

Re-Slovakisation itself was announced by the Slovak National Council in June 1946 and lasted for a year. Its terms guaranteed citizenship to everyone who declared himself to be a Slovak. Re-Slovakisation was officially a matter of free choice, but when we consider the options available to the Hungarians, we are obliged to conclude that it was a process of forcible assimilation. Opting for Hungarian ethnic identity in the census or for official purposes was highly unfavourable to a person's status. Declaring oneself to be Slovak meant being allowed to keep one's citizenship status, property and security; not doing so meant homelessness, statelessness, discrimination and financial insecurity. Thus the state institutions rudely interfered with personal identification and choice. Nor was Slovak citizenship automatically granted to everyone who applied, contrary to the provisions of the Decree. Out of over 400,000 requests, 81,142 were turned down by the Slovak authorities on the grounds of insufficient proof of Slovak origin. Every application for citizenship had to be accompanied by a 'certificate of nationality' to make sure that no person of German or Hungarian nationality would receive civil rights.[35] The Czechoslovak statistics show that 326,679 people were re-Slovakised.[36] However, in the 1960 census, 533,900 Hungarians reappeared (see Appendixes 1 and 2). Thus, re-Slovakisation was considered 'unsuccessful' in the long run. Nevertheless, it managed to worsen relations between Slovaks and Hungarians further.

The population exchange was carried out on the basis of a bilateral agreement between Czechoslovakia and Hungary of 26 February 1946, which provided for the voluntary exchange of 40,000 people. This agreement laid the foundations for an unequal trade-off. The Slovaks in Hungary were to decide freely, whilst the number of Hungarians to be transferred to Hungary from Slovakia was to be determined by the Slovak authorities. They wanted first of all to get rid of the Hungarian intelligentsia and political figures. When the Hungarian authorities were hesitant and procrastinated over carrying out the exchange, the Czechoslovak side pressured them through the deportations of Hungarians to the Czech borderlands and the policy of re-Slovakisation.

At the time, the nationalist hysteria was running out of steam, owing to international condemnation of the Czechoslovak treatment of the Hungarian minority, and the Yugoslav example of reconciliation with the Hungarians. The overall numbers given for those exchanged differ. According to Renner, the overall number of Hungarians transferred to Hungary was 89,000 (leaving behind

15,700 homes), while the Slovaks coming from Hungary reached 70,000 (leaving behind 4,400 homes).[37] The last train transport from Hungary departed on 21 December 1948. Only half of those Slovaks who had applied to be exchanged actually turned up. Usually this was due to their dissatisfaction with the property allocated to them; in many cases, they were also scheduled to be sent to the Czech borderlands, which were still suffering from a shortage of labour.[38]

'The history of Hungarians in Slovakia', states Raphael Vago, 'is clearly divided into the period before and after 1948, when the Communists reversed, albeit slowly, their line of discrimination'.[39] Unfortunately, the historical record is darker than Vago suggests. The resettlement of Hungarians in the Czech borderlands was officially stopped and the Communist government restored their Czechoslovak citizenship and allowed them to return to Southern Slovakia. In the meantime, however, their property had been confiscated, and their land and houses had been given to Slovak newcomers or those who had been repatriated. Their return thus did not represent a solution, but in many instances merely a tempering of the problem.[40] They were allowed to sue for the recovery of confiscated property and continued to do so for years. Only a few were successful, for the time was never really ripe for compensation to be paid.[41] Moreover, another wave of transfers was planned as late as 1949. 'Action South' was approved directly by the Central Committee of the Communist Party. Shortly after it was launched in Šamorín in October 1949, it had to be stopped, since it was highly unrealistic and quite obviously in flat contradiction to the Communist ideal of supranationalism.

The Communist accession to power brought with it the establishment of a totalitarian regime for the rest of Slovak society. The paradox of this era is, as Vago makes clear, that it resulted in an improvement of the Hungarians' situation. The Slovak Communists, although they had participated extensively in the persecution of the Hungarians before 1948, could no longer pursue this line, for it did not correspond with Communist ideology. The Communist Party came to power in neighbouring Hungary, and the need for reconciliation became obvious. 1948 thus marked the end of the 'years of homelessness' for the Hungarians in Slovakia and meant an improvement in the position of this minority within the state.

After their civil and political rights had been restored to the Hungarians, they were eligible for election to the national committees, the new local representative bodies combining the executive powers of the state with the Party line. In 1954, they had 4.4 per cent of representatives in the regional, 6.8 per cent in the district and 11.9 per cent in the local national committees.[42] *Csemadok*, a Hungarian cultural association of workers, was established in 1949, and *Új Szó*, a Hungarian daily, first appeared in December 1949. Hungarians were allowed to return to Slovakia from the Czech lands, where, however, approximately 13,500 of them remained because they had nowhere to return to.

As early as 1953, the Communist Party condemned the treatment of the Hungarian minority in 1945-48 as politically mistaken, and in 1956 it granted

142

minority rights to all national minorities under a constitutional law, according to which the Slovak National Council was responsible for securing adequate industrial and cultural conditions for the development of the Hungarian and Ukrainian minorities. Of course, the censorship that was imposed on the Slovak media and culture was imposed on their Hungarian counterparts, too, so that we cannot really speak of the liberation or improvement of the conditions of individual Hungarians. The oppression was especially tightened around 1956 in view of the revolutionary events then taking place in neighbouring Hungary. But the paradox of the improvement of the situation of the Hungarian minority as a group remains an important part of Slovak common history, and also contributes to the fact that Communism as such has been perceived differently in the Czech lands and in Slovakia.

Resonance of the transfers in present-day political relations between Slovaks and Hungarians

The 'solution' of the Hungarian question in Czechoslovakia proved to be inhumane, unsuccessful and largely counter-productive. In the period following the transfers, a leading Hungarian intellectual, Zoltán Fábry, wrote a manifesto addressed to the Czech and Slovak intelligentsia and entitled *The Accused Speaks Out*, in which he asked why none of them had stood up against the persecution of the Hungarians in Slovakia. Only years later did a few Slovak intellectuals admit that he was right. Among them was a Communist, Vladimír Mináč, who wrote in his memoirs in 1990:

> I remember the successive waves of hatred against the Hungarians, especially in the time after the war, when we focused on our small Slovak revenge, taking no account of political affiliation or religion, when we were willing to come to terms even with Beneš if he transferred enough Hungarians to the Sudeten lands, when we persecuted the Hungarians not as collaborators but just as unwanted aliens, when we hated, not just Hungarians, but even their language. We need to apologise humbly for each Slovak misdeed, for the suffering thus caused to every individual Hungarian. It is not of wolves, but of our citizens, that we speak.[43]

Neither the Czech nor the Slovak Republic has declared the Beneš decrees to be legally invalid. The Slovak leadership has also failed to deal with the Communist past in the way the Czech government has. The widespread restitution of nationalised property now taking place has, for example, raised the issue of the restitution of Hungarian property confiscated in the 'homeless' years. Yet the Slovak government has failed to address this topic and admit that the above-mentioned measures against the deported Hungarians were unjust. The issue keeps cropping up on the political scene today. Although never referred to directly (for a representative of a Hungarian political party would be liable to be called an irredentist, secessionist and chauvinist if he mentioned the issue of the southern borders or the transfers), these questions are implicit in the demands made by

Hungarian representatives. Slovakia is currently undergoing a process of territorial reorganisation, and a part of the Hungarian leadership has expressed a wish that a large 'Hungarian' region, approximately coinciding with the areas where the Hungarian minority is present in significant numbers, should be created. This has caused considerable turmoil on the political scene in Slovakia but, apart from the traditional general comments about 'extreme Hungarian nationalism', it has not received any further attention from the Slovak public, and has never been taken seriously or even discussed by those planning the territorial reorganisation.

I do not recall the processes described above ever being mentioned during my school days in Slovakia, and present-day historical textbooks describe the democratic principles of the post-war government in flattering colours. It is also significant that the only publication on the topic of the transfers is by a Slovak Hungarian, Kálmán Janics. This historical account was published first in English in 1982, and was brought out in Slovak only much later, in 1994, by a Hungarian publisher, in an edition numbering a few hundred copies. Yet when one looks back at the results of the simple sociological soundings that were taken in 1994 of the feelings of the communities of Slovaks and Hungarians concerned, one realises that the traumatic events of 1945–48 are far from being forgotten, despite half a century of attempts by the political leaderships to make them disappear; instead, they continue to define the nature of the relationship between Hungarians and Slovaks in Slovakia.

Appendix 1

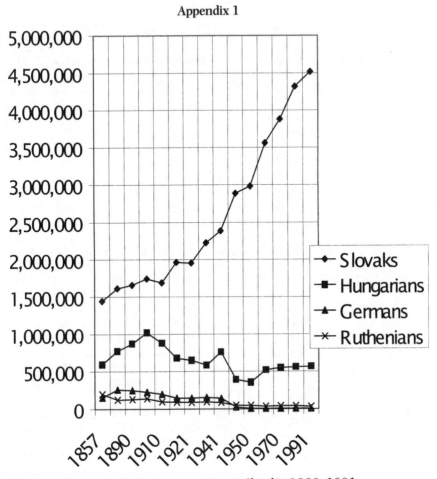

Demographic trends of ethnic communities in Slovakia 1880–1991

Appendix 2

Ethnic composition of present-day Slovakia, 1880–1991

Year	Total	Slovaks	Czechs	Hungarians	Germans	Ruthenian-Ukrainian	Other
1880	2,460,65	1,502,565 (61.1%)		545,889 (22.2%)	228,581 (9.3%)	78,402 (3.2%)	105,428 (4.2%)
1910	2,916,086	1,687,800 (57.9%)		880,851 (30.2%)	198,461 (6.8%)	97,037 (3.3%)	51,937 (1.8%)
1919	2,935,239	1,960,391 (66.8%)	72,137 (2.4%)	681,375 (23.2%)	145,139 (4.9%)	92,786 (3.2%)	55,468 (1.9%)
1921	2,958,557	1,952,866 (66.0%)	120,926 (3.7%)	650,597 (22.0%)	145,844 (4.9%)	88,970 (3.0%)	48,143 (1.7%)
1930	3,254,189	2,224,983 (68.4%)	17,443 (0.5%)	585,434 (17.6%)	154,821 (4.5%)	95,359 (2.8%)	72,666 (3.0%)
1941	3,536,319	2,385,552 (67.4%)	37,000 (1.1%)	761,434 (21.5%)	143,209 (4.0%)	85,991 (2.4%)	142,690 (4.2%)
1947	3,399,000	2,888,000 (85.0%)	40,365 (1.2%)	390,000 (11.5%)	24,000 (0.7%)	47,000 (1.4%)	13,000 (0.3%)
1950	3,442,317	2,982,524 (86.6%)	45,721 (1.1%)	354,532 (10.3%)	5179 (0.1%)	48,231 (1.4%)	11,486 (0.4%)
1961	4,174,046	3,560,216 (85.3%)	47,402 (1.0%)	518,782 (12.4%)	6259 (0.1%)	35,435 (0.9%)	7,633 (0.2%)
1970	4,537,290	3,878,904 (85.5%)	55,234 (1.1%)	552,006 (12.2%)	4760 (0.1%)	42,238 (1.0%)	11,980 (0.3%)
1980	4,987,853	4,321,139 (86.6%)	59,326 (1.1%)	559,801 (11.2%)	5121 (0.1%)	39,758 (0.8%)	6,800 (0.2%)
1991	5,274,335	4,519,328 (85.7%)	56487 (1.1%)	567,296 (10.7%)	5414 (0.1%)	30,478 (0.6%)	92,493 (1.8%)
1991*	5,274,335	4,445,303 (84.3%)	56,487 (1.1%)	608,221 (11.5%)	7,738 (0.1%)	58,579 (1.1%)	98,007 (1.9%)

Note: * Recorded by mother tongue.

Sources: 1880, 1910: Hungarian census data (mother/native/tongue); 1921, 1930, 1947, 1950, 1961, 1970, 1980, 1991: Czechoslovakian census data (ethnicity); 1991: Czechoslovakian census data (mother/native/ tongue); 1941: combined Hungarian and Slovakian census data. The data between 1880 and 1941 for the present territory of Slovakia were calculated by K. Kocsis, in Karoly Kocsis and Eszter Kocsis-Hodosi, *Hungarian Minorities in the Carpathian Basin* (Budapest, 1998), 56.

Appendix 3

Ethnic composition of Slovakia, 1857–1910

Census	Total	Slovaks	Hungarians	Germans	Ruthenian	Other
1857	2,551,935	1,441,307	599,398	154,799	199,506	156,925
		(56.5%)	(23.5%)	(6.1%)	(7.8%)	(6.1%)
1880	2,787,205	1,613,350	775,065	256,882	123,747	24,161
		(57.9%)	(27.8%)	(9.0%)	(4.4%)	(0.9%)
1890	2,958,062	1,654,917	873,166	247,189	130,433	36,758
		(56.5%)	(29.7%)	(7.1%)	(4.5%)	(1.2%)
1900	3,190,022	1,742,200	1,024,488	225,206	138,634	35,773
		(55.0%)	(32.4%)	(7.1%)	(4.4%)	(1.1%)
1910	3,350,600	1,686,712	846,271			
		(50.3%)	(25.6%)			

Source: Štefan Šutaj, 'Historický náčrt postavenia mad'arskej menšiny na Slovensku (1818–1989)', in Vladimír Paukovič, *Etnické menšiny na Slovensku* (Košice, 1991).

Notes

1 The Vienna Arbitral Award was signed on 2 November 1938 by the German and Italian foreign ministers; in return for Hungary's co-operation with Hitler's Germany, the Award granted her the territories in Southern Slovakia inhabited mainly (but by no means exclusively) by ethnic Hungarians. Out of what she had previously lost, Hungary received, under this Award, 12,700 km^2 of territory, and 1,030,000 persons, including 830,000 Hungarians, 140,000 Slovaks, 20,000 Germans, 40,000 Ruthenes and others. (C. Wojatsek, *From Trianon to the First Vienna Arbitral Award*, Corvinus Library, Hungarian history, www.hungary.com/corvinus/lib/woja/index.htm, 168.)

2 Sándor Bordás, Pavol Frič, Katarína Haidová, Péter Hunčik *et al.*, *Mýty a Kontramýty: Social and Ethno-psychological Research of Slovak–Hungarian Relations in Slovakia* (Bratislava, 1995), 46–7.

3 *Ibid.*, 47.

4 Benedict Anderson, *Imagined Communities* (London, 1991), 6–7.

5 George Brunner, *Nationality Problems and Minority Conflicts in Eastern Europe* (Gutersloh, 1996), 17.

6 *Ibid.*, 18.

7 www.coe.fr.

8 Viera Bačová, *Etnická identita a historické zmeny* (Bratislava, 1996), 10.

9 *Ibid.*, 25.

10 Robert D. Sack, *Human Territoriality, Its Theory and History* (Cambridge, 1986), 19.

11 Anderson, *Imagined Communities*, 173.

12 Dagmar Kusá, 'Tools of the state in influencing ethnic identity, state and ethnic groups on the territory of present-day Slovakia' (Bratislava, master's thesis, 1999), 28–9.

13 Sergey A. Kostya, *Northern Hungary: A Historical Study of the Czechoslovak Republic* (Toronto, 1992), 151.

14 Ján Žudel, *Stolice na Slovensku* (Bratislava, 1984), 211.

15 Kálmán Janics, *Czechoslovak Policy and the Hungarian Minority, 1945–1948, War and Society in East-Central Europe: The Effects of World War II*, IX, trans S. Borsody (New York, 1982), 30.

16 Zbyněk A.B. Zeman and Antonín Klimek, *The Life of Edvard Beneš 1884–1948: Czechoslovakia in Peace and War* (Oxford, 1997), 164–92.

17 Kálmán Janics, *Czechoslovak Policy*, 51–75; Kostya, *Northern Hungary*, 155–7.

18 Raphael Vago, *The Grandchildren of Trianon: Hungary and the Hungarian Minority in the Communist States* (New York, 1989), 27.

19 Janics, *Czechoslovak Policy*, 67.

20 See Dimond, Chapter 12 in this volume, n. 8.

21 Daniela Čierna-Lantayová, 'Vzájomné súvislosti postavenia menšín v Mad'arsku a na Slovensku po roku 1945', in J. Plichtová (ed.), *Minority v Politike* (Bratislava, 1992), 76.

22 Štefan Šutaj, 'Historický náčrt postavenia mad'arskej menšiny na Slovensku (1818–1989)', in Vladimír Paukovič, *Etniké menšiny na Slovensku* (Košice, 1991), 10.

23 Péter Hunčík and Fedor Gál, 'Historické pozadie formovania slovensko-mad'arských vzt'ahov', in Frič et al., *Mad'arská menšina na Slovensku* (Prague, 1993), 25.

24 Janics, *Czechoslovak Policy*, 43.

25 *Ibid.*

26 Marián Augustín, *Hl'adanie vzt'ahov II* (Bratislava, 1997), 102.

27 István Bibó, *Bieda východoeurópskych malých štátov: Vybrané štúdie* (Bratislava, 1996), 549.

28 Janics, *Czechoslovak Policy*, 219.

29 Samuel Campbell, quoted in Janics, *Czechoslovak Policy*, 153.

30 Janics, *Czechoslovak Policy*, 159.

31 Šutaj, 'Historický náčrt postavenia mad'arskej menšiny na Slovensku (1818–1989)', 13.

32 Karel Káplán, 'Předmluva', in Štefan Šutaj, *Akcia Juh, Odsun Mad'arov zo Slovenska do Čiech v roku 1949* (Prague, 1993), 9.

33 Šutaj, 'Historický náčrt postavenia mad'arskej menšiny na Slovensku (1818–1989)', 13.

34 Janics, *Czechoslovak Policy*, 171.

35 *Ibid.*, 185.

36 Vago, *The Grandchildren of Trianon*, 31–2.

37 Juraj Fazekas and László Szarka, 'Epilogue', in Zoltán Fábry, *The Accused Speaks Out: Documents from the History of the Hungarians in Czechoslovakia* (Bratislava, 1994), 231.

38 Čierna-Lantayová, 'Vzájomné súvislosti postavenia menšín v Mad'arsku a na Slovensku po roku 1945', 78.

39 Vago, *The Grandchildren of Trianon*, 27.

40 Šutaj, 'Historický náčrt postavenia mad'arskej menšiny na Slovensku (1818–1989)', 14.

41 Janics, *Czechoslovak Policy*, 172.
42 Šutaj, 'Historický náčrt postavenia maďarskej menšiny na Slovensku (1818–1989)', 17.
43 Vladimír Mináč, *Odkial' a kam Slováci?* (Bratislava, 1993), 115–16.

III
Youth

9

'Reforming mentalities': the Allies, young people and 'new music' in Western Germany, 1945–55

Toby Thacker

Culturally, one of the most striking aspects of the Federal German Republic in the early 1950s was its emergence as the undisputed centre of gravity of the international musical *avant-garde*. Germany had of course a proud musical heritage – not for nothing did a group of politicians there in 1950 preface one of their reports with the infinitely nostalgic statement that 'Germany *was* the world's most musical land' (emphasis added)[1] – but twelve years of Nazi repression had left that reputation in tatters. Jewish and modernist works had been stripped from music libraries and removed from publishers' catalogues. Many of Germany's most distinguished living musicians and composers had fled or been driven from their homes. Most of those who stayed were tainted by suspicion of collaboration with the Nazis. The music-loving public had been isolated from international developments and prevented during the war years from hearing works by Russian or American composers. Children had been taught that the music of other peoples reflected their racial inferiority, and largely confined to a diet of nationalistic and militaristic songs, sentimental dance music and the German classics.

Yet, by 1955, West Germany had become a Mecca for the most radical composers and performers from around the Western world. The summer school at Darmstadt and the annual festival at Donaueschingen were the centres of pilgrimage, but the support of the radio stations ensured that more 'new music' was performed and broadcast in West Germany than anywhere else in the world.[2] There was and is no more powerful metaphor for a society that had turned its back on the Nazi past, and committed itself to Western integration. The support given to 'new music' in the early Federal Republic by radio stations, *Land* and municipal authorities, and the emergence of a new generation of German *avant-garde* composers, led by Hans-Werner Henze and Karl-Heinz Stockhausen, could be read as proof of the success of at least one aspect of the 're-education' programme, that which sought to use the universal language of music to counter Nazi racial doctrine and to break the cultural isolation and stagnation of Germany in the dark years between 1933 and 1945.

There are paradoxes which force us to question this view. By 1955, it was abundantly clear that most young people in Germany were far more interested in Western popular music than in the increasingly rarified 'new music'. The prestigious Institute for Public Opinion Research in Bielefeld investigated the cultural and leisure interests of young people in the Federal German Republic in great detail, and its results indicate that only a tiny minority had any interest in 'new music'. After three years of survey work, the Institute reported in 1956 that only 1 per cent of young people questioned could name a modern composer. In 1954, 1 per cent of young people questioned said that they had been impressed by a concert of 'modern music'; in 1955 the percentage was zero. Insofar as they were concerned at all with art music, this dwindling minority of the young was apparently most impressed by the traditional German canon, and indeed by performers who had championed this canon under the Nazis, such as Wilhelm Furtwängler, and the pianists Elly Ney and Walter Gieseking.[3]

Even within the 'new music' scene, we find tensions. Henze, who had emerged in 1947 as an outstanding new talent, was by 1953 so disgusted with the estrangement of 'new music' from the wider public, and with what he perceived as the imposition of new orthodoxies, that he left the Federal Republic. He described a process of 'de-politicisation' which had led to 'the production of music that was totally mechanized and incapable of expressiveness'. He criticised particularly the practice of broadcasting 'new music' late at night. This, he argued, represented the ultimate alienation of composer from listener. Pieces of music were commissioned and composed specifically for these 'night studio' programmes, broadcast to unknown, and perhaps virtually non-existent, audiences, and never performed again. The composer in this scenario never met the audience, and was accountable only to a limited circle of fellow-professionals.[4]

Writers and commentators have reproduced this sense of paradox. On the one hand, there is a huge literature celebrating the seemingly miraculous regeneration of 'new music' in the ruins of post-war Germany.[5] More recently, historians looking at cultural continuities in twentieth-century Germany have been more sceptical. Michael Kater has used the term 'retrenchment' to characterise West German musical life after 1945, and has condemned the *avant-garde* for leading music into a cul-de-sac, describing its leading exponents variously as 'esoteric', 'elitist', 'intolerant' and 'isolated'.[6] The present chapter will address this paradox, and try to get behind the historical images of the relationship between young people and 'new music' in West Germany in the post-war period. It will outline the Allied programme to introduce contemporary international music specifically to young people in Germany after 1945, and analyse why this programme was pursued by West German authorities after 1949. It will argue that the role played by 'new music' was more symbolic than real, and suggest that the informal influences of international (and principally American) youth culture were stronger than the formal efforts of high-minded administrators and politicians in shaping the cartography of taste in this period.

In early 1945, British and American psychological warfare specialists developed far-reaching plans for the reconstruction of culture in a defeated Germany. As far as music was concerned, they dedicated themselves to the censorship of Nazi music, the exclusion of Nazi musicians and the internationalisation of the repertoire in Germany. They planned specifically to re-introduce contemporary music which had been labelled by the Nazis as 'cultural Bolshevism', and the work of banned Jewish composers. This would challenge Nazi views of German racial superiority and reintegrate Germany in an international musical culture. Unsurprisingly, the officers, administrators, and artists who planned and implemented 'music control' in post-war Germany replicated the cultural prejudices of their own societies. They believed that art music had a universal, civilising influence, and deserved official support. They believed that the Germans were a particularly musical people, and that they might be scornful of British, French and American music. The British and Americans made a straightforward distinction between high and low culture, and did not think that they should concern themselves with 'light' music or jazz, any more than they should with detective novels. The French, perhaps because of their experience of occupation, were aware of the anaesthetising way in which Goebbels had used sentimental dance music during the war, and determined to use genuine jazz in post-war Germany as an antidote to this.[7] There was a consensus amongst the Western Allies that only the very best elements of their contemporary musical cultures should be put before the German public, so that pretensions to German musical and racial superiority were not bolstered.[8]

As with all aspects of the re-education project, there was in 'music control' an emphasis on reaching young Germans. The Americans adopted several strategies in their zone to try to make contemporary music accessible to the young. In Munich they used Hans Rosbaud, a conductor known for his championship of modern music, to give introductory talks to young people before performances of 'new music'. Special concerts for young people were instituted in early 1946.[9] The American military government's *Information Bulletin* announced: 'US Music Control Officers are exerting every effort to bring musical works to German youth to which they can listen with increased enjoyment and understanding, and in which they can participate. Special symphony concerts and similar musical programs for German youth are on the increase.'[10] The Americans, for all this public optimism, were keenly aware of the prejudice they faced in trying to introduce contemporary music, particularly contemporary American music, to young people in Germany. John Evarts, the Music Officer for Bavaria, reported after a talk to young people in Regensburg that they were very patronising in their attitude to 'American culture in general'.[11] In 1947, as part of a larger 'reorientation' programme for young people, societies called 'Friends and Enemies of Modern Music' were founded in larger cities in the American zone. Meeting in the America Houses, these societies were intended specifically to challenge German hostility to new and international music by hosting discussions, seminars and concerts. Free tickets for concerts in America Houses were routinely distributed to young people, especially music students. By November 1948 a monthly average of 1,200 German students was attending these concerts.[12] After the currency reform in June 1948 the Americans channelled 'Deutschmark reorientation funds' into a number of specific 'youth and new music' projects.[13] They provided money to support two institutions which have become emblematic of West German cultural reconstruction, the *Musica Viva* concert series in Munich, and the Darmstadt summer schools. Ironically, the Americans, in attempting to develop a mass audience in Germany for new music amongst young people, were trying to create something which did not exist in the United States.

The British were less idealistic, and musical policy in their zone was aimed at an educated minority. Where the Americans were alarmed at being perceived in Germany as a people without high culture, the British were unhappy to be seen as possessing only a museum culture. The 'projection of Britain' therefore had to include the modern, to prove that Britain had a thriving contemporary culture. This cultural offensive had a clear political purpose, and was expected to have a long-lasting influence:

> The educational task is to create in the German public . . . a taste for British methods and British products and an active and convinced sympathy for the British political and moral values which they reflect. ... It is a major aim of British policy to ensure that . . . British influences in the cultural and entertainment field will outlast the period of military occupation and control.[14]

British 'Music Control' in Germany pursued precisely these aims, which meant introducing British contemporary music, and that of other countries, as was typically performed in Britain itself.[15] Within this, there was an emphasis on reaching the young. A perfect example was the series of concerts staged in the Ruhr in 1949, presenting contemporary British, French, Russian and German music to children.[16] A similar commitment to the young was shown in musical education. Like the other occupiers, the British were quick to permit the reopening of universities and institutes of higher education in their zone, but they were aware of the profoundly conservative orientation of existing German music academies. They supported the foundation in 1948 of a new Music Academy in Detmold with a specific commitment to international modernism. Brian Dunn, in charge of the musical programme in the British zone, wrote to the British Council to ask it to supply copies of British chamber works written in the last twenty years to the Detmold Academy: 'This is a newly formed and very vigorous academy comprising some of the most go-ahead teachers who have broken away from the perhaps restricted traditions of other institutions.'[17]

By common consent, the French cultural programme in Germany after 1945 was the most ambitious and well supported.[18] The French, conscious of the relative weakness of their political position in Germany, placed a particular emphasis on their *mission civilisatrice*. Convinced that, morally and culturally, they had more to offer Germany than the Anglo-Saxons, they quickly developed an energetic music programme in their zone of occupation. More directly than the other occupiers, the French linked a German sense of musical superiority to Nazi racism. They argued that, if Germans could be brought to see that they did not have a monopoly on music, 'immediately one of the fundamentals of racist and pan-German philosophy would collapse'. The French also believed music was the most potent weapon in their cultural armoury, not only because it was an international language, but because it was 'the means of expression which responded best to the most profound aspirations of the German soul'.[19] Like the Americans, French cultural officers felt that they had been presented with a unique opportunity to reform more than the tastes of a minority, and stressed the importance of changing the outlook of the young: 'It is the German soul which must be attacked, it is the mentality of the old *and above all of the young* that must be reformed, it is democracy which must be made to live in the ways and the hearts of the people, it is a humane and humanist culture which must be promoted' (emphasis added). Well before the British and Americans, the French military government sponsored tours in its zone by French musicians and ensembles. During 1946 alone, twenty-nine touring ensembles gave more than 250 concerts in the French zone to German audiences.[20] Baden-Baden, the undamaged spa town which was the seat of the French administration in Germany, was developed as a centre for international 'new music'. The French also placed great emphasis on musical education, and quickly developed international exchanges for German music students, the *'Jeunesses musicales'*. They were especially proud that the academies and schools of music they supported in Mainz, Kaiserslautern, Trossingen and Tübingen attracted many students from other zones of occupied Germany.[21] To bring French music, including that of living composers, to German schools, they used mobile discothèques equipped with supplies of French records.[22] The firm of Schotts in Mainz was quickly licensed by the French, and allocated generous supplies of paper, helping it to consolidate its position as Germany's leading publisher of contemporary music. From 1946, the French energetically exported their music programme to the other occupied zones, a policy that was continued into the 1950s. Non-governmental organisations like *A Coeur Joie*, a choral movement, joined with the Ministry of Culture in financing visits to France by young German musicians, typically carrying an explicit message of reconciliation. After a youth choir from Karlsruhe had performed in Paris on Christmas Day 1952, a Parisian choral director wrote: 'You do not know what a deep impression your Christmas trip has left on Paris. They all speak of your visit and your songs, still today. You Germans and we French are a good example that friendship among nations can exist.'[23]

It would be mistaken to view the upsurge in interest in 'new music' after 1945 solely as an Allied import into Germany. There were many individual

German musicians and German institutions which also seized the opportunity presented after May 1945 to perform 'new music'. A group of students in Berlin, led by Wolfgang Hohensee, may have been the first to perform Schoenberg and Eisler in Germany after May 1945.[24] In all four zones of Germany, supporters of 'new music' who had been marginalised under the Nazis came forward to fill important posts in radio stations, to edit musical journals and to organise concerts. In Munich, Karl Amadeus Hartmann and Hans Rosbaud worked closely with the Americans; Heinrich Strobel was given a leading role by the French in Baden-Baden; Herbert Eimert was employed by the British in Cologne; in 1946 Hans-Heinz Stuckenschmidt was employed by the Americans in Berlin. These, and others with similarly progressive inclinations, established an influence on the musical scene in Germany that persisted well into the 1950s. In 1945, when the *Land* authorities in Württemberg-Baden presented a plan to the Americans to re-open the State College for Music in Stuttgart, they stressed that the former Nazi director had been removed, and that the College's prospectus now included a commitment to teach students about international modern music.[25] In 1946, a summer school convened to study and perform 'new music' was held at Schloss Kranichstein near Darmstadt, establishing what became after 1948 an international event, and in the 1950s the practical and spiritual centre of the Western musical *avant-garde*. At the first gathering, the composer Hermann Heiss, a twelve-toner whose career had languished under the Nazis, declared: 'We have today a unique opportunity, with our experience and knowledge, to preserve young people from wrong turnings and detours.'[26] Karl Laux, a critic who subsequently committed himself to musical reconstruction in the Soviet zone and the GDR, perfectly captured this sense of contrition in 1946, arguing that atonal music should not be imagined as 'Jewish'. He listed Schoenberg, Stravinsky, Krenek, Weill, Prokofiev, Shostakovich, Britten, Walton, Elgar, Honegger and Barber as composers whom the German public needed to learn about and to judge independently.[27] The exiled composer Hindemith, who had finally left Germany in 1939 after many difficulties with the Nazi regime, was inundated in 1945 and 1946 with calls from Germany to return and make public appearances.[28] German administrators rushed to make amends for the past, and perhaps to curry favour with new masters, by staging performances of what the Nazis had called 'degenerate music'.

During 1947 and 1948, all three Western Allies devolved their control of music to municipal and regional German authorities. As the three Western zones of occupation were consolidated, these German authorities, like their economic and political counterparts, established common structures which were carried over into the Federal Republic. After 1949, at Allied insistence, control of culture in West Germany was decentralised, but *Land* and municipal authorities met regularly to articulate common approaches, and to co-ordinate policies. The *Städtetag* (Council of Towns), founded in the British zone in 1946, provided a forum where all towns with a population of 20,000 or more were represented, and its cultural committee played an active part in supporting 'new music'. It demanded in 1949 that every town ensure that a contemporary work was performed in at least every second public concert.[29] Likewise, *Land* culture ministers, represented in the Standing Conference of Culture Ministers, saw the promotion of 'new music' as a political obligation. In 1950 a joint group representing *Land* Culture Ministers and the *Städtetag* demanded that all towns place an emphasis on youth concerts.[30] The mayor of Darmstadt, writing in 1950 to thank culture ministers for their financial support of the International Courses for New Music there, provided a coded rationale for 'new music' in the Federal Republic, arguing that 'the cultural–political factor in this arrangement is particularly to be welcomed'. The courses at Darmstadt, he said, were intended to present 'a decisive contribution to the intellectual renewal, which should not be overlooked as an important factor in the new political order'.[31] Darmstadt was not the only educational centre for 'new music' to receive public monies in the early Federal Republic. Bayreuth, more usually associated with Wagner, had established an 'Institute for New Music', which was also subsidised by various *Land* authorities at this time.[32] Provincial German cities more renowned for industry than culture proudly announced their commitment to 'new music' in their concert programmes. In Bielefeld in 1952–53, the Municipal Orchestra, as well as recognising a particular obligation to its native son, Henze, was performing Bartok, Roussel, Scriabin, Khachachurian, Honegger and Hindemith.[33] The concert programme issued in Bochum in 1952 pledged 'to make the connection between the concert-goer and contemporary music ever closer'.[34] Discussions of public support for music in the early Federal Republic routinely singled out the need to introduce young people to contemporary music.[35] Another model for this was provided in Düsseldorf, where a concert association largely funded by a local banker dedicated itself after 1949 to making 'new music' accessible to the young.[36]

During the early 1950s Allied High Commissions continued to support 'new music', sponsoring tours by visiting musicians, 'record evenings' and educational courses on modern music in their respective information centres. The 1951 musical programme of the British Centre in Göttingen, *Die Brücke* (The Bridge), is a good example. As Göttingen was not one of the larger West German cities, the British Centre there hosted few concerts, but did present regular 'record evenings' and talks by local and visiting speakers. In addition to a great deal of older music, evenings in 1951 were devoted to the music of Britten, Bartok, Stravinsky and Berg. Little-known contemporary British composers such as Ferguson, Bliss, Bush, Rubbra and Moeran were played, and in September an evening was dedicated to the memory of Schoenberg, who had died a year previously.[37] This was all in accordance with British policy, which stressed that concerts in British Centres 'should have an educational purpose', as they gave 'an opportunity to perform modern, unhackneyed music'.[38] In Düsseldorf, a much larger city, the British Centre was equipped in 1949 with a concert hall seating 450, where over the next five years some 350 musical events were held.[39] American and French programmes in the early 1950s were similarly ambitious. Many young Germans were introduced to international contemporary music in this way, but there were associated problems. Certainly some Germans felt that the free or heavily subsidised concerts in Allied information centres were a threat to German concert life.[40]

The radio stations licensed by the Allies after 1945 played a critical role. By not merely broadcasting 'new music', but by acting as centres for the composition and performance of new works, stations such as the NWDR (Northwest German Radio), with separate studios in Hamburg and Cologne, the SWF (Southwest German Radio) in Baden-Baden, and Radio Munich, posed a challenge to existing municipal orchestras and their traditional patronage of music. By the early 1950s, radio stations in West Germany were typically able to pay higher salaries to musicians and guest conductors than were municipal authorities, and could therefore challenge them, particularly in the performance of technically demanding new works. The rapid development of musical technology helped to improve the quality of broadcast music, and opened up the development of a whole new genre based in the radio stations – electronic music. The radio stations finally consolidated their hold on 'new music' by sponsoring specific festivals and summer schools devoted to international modernism. The International School for New Music at Darmstadt was from its inception in 1946 sponsored by the American-licensed Radio Frankfurt. The annual festival for 'new music' at Donaueschingen, so prominent and controversial during the 1920s, had under the Nazis been used as a vehicle for the celebration of German tradition and nationalism. After 1951, the Donaueschingen festival was run by the SWF and used to showcase the international *avant-garde*. John Cage made his first appearance in Germany there in 1953.[41]

If we study internal documentation from the radio stations, from *Land* and municipal authorities, and from the Allied High Commissions in the early 1950s, a curious contradiction emerges. On the one hand, there was a shared perception that the promotion of new music, particularly among young people, was a moral and political responsibility. On the other, there was a wide acceptance that this music was not popular, and that it tended to alienate audiences. This problem was reflected in a statement made to the NWDR's Management Committee in 1951 by Dr Braunfels, Director of the State Music School in Cologne. His argument that 'programming should be influenced not so much by the wishes of listeners, but by the pedagogical duty of the radio' was accepted by his fellow committee members.[42] In similar vein, the municipal authorities in Karlsruhe in 1952 stoically reported their continuing commitment, 'despite the fact that Karlsruhe is not particularly grateful soil for contemporary music'.[43] The French Commissioner in the Rhineland-Palatinate noted in 1952 after a festival of French music and film that the concerts had been poorly attended, because 'the quality of the music offered surpassed the Mainz public's capacity for absorption'. A new formula, he argued, was needed.[44] What becomes clear is that by the mid-1950s this tension had largely been resolved by confining new music to specific times and places, and by abandoning earlier hopes of developing a new mass audience integrated with the traditional concert-going public. To understand both the reasons for the institutional commitment to new music, and its marginalisation in West German musical life, we have to be aware of the rapidly changing political and social context. Several factors should be considered here.

The earliest post-war Allied and German plans to introduce new music to the young were seen as part of an anti-Nazi programme. Modernist, atonal, or dodecaphonic music, which had been vilified by the Nazis, was understood as a language of anti-fascism. We should note in passing that there was after 1945 considerable Soviet agreement with this view, and that international modernist music was used similarly in the Soviet zone between 1945 and 1948. By 1948 the cultural Cold War was under way, and the Soviets and their East European allies renewed the call for 'socialist realism' in music, demanding an emphasis on melody, simplicity and heroism. In the Soviet zone, 'new music' was now denounced as decadent 'bourgeois music', a tool used by Western imperialists to degrade German culture and to prepare for war. The offensive was led by Stalin's cultural commissar, Andrei Zhdanov, and some sense of the tone of the attacks on twentieth-century Western music in the Soviet Union, and in the Soviet zone of Germany, can be gained from the comments made by Zhdanov's new appointee as leader of the Union of Soviet Composers, Tikhon Khrennikov, in a Soviet art journal. He argued that Western music had developed from the collision between émigré Russian composers and modernism in the 1920s, identifying Hindemith, Berg, Menotti, Krenek and Britten as composers who had followed Stravinsky and Prokofiev, creating 'concatenations of hideous sound'. 'This music', he wrote, 'openly harks back to the primitive barbaric cultures of prehistoric society, and extols the eroticism, psychopathic mentality, sexual perversion, amorality, and shamelessness of the twentieth-century bourgeois hero'.[45]

In place of this, Communists demanded new music which drew on the classical tradition, avoided unnecessary experimentation and connected directly with ordinary people by portraying the achievements of socialism. The Western *avant-garde*, preoccupied after 1945 with a rejection of tradition, with the application of mathematical principles, and the use of electronically generated sounds, exemplified for Communist critics the alienation of bourgeois art from the people.[46] During the 1950s, Communists in the GDR directed an unrelenting stream of abuse and invective at the 'new music' scene in the Federal Republic, and its alleged corruption of young people there. They provided an economic basis for their cultural critique by identifying a 'Schotts-*Melos* clique' which allegedly dictated the prevailing theoretical orthodoxy in the Federal Republic, and maintained a commercial monopoly on the printing of new music, and comment on new music in the Federal Republic. The Schotts journal, *Melos*, the voice of the West German *avant-garde*, was banned in the GDR in 1951. Individual composers, conductors and critics were singled out for criticism, and although the GDR actively encouraged many other musical links with the Federal Republic, it rejected any official involvement with 'new music' institutions there. In 1954, the new GDR Ministry for Culture issued a manifesto calling for more all-German artistic co-operation. The manifesto wanted nothing to do, though, with 'new music' in West Germany, which it described as engendering 'anxiety, alarm, war, and emptiness'.[47]

From 1948, therefore, it became increasingly clear in the West that new music could also serve as a language of anti-Communism, and that tolerance extended to even the most challenging and bizarre forms of musical experimentation served to demonstrate a larger commitment to artistic and personal freedom. This was undoubtedly what the mayor of Darmstadt meant when he referred cryptically to 'cultural–political factors' in the 'new political order'. It is in this light that German and Allied support for the Darmstadt summer schools and other 'new music' institutions after 1948 should be understood. After the formal division of Germany in 1949, new music also served as a symbol of commitment to Western integration. The *avant-garde* music scene in the early Federal Republic was notably international, its leading lights drawn not just from Germany, but from all over Western Europe, North and South America. In 1945, a prime concern of the Western Allies had been to decouple the arts in Germany from politics, and therefore, once it became clear that there would be no immediate resurgence of Nazism in Germany, music was relocated to an idealised discursive arena which typically avoided mention of politics. The British, as early as 1946, in transferring various aspects of broadcasting at the NWDR to German control, described music as 'non-ideological'.[48] The West German politicians who in 1950 demanded regular performances of 'new music' and 'youth concerts' also stressed that the direction of these concerts should be free from 'ideological and political influences'.[49] The increasingly abstract forms favoured by composers after 1948 aided this process, and it is notable that, when individual works did carry overt political and social messages, they were almost invariably controversial. One example which demonstrates this, and shows how some interpreted 'new music' in even the most receptive environments in the Federal Republic, is the first performance, in 1950, in Darmstadt, of Schoenberg's *A Survivor from Warsaw*. Even members of the choir and orchestra assembled to perform the work were unhappy, making comments like 'the Amis [Americans] should sing that themselves', or even 'the Jews should sing that themselves'.[50]

Finally, 'new music' took on an added layer of meaning as the '*Wirtschaftswunder*', or economic miracle, gained pace in the 1950s, and West Germany developed as a consumer society. One salient aspect of this development was the emergence of young people, now dubbed 'teenagers', as a distinct consumer group with ever greater disposable income and with specific desires, typically for commodities linked with fashion. Music, and music-related products such as records and radios, became iconic symbols of the consumer boom of the 1950s. 'New music', as Adorno had noted thirty years previously, was highly resistant to commodifi-cation, and appeared in the 1950s as one area of cultural production that was not subject to the relentless simplification and mass production that were the hallmarks of commodified consumer culture.[51] 'Appeared', because there was no inherent reason why a piece of music by Stockhausen was any less susceptible to mass production than one by a dance band or folk singer. The difference lay chiefly in popularity. As long as 'new music' remained of interest only to an edu-cated, largely male, urban minority, it was not worthwhile for any individual or corporation to attempt to market it in mass-produced forms. The radio stations and public authorities which financed new music in the 1950s used taxpayers' money to do so, justifying this as an artistic and political duty.

So, while the majority of West German youth developed its passion for sen-timental dance music, boogie-woogie, and, after 1956, for rock 'n' roll, a tiny minority immersed itself in the arcane, nocturnal world of 'new music'. The early 1950s witnessed a headlong rush from Schoenbergian dodecaphony, Webernian serialism and electronic rationalism to the aleatory experimenta-tion of Cage and Stockhausen. This was the period of the most dramatic and far-reaching change in music, and coincidentally the high point of the cultural Cold War. After 1955, Allied High Commissions in Germany no longer main-tained so many information centres and cultural journals; the British Centre in Göttingen, for example, held its last talk in March 1955. American interest, and money, shifted slowly from Europe to the Pacific and the 'Third World'.[52] The suppression of popular uprisings in the GDR and in Hungary demon-strated more clearly than the rather inept censorship of music in Soviet bloc countries that Stalinism was profoundly hostile to political and artistic free-dom,[53] and moves towards the foundation of the European Economic Commu-nity (EEC) made it clear that the Federal Republic was firmly set on a path of Western integration.

Unfortunately for those who believed in the civilising power of music as a living art form, West Germany was not immune from wider developments. 'New music' there, as elsewhere, was indeed in a cul-de-sac, its theory and prac-tice now so intellectualised as to be incomprehensible to all but the most devoted connoisseur. Hans-Heinz Stuckenschmidt, who as a critic and publicist had tirelessly championed the cause of 'new music' since the 1920s, earning in the process the enmity of both Nazis and Communists, confronted this prob-lem squarely in 1955. Writing in *Melos*, he admitted that this was a music which now seemed to be, not for everyone, but *against* everyone. After survey-ing various political, sociological and commercial demands for composers to write for mass audiences, he rejected them all. He suggested instead that com-posers should be freed from the obligation to write for any audience whatsoever, declaring: 'A music against everyone, which consciously seeks to reduce its circle of potential admirers to vanishing point, would be a perhaps paradoxical, but psychologically and aesthetically equally interesting goal.' Quoting Ravel, and recalling a long tradition in French cultural criticism, he argued that music

163

written with this purpose would fulfil the one objectively demonstrable crite-
rion for art, 'the joy of creativity', or 'le plaisir délicieux d'une occupation
inutile'.[54] Stuckenschmidt was perhaps here being slightly ironic, but his enemies in the GDR certainly took his comments at face value, seizing upon them
as confirmation of their cultural critique of the West. Hans Pischner, the GDR's
Deputy Minister of Culture, and himself a notable musician, denounced Stuckenschmidt as the 'apostle of inhumanity, of esotericism, and of nihilism'.
Goethe himself, claimed Pischner, had stressed that art must have ethical
goals.[55] Pischner and Stuckenschmidt were old antagonists, and were both here
going over familiar ground. One has the sense, though, that not many others
were listening, or cared much one way or the other.

By 1955, the idea that 'new music' might play a significant role in shaping
the political consciousness of the younger generation in West Germany was
manifestly redundant. If any music was doing this, it was popular music from
America, widely held to be responsible for the youth riots that had become a
focus for debate in East and West Germany by this time, or sentimental dance
music, equally considered on both sides of the 'Iron Curtain' to be a cause of
widespread political apathy.[56] If the intention of the Western Allies and German
administrators after 1945 had been to foster a mass audience for international
'new music', they had clearly failed. If it was to create in the Federal German
Republic a cultural environment which tolerated and indeed supported diversity,
they could claim success.

Notes

1 Nordrhein-Westfälisches Hauptstaatsarchiv, Düsseldorf (hereafter NWHD), NW
60/861, 'Vorbericht für die Gemeinsame Sitzung des Kunstausschusses der Kultusministerkonferenz und des Kulturausschusses des deutschen Städtetags am 7.12.
1950 in Hannover, Konzertwirtschaft', 15 December 1950. All translations, unless
otherwise indicated, are the author's.
2 The term 'new music' is potentially confusing, as the German usage does not have an
equivalent in English. In Germany, the term 'neue Musik' was used in the 1920s to
refer to a wide range of contemporary music, from the neo-classical to the atonal and
dodecaphonic. It was still used in this wide sense in the 1940s and 1950s, particularly in the Federal Republic, to describe music that in English would be called *avant-
garde*, modern, or merely contemporary. This persistence was noted by the
Communists in the Soviet zone and early GDR, who after 1948 frequently pointed out
in their criticism of cultural developments in the West of Germany that what was
called there 'neue Musik' was typically not new at all, but music written before 1933.
3 Karl-Georg von Stackelberg (ed.), *Jugend zwischen 15 und 24: Untersuchungen zur
Situation der deutschen Jugend im Bundesgebiet* (Bielefeld, 1956), 370, 363, 365.
4 Hans Werner Henze, *Music and Politics: Collected Writings 1953–81*, trans. P.
Labyani (London, 1982), 41–4.
5 Much of this literature is in the form of biographies celebrating individual composers; much is in the form of musicological analysis; typically the most bland and

complacent versions of this narrative appear as chapters or sections on music within larger histories of 'culture' in the Federal Republic. For a recent account which places the resurgence of 'new music' in a specifically political context, see Amy Beal, 'Negotiating cultural Allies: American music in Darmstadt, 1946–1956', *Journal of the American Musicological Society*, 53:1 (2000), 105–39.

6 Michael Kater, *Composers of the Nazi Era: Eight Portraits* (Oxford, 2000), 275–6.

7 Centre des Archives de l'Occupation Française en Allemagne et en Autriche, Colmar (AOFC), AC 857/5, Rapport sur l'oeuvre de démilitarisation, dénazification et de démocratisation entreprise par la Direction de l'Information, 8 January 1947, 17.

8 For a comparative study of 'music control' in all zones of occupied Germany, see Toby Thacker, 'Music after Hitler: politics, society, and the reconstruction of an art in Germany 1945–1955' (Cardiff University, PhD thesis, 2002).

9 Bayerisches Hauptstaatsarchiv, Munich, Office of Military Government, Bavaria (hereafter BHM OMGB), 10/48–1/4, Contribution of Music Section OMGB to Education, 3 April 1947.

10 *Military Government Information Bulletin (United States)* (10 February 1947), 36, 'Information Control',

11 BHM OMGB 10/48–1/5, 'Music Weekly Report', 22 December 1946.

12 BHM OMGB 10/48–1/4, 'Cultural Affairs Branch – Land Directors Briefing', 19 November 1948.

13 BHM OMGB 10/48–1/9, 'Music DM Reorientation Projects', undated.

14 Public Record Office, Kew, Foreign Office Correspondence (hereafter PRO FO) 898/401, 'British Information Services to Germany', 20 September 1945.

15 For a concise summary of the British musical programme, see PRO FO 898/415, 'Draft Notes on Music for Germany', 21 March 1945.

16 *Monthly Report of the Control Council for Germany (British Element)*, 4:2 (1949), 29; see also Edith Davies, 'British policy and the schools', in Arthur Hearnden (ed.), *The British in Germany: Educational Reconstruction after 1945* (London, 1978), 95–107.

17 PRO FO 1056/253, Dunn to Denison, Music Department, British Council, 30 April 1948.

18 For an early expression of this view, see Paul Bidwell, 'Reeducation in Germany: Emphasis on culture in the French Zone', *Foreign Affairs*, 27 (1948), 78–85.

19 *La France en Allemagne, Numéro Special: Information et Action Culturelle*, August 1947, 48 and 46.

20 *La France en Allemagne*, August 1947, 9 and 42.

21 AOFC AC 505/3, 'Inspection des Conservatoires et écoles de Musique', 25 October 1948.

22 AOFC AC 332/1, Directeur de l'Education Publique to Directeur du Personnel, du Matériel, et du Budget, 10 December 1947.

23 *Military Government Information Bulletin (United States)*, March 1952, 'Musical Ties'.

24 See Daniel zur Weihen, *Komponieren in der DDR: Institutionen, Organisationen und die erste Komponistengeneration bis 1961* (Cologne, 1999), 394.

25 Institut für Zeitgeschichte, Munich, Office of Military Government, United States (hereafter IfZ OMGUS), 5/301–3/9, Landesverwaltung für Kultus, Erziehung und Kunst, Württemberg-Baden, to Military Government, Stuttgart, 12 December 1945.

26 Gianmario Borio and Hermann Danuser (eds), *Im Zenit der Moderne – Die internationalen Ferienkurse für neue Musik Darmstadt 1946–1966* (Freiburg-im-Breisgau, 1997), I, 71.

27 See H. von Lutz and D. Meisz (eds), *Theater hinter Trümmern: Theater und Theaterpolitik in der Landeshauptstadt Düsseldorf 1945–1955* (Düsseldorf, 1995), 159–60.

28 See Kater, *Composers of the Nazi Era*, 31–56.

29 Bundesarchiv Koblenz (hereafter BAK), B105/192, 'Betr.: Lage der Kulturinstitute nach der Geldneuordnung IX', 9 May 1949.

30 NWHD NW 60/861, 'Vorbericht für die gemeinsame Sitzung des Kunstausschusses der Kultusministerkonferenz und des Kulturausschusses des deutschen Städtetags am 7.12.1950 in Hannover, Konzertwirtschaft', 15 December 1950.

31 NWHD NW 60/861, Bürgermeister, Darmstadt, to Kultusminister von Nordrhein-Westphalen, 30 October 1950.

32 See, for example, NWHD NW 60/885, Kultusminister des Landes Nordrhein-Westphalen to Ministerialrat Dr. Busley, 14 June 1948, in which the importance of paying for students from Detmold to attend the Institute in Bayreuth is stressed.

33 Westdeutscher Rundfunk, Historisches Archiv, Cologne (WDR HAC), 07362, *Städtisches Orchester Bielefeld, Abonnementskonzerte 1952/1953*.

34 WDR HAC 07362, *Das Orchester der Stadt Bochum, Spielzeit 1952/1953*.

35 See for example, Reinhard Limbach, 'Musikpflege – von Staat und Stadt gelenkt', *Das Musikleben*, 4:10 (1951), 273–5.

36 See Hans-Hubert Schieffer and Hermann Josef Müller, *Neue Musik in Düsseldorf seit 1945* (Cologne, 1998), 82–5.

37 See the 1951 programmes for *Die Brücke*, in Stadtarchiv Göttingen, III B 146.

38 PRO FO 1050/1344, Director, Cultural Relations Branch, to Heads of Cultural Relations Branch, Düsseldorf and Berlin, 5 January 1950.

39 Schieffer and Müller, *Neue Musik in Düsseldorf*, 67–9.

40 See Limbach, 'Musikpflege', 273.

41 Hans-Heinz Stuckenschmidt, 'Modern music festival at Donaueschingen shows vivid contrasts', *Musical America* (15 December 1954), 18, 33.

42 WDR HAC 10070, 'Protokoll der 15. Sitzung des Hauptausschusses des NWDR am 10. März 1951 in Hamburg', 11.

43 Generallandesarchiv Karlsruhe 481/398, 'Stadtverwaltung Karlsruhe an den Regierungspräsidenten von Nordbaden', 8 September 1952, 8.

44 AOFC AC 28/2, Gouverneur Commissaire du Land de Rhénanie-Palatinat to l'Ambassadeur, Haut Commissaire de la République Française en Allemagne, 23 May 1952.

45 Cited in Virgil Thomson, *Music Right and Left* (New York, 1951), 161–2.

46 The first attacks of this nature in Germany were made in the Soviet-licensed press in February 1948, provoking lively debate and, it should be said, scorn in other zones. By 1951, the SED in the GDR was articulating its own distinct criticism of 'new music' in Adenauer's Germany. See Ernst Hermann Meyer, 'Realismus – die Lebensfrage der deutschen Musik', *Musik und Gesellschaft*, 1:2 (1951), 38–40; for a concise summary of the SED's view in English, see Everett Helm, 'Germany', *The Musical Quarterly*, 37:10 (1951), 590–7.

47 'Programmerklärung des Ministeriums für Kultur', *Sinn und Form* (1954), 279–95, here 294.

48 PRO FO 1032/759B, 'The Future Organisation of ISC Activities, CCG (BE)', 9 September 1946, Appendix A, 3.

49 BAK B105/192, 'Betr.: Lage der Kulturinstitute nach der Geldneuordnung IX', 9 May 1949.

50 See Berndt Leukert, 'Musik aus Trümmern. Darmstadt um 1949', *Musik-Texte: Zeitschrift für neue Musik*, 45:7 (1992), 20–8, here 25.
51 Adorno's own thoughts are notoriously resistant to simplification. See Max Paddison, *Adorno's Aesthetics of Music* (New York, 1993).
52 For a wider perspective on this shift, see Volker Berghahn, *America and the Intellectual Cold Wars in Europe: Shepard Stone between Philanthropy, Academy, and Diplomacy* (Princeton, NJ, 2001).
53 See Toby Thacker, '"Anleitung und Kontrolle": Stakuko and the censorship of music in the GDR, 1951–1953', in Beate Müller (ed.), *Censorship and Cultural Regulation in the Modern Age* (Amsterdam, 2003), 87–110.
54 Hans-Heinz Stuckenschmidt, 'Musik gegen jedermann', *Melos*, 22:9 (1955), 245–8, here 248.
55 Stiftung Archiv der Akademie der Künste, Berlin, Hans-Pischner-Archiv 874, 'Zur Krise des musikalischen Avantgardismus', 18.
56 See Uta Poiger, *Jazz, Rock, and Rebels: Cold War Politics and American Culture in a Divided Germany* (Berkeley, CA, 2000); and Toby Thacker, 'The fifth column: dance music in the early GDR', in Patrick Major and Jonathan Osmond (eds), *The Workers' and Peasants' State: Communism and Society in East Germany under Ulbricht, 1945–71* (Manchester, 2002), 227–43.

10

Saints and devils:
youth in the SBZ/GDR, 1945–53[1]

Mark Fenemore

As the Communist leaders of East Germany struggled to find their feet, youth acted as the focus for enormous hope and fear. But while youth held an important place in the regime's preoccupations, it was by no means a united or homogeneous group. Although the 'youth' category officially embraced everyone between the ages of fourteen and twenty-five, important divisions resulted from differences of class, gender, age, upbringing and education. Taking Leipzig as an example, this chapter points to the diversity of young people's outlooks and responses as they emerged from the enforced uniformity of the Third Reich and struggled to adapt to life in the new, avowedly anti-Nazi state. Focusing in particular on cultural differences between 'rough' and 'respectable' groups, the chapter examines how social realities collided with 'high politics' in the spring and summer of 1953.

In the immediate post-war period, the Soviet occupation forces and their Communist allies were faced with the task of overcoming the chaos and destruction wrought by the war. In addition, they had set themselves the goal of fundamentally transforming society and eliminating once and for all what they saw as the roots of Nazism.[2] In the context of restoration and reconstruction, young people were seen ambivalently as a source of hope, and yet, at the same time, as a major threat to stability and order. Youth was presumed to be idealistic and forward-looking, ready to make sacrifices and to act as the driving force for reform and rebirth. But this vision of youth as positive energy for change hardly chimed with the fervent support many hundreds of thousands of young people had given to the Nazi cause. Even when it was clear that the Third Reich was in its death-throes, youngsters barely old enough to shave had been throwing themselves in front of Soviet tanks. Hatred of Communism and blind loyalty to Hitler were qualities which did not necessarily make for easy absorption into the new regime.

The most immediate task facing the Soviet occupiers was that of getting society functioning again. Whole cities had been reduced to rubble. The destruction of homes and factories left thousands cold, hungry and without work. With the normal distribution network disrupted, families could feed themselves only by making foraging trips out to the surrounding countryside to barter with farmers for food at exorbitant prices. Young men played a particularly prominent role in black-market activities. In part, this reflected their increased importance within the family. In the absence of fathers (killed or taken prisoner), they were forced to grow up quickly. While, to younger boys and girls, the rubble landscape offered a huge adventure playground, for their older siblings it formed an urban jungle in which they had to become a lot more canny and streetwise. The marauding of the Soviet occupiers (committing untold numbers of robberies, rapes and murders) helped create a sense of menace and of impotence in the face of an omnipresent threat. The mass rapes left a vast legacy of suffering, affecting children as well as adults. Although subsequently ignored and denied by the Communist authorities, large numbers of incidents are documented in the Soviet archives.[3] With so many families torn apart by war, the immense burden of keeping things going fell to women. Not only were they potential prey to roaming packs of occupying soldiers, but they were often faced with the task of supporting parents as well as children.

Given the pressures on the family and society, it is not surprising that the period immediately after the war saw an escalation in crime, notably among young people. Despite their best efforts, the Nazi authorities had been unable to stamp out juvenile delinquency and expressions of dissent and disorder. The requirement to adhere to the monotonous agenda of the Hitler Youth had spawned a series of youth subcultures. These ranged from the upper echelons of youth society, involved in the Hamburg Swing scene, down to the proletarian and allegedly politicised Leipzig packs, passing through the semi-delinquency and macho rebellion of the Edelweiß Pirates.[4] To prevent a more general upsurge in uncontrolled and potentially delinquent youthful behaviours, the Nazi authorities issued a decree in June 1943 which forbade young people from engaging in all sorts of otherwise harmless activities.[5]

After the war, juvenile delinquency and the threat it was said to pose became emblematic of the need to restore order. Keen to re-establish their authority, the police in Berlin instituted a policy of 'zero tolerance'. But the regulation on which it was based remained the police order of 1943. The first to fall foul of the crackdown were young men calling themselves Edelweiß Pirates.[6] Their collective physical strength and propensity for violence gave them a bargaining power in the new, levelled condition of post-war Germany. The emergence of the black market brought them into competition for territory with Poles and displaced persons. They did not shy away from using Nazi notions about racial superiority to taunt their opponents and justify their attacks on them.[7] For Allied occupiers in East and West, there was little to distinguish them from the so-called 'Werewolf' groups of die-hard Hitler supporters who were supposed to (and in a few cases did) conduct guerrilla warfare against Allied occupation. Although all the Allies rounded up youths they suspected of being Werewolves, the reaction was most extreme in the Soviet zone.[8]

Despite of, or rather because of, their fears about delinquent youth, the Communists were keen to re-establish the 'happy youthful life'. In part, they wished to ensure that young people had something preoccupying and productive to do. They also sought to win young people for the task of (re)construction. Because of the Communists' desire to ensure that it appealed to the great majority of young people, the FDJ (*Freie Deutsche Jugend*) organisation which emerged was a hybrid, combining the traditions of the Communist youth organisation with what were seen as the best traditions of German youth. Although the camping and hiking expeditions were ostensibly modelled on those of the *Wandervögel* movement, in reality they were more likely to appeal to former members of the Hitler Youth. Indeed, the earliest debates within the FDJ leadership reveal the difficult balancing act they faced between preventing former Hitler Youth cadres from having a negative effect on youth, and utilising their leadership and organisational skills within the new, avowedly anti-militaristic and anti-Nazi organisation.[9] As a sop to inclusivity, the early FDJ even strove to incorporate Christian youth leaders and their ideals.[10]

For early recruits to the FDJ, the organisation did act as a conveyor belt towards positions of responsibility. The campaigns of (re)construction and denazification offered important opportunities for social mobility to those willing to profess that they had broken with the past. How much deep-down internalisation and soul-searching took place is questionable, particularly considering the speed with which people like the *Neulehrer* ('new teachers') were recruited, trained and thrown into their new functions. Conversion was measured in terms of commitment and hard work. The more time spent winning approval, the less there was for genuine inner reflection. Soul-searching, in any case, would increasingly prove a dangerous exercise as the Cold War intensified, and with it the suspicion of any deviations from the (itself increasingly erratic) Party line.

The new republic

The birth of the new republic (on 7 October, 1949) coincided with a shift away from conciliation and bridge-building towards rupture and conflict. In the West, the new federal German authorities put pressure on the Western FDJ to liquidate itself. In the East, the FDJ leadership ceased to strive for inclusivity and openly broke with the churches and the so-called 'bourgeois parties'. The *Junge Gemeinde* (Youth Congregation), which grouped together young Christians in the countryside and in the higher schools (*Oberschulen*), became the FDJ's biggest rival in providing the 'happy youthful life' to young people.[11] Attacks on the *Junge Gemeinde* coincided with discrimination against those in the *Oberschulen* labelled 'bourgeois' or 'Christian'. Within the FDJ itself, recreation and leisure increasingly took a back seat to militarisation and indoctrination.

Although the threat of repercussions in the event of non-membership ensured that, on paper, membership figures remained high, the organisation lost much of its room for manoeuvre and ability to respond to local needs. Genuine enthusiasm was increasingly replaced by feigned conformity. The most energetic youth leaders moved into important cadre positions in industry and the Party.

In the education system, the mass recruitment of *Neulehrer* was supposed to bring fresh ideas and new attitudes into the schoolrooms. Drawn from the lower classes, these 'new teachers' were to make up in energy and vigour what they lacked in formal education and training. But, while some remember their 'new teacher' with fondness and appreciation, many others regarded them as inflexible and doctrinaire. Their recruitment coincided with attacks on liberals within the education system and the imposition of overtly Communist formulae and demands. For many, brought up to view teachers with the same respect as pastors and priests (in rural areas churches and schools were closely interlinked), the introduction of 'new teachers' seemed unnecessarily radical and likely to result in a decline in educational standards. For those within the education system, the efforts to improve and reform it were marred by the overt attempts at politicisation and indoctrination. For a generation rendered cynical by the collapse of Nazism and the aftermath of the war, such attempts to exert influence and control were perceived as bullying and intimidation.

For those who had already left school and started work, there had been a slow improvement in the conditions of material existence. But while there was no question that the population was materially far better off than the near-starvation experienced at the end of the war, there was an increasing divide between expectations and reality. While the Western Allies were keen to re-establish prosperity and productive capacity in their zones, in the East, the Soviets seemed interested only in extracting the maximum possible in reparation for Germany's aggression and unleashing of wholesale destruction on Soviet soil. From 1950 onwards, aided by currency reform and the Marshall Plan, the Western zones began visibly to move ahead and away from their counterpart in the East. For many in the East, employment and affordable housing remained potent symbols of security but, among young people in particular, there was an increasing desire for the status symbols and leisure products which were beginning to become available in the West. Particularly for young men, emigration was the most direct way of achieving their ambitions. For those 'honest workers' who remained behind sweating it out in the factories and on the construction sites, however, the divide between their expectations and reality was heightened by the increases in prices and hikes in work norms.

The rough and the respectable

Despite the Communists' attempts to establish Moscow as their point of reference, the presence of several hundreds of thousands of Allied troops on

171

German soil served to open up cultural horizons and boundaries of experience for many young Germans in the East. The trend in the West for bebop music spread to the East. A report of March 1953 described the latest trend in West Germany as a covert attempt to influence German youth with 'American ape culture (*amerikanische Affenkultur*)'.[12] Fans made up for their lack of numbers with the brightness of their clothing, contrasting as it did with the drab and decayed backdrop of war-torn Germany. Checked shirts, long swept-back hair and stripy socks characterised the bebop look. The reopening of the cinemas added a little more colour and excitement to young people's lives, albeit heavily censored and controlled by the government. The revival of popular festivities such as *Fasching* and Leipzig's annual *Tauchscher* festival provided a source of amusement and an outlet for pent-up energy. Unfortunately for the authorities, the traditional function of these festivals as periods of licensed misrule allowed them to become vehicles for outspoken criticism and physical clashes with the new and not particularly popular agents of law and order, the People's Police.[13]

For young Christians who were members of the *Junge Gemeinde*, the reason they existed on earth was to observe God's laws and to work for the spiritual renewal of Germany. Free time was taken up by religious observance, doing good works in the community and taking part in the 'happy youthful life' organised by the local pastor. The emphasis was on engaging in activities of a 'sensible' and 'meaningful' nature which combined innocent enjoyment with the development of a sense of togetherness. The sorts of activities (ranging from choir practice to parlour games) typically offered by the *Junge Gemeinde* tended to attract more girls than boys. Party officials only became seriously alarmed when pastors branched out into outdoor sports and hiking, thereby aiming beyond the 'Hallelujah girls' and attracting boys.

For youngsters from working-class neighbourhoods, particularly boys, leisure time was about escape from, rather than observance of, adult-imposed restrictions and norms. The street traditionally provided freedom from the confines of domesticity. There, boys learned to become men by standing up for themselves, physically in fights and verbally through jokes and repartee.[14] As they grew older, they sought to demonstrate their maturity and masculinity by smoking, drinking, going to dances and chasing girls.

If the outlook and beliefs of young Christians posed an ideological threat to Communist hegemony, the less high-minded activities of working-class street gangs posed a threat above all to the regime's fragile authority. Just as the Christians expressed their difference by wearing crosses hung on neck-chains, so too did gang members wear emblems of their allegiance – only in their case these were coins with holes drilled through them, a favourite having Hindenburg on one side and the swastika on the other. While the Christians had well-established rites and rituals, the gangs tended to make theirs up as they went along, often as a means of combating boredom. Gangs no longer engaged in their traditional activity of 'wild hiking'. Instead, they took to cycling together. Their added mobility served to heighten the authorities' fears. They were also becoming less provincial in outlook, embracing jazz with English and American lyrics.

For young Christians and other members of respectable society, the vulgarity of the gangs, together with their wild drinking and dancing, made them a group to give a wide berth to. There was little to distinguish their heathen antics from the atheist idolatry pursued by the Party. Young Christians responded to both official and unofficial pressures by keeping to themselves, avoiding the youth organisation and state-sponsored leisure activities. For youngsters from less respectable backgrounds, there was little to distinguish the holier-than-thou attitudes of local pastors from those of the SED functionaries and teachers loyal to the regime. As one pastor remarked to an SED functionary, 'I wish you much fun and success with the young people in our village. The youth of today is rotten . . .. They're only interested in two things – drinking and dancing'.[15]

Vilification

Starting in January 1953 and continuing until May, the SED engaged in a campaign of repression against the *Junge Gemeinde*. The popularity of Christian youth groups, particularly in rural areas, was taken as proof that the Church was engaged in 'unfair competition' and was using underhand tactics to keep young people away from the official youth organisation. To explain why the *Junge Gemeinde* was so successful in poaching members from the FDJ, the SED argued that young Christians had infiltrated the youth organisation in order to render it dull and uninteresting.[16] In a campaign with strongly Stalinist overtones, a series of show trials and purges was instituted in which young Christians who had 'infiltrated' the youth organisation were to be 'exposed' and publicly denounced.[17] In their attack on the alleged Christian subversion of the youth organisation, Party leaders could fall back on the tried and tested language of 'spies', 'agents' and 'traitors'. The campaign of vilification and public humiliation took on other aspects, however, which bore more resemblance to attacks by the Nazis on 'community aliens'.

An article printed in the *Leipziger Volkszeitung* on 19 April 1953 gives an example of the type of emotive and defamatory language used. The headline runs: '*Junge Gemeinde* – Cover organisation acting on the orders of the USA'. The newspaper then sets out to explain 'how young people are incited to commit crimes through the misuse of religious feelings'. Examples of the *Junge Gemeinde*'s misdeeds are summarised under headings which sound more like the titles of pulp fictions: '*Agents provocateurs* in priests' frocks', 'The SS Death's-head was their symbol', and 'Fascist songbooks for "spiritual edification" '.[18]

Members of the *Junge Gemeinde* were variously accused of being fascist, racist, dirty, unhygienic, criminal and potentially sexually deviant. Evidence to support the accusations of pro-fascism came in the form of a photograph purportedly showing a death's-head symbol. The caption reads: 'SS Death's-head, the symbol of the fascist murder organisation [which] members of the *Junge Gemeinde* painted on the doors when they were amongst themselves.' The *Junge Gemeinde* was no religious community, but an illegal terror organisation. 'Under the flag of supposedly religious activity', it tried to lure young people into 'banditry' so that they would later become part of the network of agents and subversives under American secret service control.[19] Most of the information contained in the article was pure fantasy. But, as far as the SED was concerned, the *Junge Gemeinde* was not only seeking to undermine the unity of young people. It was also inciting them to commit hostile acts against the state.

In a lengthy tabloid-style exposé, the newspaper recounted what had been discovered during a raid on a retreat (described as a 'training camp') run by the *Junge Gemeinde* in Sehlis.[20] The inspection had supposedly revealed a dummy hanging from a tree with a red tie around its neck. 'What has the symbolic hanging of a man with a red tie to do with the principles of Christianity and religious activity? This outrageous provocation is closely related to the notorious methods of the American lynch organisation, the Ku Klux Klan, and the brutal terror of Ami-soldiers in Korea.' In short, the newspaper argued, the *Junge Gemeinde* was nothing but a cover for American and CIA interests, a 'nesting place' for 'the sworn enemies of our young people and our republic, disguised as Christians'. Those in charge of the SED witch-hunt sought to alert parents to the shocking 'hygiene conditions' and promiscuous proximity they had discovered in the camp. 'Do the parents of 17-year-old Brigitte N. or Gisella R. [their names and addresses printed in full] approve of their daughters sleeping two to a bed so as to keep one another "warm"?' (*um sich zu 'erwärmen'*), the article asked.[21] Unable to cite any evidence of 'misdemeanours', let alone real crimes, having been committed, the authorities sought to present the *Junge Gemeinde*'s activities as something dirty and shameful. The young people in the camp were 'packed together like veal calves', with considerable risk not just to their health, but also their morals.

The fact that much of the 'evidence' used against the *Junge Gemeinde* was fairly flimsy did not prevent the SED from finding FDJ members prepared to assist in 'unmasking' the Christian youth organisation. As Manfred Klein suggests, in some cases the uniforms and ideological training had proved 'psychologically effective' in creating and heightening divisions between 'them' and 'us'.[22] The opportunities for actionism and aggressive posturing offered by attacks on the middle classes and purges of young Christians were capable of mobilising those in the FDJ who felt hostility towards their more privileged and respectable neighbours. Even after the campaign had been called off (under pressure from the Soviets), there were reports of residual hostility to the Christians and disgust at the U-turn: 'I voted for members of the *Junge Gemeinde* to be expelled from the *Oberschule* and now I'm supposed to sit next to them on the same bench. I can't go along with that!'[23]

The uprising, June 1953

However hostile the SED was to the *Junge Gemeinde*, its attitude to the working-class street gangs was highly ambivalent. The SED claimed to represent young-sters from working-class backgrounds, yet it espoused a set of values that had more in common with those of respectable society. It is true that, on the eve of the Nazi seizure of power, the Communists had turned to the gangs as a means of providing local defence against intrusion by the SA and Hitler Youth.[24] But, in the immediate aftermath of the war, this one-time affinity had been forgot-ten and the gangs were seen merely as a nuisance and as a threat of disorder. It was only with the uprising of 1953, however, that the SED realised the true threat posed by 'rowdy', working-class young men. The day of strikes and mass unrest saw the various sections of the working-class community responding in different ways to the constraints imposed by the SED leadership. It might have been expected that older male workers, steeped in the traditions of the organ-ised labour movement, would be principally involved in organising strikes and political demonstrations. But, as Heidi Roth argues, though the age-range of 'provocateurs' was anywhere between twenty and sixty, the strike committees and 'ringleaders' were dominated (80:20) by the under-forties.[25]

In Leipzig, the first to strike were building workers on Windmill Street, an important new housing development. While one part formed a procession and marched to the Karl-Marx-Platz, others, 'mainly teenagers with their Western bicycles, rode in various directions and to different parts of town, presumably in order to call the workers in other factories out to the demonstrations'.[26] Later, a 'column of twenty bicycle outriders' was seen collecting stones in the Ni-kolaistraße. In all, eighty-one firms and an estimated 27,000 workers were involved in the strike. Around midday on 17 June, a huge crowd of strikers and protesters (estimated to number 25,000) gathered on Leipzig's main square.[27] Political demands merged with social and economic protest, creating an atmosphere of tense expectancy and anger against the authorities. After attacking a statue of Stalin and attempting to topple it, the crowd moved into the town centre, pushing its way into public buildings and forcing the authori-ties to barricade themselves in.[28] Events ceased to be planned or controllable. At certain points, stand-offs occurred between an angry crowd and nervous, heavily outnumbered policemen. The various police units were cut off from contact with headquarters and one another. Many telephone lines were down and couriers had difficulty getting through road-blocks.[29] This gave young workers the chance to play their traditional role as 'guerrilla fighters' and 'defenders' of the working-class community.[30] From within the crowd, young-sters made rapid and daring forays, attacking symbols of the regime, storming into official buildings and throwing their contents out into the street. Blow-by-blow police reports described up to 2,000 people trying to storm buildings such as the Ernst Thälmann House.[31] Members of the street gangs were 'naturals' for this kind of confrontation and conflict. In a tense situation, in which everyone involved belonged to the working class, it was sometimes difficult to know how to react. One policeman described being kicked and spat on as he lay on the ground. 'An older worker came along and said, "Let the poor swine go, he's only a prole [like us]".'[32] In another instance, a former policeman led an attack on a police station to disarm those inside and seize their weapons.[33]

The widespread support for strikes and demonstrations was deeply embarrassing for the self-proclaimed party of the working class: 'These workers have acted against their own interests and the interests of the working class . . . the victory of working-class interests must be secured against them.'[34] In the aftermath of the uprising, the SED desperately needed an explanation for what had happened and a scapegoat on whom to pin the blame. Within hours of the uprising in Berlin, SED leaders were already formulating a story about how the events were actually part of a 'fascist *Putsch*', planned and accomplished by Western intelligence agencies with the aid of '*provocateurs*' and 'bandits' infiltrated from West Berlin. In Leipzig, too, in spite of the overwhelming working-class support for the strike, it was decided to argue that the workers had been led astray:

> As a result of continual stirring up by fascists working in the factory, a large part of the workforce had lost its belief in the strength of the working class. Through their hypocritical manner, a few enemies of our Workers' and Peasants' State were able to use a whole workforce to serve their interests. For these elements, the power of the workers was a barrier to achieving their old or dreamed-of positions.[35]

Party leaders sought to drive a wedge between their opponents by creating and emphasising a distinction between 'legitimate', purely economic demands, and the chaos and disruption that had resulted from mass insurrection. 'In order to put a stop to these rowdy activities and to divide those engaging in them from the working masses [they] currently lead, the People's Police must carry out quick and consistent measures.'[36] The SED leadership sought to use its control over the media to create a false gulf between older and younger workers. In fact, over half those who left the SED in the months following the uprising were over fifty. The commonest reason given was the use of firearms against unarmed, defenceless workers.[37] Nevertheless, the most visible legacy of the uprising, the burned-out, ransacked buildings, was blamed not on the huge crowd, but on a small band of fascist *provocateurs*. Although there were reports of 'bandits' being parachuted out of planes, for the most part the Western agents were easy for the authorities to spot. What gave them away were their bright T-shirts and other Western garments.[38] The imposition of a curfew by the Soviet troops made them stand out even more. While most people had the sense to stay indoors, over a thousand young people remained on the streets, mostly in small groups of fifteen–twenty. 'In the evening, a few collections of young people could be seen, but they quickly scattered.' One young man was given three years for taking part in such 'rioting' and for calling the policemen pigs. Another was arrested for answering back to police as he stood talking with his gang about a portable record-player he wanted to buy.[39] A number of groups of 'Western-influenced young people', equipped with bikes and dressed according to the 'Bubi-style', were encountered in the countryside in the week following the Uprising.[40]

Youth subculture – in the form of distinctive clothes and haircuts – provided the regime with an easy way of identifying and 'revealing' the agents who had led ordinary workers astray. Existing rhetoric about the dangerous influence of Western music could easily be redeployed to present the whole uprising as a pre-meditated imperialist plot. It did not matter whether the offending music was supposed to be samba-influenced *Schlager*, tango or bebop. The rising was the direct consequence of the cultural subversion of youth. The *Stasi* issued precise instructions about which suspects should be first to suffer retribution.[41] Not surprisingly, their investigations revealed that the ringleaders of the uprising were 'inferior types (*minderwertige Subjekte*)' inflamed by listening to RIAS (Radio in the American Sector).[42] The *Leipziger Volkszeitung* printed mugshots and potted biographies of these once marginal, now key figures, claiming that they had been responsible for turning the uprising into a violent counter-revolutionary *Putsch*. Urging the population to 'judge for themselves', the paper declared, 'here and there, workers and a few citizens forgot that that which the warlike rowdies were destroying they themselves had created, and by the time they remembered, the rooms were already burnt out and the furnishings reduced to wreckage'.[43] The authorities also made a distinction in the punishment of participants. Seeking to avoid 'mass reprisals', they decreed that 'fascist *provocateurs*' should receive hard sentences while 'workers who had been led astray (*irregeleitete Arbeiter*)' should receive 'extremely mild' treatment.[44]

One picture in particular, printed in *Neues Deutschland*, summed up the message the Party wanted to put across. It showed a young Berlin worker with a close-up of his socks. This was conclusive proof, the caption stated, that he could not be a genuine worker. For what kind of a worker would wear 'samba socks' and crepe-soled shoes underneath his overalls?[45] Another widely published picture showed a young man wearing a cowboy T-shirt and a tie, illustrated with a picture of a naked woman, draped tastefully over his shoulder.[46] Blind to the alien young people who had infiltrated their ranks, older workers had allowed themselves to be led astray. 'So many an old worker disgraced himself by the way he acted against the working class on 17 June.' The whole workforce was to be made to understand 'how on 17 June they fell into the trap set by the agents of American and German monopoly capitalism'.[47]

Workers who had taken part in the rising knew very well, of course, what had really happened and why. One of their 'fascist actions' after 17 June had been to criticise 'elected representatives of the Party and the Trade Union' as 'criminals and blackguards'.[48] A twenty-one-year-old worker said that he and his colleagues felt insulted that their lawful laying down of tools was 'made to look like a fascist adventure'. In Erfurt, they said that the so-called '*provocateurs*' were nothing more than harmless young people: 'The police got these T-shirts out of their wardrobes at home and made them put them on to be photographed at the police station.' A teacher dismissed the official propaganda, saying that 'the acts of violence in Berlin and other towns weren't a planned provocation, but a popular movement'. Likewise, a member of the FDJ leadership in the Leuna works declared that she was leaving the organisation, saying, 'All this talk about a *putsch* organised by the Western imperialists is a load of rubbish. The workers alone were the authors of the provocation.' Young women in Köpenick responded to the attacks on Western youth culture by decorating their workplace with pictures of 'tango-boys in T-shirts'.[49] Although the *Leipziger Volkszeitung* did allude to girls who belonged to the bebop scene, it did not deem it necessary to describe them beyond referring to their 'doubtful' morality.[50]

Of the 20,000 workers who took part in the demonstrations of 17 June 1953 in Leipzig, between 40 and 50 per cent are estimated to have been under the age of twenty-five.[51] Following the uprising, a small number of the *junge Burschen* (young lads) who had taken part were singled out in the campaign of defamation. By drawing attention to their Western-style dress, the authorities sought to present them as alien intruders and thereby to deny them membership of the working class. The propagandists sought to divide the working class into 'decent workers' who had only wanted a reduction of the work norms, and the 'scum' (*Abschaum*) who had carried out the work of Western agents, looting and burning buildings and paying heed to 'fascist' demands for an end to the regime. Older workers, it was claimed, had allowed themselves to be led astray by common 'street thieves' and 'criminal elements' infiltrated from the West. By falling prey to youngsters 'dressed Bubi-style', the working class had acted against its own interests. But although the authorities were able to find a number of 'checked shirts' and 'Texas trousers' to parade in front of the public, a greater number of young people arrested on 17 June were actually members of the FDJ.[52]

While it is true that young workers were usually to be found in the lead in attacks on official buildings, their involvement fitted into a tradition of street-based working-class protest. Although individuals became involved for a wide range of reasons – some of them far removed from the political goals of the 'party of the working class' – as a crowd they were nevertheless governed by a shared sense of class identity. Evidence of the interventions of older workers suggests that they provided younger participants not only with a sense of legitimacy, but also with direction and encouragement. Far from being wild and indiscriminate, the actions of the crowd showed a significant degree of discrimination, lending them a highly symbolic character. Underlying their acts was a shared vocabulary of resistance uniting old and young. They were united not least by the actions of the police in firing indiscriminately into the crowd (killing and wounding not just young workers, but a female old-age pensioner). East German workers suffered for being the first to rise up against their Soviet-imposed leaders. In 1956 in Hungary and in 1968 in Czechoslovakia, young workers again risked their lives in challenging Soviet occupation and Stalinist domination. In the name of the working class, they were denounced anew as gangsters and criminals.[53]

Conclusion

The young did have the potential to act as agents of change. But the changes they desired were often diametrically opposed to those planned by the Party. The 'events of 1953' offer an important demonstration of the diversity of youth. Both Christian and working-class youth found themselves targeted by the SED for their dissent from the socialist ideal. But while young Christians attempted to preserve their respectability and religious beliefs by remaining aloof from the regime, actionism and machismo pushed working-class street youth to the forefront of events. Although the two groups were poles apart in terms of 'respectability' and their attitudes to consumer culture, the authorities drew on a common store of libel and innuendo to typify them as alien and other. Though the Communists' original aim had been to transform society and make a fundamental break with the Nazi past, their intolerance of difference and the methods they used to vilify nonconformity inevitably led people to make comparisons between them and the Nazis.

Notes

1 Research for this chapter was generously supported by the British Academy, the DAAD and the Institute for Historical Research.
2 Michael Buddrus, 'A generation twice betrayed: youth policy in the transition from the Third Reich to the Soviet Zone of Occupation (1945–1946)', in Mark Roseman (ed.), *Generations in Conflict* (Cambridge, 1995), 247–68; Arno Klönne, *Umerziehung, Aufbau und Kulturkonflikt: zur Geschichte der Jugend im geteilten Deutschland von 1945 bis in die fünfziger Jahre* (Hagen, 1998); Sonja Häder, *Schülerkindheit in Ost-Berlin: Sozialisation unter den Bedingungen der Diktatur, 1945–1958* (Cologne, 1998); Ulrich Mählert, *Die Freie Deutsche Jugend 1945–1949* (Paderborn, 1995).
3 Norman Naimark, *The Russians in Germany: A History of the Soviet Zone of Occupation, 1945–1949* (Cambridge, MA, 1995).
4 For the best account of these groups, see 'Young people: mobilisation and refusal', in Detlev Peukert, *Inside Nazi Germany: Conformity, Opposition and Racism in Everyday Life* (London, 1993).
5 *Polizeiverordnung zum Schutze der Jugend vom 10.6.1943.*
6 'Bekämpfung von Unrühen & Bandenunwesens' (1945–47), Landesarchiv Berlin, STA Rep. 303/9, 80.
7 Alfons Kenkmann, *Wilde Jugend. Lebenswelt großstädtlicher Jugendlicher zwischen Weltwirtschaftskrise, Nationalsozialismus und Währungsreform* (Essen, 1996), 362.
8 Jan Foitzik, 'Bemerkungen zur Jugendpolitik der SMAD', in Helga Gotschlich, Katharina Lange and Edeltraud Schulze (eds), *Aber nicht im Gleichschritt* (Berlin, 1997), 117–24; Kenkmann, *Wilde Jugend*, 334–6, 350–4.
9 Ulrich Mählert and Gerd-Rüdiger Stephan, *Blaue Hemden – Rote Fahnen: Die Geschichte der Freien Deutschen Jugend* (Opladen, 1996), 28.

10 See, for example, the experiences of CDU member Manfred Klein as recounted in his book, *Jugend zwischen den Diktaturen, 1945–1956* (Mainz, 1968).

11 Members of the *Junge Gemeinde* were Lutherans, as were the majority of churchgoers in the GDR. Important pockets of Catholic belief existed in major towns and on the southernmost fringes of the State. But while Catholics were also seen as obstacles to the SED's atheist mission, Catholicism's status as a minority religion ensured that its youth organisations occupied less attention in the regime's struggle against 'Christian influences'.

12 Sächsisches Staatsarchiv (SStA) Leipzig, Bildung, Kultur und Sport, 3717, 16.

13 See Mark Fenemore, 'Nonconformity on the borders of dictatorship: youth subcultures in the GDR, 1949–1965' (University of London PhD, 2002), 126–32.

14 Paul Willis, *Learning to Labour: How Working Class Kids Get Working Class Jobs* (London, 1977), 30.

15 Stiftung Archiv der Parteien und Massenorganisationen der DDR (hereafter SAPMO-BArch), DY 24/3710.

16 'Arbeit der Jungen Gemeinde unter der Jugend' (January–October 1952), SAPMO-BArch DY 24/A-FDJ 11.893.

17 For eye-witness accounts of these mini show trials see Patrik von zur Mühlen, *Der Eisenberger Kreis: Jugendwiderstand und Verfolgung in der DDR, 1953–1958* (Bonn, 1995), 27–8.

18 '"Junge Gemeinde" – Tarnorganisation im USA-Auftrag', *Leipziger Volkszeitung* (19 April 1953).

19 *Ibid.*

20 *Ibid.*

21 *Ibid.*

22 Klein, *Jugend*, 79.

23 Report of 15 June 1953, SAPMO-BArch, DY 24/2301.

24 Eve Rosenhaft, *Beating the Fascists? The German Communists and Political Violence, 1929–1933* (Cambridge, 1983).

25 Heidi Roth, *Der 17. Juni in Sachsen* (Cologne, 1999), 580–1.

26 SStA Leipzig, IV-2/12/588, 7, 140.

27 'BDVP Fernschreiben' (17 June 1953), SStA Leipzig, BDVP 24/42, 8.

28 Roth, *Der 17. Juni in Sachsen*, 115–16.

29 SStA Leipzig, BDVP 24/42, 172.

30 Thomas Lindenberger, *Straßenpolitik: Zur Sozialgeschichte der öffentlichen Ordnung in Berlin 1900 bis 1914* (Berlin, 1995), 391.

31 SStA Leipzig, IV-2/12/588, 139.

32 SStA Leipzig, BDVP 24/42, 192.

33 *Ibid.*, 165.

34 SStA Leipzig, IV-2/12/588, 206.

35 'Die Belegschaft des VEB Schrott trennt sich von den faschistischen Provokateuren des 17. Juni 1953' (8 September 1953), SStA Leipzig, IV-5/01/483.

36 SStA Leipzig, BDVP 24/42, 141.

37 SStA Leipzig, BDVP 24/42, 89-91; Roth, *Der 17. Juni in Sachsen*, 583.

38 Federal Office for the Documents of the State Security Services of the Former GDR (BstU), Leipzig Branch (Ast Lpz), Leitung 240/2 and 240/3.

39 SStA Leipzig, BDVP 24/42, 118; BstU, Ast Lpz, Leitung 243.

40 SStA Leipzig, IV-2/12/588, 76 and 81.

41 BstU, Ast Lpz, Leitung 300/01.

42 BstU, Ast Lpz, AU 129/55, 95.

43 *Leipziger Volkszeitung* (24 June 1953)

44 Roth, *Der 17. Juni in Sachsen*, 550.

45 *Neues Deutschland* (22 June 1953)

46 *Ibid.*

47 'Die Belegschaft des VEB Schrott trennt sich von den faschistischen Provokateuren'.

48 Reports (June 1953), SAPMO-BArch, FDJ 24/2301.

49 *Ibid.*

50 *Leipziger Volkszeitung* (24 June 1953)

51 SStA Leipzig, IV-2/12/588, 7.

52 *Ibid.*, 25.

53 See, for example, Sandor Kopacsi, *In the Name of the Working Class* (New York, 1987).

11

Austrian youth in the 1950s

Karin M. Schmidlechner

Post-war Austria was paternalistic, authoritarian, submissive to authority and pious.[1] In particular, the immediate post-war period in Austria witnessed a strengthening of traditional religious institutions and, at least in rural areas, the Church defined the rhythms of people's everyday lives, including their holidays.[2] The influence of the Church on the population began to wane only in the mid-1950s, a development related to the triumph of consumer and leisure culture.[3]

After a temporary relaxation of gender roles in the immediate post-war era, the reinstatement of gender polarisation moved to the centre of the political agenda in the 1950s.[4] The family was at this time regarded as a shelter for its members from the pressures of the outside world, as a safe retreat. This way of life – idealised and propagandised – addressed the needs of a large portion of the population after the strains of the war and the immediate post-war period. Women's economic independence and self-realisation beyond typical female roles was not part of this model.[5] The dominant social ideal also conformed to the familial socialisation of young women around the single goal that was perceived as worthwhile, namely, marriage. In preparation for marriage, girls were already trained at young ages to carry out gender-specific household tasks. Alternative conceptualisations of femininity were not available for developing girls, and would not have been accepted in any case.[6] Socialisation in schools also conformed to this general emphasis on marriage as a goal. The schooling of girls was intended to contribute to ensuring that they fulfilled their all-important household duties. This was to be achieved through single-sex classes and appropriate curricula.[7]

The watchword of Austrian society at that time was 'respectability'. 'Respectable' behaviour was the decisive precondition for upward social mobility, and was therefore more important than ever before. This explains the unusually high number, and unprecedented success, of etiquette books published at this time.[8] 'Respectable behaviour' was incompatible with sexuality. This was the message provided by the advice books for young people which appeared in large numbers on the Austrian market, many of them traceable to the initiative of the Catholic Church, which was particularly concerned with this issue.[9] Questions of the body and of sexuality were either not addressed in these books and brochures, or else they were treated in a purely negative way. Above all for girls, but for boys as well, the prescribed rules of behaviour in regard to morality and sexuality to be found in these 'advice' manuals were unambiguous: Sexuality in general, but especially pre-marital sex, was treated as dangerous and sinful.[10]

This negation of sexuality permeated the general social climate, and as a result sexuality was correspondingly not addressed in schools at all, or only negatively.[11] The public hostility to sex found its counterpart in the family, where authoritarian fathers in their role of family heads were also responsible for this aspect of socialisation.[12] According to the understanding of the time, this was limited to protecting in particular their daughters from the dangers of sexuality. For this reason, young women were kept at home after puberty, in the arena of parental control, in contrast to their childhood during the war and the immediate post-war period, when some of them had enjoyed a relatively high degree of freedom outside the home.[13] The repression of girls' sexuality worked not only indirectly through restrictions on their physical freedom beginning at puberty, but also through prescriptions hostile to sexuality designed to prevent pre-marital sexual intercourse and the possibility of pregnancy. Getting pregnant was the major problem for girls who had sexual relations with boys, since the birth control pill did not yet exist and buying other forms of contraception was embarrassing and practically unthinkable for girls.[14] Pregnant girls were cast out by society and even by their own families. Girls were constantly reminded that they would never be allowed to return home in the event of a pregnancy.[15] That this was a matter not just of threats, but also of actions, is demonstrated by the fact that homes for unmarried mothers were established at this time to alleviate at least in some degree the plight of girls cast off by their families.[16]

But it was not just pregnancy and its consequences for their own future that girls might expect as a result of early sexual encounters with boys. Because pregnancy made their misbehaviour public, they also had to fear for their good reputation and their future chances of marriage. The only possibility of preserving their good reputation in the event of pregnancy consisted in marriage, which everyone was aiming for anyway, even if at a later point in time. Sex with a 'fiancé' was thus the only even implicitly tolerated form of pre-marital sex because, in the event of a pregnancy, a potential husband was already lined up. Very often, sex was even traded for the promise of a steady relationship with the ultimate goal of marriage. As the high illegitimacy rates indicate, however, pregnancy often did not lead to marriage, at least not immediately, either because the necessary financial security or place to live were lacking, or because the 'intended' husband decided otherwise. In the former case, premarital sex resulting in pregnancy frequently led to a shotgun wedding, and therefore from dependency on parents seamlessly to dependency on a man.[17]

For working-class girls, marriage was very important not only for social but also for economic reasons; life without a partner would be nearly impossible for them because of low wages – above all since they wanted, and were also supposed to have, children. Very often, marriage was seen as offering escape from a job that they did not really value, and the opportunity to devote themselves after marriage more fully to the household and childcare. In reality, a large number of young women had to continue working outside the home after marriage. The ideal cherished by society at that time, however, even among the working class, did not address this prospect.[18]

Many of these girls displayed a remarkable realism concerning their future as wives. They hoped that their partners would treat them well (a good husband was expected to be faithful and not to drink), and that there would not be too many problems, in particular financial ones. The romantic notions of love depicted in many films of that period were not part of their expectations.[19]

For working-class boys, marriage was not attractive. The prospect of a permanent bond was daunting, and marital responsibilities were incompatible with their favourite pursuits. On the other hand, they knew that marriage was part of the life mapped out for them, and that they would eventually end up getting married. The girls they hoped to marry sometime should be attractive but above all decent and should know how to cook and clean.[20]

Since girls were dependent on the marriage market, they had to make sure they prepared themselves for it. In addition to possessing the appropriate moral qualities, they needed to acquire skills such as the ability to run a household, as well as material qualifications. In this era the dowry that a girl customarily brought to marriage – which mainly involved household items such as dishes, kitchen utensils and bedding, but also furniture – really mattered. In some families, the assembly of items for the dowry began at the time of the daughter's birth. There were also businesses which specialised in meeting this need; dowry contracts specified the commitment either to save a certain sum of money each month or to purchase goods of a set value.[21] As soon as a girl started earning her own money, a portion of her income was applied to the purchase of the dowry goods that would be so important for her future life as a wife. In contrast, young men spent their money on radios, motorcycles and sporting goods.[22]

Neither an academic nor a professional training was seen as necessary for girls – not only because of limited financial means but also because women would withdraw from the labour market after marriage anyway;[23] instead, the expansion of home economics courses was further accelerated. Additionally, the high rate of unemployment among youth in Austria at the time, which affected a significant proportion of the roughly 80,000 annual secondary school-leavers, narrowed girls' choice of occupation.[24] The girls' dream job of secretary was scarcely attainable. It was also extremely difficult to get an apprenticeship as a seamstress or hairdresser.[25] Work as a chambermaid, housemaid, or waitress, and particular jobs in agriculture (farm domestic, farmhand), were the only uncontested female occupations.[26] If girls did resist societal prejudices and worked outside of agriculture, they went into either unskilled, poorly paid training positions or low-status, typical women's employment – as, for example, carers – which they only reluctantly accepted. Besides the unfavourable working conditions, these jobs were extremely poorly paid and offered no chance of promotion.[27] Many girls had no other choice than to work in a factory. However, the decision to work in the factories was not made merely because of the lack of other opportunities, but also because girls could earn more there than in jobs requiring an apprenticeship.[28]

Although boys were affected by youth unemployment, too, they were better off than girls. Parents were more ready to invest money in their professional education, employers preferred hiring boys to girls and boys' job interests were not concentrated in only a few fields.[29]

The economy

In economic terms, the 1950s in Austria were characterised by rapid growth in per capita productivity, as well as changes in the economic structure. The primary goal of economic policy at the time was to make the Austrian economy competitive, to equalise the balance of payments, and to secure 'a socially acceptable standard of living' for the population.[30] The 'standard of living' became the new mantra, according to which the individual was to be pushed towards greater achievement and personal effort for the good of the national economy.[31] This campaign would appear to have been successful. Between 1950 and 1960, Austria's gross national product (GNP) grew by nearly 75 per cent,[32] and this resulted in a higher standard of living for all politically significant sectors.[33] Economic opportunity increased as never before. Between 1958 and 1961, Austrian per capita income increased by 21 per cent in real terms. In the years 1954–60 alone, the net per capita wages of workers increased by over 30 per cent. Concurrently, the growth of the workforce was such that the resultant increase in spending capacity caused private consumer spending to rise at the same time by 45 per cent.[34] In 1956, living standards in Austria were double what they had been in 1950.[35] Private consumption increased by 71 per cent in the decade between 1950 and 1960.[36] Spending on basic necessities and semi-luxury goods rose by 50 per cent, on clothing by 68 per cent, on education and entertainment by 81 per cent and on transportation by 169 per cent during the same period. In the immediate post-war years, the main demand had been for foodstuffs, but this shifted to textiles in 1950 and to shoes in 1951. Beginning in 1954, demand focused on consumer durables, especially motor vehicles, electrical goods and other household equipment. Between 1950 and 1960, the scooter and the motor-cycle symbolised success and the spirit of the times.[37]

The development of the welfare state also made progress during this era. In 1955, a law on general social insurance was passed; five years later, the 45-hour working week was established.[38]

Americanisation

With the increase in leisure time and the economic upswing beginning in the mid-1950s came a transition to an Americanised consumer culture which contributed significantly to the changes in everyday life experienced by Austrian women and men.[39] American food and consumer goods became essential components of the quality of life in Austria. Spending more and more, and faster and faster, became the hallmark of prosperity.

American popular culture and the goods associated with it became an essential part of the lifestyle and everyday cultural experience of young people in particular. For them, these things symbolised freedom and independence. Young people in Austria, sold on America, took greedily to Coca-Cola, petticoats, leather jackets, Las Vegas-style slot-machines, jukeboxes and blue jeans. Living out this cultural fantasy was a phenomenon that had never been seen before in the everyday world of Austria, and it signalled a new attitude towards life.[40]

Above all, young people working in factories were drawn to this new lifestyle. As unskilled workers, they were in a better position to afford the increasing range of goods offered them by the consumer industry that was then taking off.[41] A newspaper article of 1957 ran as follows:

> A propos hours and wages: Here, industry has most to offer, and its power of attraction, and the number of young people who elect to work in this area, are correspondingly substantial. The five-day working week buys a moped, nice clothes, a portable radio, and the possibility of frequently going to the movies. There is a certain danger in this trend, namely, that many professional talents are being pulled away from where they are urgently needed.[42]

Popular culture

The adoption of American popular culture was greatly promoted by the media. Movies especially had a very strong influence on the young.[43] The cinema was the most readily available leisure-time interest for the young outside the family, 'the place of contact and specific development of social relationships'.[44] Through visiting the cinema they could obtain a 'certain breaking away from the parents and manifest elements of independence'.[45] In these years, besides youth-specific German and Austrian musical films, the cinemas mainly showed American films about youthful rebellion. The first film on this theme – 'The Wild One' – dates from the year 1953 and describes the doings of a youthful motorbike gang that oppresses an American small town. The film starred Marlon Brando, who became one of the great idols of the young. Later films in similar vein were 'Rebel Without a Cause', starring James Dean, and 'Blackboard Jungle', which deals with a gang and its adolescent boss in a school in Chicago.[46]

According to statistics and oral reports, going to the cinema was a favoured leisure-time pursuit for girls as well as boys. A newspaper poll found that the chief ways in which boys spent their time was doing sports, going to the movies, or hiking, while for girls it was dancing, going to the movies and reading.[47] Girls as well as boys cherished the American teen rebel films which were shown in Austria from the mid-1950s and offered stiff competition to German and Austrian films, while working-class girls living in the country clearly preferred the so-called 'light entertainment' films.[48] American movie stars such as James Dean and Marlon Brando were not just trend-setters in tastes in music and fashion, but also in a readiness to go against the social grain. In this regard the effect was twofold – on the one hand through the girls' own heightened tendency toward rebellion, and on the other hand through their preference for 'rebels' as boyfriends.

According to one particular study, trainees went to the cinema more often than grammar-school students. Only 25 per cent of trainees, but 50 per cent of grammar-school students, visited the cinema less than once a week.[49] This difference was mainly attributed to social background; grammar-school students were more strongly encouraged – by the school as well as by their parents – to engage in other forms of recreational activities, going rather to the theatre, concerts and exhibitions. In addition, there was the financial factor. Trainees had at least some money of their own, whilst grammar-school students were dependent on their parents.[50] 33 per cent of trainees and 14 per cent of grammar-school students belonged to the category of the juvenile frequent cinema-goer. Typical for this category was that they tried, more than other persons of the same age, to act grown-up, and were the most willing to subscribe to the messages conveyed by advertising and the entertainment industry. These youths were also the readiest to attach themselves to a congenial group of friends, even against parental prohibition. They were also more likely to have close relationships with girls.[51] Marked regional differences were found, but the difference in frequency of cinema visits was most pronounced and strongest especially in medium-sized towns. In second place came cities, followed by villages.[52] There was a clearly negative correlation between frequency of cinema-going and of church-going. Especially among young workers, religious observance proved to be 'one of the most effective factors militating against overly numerous cinema visits as well as the reading of sensational papers, visits to cafés or espresso-bars, dancing, smoking and drinking' – behaviour patterns that were all connected with cinema-going in general.[53] The standard of the films attended stood in a complex relationship to the standard of other cultural occupations. The more a juvenile's taste in general was already formed to some degree, whether through the influence of parents and school or due to initiatives of his or her own, the more mature was his or her taste in films.[54]

Indicative of the huge interest in information about films and actors, pop songs and pop singers, was the popularity of youth magazines such as *Bravo*.[55] Out of 100 trainees interviewed, sixty-two read one or more magazines.[56] At that time young people in Austria also became acquainted with the 'comic', an American form of the picture story possessing no literary value, which was produced in huge quantities, and dismissed as 'filthy trash' by conservative educators. Comic-book heroes endowed with superhuman powers appealed to young minds and satisfied the dreams of power and desires for independence, especially of male youths.

The youth-specific music scene in Western Europe in these years was also chiefly influenced by commercialised cultural imports from the United States. This music scene involved the organisation of big concerts that gave thousands of fans the opportunity to see their idols live on stage, and to rebel against adults' ideas of discipline.[57] In Austria such events did not take place very often, as there were no big cities except Vienna. So the young people became acquainted with the new music mainly through films, (foreign) radio programmes and records. Very often, it was quite difficult for them to get an opportunity to listen to this music, because only a few of them owned radios or record-players.[58]

In particular, rock 'n' roll was an important part of American popular culture and something completely new in Austria in the mid-1950s. Through it, commercial culture offered young people a way to express their own ideas, and a channel, if only a symbolic one, through which to articulate discontent against authoritarian structures at work or at home. Rock 'n' roll – with its emphasis on physicality and its strong flavour of sexuality – clearly offended against the norms of female gracefulness and male chivalry. It did not fundamentally change traditional gender relations, though, because the man still asked the woman to dance, steered her and caught her after a somersault handspring, but its frank energy gave girls a chance to express their sexuality, at least in an indirect way, and a means of circumventing existing norms concerning masculinity and femininity.[59] Girls who declared themselves Presley fans also influenced young men's self-construction and so contributed to the formation of new ideals of masculinity.[60] Boys from the city, no matter whether trainee or student, favoured rock 'n' roll more than did youths from country regions, where generally tear-jerking German hit songs still had still a lot of fans among juveniles.[61] As regards the top-ranking hits, there was considerable unanimity right across the board. While in the United States Pat Boone led, followed by Perry Como and Elvis Presley, juveniles in Austria put Elvis Presley first, followed by the German singer Freddy Quinn and, in third place, Pat Boone.[62]

Grammar-school students could only occasionally be counted among the rock 'n' roll fans. They very often shared the opinion of their parents and teachers that rock 'n' roll was worthless noise. Allowable at best was an enthusiasm for jazz, which still stands out in its quality and virtuosity from the rock 'n' roll hullabaloo.[63] Boys who preferred classical music and jazz to the hit songs used the mass media very rarely and for different purposes compared to the hit song fans. They, rather, played instruments themselves and went to concerts.[64] In addition, the fans of classical music and jazz did not go to the cinema as often as did hit fans, and preferred social commentary, cultural and historical films, while hit fans watched detective and comedy films, westerns and sentimental films in regional settings.[65]

A further local characteristic of these years was the start of the motorisation of Austrian youth and the cult that accompanied this.[66] In Austria, trainees and young workers needed the moped to get to work or training school, but especially in their spare time. While for grammar-school students the moped was – for reasons of status – taboo as a cultural object as well as too expensive,[67] for young workers, who were especially constrained by the compulsions of the working day, the moped represented the freedom and independence they longed for, but did not have in reality. It also represented an important status symbol within their circle of friends.[68]

Teenagers

With the adoption of American mass culture in Austria, a new type of youth emerged under the label 'teenager'. The word itself appeared around the same time as phrases such as 'blue jeans' and 'Coca-Cola' and, like these phrases, it expressed a new attitude towards life. At first, only the female Elvis Presley fans were labelled as teenagers, but from 1957 young females in general started to be classified under this heading. Beginning slightly later, in 1959, male youths also began to be called teenagers.[69]

For the newly established teenage leisure market, which was originally oriented toward male demand, girls emerged as a new and attractive target group – especially young working girls who had money to spend. In this way, new youth cultures such as the teenage culture not only attested to new consumer preferences, but also mirrored the changing conditions of production and the labour market.[70]

The girls and boys in this new category differentiated themselves in clothing, hairstyle and behaviour. Female 'teenagers' were much interested in fashion, and enjoyed spending money on clothing, cosmetics, accessories, movie tickets and records. Information about new products and styles was provided primarily by the mass media.[71] The media also supplied images of the 'ideal female body', for which American actresses like Jayne Mansfield and Marilyn Monroe served as models which were sedulously imitated by many girls.[72] Through the mass media, young girls learned not only how to attain or keep the perfect body, but also how important it was to have a perfect appearance and, to that end, the right clothing and appropriate make-up. This all required money and a certain amount of self-discipline. The measure of the degree of perfection their appearance reached was, as before, the attention and recognition they received from men, which was indicative of their chances on the marriage market.[73]

The attractions of the American market also offered those girls who first took them up – and in the first instance this meant working-class girls – multiple opportunities to articulate their rebellion against authoritarian structures and the conventional expectations about clothing and respectability established by their parents and by society as a whole, and this made these attractions even more appealing. The American lifestyle furnished these girls with an alternative to the ascetic morality of self-denial and the traditional image of girlhood. Thus American mass culture undoubtedly offered girls the possibility of taking their first steps toward self-determination, even if this was an unintended consequence and operated only for a limited period.[74]

Hooligans

As already mentioned, American consumer culture also offered young people the chance to rebel against the conservative society of that time. Young workers, in particular, developed a special form of rebellion in the shape of street riots. These young workers were called 'hooligans' and viewed as conspicuous and provocative. According to contemporary reports, there were riots all over Europe, though of course they did not take on the same dimensions in all countries. In Switzerland and Italy, the phenomenon was scarcely noticeable. After a few insignificant riots in 1956, Austrian hooligan riots occurred only in the summer of 1957, with those in Vienna creating the greatest sensation.[75] These riots also point up another characteristic of those born around 1940 – namely, rebellion. In addition, they can be seen as precursors of a more general tendency toward violence in youth culture.[76]

Hooligans articulated their disaffection with society and their rejection of dominant societal values primarily through the adoption of American mass culture. They wore blue jeans, rode motorbikes and enthusiastically followed rock 'n' roll.[77] The actions of the hooligan gangs were defined by masculine norms of interaction, even though some of these gangs – albeit very few – included girls, most of whom participated only for a short period of time and not as members in their own right, but as the girlfriends of boy members. Nevertheless, solely by reason of the fact that they undertook activities in common with the boys, these girls called into question the dominant gender-specific norms. Female hooliganism offered girls a potential for rebellion in the context of a time when all forms of oppositional behaviour were discouraged and when society sent girls very clear signals about how to behave and conform.[78] To the parents of girls linked to gangs it was unacceptable that their daughters should ignore gender norms so blatantly.[79] Hence they often resorted to drastic measures in order to keep their daughters from joining gangs. Interviewees mentioned the imposition of curfews and not infrequently even beatings and other draconian measures such as hair-shearing.[80] Not all girls were intimidated by these repressive tactics, however. By contrast, boy gang members, although they rejected society and its values, accepted the established conventional moral standards for girls.

The divergent behaviour patterns of juveniles were mainly seen as an ethical and moral danger, and hooligans were almost universally criminalised by society and the mass media. In general, it was argued that the disturbing influences of the war on children born during that time – absent fathers, evacuation and other interruptions of normal family life, as well as omnipresent violence – and the experience of repressive education as soon as conditions had been consolidated, at the latest with the return of the fathers, taken together, were

190

responsible for the new 'juvenile delinquency' in the mid-1950s.[81]

The following excerpt from a 1956 issue of the Graz *Tagespost* is typical:

> Residents of Graz crowd in front of the Annenhof cinema. For the most part these are not the patrons who usually attend this movie theatre, seeking relaxation, looking to forget their everyday worries for a couple of hours. The people whom the film *Rififi* has been drawing to the box office for several days now find everyday life boring. They think it's necessary to seek unusual thrills; they want to see how people kill and are killed, how they commit the perfect crime. And the young boys who crowd the entrances want to experience this to the full; they all look as if they were eighteen, these fifteen- and sixteen-year olds. 'Rififi', a word which comes from the Parisian underworld, and is a technical term for 'pulling off a crooked plan and slaughtering people', attracts both boys and girls, whether in Paris, London, New York, Berlin, Vienna or Graz. *Rififi* is the 'proof' that criminals are heroes, that the gangsters have honour; the film sings the 'anthem' of gang solidarity, the 'law of honour' against the betrayer, and depicts also the gangster's moll, just as imagined by the little gangsters, the hooligans from [our] city on the Mur.
>
> These young people, whether in corduroy trousers, pullover and sports cap, or with teddy-boy hair-do and a cigarette hanging from their lips, have all found the idol of their fantasy in *Rififi*. These hooligans, who are already potential criminals today, lack the opportunity rather than the nerve to imitate their models. They can't crack safes in which millions lie waiting, because they lack the professional training necessary even for that. So they travel in packs, harass passers-by, rape, defile, and steal . . . Quivering with excitement, feeling in every muscle the horrible events depicted on the screen, they sit on the edge of their seats, the girls in their tight Lollobrigida sweaters, the boys in their narrow 'drain-pipe trousers'.[82]

In some ways, hooligans served as a kind of symbolic battlefield for the generational conflict over parental authority and juvenile autonomy, money and obedience.[83] Towards that which the commercial culture had to offer, hooligans behaved in a culture-affirming and opportunistic manner. They realised that it promised them a hedonistic way of life, and exploited it whenever possible. Much of what the hooligans had demonstrated in practice inspired further youth styles around the end of the 1950s and early 1960s: their aspirations as consumers, their hedonistic attitude of having fun while you are young, their habit of spending leisure time in the public sphere and at commercial locations such as cinemas, concerts, cafés and dance halls rather than in the intimate space of the family.[84]

Backlash

In Austria, there was a consensus that the new trends adopted from America – as apparent above all in comics and movies – were the main causes of various problems with young people:[85] 'Our youth is being flooded with trashy literature, by-products of which – comics – are designed to turn the thoughts, feelings and fantasies of our young people in the worst possible direction . . . We know that our youth are unusually strongly influenced by trashy American movies.'[86] Anxieties centred on the waywardness of youth and the displacement of national culture by gangsterism and kitsch from Hollywood. Crime and Wild West novels were suspected of leading young people into criminal ways, and the predominant reaction to the 'erotically charged image' of the new teenager 'in tight pedal-pushers, ponytail or short hair, polished nails and finely plucked eyebrows' as presented in American movies and magazines such as *Bravo* was sheer horror. Observers denounced the contamination of youth 'through striptease as a means of American propaganda' and indicted 'half-naked pin-ups' as a 'cunning form of sexual provocation' and as a 'moral danger'.[87] There was also anxiety lest this 'erotically provocative image' of young women should call into question the 'natural gender order'.[88] The new type of woman displayed in these media, embodied by curvaceous and provocative female 'sex-bombs' such as Marilyn Monroe and Brigitte Bardot, must absolutely not be allowed to become the model for Austrian girls and young women. They were supposed to model themselves after the 'young lady' or the 'innocent girl' type associated with Romy Schneider, but definitely not after the 'sex-bomb'.

In this connection, the emphasis on the body, and the transparently sexual aspects of rock 'n' roll, were also perceived as a provocation, and thus as clashing unmistakeably with the norms of female sweetness and male chivalry. Through rock 'n' roll, the conventional polarisation of roles was also called into question, though not because of what the dancing itself involved, since the man was still the one who initiated, led and directed the moves, but rather because it encouraged the girls to adopt aggressive, masculine behaviour.[89]

For the guardians of order and morality, precisely targeted responses were called for to combat these new trends.[90] The means by which the 'moral decadence' of the young in general, and of the hooligans in particular, was to be attacked 'from above' fell into two different categories. First, relevant legal measures were enacted in this era and, second, increased organisation of youth leisure time was introduced. The Styrian parliament, for example, passed a youth welfare law in 1957 which provided for voluntary youth workers. The activities of these voluntary workers not only included the inspection of homes maintained by the provincial authorities, but also assistance in special charitable and other welfare measures. Also in 1957, a law designed to ensure the protection of young people again immoral influences was enacted. This law included measures to protect minors under the age of eighteen against 'the dangers of the street, patronising bars and establishments, the use of alcohol and nicotine, and all harmful external influences including movies'.[91] Among other things, it prohibited juveniles under sixteen from attending public dances (this prohibition did not apply to juveniles between sixteen and eighteen accompanied by a parent); it also regulated the consumption of spirits by minors under eighteen, and the consumption of every kind of alcohol by juveniles under sixteen. Moreover, juveniles under sixteen were not allowed to smoke at all, whilst sixteen- to eighteen-year-olds were forbidden to smoke in public.[92]

That same year, several provinces raised the minimum age limit from sixteen to seventeen to protect juveniles against the harmful influence of unsuitable films. A film advisory board, consisting of five experts from the regional government and one representative each from the regional school board, the state police department, the Catholic church, the Lutheran church, the cinema owners, the agricultural chamber, the youth welfare bureau and others, was to decide which films could be seen by juveniles.[93]

The second measure in this war against 'filthy trash'[94] was the organisation of youth leisure. It involved different initiatives by a variety of institutions, interest groups and organisations such as the Church, political parties, schools, etc., which aimed to prevent young people becoming too influenced by commercial culture and the leisure industry, with the corresponding consequences, one of which was thought to be the hooligan movement. As a deputy to a provincial assembly declared in 1957:

> We have a duty, not just to hold young people accountable for misdemeanours, but also to provide them with opportunities for leisure-time activities in centres, clubs, and so on, so that the youth does not need to go and see banned films, so that he does not have to hang about in the streets, but instead can spend his leisure time usefully in specific organisations or facilities.[95]

To these initiatives belonged also sweeping campaigns to promote good literature which were organised in all fields by such protectors of youth interests as the '*Buchklub der Jugend*' (youth book club) as well as by newspapers and periodicals. The latter propagated books designed especially for adolescents which were insipid, glossy and far from realistic.

Parallel with the emergence of a new image of girls in the form of the female teenager, efforts were also made, right from the start, to minimise the oppositional and confrontational elements of the new style, as is, for example, illustrated by a campaign in the youth magazine *Bravo*, started in 1956, 'against the reprehensible erotic star image and advocating instead the modest home-loving and girlish teenage type who would rather wear skirts than blue jeans'.[96] In brochures for teens of this time, which specifically targeted young girls, prominence was given to the image of the ladylike teenager who retained control of her body and could behave according to civilised standards of conduct.[97] Efforts were made to disarm rock 'n' roll and to rob it of its expressiveness and lack of restraint. In a modified version, it was elevated to the status of an acceptable form of social dancing, and was taught in dance schools along with the foxtrot and the waltz. The American rebel films and songs were replaced by innocuous German films and hit songs sung by well adjusted, nice young stars such as Peter Kraus and Conny Froboess.[98]

The result of these developments was that by the end of the 1950s an autonomous, cross-class female teenage subculture had begun to establish itself, which was largely an 'indoor' culture. In other words, it was pursued largely at home, where girls would listen to music, read magazines and chat with friends. These activities were such as could 'readily be fitted into the traditionally defined cultural space of the home and organised through girls' culture embracing same-age groups'.[99] In this way, the teenager type became 'domesticated' in the course of the 1950s, so that the conventional picture of the future wife and mother – with its emphasis on the ladylike and feminine – was re-established. And the teenager could thus be seen as nothing more than a new version of the traditional image of girlhood, albeit in a somewhat more modern form, and one more appropriate to the altered social conditions.[100] In this form, the phenomenon of the 'teenager' eventually became acceptable to the majority. Compared to the male youth, where the class-specific differences in behaviour did not undergo major changes in the 1950s, it seems that (at least in some fields such as tastes in clothes, etc.) there was a cross-class approach by the female young, mainly involving girls from the middle and working class. The creation of a modern youth culture also served the interests of those industries engaged in the production of consumer commodities, which did not wish the merry-go-round of fashions and fads to come to a halt.[101] Nevertheless, it is in general the case that Austrian youth was still comparatively far from establishing a uniform youth culture.

Notes

1 Karin M. Schmidlechner, *Frauenleben in Männerwelten: Ein Beitrag zur Geschichte der steirischen Frauen in der Nachkriegszeit* (Vienna, 1997); Hanna Schissler (ed.), *The Miracle Years: A Cultural History of West Germany, 1949–1968* (Princeton, NJ, 2001).

2 Especially in regard to its favourite subject, the control of sexual morality, the Church held unbroken power and could control a large proportion of young people. Ernst Grissemann and Hans Veigl (eds), *Testbild, Twen und Nierentisch: Unser Lebensgefühl in den 50er Jahren* (Vienna, 2002); Hans Veigl, *Die 50er und 60er Jahre: Geplantes Glück zwischen Motorroller und Minirock* (Vienna, 1996), 36.

3 Ernst Hanisch, *Der lange Schatten des Staates* (Vienna, 1994), 247.

4 Edith Saurer, 'Schweißblätter. Gedankenfetzen zu Frauengeschichte in den fünfziger Jahren', in Gerhard Jagschitz and Klaus-Dieter Mulley (eds), *Die 'Wilden' fünfziger Jahre: Gesellschaft, Formen und Gefühle eines Jahrzehnts in Österreich* (St Pölten, 1985), 42.

5 Erika Thurner, 'Die stabile Innenseite der Politik: Geschlechterbeziehungen und Rollenverhalten', in Thomas Albrich, Klaus Eisterer, Michael Gehler and Rolf Steiniger (eds), *Österreich in den Fünfzigern* (Vienna, 1995), 53–66.

6 Films produced in Austria at this time provide a good illustration of this; 267 feature films were made in Austria between 1950 and 1960, the year of peak production was 1956, with 37 films. Christine Leinfellner, 'Silberwald, Sissi und Sexbomben', in Jagschitz and Mulley (eds), *Die 'Wilden' fünfziger Jahre*, 54. 40–50 per cent of films shown in Austria originated in the United States. Reinhold Wagnleitner, 'Die Kinder von Schmal(t)z und Coca Cola', in Jagschitz and Mulley (eds), *Die 'Wilden' fünfziger Jahre*, 148.

7 Saurer, 'Schweißblätter', 44.

8 Peter Huemer, 'Die Angst vor der Freiheit', in Jagschitz and Mulley (eds), *Die 'Wilden' fünfziger Jahre*, 210.

194

9 *Ibid.*

10 Pius Frank, *Führung durch die Reifejahre* (Linz, 1956), 68, cited in Huemer, 'Die Angst vor der Freiheit', in Jagschitz and Mulley (eds), *Die 'Wilden' fünfziger Jahre*, 212.

11 Huemer, 'Die Angst vor der Freiheit', 208.

12 This area of paternal responsibility continued to exist in the 1960s in Austria, with few exceptions.

13 Schmidlechner, *Frauenleben*, 255; Yvonne Schütze and Dieter Geulen, 'Die Nachkriegskinder und die Konsumkinder: Kindheitsverläufe zweier Generationen', in Ulf Preuss-Lausitz *et al.* (eds), *Kriegskinder, Konsumkinder, Krisenkinder: Zur Sozial-isationsgeschichte seit dem Zweiten Weltkrieg* (Weinheim, 1983), 29–58. The control exercised over girls, especially by authoritarian fathers, cut across classes, although there were differences in the means by which authority was exercised. In contrast to middle-class families, the pressure on daughters in working-class families was publicly and aggressively manifested.

14 Peter Kuhnert and Ute Ackermann, 'Jenseits von Lust und Liebe – Jugendsexualität in den 50er Jahren', in Heinz-Hermann Krüger (ed.), *Die Elvis-Tolle hatte ich mir unauffällig wachsen lassen* (Opladen, 1985).

15 Even when a mother had had children out of wedlock, this did not lead to greater leniency towards her daughters.

16 That this problem was relevant is revealed by the rate of out-of-wedlock births in Austria, which in the mid-1950s was about 20 per cent. *Neue Zeit* (5 June 1955).

17 Female sexuality was considered legitimate only within marriage.

18 Karin M. Schmidlechner, 'The construction of gender roles, gender relations, and political representation in Austria since 1945', in Katherine Isaacs (ed.), *Political Systems and Definitions of Gender Roles* (Pisa, 2001), 235–44. A man proved himself to be a 'suitable' husband by being able to support his family single-handedly. Many husbands therefore forbade their wives to work, although work for cash-in-hand, such as cleaning or ironing, was grudgingly tolerated. Oral reports.

19 Jos Perr and Helene Vossen, 'Old problems, new solutions: working class youth cul-ture and some efforts to change it, 1945–1955', in Lex Heerma van Voss and Frits van Holthoon (eds), *Working Class and Popular Culture* (Amsterdam, 1986), 213.

20 Perr and Vossen, 'Old problems', 214.

21 Oral reports.

22 Erica Carter, 'Alice in the consumer wonderland: West German case studies in gender and consumer culture', in Angela McRobbie and Mira Nava (eds), *Gender and Generations* (Basingstoke, 1984), 200.

23 Although, as mentioned above, this was not always the case.

24 Veigl, *Die 50er und 60er Jahre*, 36. In comparison with the inter-war period, the sit-uation for working girls had noticeably improved, not least because of their refusal to submit to gender-specific handicaps. Schmidlechner, *Frauenleben*, 199.

25 In comparison with the early twentieth century, when girls primarily from the upper and middle classes stormed these occupations, girls from the working class also now made their way into these jobs. Erna Appelt, *Von Ladenmädchen, Schreibfräulein, und Gouvernanten: Die weiblichen Angestellten Wiens zwischen 1900 und 1934* (Vienna, 1985). Between aspiration and realisation, however, there was a difficult path.

26 Leinfellner, 'Silberwald, Sissi und Sexbomben', 60.

27 *Neue Zeit* (4 July 1957).

28 Dorothea-Luise Scharmann, *Konsumentenverhalten von Jugendlichen* (Munich, 1965), 25.
29 In Styria, at the end of 1949, there were 659 vacancies for office jobs and 1,470 people looking for work (of whom 1,071 were female). In 1951, the percentage of female trainees in professional occupations in Styria stood at 1.5 per cent; 35 per cent of girls wanted to be seamstresses, 30 per cent saleswomen, and somewhat fewer hairdressers. Schmidlechner, *Frauenleben*, 198.
30 Klaus-Dieter Mulley, 'Wo ist das Proletariat? Überlegungen zu "Lebensstandard und Bewußtsein" in den fünfziger Jahren', in Jagschitz and Mulley (eds), *Die 'Wilden' fünfziger Jahre*, 22.
31 *Ibid.*
32 Bernd Riessland, 'Das "Wirtschaftswunder"', in Jagschitz and Mulley (eds), *Die 'Wilden' fünfziger Jahre*, 90.
33 Mulley, 'Wo ist das Proletariat?', 25.
34 Riessland, 'Das "Wirtschaftswunder"', 94.
35 Hanisch, *Der lange Schatten des Staates*, 440.
36 Roman Sandgruber, 'Vom Hunger zum Massenkonsum', in Jagschitz and Mulley (eds), *Die 'Wilden' fünfziger Jahre*, 118; Arnold Sywottek, 'From starvation to excess? Trends in the consumer society from the 1940s to the 1970s', in Schissler, *The Miracle Years*, 341–58.
37 The number of motorcycles increased by 204,000 (from 123,000 to 327,000).
38 Hanisch, *Der lange Schatten des Staates*, 440.
39 Without a doubt, this came very opportunely for American business interests, and was strongly driven by the relevant American institutions. Reinhold Wagnleitner, *Coca-Colonisation und Kalter Krieg: Die Kulturmission der USA in Österreich nach dem zweiten Weltkrieg* (Vienna, 1991). The situation in Austria was also heavily influenced by West Germany, which was always a few steps ahead in terms of development. Wagnleitner, 'Die Kinder von Schmal(t)z und Coca Cola', 154.
40 Kasper Maase, 'Establishing cultural democracy: Youth "Americanization" and the irresistible rise of popular culture', in Schissler, *The Miracle Years*, 428–50.
41 Thurner, 'Die stabile Innenseite der Politik', 60.
42 Even if the financial resources of Austrian youth were rather limited because of the low wage levels, youth disposed of more money in total, and also of more spare time, and became interesting to the market as a social group. In many cases, this development was inverted, in so far as the youths first had the new needs but not the necessary money and chose their professions mainly according to financial considerations. *Kleine Zeitung* (4 July 1957).
43 The cinema was also important as a venue that accommodated many patrons. This was the case only from the mid-1950s onwards, when adults did not supervise this spare-time occupation as intensively as previously. Jürgen Zinnecker, *Jugendkultur 1940–1985* (Opladen, 1986), 85.
44 *Ibid.*, 171.
45 *Ibid.*, 172.
46 Karin M. Schmidlechner, 'Jugendliches Protestverhalten in der Nachkriegszeit', in *Tagungsbeiträge zum 20. Historikertag* (Vienna, 1992).
47 Oral reports suggest that urban girls preferred American 'rebel' films, while girls from rural areas mostly wanted to see Austrian and West German films. Both groups enjoyed musicals.

48 Oral reports.
49 Leopold Rosenmayr, Eva Köckeis and Heinrich Kreutz, *Kulturelle Interessen von Jugendlichen: Eine soziologische Untersuchung an jungen Arbeitern und höheren Schülern* (Vienna, 1996), 174ff.
50 *Ibid.*, 175.
51 *Ibid.*, 177.
52 *Ibid.*, 176.
53 *Ibid.*, 178.
54 *Ibid.*, 258.
55 *Bravo*, founded in Austria in 1956, was first conceived as a magazine for adults. Kasper Maase, *Bravo, America* (Hamburg, 1992), 107.
56 The connection between the reading of these magazines and the frequency of cinema visits shows clearly how much films influenced interest in film-orientated magazines and how these magazines in turn encouraged further visits to the cinema. Rosenmayr, Köckeis and Kreutz, *Kulturelle Interessen von Jugendlichen*, 113.
57 Zinnecker, *Jugendkultur*, 87.
58 In 1959, 38 per cent of trainees and 40 per cent of grammar-school students in Vienna owned a portable radio. 39 per cent of trainees and 42 per cent of grammar-school students wanted to have one. 14 per cent of trainees and 25 per cent of grammar-school students owned a record player. 6 per cent of trainees and 11 per cent of grammar-school students had a tape recorder of their own. Rosenmayr, Köckeis and Kreutz, *Kulturelle Interessen von Jugendlichen*, 171. Just under half of grammar-school students and a little less than one-third of trainees owned records, juveniles who had close relationships with girls being more likely to own records than the rest. *Ibid.*, 194. In West Germany only about one-third of fifteen- to twenty-four-year-old youths did not own a record player or a tape recorder in 1953. Zinnecker, *Jugendkultur*, 88.
59 Christine Bartram and Heinz-Hermann Krüger, 'Vom Backfisch zum Teenager – Mädchensozialisation in den 50er Jahren', in Krüger (ed.), *Die Elvis-Tolle*, 95. Uta G. Poiger, *Jazz, Rock, and Rebels: Cold War Politics and American Culture in a Divided Germany* (Berkeley, CA, 2000), 180.
60 Maase, *Bravo, America*, 132.
61 Veronika Ratzenböck, 'Expeditionen in eine exotische Heimat', in Jagschitz and Mulley (eds), *Die 'Wilden' fünfziger Jahre*, 264–72. Rosenmayr, Köckeis and Kreutz, *Kulturelle Interessen von Jugendlichen*, 209.
62 *Ibid.*, 346.
63 Kasper Maase, 'Antiamerikanismus ist lächerlich, vor allem aber dumm. Über Gramsci, Amerikanisierung von unten und kulturelle Hegemonie', in Johanna Borek, Birge Krondorfer and Julius Mende (eds), *Kulturen des Widerstands: Texte zu Antonio Gramsci* (Vienna, 1993), 20.
64 Rosenmayr, Köckeis and Kreutz, *Kulturelle Interessen von Jugendlichen*, 220.
65 *Ibid.*
66 Even for Austrian adults, the main means of transport in the 1950s were the motorbike and the moped. In 1954 1 in 60 in Vienna, 1 in 48 in Linz, 1 in 47 in Innsbruck, 1 in 38 in Salzburg, 1 in 37 in Graz, 1 in 34 in Klagenfurt and Bregenz and 1 in 22 in Feldkirche owned a motorbike. Motorbikes were most common in Dornbirn, Feldkirch and Lustenau. *Frau* (20 June 1954). Only in the second half of the 1950s had living standards risen to the point where – decades after the United States – car

ownership was affordable. Paul Willis, *Learning to Labour: How Working-Class Kids Get Working-Class Jobs* (London, 1978).

67 A study of the aspirations of trainees showed that they wished to own a moped more often than grammar-school students. At 53 per cent, this aspiration stood in third place with trainees, while it took only eleventh place with grammar-school students (22 per cent). Rosenmayr, Köckeis and Kreutz, *Kulturelle Interessen von Jugendlichen*, 89.

68 H.Schimetzke, *Der jugendliche Motorradfahrer* (Munich, PhD thesis, 1958).

69 Poiger, *Jazz, Rock, and Rebels*, 191.

70 Zinnecker, *Jugendkultur*, 83. Simon Frith, *Jugendkultur und Rockmusik* (Reinbek, 1981), 226.

71 This can be clearly seen in the increased production of socks made from synthetic materials (nylon, perlon), which doubled within one year. *Arbeiter-Zeitung* (5 September, 1957).

72 Joan Jacobs Bumberg, *The Body Project: An Intimate History of American Girls* (New York, 1998).

73 Erica Carter, *How German is She? Post-war German Reconstruction and the Consuming Woman* (Ann Arbor, 1997); Victoria de Garcia and Ellen Furlough, *The Sex of Things: Gender and Consumption in Historical Perspective* (Berkeley, CA, 1996); Carter, 'Alice in the consumer wonderland', 205.

74 This would be reversed at the latest with marriage.

75 The proportion of male hooligans in the general population of young people was 1–2 per cent. Curt Bondy *et al.*, *Jugendliche stören die Ordnung* (Munich, 1957), 52–5.

76 There were hooligans throughout Europe. Zinnecker, *Jugendkultur*, 19. In Austria, their predecessors can be found in the 'Schlurfs' of the Nazi period. Here, 'hooligan' applies to male, working-class youths who adopted American styles. Christian Gerbel *et al.*, 'Die "Schlurfs": Verweigerung und Opposition von Wiener Arbeiterjugendlichen im Dritten Reich', in Emmerich Tálos *et al.* (eds), *NS-Herrschaft in Österreich 1938–1945* (Vienna, 1988), 243–68.

77 Maase, 'Establishing cultural democracy', 428–50.

78 These included readiness for physical confrontations.

79 Poiger, *Jazz, Rock, and Rebels*, 179.

80 Oral report.

81 Schmidlechner, 'Jugendliches Protestverhalten in der Nachkriegszeit'.

82 *Tagespost* (4 April 1956).

83 Maase, 'Establishing cultural democracy', 428–50.

84 *Ibid.*

85 There is a suggestion here of the not insignificant anti-American sentiment concealed in Austrian society. Thurner, 'Die stabile Innenseite der Politik', 60.

86 Tito Pölzl, Stenographic report of the Styrian state parliament, Period III, 37th session, 19–29 December 1955, 846ff. This hostility to Americanisation on the part of a Styrian elected official may be considered atypical, as the official position on these issues was generally more reserved.

87 Maase, 'Antiamerikanismus ist lächerlich, vor allem aber dumm', 27.

88 Bartram and Krüger, 'Vom Backfisch zum Teenager', 94.

89 Poiger, *Jazz, Rock, and Rebels*, 179.

90 This even went so far that the Catholic youth went out on to the streets to protest against this 'filthy trash'. Veigl, *Die 50er und 60er Jahre*, 36.

91 Stenographic reports of the Styrian state parliament, Period IV, 12th session, 4 December 1957, 100.

92 Karin M. Schmidlechner, 'Youth culture in the 1950s', in Günter Bischof, Anton Pelinka and Rolf Steininger (eds), *Austria in the Nineteen-Fifties, Contemporary Austrian Studies* 3 (New Brunswick, NJ, 1995), 125.

93 Stenographic reports of the Styrian state parliament, Period IV, 14th session, 18 and 19 December 1957, 118.

94 For example, the Austrian book club for youth, which advertised 'good, decent books'. Veigl, *Die 50er und 60er Jahre*, 36.

95 Stenographic reports of the Styrian state parliament, Period IV, 12th session, 4 December 1957, 103.

96 Bartram and Krüger, 'Vom Backfisch zum Teenager', 94.

97 *Ibid.*

98 Maase, *Bravo, America*, 168.

99 Angela Robbie and Jennie Garber, 'Mädchen in den Subkulturen', in John Clark (ed.), *Jugendkultur als Widerstand* (Frankfurt/Main, 1981), 224.

100 The difference between this new model of the teenager and the traditional model of girlhood of the immediate post-war period in Austria lies principally in a different attitude towards girls' employment.

101 In contrast to earlier years, it was seen as legitimate for young women to prolong their time in the workforce before getting married. In fact, this option was realistic only for middle-class girls who, because of their better education, had access to more interesting professions, providing them with an attractive alternative to an early marriage.

12

Sokol and the Communists: the battle for Czech youth, 1945–48

Mark Dimond

The Communist Party failed to win the hearts and minds of Czech youth between 1945 and 1948, despite the fact that it won over much of the rest of Czech society. Indeed, the Communist take-over of Czechoslovakia between 1945 and 1948 has often been seen as the textbook take-over, or, as one historian noted, the 'elegant' take-over.[1] Although some Czechs suspected that the Communists were bent on achieving power by unscrupulous means after Stalin forced the Communist Party leader, Klement Gottwald, to recant his acceptance of the Marshall Plan in July 1947, the Communist coup of February 1948 still came as a shock to most Czechs. Yet many young Czechs had their suspicions about the Communist Party's intentions in 1945. In demonstration against its rising power, many of them soon deserted the communist-inspired youth movement, the *Svaz české mládeže* (Czech Youth Organisation – SČM) and joined the Sokol gymnastics and athletics movement instead.

Sokol was not just a gymnastic outfit; it was also a guardian of national identity. From its establishment in 1862 Sokol trained its members on the basis of the Roman proverb, *mens sana in corpore sano* (a sound mind in a sound body). Collective spiritual and physical discipline would form the foundation of a national identity, which the Czechs felt they were lacking. The ultimate aim was nationhood itself, for before 1918 Czech politicians struggled to win concessions on the question of autonomy from their Habsburg rulers in Vienna. Sokol reaped the benefits of its discipline in 1918 when Czechoslovakia was established: the organisation acted as gendarme during the transfer of power from Vienna to Prague. Sokol became a kind of presidential tool of last resort, for in 1926 President Masaryk considered using Sokol to combat the Gajda fascist threat. Sokol's contribution to nation-building was most notable at the Sokol gymnastics festival (*slet*) of 1938 when the Nazi threat loomed ominously over central Europe. The two-week *slet*, which had traditionally taken place every six years and had been, in more modern times, attended by as many as 300,000 spectators, was festooned with defiant national imagery. The theme of 1938 was 'Build and Defend' (*Budovat a bránit*) in reference to the inviolability of Czechoslovak borders. The moral uplift generated by the *slet* gave Czechs hope in the dark days of the ensuing Nazi occupation. Despite the Nazi clampdown on Sokol, the movement still worked alongside Czech resistance groups during the Second World War, helping, *inter alia*, to support the logistical operations behind the assassination of Reinhard Heydrich, the acting *Reichsprotektor* of Bohemia and Moravia. Having survived the war, Sokol reached its height of popularity on the eve of the 1948 coup, gaining over a million members, half of whom were under eighteen years of age. The scheduled *slet* of June–July 1948 was not cancelled, lest the Communists might face a national backlash at their seizure of power. The *slet* was still marked by a series of anti-Communist protests, many of which were engineered by young Sokol members. Despite the disturbances, the Communists regained control of Sokol, arresting over 11,000 members in the process.[2] In all, Sokol acted as a national unifier during times of political adversity.

In 1945 the Communist Party had also presented itself as a national unifier in the name of anti-fascism. From this perspective, the Communist failure to gain the allegiance of young people was remarkable, and all the more so given that in 1945 the Communists put a priority on winning them over. What is more, the Communist Party was, for a number of reasons, in an advantageous position to do this. Firstly, as Lenin once declared: 'We are the party of innovators, and innovations are always followed more willingly by youth.'[3] Socialism, the new international *Leitmotif* that followed the fall of Nazism, would be more likely to capture the imagination of the younger generation. Secondly, as the historian Zdeněk Mlynář recalled, the 'children of war', who had not actually fought against the Nazis during the occupation, had been deeply affected by it and now wished to channel their anger into building a new ideological vision.[4] Thirdly, Josef Hromádka, a contemporary Christian evangelical writer, wrote that youth was the only social sector that would rid society of the 'cynicism, apathy and lack of principles' that had characterised the First Republic of Czechoslovakia, because it was the least tainted of all generations and it had fresh ideas.[5] He believed the Communists would lead a campaign of de-fascisation of Czech society.[6]

The failure to win over young people is significant – in terms of 'high politics' – because it was one factor that impacted on Gottwald's decision in late 1947 to abandon an evolutionary path to power through parliamentary means and to resort to a coup d'état. An alternative explanation for this decision is that Stalin had, in any case, forced Gottwald to take more radical measures after the Marshall Plan débâcle. Later, at the Cominform conference in September 1947, Czechoslovakia was singled out by other east European Communists as being lackadaisical in bringing about a new Communist order. As late as the autumn of 1947, Gottwald, however, believed that the Communist Party was succeeding in Czechoslovakia, and that it would gain over 50 per cent of the vote in the parliamentary elections scheduled for the summer of

1948.[7] Moreover, youth had become a crucial target in the Communists' electoral strategy, for, under the Košice Programme of April 1945,[8] the franchise had been widened to include anyone above the age of eighteen, in accordance with a proposal originally made by the Communists. The number of votes to be gained from the eighteen- to twenty-five-year-olds, whom the Communists considered as constituting the upper end of the youth bracket, was large. To be precise, 2 million new young voters had been added to the national electoral register since the elections of 1935.[9] This equated to about 20 per cent of the total Czechoslovak population, or 13 per cent of the total population of the Czech Lands. In psephological terms, this was roughly 30 per cent of the total voting population. The support of youth was therefore crucial for the Communists, particularly because they had no idea how successful they would be in the May 1946 elections; they had never managed to acquire a significant electoral allegiance beyond some workers and disenchanted Sudeten Germans and Hungarians.

The Communists decided to target young people in the first days after liberation by establishing the SČM which, under the banner of anti-fascism, was designed to unite the nation's youth. Although the organisation appeared to have been formed spontaneously by some home-grown Communists in early 1945, there is strong evidence to suggest that Moscow-trained Communists helped to expand it from the beginning.[10]

Believing that the Czechs held the Russians in veneration, the Communists had no qualms about using Russian in the banner headlines of the SČM's new mouthpiece, *Mladá fronta*. One banner read, in cyrillic: '*etot kto s nami po zhizni shchagaet – etot nikogda i nigde ne propadet*' ('Whoever walks with us through life will never and nowhere go astray').[11] This approach was highly successful: the first edition of *Mladá fronta*, issued on 9 May 1945, sold 125,000 copies, which was possible only because of the Red Army's generosity with supplies of paper. Within a few days, the SČM had attracted 600,000 members, corresponding to roughly 6 per cent of the population of the Czech Lands. Other socialist parties, including the Social Democrats and the Czech Socialists,[12] endorsed the organisation on 7 June 1945. The SČM was therefore able to attract broad support.

However, once the euphoria of liberation receded, the Czech Communists attempted in September 1945 to consolidate their grip on youth by forcing the SČM and the scouting organisation, the Junák, to fuse. The repercussions of this were twofold. Firstly, many Junák members started to leave,[13] and its membership fell from 144,922 in 1945 to 99,176 in 1948.[14] In the medium term, the SČM–Junák merger aroused suspicions among other political parties that the Communists were not respecting the democratic rights of social organisations, as stipulated in the Košice Programme. Before long, the SČM encountered further difficulties: Czech Socialist Party youth members left it *en masse* on 7 May 1946, following allegations that the Communist Party had packed the SČM executive with sympathisers.[15] The SČM executive was accused of 'swapping two Czech Socialists for two Communists'.[16] The Communists managed to conceal their political intentions by ensuring that the appointed representatives from the twelve SČM regions did not have party labels; J. Čech, a member of the SČM executive who was a Communist sympathiser, wrote that those elected were from the Junák and the student trade union, the *Svaz vysokoškolského studentstva* (SVS), not from named political parties. But, as the Communists had large influence within the both these youth organisations, they were in a strong position to vet appointments to the SČM executive.

The Czech Socialists launched their first major anti-Communist propaganda campaign in the newspaper *Svobodné slovo*. A Czech Socialist Party rally of 80,000 youths, which took place on 12 May 1946, just days before the national elections, dwarfed a parallel effort made on the same day by the SČM.[17] The Communists had thus lost their battle for a united youth movement as early as May 1946, despite the fact that a year earlier they had managed to bring together 30 per cent of the fifteen- to twenty-five age-group.[18] Communist tactics played into the hands of the other parties; the Czech Socialist Party and the People's Party were now willing to forge links between their respective youth organisations, something they had not previously sought to do.[19] By the summer of 1946, the fate of the SČM was sealed, and membership plummeted from 600,000 at its peak in 1945 to 289,000 by early 1948.[20]

The Communists had believed that the SČM would work closely with other youth organisations, particularly the SVS and the Sokol gymnastics organisation, the latter of which had a youth section. But the failure of the SČM had a direct impact on the ability of the Communists to attract other sectors of youth. Those students who had initially flocked to the SČM in 1945 had at that time signed up to the Communist Party vision. This was unsurprising as Czech students had been deeply anti-fascist; they had, for example, initiated the first clashes with the Gestapo around Prague's Charles University as early as November 1939, with the result that Czech universities were shut down for the duration of the war. Many students were full of pent-up anger in May 1945. Some packed themselves on to trains marked with hammers and sickles to join labour brigades in places like Most in the industrial north-east of the Czech Lands.[21] Some stood in the streets carrying banners proclaiming 'students are with the Communists'.[22] Others joined community committees whose task was to purge the university establishment of war-time traitors.[23] These actions were reflected in the appointment of the Communist sympathiser, Jan Kazimour, as leader of the newly established *Studentský narodní výbor* (Students' National Council) (SNV) in May 1945 (renamed SVS in June 1945).[24]

The Communist Party was already in a good position to woo the students, having successfully gained control of the Ministry of Education in all-party negotiations which took place in Moscow in March 1945, before Czechoslovakia had been liberated. The main reason why the Communists wanted to secure the post of Minister of Education was to ensure that they could determine the ideological contents of textbooks. The Communists were thus able to implement educational policies that would help the position of students who, in theory, would reciprocate by supporting the Communist Party.

In practice, however, the new Communist Minister for Education, Zdeněk Nejedlý, faced an uphill struggle. The massive intake of 45,000 students into establishments of higher education in 1945,[25] almost double the intake in 1938, put a severe strain on teaching resources, and was caused by the backlog of students that had accumulated during the war when, as has been seen, the Nazis had closed down all establishments of higher education.

Students quickly became disenchanted. One major problem was the lack of teaching space arising from wartime damage to lecture halls; lectures were often held in Prague's Lucerna cinema or even at the Letná circus.[26] The total damage to university property during the war was estimated at 300 million crowns based on 1938 currency value,[27] and money for rebuilding was in short supply. These conditions led to student protests, the first of which was staged by law students on 19 July 1945.[28] This was followed by a protest staged by science students on 11 December 1945 about the lack of textbooks.

However, the Communists were less concerned with student welfare than the creation of an all-encompassing youth body under their control. The Communists had already encouraged students to accept the SČM, for example by promoting student representation on the SČM executive. But it was the Communists' idea of a joint trade union body linking the SVS, the SČM and the workers's union (*Revoluční odborové hnutí* – ROH) under an umbrella organisation called the *Ústřední rada odborů* (ÚRO), or the Central Council of Unions, that irked many students.[29] In October 1945 the SVS decided that it wanted to become a 'political-cultural' body rather than a trade union movement, thereby deviating from Communist policy. While some students wished to become involved in the industrial reconstruction of Czechoslovakia by becoming student workers, most preferred to pursue their true objective, namely, a higher level of education. In any case, many of these students could not understand the logic of 'collectivising' the student body in a large trade union structure, when professions such as engineering, the law, medicine and architecture were not part of the ROH.[30] But the pivotal event that made the SVS move away from supporting the Communists was the revelation that the latter had packed the SČM with their own sympathisers. As a direct result of this, the Socialist sympathiser Jan Zajíček replaced the Communist Kazimour at the student congress of 8 April 1946. Not long after this, the Communist Party, despite its resounding success in the May 1946 elections, surrendered control of the Ministry of Education to the Czech Socialists. Its main priority was now to build the Two-Year Plan, and so, in a strategic move, the Ministry of Education was sacrificed in exchange for control of the Ministry of Domestic Trade. Handling students had proven to be too difficult, and a continued rift with them would have been a political thorn in the side of the Communists, especially as the students were particularly good at publicising their views. The decision to abandon the Ministry of Education was a signal that the Communists had compromised on their original vision for Czech youth.

By 1947 the collapse of student support for the Communists had become clear. In the November 1947 student elections, 74 per cent of those elected were democrats and only 20 per cent were Communists.[31] According to Josef Korbel, this election reflected the genuine mood of the nation,[32] a psephological indication that the Communists were losing public support. This mood was the result of a concatenation of Communist Party tactical gaffes during the autumn of 1947, such as the attempted murder by parcel bomb of the senior politicians Jan Masaryk and Prokop Drtina. Such tactics had been employed after the Czech Communist Party was forced by Stalin in the wake of the Marshall Plan débâcle to take radical steps in order to secure a monopoly of power. According to Paul Zinner, however, the anti-Communist mood was attributable to the disparaging remarks about 'Czech culture' made by Václav Kopecký, the Communist Minister of Information,[33] concerning the election of the new democratic-minded rector of Charles University, Karel Engliš. On 12 December 1947, Kopecký made a public statement to the effect that the six hundredth anniversary of the founding of the Charles University, which was to occur the following year, 'will be taking place based under false pretences'.[34] The students believed the very cornerstone of Czech culture – intellectual culture – was being threatened.

Just as the Communists failed to attract many students to their cause, they were also unable to lure Sokol. Sokol also benefited from the Communist decision to merge the SČM and the Junák, for this merger had directly disrupted talks taking place in the summer of 1945 between Zdeněk Nejedlý, the Communist Minister of Education, and the sports and gymnastics organisations. The aim of the talks was to create a state-run gymnastics movement but, fearing that they, like the Junák, would fall prey to the Communist Party, many organisations pulled out of the negotiations. Sokol withdrew in December 1945 and managed to remain an independent body.

Sokol was particularly important to the Communists because it had a massive youth section. The youth, or *dorost*, section was a key part of the organisation, one of the three levels of membership, the other two being *žactvo* (pupils) and *členstvo* (full membership). Anyone under fourteen could join the *žactvo* section, anyone between fourteen and eighteen was eligible for the *dorost* section and all other adults could join the *členstvo* section. Roughly 119,000 young people were members of Sokol in 1937, and as many as 24,000 male youth members and 33,000 female members took part in the 1938 *slet*.[35] Sokol membership amounted to over 1 per cent of the total population of the Czech Lands, and around 20 per cent of the total fourteen–eighteen age group. It therefore formed a significant proportion of a future electorate. By extrapolation, it can be seen that the young gymnasts of 1938 would have been twenty-one–twenty-seven in 1945, and therefore most of them would still, after 1945, fall within the youth age-bracket as defined by the SČM, which was fourteen–twenty-eight. But many young Czechs had been imbued with pre-war Sokol values, and would therefore not readily be attracted to the SČM, for reasons of both nostalgia and loyalty. Just as significantly, during the inter-war period there was an increase in Sokol membership at the *žactvo* level, which consisted of six- to fourteen-year-olds. This section grew from 155,522 members in 1920 to 288,174 in 1937, and its members would have been between fourteen and twenty-two in 1945. Most of them renewed their membership of Sokol, in either the youth section or in the adult section. The advantage of Sokol's three-tiered system of *žactvo*, *dorost* and *členstvo* was that it allowed a seamless development from tots to teens to adults, something that the Communists found impossible to replicate quickly. As a result, in late 1945 the Communists fused the SČM and the Junák so that they could start Communist indoctrination at a younger age.

Those who had joined Sokol before the war did, on the whole, remain members after 1945. The evidence suggests that the biggest growth in membership after 1945 was in the *dorost* and *žactvo* sections. At the end of 1945, there were 73,270 youth members; by December 1947 there were 132,430.[36] During the same period, the *žactvo's* numbers increased from 179,343 to 303,340.[37] One conclusion we might draw is that the growth in both these categories was due to the increasing political tensions in the latter part of 1947, a period of political polarisation during which many Czech parents may have urged their children to consider joining Sokol in the face of the rising tide of Communist power. Yet statistics show that there was a steady increase between 1945 and 1947, not a sudden jump between July and December 1947. For example, the boys' membership of the *dorost* section increased from 32,533 in December 1945 to 47,926 in November 1946, and then to 56,660 in December 1947. If anything, there was a bigger jump in the numbers in 1946 than in 1947. Much has also been made of the link between Sokol and the Czech Socialist Party to explain why Sokol's membership grew so quickly after 1945. But the Czech Socialist Party benefited in membership terms only after the Marshall Plan episode, while Sokol was already growing steadily before this. This would suggest that the choices made by Sokol youths were not linked to political allegiances but had more to do with apolitical considerations. Many youths were attracted to Sokol because of its non-partisan philosophy.

Many *Junáci*, or boy scouts, who left the SČM in 1946 and 1947 joined Sokol. The number of *Junáci* declined from 177,589 in 1946 to 135,819 in 1947.[38] The minutes of a Sokol male youth committee meeting of early 1946 suggest that the merger of the SČM and the Junák in September 1945 directly helped Sokol's cause: 'We have brought to your attention the fact that in September and October a large wave of [Junák] youths entered our local branches, which is a more favourable development . . .; it's therefore important that these new boys stay with us and gain something from us. They must enjoy being with us, they must occupy their time with us according to their particular interests.'[39] This was the second time that Sokol had benefited from an influx of Junák members. The term 'Sokolský Junák' had already been coined for those who had joined Sokol when Junák was split up soon after the Nazi takeover of

Bohemia and Moravia in 1939. As it was, the Nazis disbanded Sokol soon after, in 1941.[40] The main reason why the ex-*Junáci* joined the Sokol was because the differences between the two organisations were small. The Junák had been established in 1918 in the spirit of Miroslav Tyrš, the original founding father of Sokol. Both organisations were geared towards introducing their respective members to rural life, or *příroda*, and Sokol put as much emphasis on non-gymnastic activities as gymnastic ones in its youth programme. Those *Junáci* who left the SČM after 1945 therefore had little alternative but to join Sokol if they were still interested in organised camping trips.

The Czech Communists obviously made some early tactical mistakes, but there was an underlying problem with their whole strategy for winning over young people. Firstly, they had absorbed the wrong lessons from the Soviet model. Most of the higher echelons of the Czech Communist Party had spent the war years in Moscow, and had learnt a great deal about the role of the Soviet youth organisation, the Komsomol. However, their observations were based on a mistaken analysis of the history of Soviet youth. Lenin had underlined the importance of youth in helping to sustain the Communist regime, and in 1918 it looked as though young people would be treated well: the Bolsheviks proposed a maximum six-hour working day, free education and paid vacations for minors.[41] Such bright prospects helped the Komsomol to increase its membership from 22,000 in October 1918 to over 400,000 in October 1920.[42] Moreover, the Soviet authorities were also aware of the dangers of over-politicising the young too early on in the new Communist era. Indeed, it was Lenin's wife, Nadezhda Krupskaya, who suggested that youth movements could become mass movements only if they were independent (samostoiatel'ny) – that is autonomous within the Communist political set-up. She wrote that 'inculcating discipline' was important, but that it should be done 'without eliminating initiative'.[43] Lenin agreed. One Komsomol delegate suggested that young people had developed 'a hatred towards adult organisations in general'.[44] The Komsomol was initially autonomous; rather than ruling the Komsomol, the Party Secretariat merely planned to patronise it.[45] Lenin, in this respect, did well to identify the attitudes of youth; he understood that the youth often distanced itself from adulthood, engaging in a generational conflict as opposed to a 'class' struggle.

It was only after the Civil War, the consequent radicalisation of Bolshevik policy and the death of Lenin in 1924, that the Komsomol lost its 'freedom of action'.[46] Six of the seven Komsomol leaders in the period 1918–28 were executed by the *Narodnyi Kommissariat* (People's Commissariat for Interior Affairs – NKVD).[47] Stalin appointed party nominees to the leadership of the Komsomol but, each time he felt that the Komsomol was diverging from his political line, the leadership was replaced.

From 1926 onwards, the Komsomol was the only legal youth organisation in the USSR. By 1936, its ranks comprised 15 per cent of the total youth population, and this figure reached 20 per cent after the Second World War.[48] The

Komsomol had also become highly politicised. It played, for example, a key role in the introduction of the *kolkhoz* (collective farm) into the Soviet countryside and led the campaign to educate village folk about Communist doctrine. By the start of the Second World War, it had become involved in Stalin's new Factory-and-Plant training schools, and many members volunteered for the Labour Reserves. But Stalin measured the success of this movement primarily by its growth in membership. This is why the Komsomol stretched the age-range of youth to the point of absurdity. Rather than taking the age of eighteen as its upper limit, membership was widened to include young males and females from the ages of fourteen to twenty-six, a vast segment of the population that bracketed pubescents together with young adults.[49] What is more, the age qualifications changed frequently. In 1942, for instance, the minimum age of entry was lowered to make up for the shortfall in membership.[50] The Soviet experience suggests that for Stalin the concept of 'youth' could be defined arbitrarily to produce the numbers required.[51] In October 1943, the twenty-fifth anniversary of the founding of the Komsomol was celebrated, and Gottwald and the other Moscow-trained Czech Communists would have been well aware of the publicity surrounding the anniversary.

The Czech Communists seem to have been overawed by the razzmatazz surrounding Soviet youth and tried to impose this model on Czechoslovakia. However, the political circumstances prevailing in the Soviet Union were entirely different from those in Czechoslovakia. Czech youth movements had developed in a democratic system. A state-run youth organisation was incompatible with the democratic ideal, which many Czechs after 1945 still held dear. Moreover, Czech Communists were also pursuing a dangerous strategy because the youths had already been dragooned into a kind of Nazi *Hitlerjugend*, in the form of the Curatorium for the Education of Youth in Bohemia and Moravia (*Kuratoria pro výchovu mládeže v Čechách a na Moravě*),[52] and were therefore hardly likely to accept another form of *Diktat*.

But the greatest mistake the Communists made was in underestimating the strength of Czechoslovakia's own youth traditions. In inter-war Czechoslovakia, youth movements had not been run on a centralised political basis, as was the case in the Soviet Union. Czech youth movements were fragmented, with some affiliated to political parties and others acting independently. For instance, Orel was a Catholic youth athletic body linked to the Czech People's Party, which had particular appeal in rural areas, especially in Moravia. Its membership had increased from 12,000 in 1914 to 92,736 in 1921.[53] By 1948, despite the disruption of the war, this had risen to approximately 150,000.[54] The Czech Socialist Party also had its own youth section, which continued to operate after 1945. Sokol and the Junák both had non-partisan youth sections. The latter, which had been established in 1918, still had as many as 144,922 members in 1945.[55] Sport in general continued to be extremely popular among youth after the war, and 2 million people had joined sports organisations by 1947.[56] There had never been one overriding Czech 'youth movement' in the Soviet sense.

Nevertheless, the purpose of the SČM was to unite young people politically. It laid out its vision on 22 June 1945, the main aims of which were: 'to adapt the relationship of the SČM to the organs of the "People's Democracy"'; 'to ensure the influence of youth on, and representation in, the National Committees and the Provisional National Assembly, as well as other central institutions'; 'to look after the political and ideological education of activists and members'; 'to take advantage of all opportunities, especially the press and radio, for the distribution of information on the principles and work of the SČM'; 'to deepen and to define relations with the Slovak youth organisations, and to build a truly united Czechoslovak programme'; and 'as an immediate and main goal . . . [to concentrate] all efforts on competition to help in the collection of the harvest'.[57] All these aims were linked to 'high politics', whether they concerned building links with political institutions or helping in the reconstruction of Czechoslovakia.

The slogans of the SČM in this period also reflected these political tasks. They included: 'Against the Enemies of the Republic!', 'For the Fulfilment of the Two-Year Plan!', 'After Good Work, Leisure and Relaxation!', and 'For the Socialist Enlightenment of Youth!'.[58] SČM flags were intermingled with trade union banners.[59] Images of the SČM also reflected the political tasks involved. One SČM pamphlet contained graphs of industrial development, demonstrating the need to increase the production of, for example, coal and electricity.[60] In another pamphlet there were images of young men bearing axes and women holding financial reports under their arms; another picture showed men with scythes, and women with bundles of hay.[61] These images were intended to motivate young Czechs in their efforts to fulfil Czechoslovakia's first production plan, the Two-Year Plan, which was rolled out in January 1947. Amongst other things, SČM youths were organised into volunteer brigades, whose task was, for example, to construct houses under the mass housing programme, since there was a shortage of labour in this sector.[62] In order to bring some light-hearted aspects to these serious types of duties, SČM members were invited to think creatively, as in the case of singing competitions held in factories; the lyrics were the creative part, as this verse demonstrated: 'Something will happen that exists nowhere else/Singing factories/Factories which not only compete in work, in productivity and especially in attendance, but also in singing/You know that somewhere I've read that the machinery will be singing too.'[63] Such were the lengths the Communists went to in romanticising the otherwise drab task of increasing industrial production.

So what motivated some young people to join the SČM? Firstly, joining was easy. It was only necessary to bring along five Czech crowns to the nearest branch, and then the new member would enter, with few questions asked, the SČM's so-called 'card index'.[64] Like many Czechs who joined the Communist Party, some joined the SČM in order to enhance their chances of employment. The Communists had control of the key ministries devoted to the economy, including both internal trade and agriculture, sectors that offered large scope for work. Others simply viewed reconstruction as a 'national' duty, overriding any private commitment. This was especially the case when many politicians and academics – Communists and non-Communists alike – were demanding that young people should help in the reconstruction of Czechoslovakia because they had 'considerable energy'.[65] One commentator, supposedly paraphrasing former President Tomáš Masaryk, argued that 'it is necessary to make use of the natural radicalism of youth as a social force behind the political life of the nation'.[66] But the Communists' chief mistake was to make the SČM a political force, which served the needs of a particular party.

Sokol, on the other hand, was a social force, and non-partisan in outlook. Its activities served the development of youth for the sake of youth, not for the sake of politics. Sokol surveys in the late 1920s had already found that sporting activities were more likely than any other to attract young people. Two of the post-war objectives set out in January 1946 included the organisation of the eleventh *slet* in 1948 and preparation for the London Olympic Games in the same year, both of which attracted the attention of young people in 1946 and 1947. Through its vast network of gymnastic halls, athletic fields and mountain retreats,[67] Sokol offered numerous sporting activities, from canoeing to ice-skating. The organisation had been a seedbed for Olympic talent, and had produced world-class gymnasts who had won a large number of gold, silver and bronze Olympic medals in the inter-war period. The Czech men's gymnastic team had won the World Championships in 1938, acquiring cult status at home, especially for one of its leading gymnasts, Gajdoš, who, with his well-chiselled physique, was highly popular. Sokol youths were put through athletics trials, and the most talented were considered for the Czechoslovak athletics championships.[68] In order to attract as many young people as possible, Sokol made deals with other sporting organisations. For example, on 1 November 1946 an agreement was signed with the Czech Basketball Organisation offering dual membership in return for the basketball organisation's right to use Sokol's venues for its own training and competitions. This was the first of many joint membership agreements between Sokol and other sports organisations, which extended its web of influence. The Communists, by failing to introduce sport into the activities of the SČM, lost out in terms of membership.

But many young people also joined Sokol simply because of its competitive spirit. It was like joining an elite. Although a fee-paying organisation, those who joined still had to work hard to stay within its ranks. Moreover, unlike the SČM, membership was not automatic. The incentive to join was great. New members underwent a probationary period of six months, during which they had to participate in gymnastic exercise groups on a weekly basis and to pass exams. Not all were successful.[69] Having completed the probationary period, new entrants could compete in various activities, which included everything from gymnastic routines to flag signalling, from knowledge of Morse code to first aid. In the girls' sections, there was emphasis on 'home-making' (*domácnost*), including cooking. There were different levels of attainment and with them came different rewards.[70] In terms of general performance within Sokol, average achievers would receive bronze badges, high achievers would gain silver ones and the best were awarded gold. In specific activities, such as exercises on the gymnastic apparatus, the reward was a red Sokol belt. Those who mastered the Sokol ideal through the rote learning of its history won a special badge in the form of a belt buckle, and those who acquired skills in special emergency training wore red epaulettes. All these motivational aspects formed part of the 'Badge of Efficiency' (*Odznak zdatnosti*) scheme, which Marie Provazníková, the women's section leader, had devised just before the war. As a further incentive to youth members, those who became gymnastic leaders were given full membership rights, even if they had not yet reached the age of eighteen.[71] Moreover, behind these competitive schemes lay a highly organised body that, over the years, had become experienced in event management. For the youth section, a comprehensive training programme for all male youth leaders (*vedoucí dorostenců*) was planned for 1946, with provision for those with a special talent for skiing or a desire to lead day-outings or those who simply wished to learn about the countryside.[72] More than anything, it was the variety of practical experience made available to young people, which they could not easily enjoy elsewhere, that attracted so many to the movement.

Sokol's role as a social centre in town and village was equally important. Its branches were more accessible than those of the SČM in rural areas. By December 1947, there were 3,391 branches, equating to one branch for every 9 square miles. The SČM was predominantly an urban phenomenon. Young Czechs in most cases needed to be close to major towns in order to consider joining the SČM. It was, in fact, Sokol's rural network that allowed young people to take advantage of its weekend retreats, away from the gloom of post-war city life.[73] Indeed, the attraction of the countryside was one of the reasons why the SČM decided to merge with the Junák, which also had a rural presence. Moreover, in most local Sokol branches there was the opportunity for young members to set up self-governing youth units (*samosprávy*), enabling them to organise such things as poetry recitals, dancing events or chess tournaments. With so many branches, Sokol was an obvious meeting-place.

In all, Sokol gave young people access to a world which differed from the one offered by the SČM. It promoted itself as an oasis of leisure in an austere environment where politics pervaded almost every corner of life. According to one young commentator, participation in the SČM left little time for young people to do anything else.[74] In the evenings, young people often had to choose between participation in the public affairs of youth, and more pleasurable pursuits such as drinking, socialising or visiting the cinema.[75] On the other hand, although Sokol had strict rules on the consumption of alcohol, and many of its cinemas had been seized by the Communists in 1945 (perhaps in an attempt to deny the organisation at least one means of recruiting young members) it continued to attract youth because of its cultural character. This differed markedly from the political character of the SČM. Sokol sheltered the young from this politicisation, offering instead an array of activities. The other advantage it had over the SČM was that its youth section was focused on the biologically more appropriate age-range of fourteen to eighteen, not the SČM's unwieldy four-teen to twenty-eight age-bracket.

Sokol and the SČM differed in one other fundamental way. Sokol concerned itself with the cultivation of the well-rounded individual by encouraging its youth members to develop physically, mentally, socially, practically and ethi-cally. Its avowed aim was simply that each member should become 'a healthy, beautiful and decent person'.[76] The SČM, by contrast, sacrificed the individual to the greater collective good, as defined by the Communist Party. Sokol contin-ued to adhere to the maxim of its founding father, Miroslav Tyrš, that 'the indi-vidual is nothing, the whole is everything' (*Osobnost mu není nic a celek vše*), but argued that the 'whole' could only become 'everything' once the individual had been properly formed. It realised that young people were fickle, emotional and inexperienced beings, who required different, preferably non-political, activi-ties to keep them mentally and physically challenged.

In conclusion, there is a semantic lesson to be learnt about the development of Czech youth movements after 1945: the Soviet model of youth culture could not be so easily imposed on other national cultures. For instance, Czechs used the noun-adjective *youth* in the sense of 'youth culture', implying heterogene-ity, whilst Communists considered *youth* to be *the youth*, a collective noun, implying homogeneity. After the euphoria of liberation had died down, Czech youth lost confidence in the Communist Party, not least because it had become aware that it was the object of politicisation. This politicisation had the effect of re-invigorating the youth sections of other political parties, which was the opposite of what the Communists had intended. The Communists felt that to sustain themselves in power they needed to impose a strong socialist culture on the younger generation, who would, in turn, pass on this culture to future gen-erations. The SČM was, therefore, seen as an agency of 'political socialisa-tion';[77] the Communists intended to build for the future as much as the present. Also, by linking youth and students in one movement, the Communists put all their political eggs in one basket; the decline of the SČM precipitated declining student support for the Communist Party. As a result, the Communists also lost the support of the backbone of a future intelligentsia.

After the coup of February 1948, however, the Communist Party resumed its attempt to unite youth from above. By May 1950, the task of universities was primarily to educate the future intellectual 'workers'.[78] The Soviet cult of Stakhanov arrived in higher education in the person of the renowned Czech 'superworker', Kyzlink, who joined the State Council for High Education to offer advice on the direction of the student movement.[79] The SVS was also forced to liaise more closely with the SČM (now reconstituted as the Czechoslovak-wide ČSM). University professors had to register all students attending their lectures in a booklet called the *index lectionum*, but were told not to register students who refused to join the reconstituted ČSM.[80] If the students lost their liberties, the

Junák was deprived of its existence; the Communists replaced it with the *Pionýrské organizace* (Pioneers' Organisation), which reported to the ČSM. Sokol survived, though in a limited form, until the late 1950s. It constituted only one part of a wider state-run organisation, and its chief role was to represent rural areas. The main urban Sokol branches were converted into trade union (ROH) gymnastic centres. Sokol had been so highly regarded by the Czech people that it was difficult to shut it down completely, in case this led to public reaction, as had taken place at the last Sokol *slet* of 1948 when anti-Communist demonstrations took place.

The suppression of a free and independent youth movement was to cause the Communist Party great difficulties in the 1960s. On almost every May Day parade from 1962 until the Prague Spring of 1968, students and young workers congregated at the poet Karel Mácha's statue on Prague's Petřín Hill and then on Wenceslas Square to voice their protests against the Communist regime. Twenty-three years after the end of the Second World War, the Communists were no closer to winning the hearts and minds of Czech youth.

Notes

1 Pavel Tigrid, 'The Prague coup of 1948: the elegant takeover', in Thomas T. Hammond (ed.), *The Anatomy of Communist Takeovers* (Yale, 1975), 399–432.

2 Marek Waic and Jan Uhlíř, *Sokol proti totalitě, 1938–1952* (Prague, 2001), 149.

3 V.I. Lenin, quoted in Ralf Talcott Fisher, *Pattern for Soviet Youth* (New York, 1959), 1.

4 Quotation from Mark Mazower, *Dark Continent: Europe's Twentieth Century* (London, 1999), 259–60.

5 Josef Hromádka, *O nové Československo* (Prague, 1946), 42.

6 Hromádka pointed, in many of his books, to the Soviet Union as the model state. For example, he declared that it was important to look up to the model of the Soviet Union of 1945, which was totally different to the one of 1917 and 1918. Josef Hromádka, *Naše dnešní orientace* (Prague, 1945), 15. See also Josef Hromádka, *Mezi Východem a Západem* (Prague, 1946), 54–60.

7 Karel Kaplan, *The Short March: The Communist Takeover in Czechoslovakia, 1945–1948* (London, 1987), 106.

8 The Košice Programme laid out the major political tasks awaiting Czechoslovakia once the Nazi occupation was over. The agreement was actually concluded in Moscow in March 1945 by representatives of all the Czechoslovak political parties, but was influenced to a large extent by the Czech Communists. Košice is located in eastern Slovakia, and was the first major town to be liberated by the Red Army.

9 Martin Myant, *Socialism and Democracy in Czechoslovakia, 1945–1948* (Cambridge, 1981), 125.

10 See *Mladá fronta* (31 May 1945), 1. As the Red Army moved into Moravia in April 1945, some young Czechs managed to establish the SČM in Moravia before setting up headquarters in Prague – see Václav Hájek, *Funkcionářská rukověť SČM* (Prague, 1948), 6.

11 *15 let Mladé fronty* (Prague, 1960), 11.

12 In this chapter, the term 'Czech Socialist' will be used instead of the official title 'National Socialist' so that there is no confusion with German National Socialism.

13 Státní ústřední archiv (SÚA), Vznik a vývoj junáctví Junák, č.k.: 1.

14 *Ibid.*

15 Jan Renner, *Československá strana lidová, 1945–1948* (Brno, 1999), 81.

16 J. Čech, 'Pravda o volbách do Ústředního výboru SČM', *Svobodné slovo* (16 May 1946).

17 *Svobodné slovo* (22 May 1946), 3. The SČM managed to assemble only 20,000 demonstrators for its rally.

18 Myant, *Socialism and Democracy*, 117.

19 Renner, *Československá strana lidová*, 84. The Czech Socialist Party and the People's Party did not manage to form an alternative youth movement, but they did share a strategy of destroying the base of Communist representation in the students' unions in the university elections in the autumn of 1947: the two parties did not put forward a joint list of candidates, but rather fielded separate candidates so as to offer more alternatives for students now out of sympathy with the Communists.

20 Paul Zinner, *Communist Strategy and Tactics in Czechoslovakia* (London, 1963), 170.

21 Blanka Zilynská, 'Poválečná obnova a zápas o character univerzity', in Jan Havránek and Zdeněk Pousta (eds), *Dějiny univerzity Karlovy, IV: 1918–1990* (Prague, 1998), 243.

22 *Ibid.*, 256.

23 *Ibid.*, 240.

24 John Connelly, 'Communist Higher Education Policies in Czechoslovakia, Poland and East Germany', in Norman Naimark and Leonid Gibianskii (eds), *The Establishment of Communist Regimes in Eastern Europe, 1944–49* (Boulder, CO, 1987), 194.

25 Jiří Pešek, 'Kontinuita a diskontinuita české kultury, 1945–1965', in Gernot Heiss, Alena Míšková, Jiří Pešek and Oliver Rathkolb (eds), *An der Bruchlinie* (Vienna, 1998), 445.

26 *Ibid.*

27 Zilynská, 'Poválečná obnova a zápas o character univerzity', 245.

28 *Ibid.*, 249.

29 *Svobodné slovo* (6 November 1947).

30 *Ibid.*

31 Josef Korbel, *The Communist Subversion of Czechoslovakia 1938–1948: The Failure of Co-existence* (London, 1959), 244.

32 *Ibid.*

33 Zinner, *Communist Strategy and Tactics*, 170.

34 Zdeněk Pousta, 'Univerzita Karlova v letech 1947–1953', in Jan Havránek and Zdeněk Pousta (eds), *Dějiny univerzity Karlovy, IV: 1918–1990* (Prague, 1998), 267.

35 Marie Provazníková, *To byl Sokol* (Munich, 1988), 141. The *slet*, literally meaning 'flocking of birds', was a two-week gymnastics festival that the Sokol had organised and that had taken place every six years or so since 1882. By the 1930s thousands of Czech gymnasts would perform synchronised routines in front of as many as 250,000 spectators at the Strahov stadium in Prague.

36 SÚA, ČOS, Statistické výkazy členstva ČOS 1947–1948, č.k.: 338.

37 *Ibid.*

38 SÚA, Vznik a vývoj junáctví Junák, č.k.: 1.

39 SÚA, ČOS, Dorostový odbor 1945–1948, č.k.: 397.

40 *Sokolský věstník* (21 April 1947), 'Co víš o Sokole?'.

41 Fisher, *Pattern for Soviet Youth*, 5.

42 *Ibid.*, 112.

43 *Ibid.*, 7–8.

44 Jim Riordan, *Soviet Youth Culture* (London, 1989), 17.

45 *Ibid.*

46 *Ibid.*

47 *Ibid.*, 18.

48 *Ibid.*, 22.

49 The age eligibility of British youth organisations varied in the late 1940s, but few offered membership to those over twenty-one. See Gordon Ette, *For Youth Only* (London, 1952), 85.

50 Fisher, *Pattern for Soviet Youth*, 221.

51 By the late 1980s the Komsomol appeared to encompass thirtysomethings too. A.I.Yakovlev, the Secretary of the Party Central Committee, stated that Soviet youth comprised fourteen to thirty-two-year-olds. See Riordan, *Soviet Youth Culture*, ix.

52 SÚA, ČOS (1862) Inv.1 díl, Úvod (1978).

53 Marek Waic, 'Orel', in Jitka Beranová and Marek Waic (eds), *Kulturně výchovná a vzdělávací činnost českých tělovýchovných organizací* (Prague, 1998), 36, 45.

54 Karel Kaplan, *Socialismus a demokracie* (Prague, 1968), 108.

55 SÚA, Vznik a vývoj junáctví Junák, č.k.: 1.

56 *Sokolský věstník* (6 May 1946), 'Kolik nás je?'.

57 *Mladá fronta* (25 July 1945), 'Úkoly vedení Svazu české mládeže'.

58 Hájek, *Funkcionařská Rukověť SČM*, 9.

59 *Ibid.*, 13.

60 *Mládež a dvouletka: SČM* (Prague, 1946), 11–13.

61 *Working Youth in Czechoslovakia* (Prague, 1948), 2–3.

62 *Ibid.*, 14.

63 *ABC Propagace SČM, Funkcionářská rukovět*, Part 2 (Prague, 1948), 16.

64 *Ibid.*, 90.

65 Jan Bělehrádek, 'Vliv mládeže na politiku', *Mladá fronta* (11 May 1946).

66 *Ibid.*

67 SÚA, ČOS, č.k.: 872. By 1948, the Sokol owned as many as 1,170 gymnasia and libraries as well as 1,180 summer training facilities.

68 SÚA, ČOS – Dorostový odbor 1945–1948, č.k.: 397. For instance, if those aged between sixteen and eighteen could meet the following standards, they could perform at the national athletic championships: 100m: 12.2 sec.; 200m: 25.3 sec.; 1200m: 3:40 min.; 80m hurdles: 14.2 sec.; long jump: 5.50m; high jump: 1.60m; pole vault: 2.80m; shot putt: 12m; discus: 32m; javelin: 40m; 4 × 100m relay: 49 sec.; 3 × 1000m relay: 9:02 min.

69 *Sokolský věstník* (7 July 1947), 'Ze života našich žup a jednot'. In some regional branches of the Sokol, only half the candidates for membership managed to complete the probation and to take Sokol vows at the end of it.

70 SÚA, ČOS, Dorostový odbor 1945–1948, č.k.: 397.

71 Provazníková, *To byl Sokol*, 206.

72 SÚA, ČOS, Dorostový odbor 1945–1948, č.k.: 397. Eleven separate youth training

programmes were scheduled to be run in 1946 at different locations around Moravia and Bohemia.

73 *Sokolský věstník* (18 February 1946), 'Největší péči mládeži!'
74 *Mladá fronta* (10 May 1946).
75 *Ibid.*
76 SÚA, ČOS, Dorostový odbor, 1945–1948, č.k.: 397.
77 Zilynská, 'Poválečná obnova a zápas o character univerzity', 256.
78 Ivan Gadourek, *The Political Control of Czechoslovakia: A Study in Social Control of a Soviet Satellite State* (Leiden, 1953), 121.
79 *Ibid.*, 122.
80 *Ibid.*, 123.

IV

Women

9

13

Women, work and unemployment in post-war West Germany[1]

Vanessa Beck

The recently defunct National Socialist regime, the war and the Allied occupation all had a profound effect on women's everyday lives in the immediate post-war period in Germany, which many women did not experience as peace-time, in either political or in personal terms. They were primarily concerned with survival in face of the scarcity of goods and basic amenities, whilst, in the absence of men, they also often took on the role of head of the household. In the late 1940s and early 1950s women's position in the family, the labour market and society again changed, as men returned to reclaim positions in both the private and the public sphere, and especially in the state that was in process of being established. As had happened in the aftermath of the First World War, women now partly withdrew from and were partly forced out of the labour market. For a limited time women were a significant driving force, but were ousted from this role prior to and with the establishment of the Federal Republic, which ultimately reinforced traditional female roles in the household and family.

This chapter will consider the position of women in the Western zones of occupation in post-war Germany, particularly with regard to the labour market and unemployment. Female joblessness was a public concern of the day, as is evident from the number of newspaper articles dealing with this issue which appeared in the early and mid-1950s especially, though mention was also being made of redundancies as early as 1946. Despite this, and despite the detail in which the economic upheavals and subsequent *Wirtschaftswunder* ('economic miracle') in West Germany have been examined, joblessness amongst women in the post-war period has not been treated as a distinct research area. We shall therefore outline the changes in female participation in the labour market, highlighting in particular problems of access, training and promotion, which in many cases explain subsequent unemployment. Examples of these developments will be given at sectoral level. In the post-war period, demand for additional labour was high, especially in industries such as agriculture and construction, as the main priorities were to provide food and shelter for the population. The construction industry provided a new opening for women, but female participation was traditional in agriculture, albeit at the lowest levels or as casual labour. The case of the transport sector, or more precisely the railways (*Reichsbahn*), will be used to show how a reliance on women turned into an overt refusal to employ them, despite some trade union attempts to hinder or at least mitigate such open discrimination. The increase in female unemployment in the later 1940s is evident both within these sectors and at national level. Finally, this chapter will look at some contemporary palliative measures, but will conclude that the socio-political context was not conducive to finding a solution that would enable women to remain in the labour market. The fact that female involvement in the economy in wartime can drastically change partici-pation rates has been adduced when putting forward the 'reserve army of labour' hypothesis,[2] in other words, the idea that women can be brought into or thrown out of paid employment as desired.[3] The present analysis will adopt this approach, but will at the same time seek to show the diversity of individual sit-uations and choices which is obscured by general trends. The developments of the post-war period had long-term consequences for the position of women in the West German state and economy, as these were dominated by a strong male-breadwinner model. There were also, however, repercussions in the immediate post-war years, which can be fully understood only through an appreciation of the situation of West German women.

One of the main characteristics of post-war Germany was a greatly altered demographic structure. An estimated 7 million Germans had been killed or were presumed dead, though some of the latter subsequently returned from POW camps. The numerous displaced persons, especially from the East, and former forced-labour workers added to the extent of the disruption. It was estimated that there was a surplus of 7 million women over men in Germany.[4] The war had created some 2.5 million widows, whilst many more women did not know the whereabouts of their husbands.[5] At a time when a woman without a husband was seen as in some sense 'superfluous' (the term current at this time, *Frauen-überschuß*, refers to a 'superfluity' of women), this was publicly proclaimed to be a problem. The state could not provide for all single women, who were instead encouraged to enter the labour market,[6] although the ideal role for women con-tinued to be seen as that of housewife and carer. Despite this common context, German women in the post-war period were a heterogeneous group. A woman's situation would vary depending on age, social class, political involvement during the Third Reich, in what region of Germany she had lived or whether she had experienced bombing, flight and displacement, what her position in the family was and whether she had children.[7] The zones of occupation provided different economic circumstances and, in particular, varied in the degree to which they encouraged economic and political activities.[8] Whereas for some the end of the war meant an end to fear and repression, for many, especially members of the younger generations, the demise of the Nazi regime spelt the end of their political identity because they had been committed National Socialists and/or did not know any other system.[9] These factors often determined what kind of life a woman would be able to (re-)establish, and, in the first years after the war, whether she chose or was compelled to enter or remain in the labour market.

Despite their differing backgrounds, many women in post-war Germany faced similar situations in that they bore a double responsibility. In addition to their domestic role, women also had to provide for families either by becoming gainfully employed or by other means, such as involvement in the illicit economy. The re-establishment of the German economy was, at least initially, based on this 'double burden'. Without heating, and sometimes electricity or water, women were catapulted back into pre-industrial times where family and household were materially self-sufficient.[10] Running a household and providing for children, the elderly or other relatives was even harder work than usual at the end of and after the war. Scarcity made everyday life and survival difficult. Until the currency reform, money was almost worthless and many women bartered with whatever they had, got involved in subsistence production, worked in return for payment in kind, and went on 'hamster tours' (*Hamsterfahrten*) to the countryside to barter directly with farmers. Women were heads of households and took on responsibilities previously borne by men. Yet, even when men started to return from the war and then from POW camps in the late 1940s and early 1950s, women's workload was not necessarily reduced. On the contrary, many men returned home bearing physical and psychological scars, and often proved to be genuinely incompetent in terms of work in the illicit economy, childcare and household tasks. Women were critical of men's failure to contribute and the dissatisfaction felt extended beyond the division of labour to include men's claims to authority.[11] Some women resented giving up their positions as heads of the household, whilst others found that their husbands were incapable of lightening their burden. Women, too, had been physically and mentally scarred by the war and often found it difficult to cope with everyday life.[12] To make matters worse, women's contribution often went unrecognised and unrewarded – for example, in terms of their ration card, which allocated them a far smaller allowance than that made available to those categorised as doing heavy work.[13]

Women's position in public life had changed during the war in that, as during the First World War, they had entered previously male-dominated professions in response to the requirement for additional labour. The emphasis on the production of essential and (some) investment goods had resulted in the employment of females in relevant industries. Yet, given that at the same time attempts were being made to confine women to children, kitchen and church (*Kinder, Küche, Kirche*),[14] there was a distinct ambiguity towards both employment and motherhood. Women had thus hesitated to allow themselves to be recruited. Considering the altered demographics, the dual responsibility for household and income, which often resulted in a woman's having to head a household, as well as the ambiguity of women's position in society, any involvement in the labour market was bound to be fraught with conflicting demands.

Women and work in the post-war period

Germany had seen a long-term increase in female participation in the labour market, which rose from 25 per cent in 1882 to 36 per cent in 1939 and then, according to the West German census of 1950, sank slightly to 31 per cent, though this fall was mainly due to the drastic changes in population figures during and after the war. The main concern here is employment overall, as figures provided in newspaper articles did not distinguish between full- and part-time work immediately after the war, though it should be added that part-time work was later to become the chief entry route for West German women, and today part-time women workers conform most closely to the model of women as a disposable reserve army.[15] The 5.8 million female workers registered on 31 March 1956 can be disaggregated as follows: industry and trades 41 per cent, services 19 per cent, trade, finance and insurance 19 per cent, public services 14 per cent, agriculture 5 per cent and transport 2 per cent.[16] These figures underwent considerable changes over the post-war years, as the sectoral examples given below will demonstrate. It should also be mentioned that women filled a range of positions required by the occupation forces for the day-to-day running of their operations. Employment of German women by the American forces, for example, rose from around 1,000 in mid-July 1945 to 25,000 by November of that year.[17] Employment opportunities ranged from unskilled technical support to ancillary and clerical work.

Despite the wide range of jobs undertaken by women, they did not necessarily see their work as 'employment', because to them it was a 'practical necessity', a means of survival rather than waged labour or an occupation. The present-day terminology employed in this chapter may therefore not always reflect contemporary understanding of the roles filled. Both women and men emphasised that women's work in male-dominated professions represented a temporary solution until men returned home and the economy was re-established.[18] This view of the social division of labour was not based merely on the views of individuals, but was enshrined in law. Under the civil code, women were required to do the housework and were permitted to enter employment only if this did not interfere with their duties in the household. At the same time, women were required to take on gainful employment if the husband could not provide for the family on his own. Men, on the other hand, were not required to help with the housework if women could not cope. These regulations remained in place until 1977.[19] Recruitment of female employees was half-hearted because it conflicted with ideas about women's proper role, resulting in contradictory and inconsistent measures despite the continued labour shortage. In the British zone, a circular dated 1947 stated the ultimate goal to be the re-establishment of the 'natural order of the labour market',[20] with 'natural order' here meaning the restriction of women to household and family. Whilst women may not have been aware of the social and historical importance of their work, many did discover their own capabilities. Those women, however, who saw their future as independent from a husband or thought they would not marry and hoped to be self-sufficient via the labour

market, found it difficult to maintain their claim to employment. Policies continued to promote housewifery by encouraging the release of married women from
public services or by granting money to dependent wives and their children.
The 1950 'Law to Aid the Victims of War', for example, complemented West
German family law by enabling widows as well as wives to fulfil the ideal female
role of housewife.[21]

While women's legal responsibility to the labour market was thus limited,
women who withheld their labour incurred resentment.[22] It must be emphasised that there were always a considerable number of women who did want to
work and who would not voluntarily confine themselves to household duties.[23]
Women were torn, however, between family and employment, with some not
wanting to make a choice between the two. At the policy-making level, expectations were similarly divided between the need for additional labour and wanting women to be housewives and mothers. With discontent in both spheres on
the increase, Strecker described the situation as one of 'female unrest'.[24] From
the late 1940s onward, difficulties in the labour market, which made it harder
to enter into employment, further complicated women's position.

Training and entry into the labour market

Berghahn suggests that there was an abundance of labour and of skilled people
who were eager to work, and that the war effort had created a more highly
skilled population.[25] This may explain why women were usually refused (re-)
training or found it difficult to enter and remain in the labour market.
Although women could work as labourers (*Hilfsarbeiter*) even where this meant
very heavy work, they were refused training for specialist occupations, often on
the grounds that they would not be able to cope with the physical demands,[26]
or that they would not be accepted in leading positions. Given these obstacles in
the way of achieving equal access to vocational training, it is not surprising
that employed single women would have difficulty in claiming anything more,
such as positive recognition of their contribution. Despite an Allied Control
Council directive *permitting* equal pay for equal work, women were usually paid
less. The largest portion of the pay gap, however, was due to women's inability
to rise above unskilled, entry-level positions.[27]

One of the main concerns of labour exchanges was thus the qualification of
women for the labour market. It seems that women were mainly regarded as
qualified for light or easier occupations, whilst men were redirected into heavy
industry and (re-) construction, although women also worked in what were
termed 'men's jobs'. In February 1947 the women's magazine *Die Welt der Frau*
(*Woman's World*) gave an overview of possibilities for women in the Stuttgart
area, indicating that popular occupations such as seamstress, hairdresser,
florist, sales assistant or employee in the beauty industry were oversubscribed,
so that women found it difficult to access the necessary training. At the same
time, labour exchanges were finding it difficult to fill positions as domestic work-

ers and also as textile workers, typists and interpreters. All these jobs fell within the range of what was commonly described as 'women's jobs', but were in contradiction to what was the workaday reality for a large number of women in the post-war period. This disparity shows the extent to which this magazine considered the presence of women in male professions as temporary – and possibly unacceptable. It should be mentioned, however, that the magazine ran a series designed to introduce 'women's occupations with a future' (*Frauenberufe, die Zukunft haben*), which included those of architect, doctor, glazier, lawyer and electrician. Nevertheless, the article repeatedly advised women waiting for appropriate training to fill their time with practical work in the household, as these skills would prove useful in every occupation.[28] It is noteworthy that the next issue of *Die Welt der Frau* included a letter from a reader criticising the underlying but clearly recognisable assumption that women would have to fight to enter typical non-female occupations such as that of university lecturer. The letter takes exception to the expectation that women should give way to (wounded) men returning from the war. Social norms were thus not necessarily accepted across the board.

The obstacles to employment or training that women faced included the expectation that they would get married anyway, so that any training would be wasted. An occupation was not considered to be 'the sole purpose of life' for a woman. Despite talk of equality there was a feeling that it was more important for men to have jobs and it was taken for granted that women would give way to unemployed men and those returning from the war.[29] It was furthermore assumed that women were 'additional earners' (*Zusatzverdiener*) and that removing them from the labour market would free more employment openings for men. What was not taken into account, however, was that, due to the higher proportion of women in the population as well as the high incidence of invalids amongst men, women were often the sole or at least the main family breadwinners.[30] Many women had lost their families, wholly or in part, their belongings and their employment, and were entirely without means of subsistence. Moreover, there were many women who were refused training or were otherwise unable to enter employment because, as the *Hamburger Freie Presse* (*Hamburg Free Press*) put it, they had 'fulfilled the most varied range of functions during the war', and after 'years of carrying out their occupations in a biased manner [*nach jahrelanger einseitiger Berufsausübung*]' were no longer serious contenders in the labour market.[31] Finally, there were increased problems with the 'silent reserve', a group that had perforce become active following the currency reform but had found it difficult to enter the labour market. However, there were also increased redundancies amongst women already in employment,[32] and these changes are clearly visible in some of the sectors under consideration here.

Sectoral developments: not just rubble women

Some of the most important work undertaken immediately after the war involved clearing destroyed cities and towns and reconstructing them. A distinction needs to be made here between the work done in this context, especially the clearing of rubble, and formal employment, although both activities were considered to be part of the construction sector. This is in contrast to agriculture and the transport sector, which will be discussed below. Women's involvement in clearing the rubble from bombed cities became a symbol of German reconstruction, despite the fact that female labour in the construction industry was forbidden under the 1938 working hours regulation. But the number of women working in the sector was high, even before the law was changed. In July 1946, Allied Control Council Regulation No. 32 revoked all restrictions on female employment in the industry due to the lack of male labour.[33] Although health and safety regulations existed (from 1947 onwards), it is doubtful whether these were adhered to, and rubble women (*Trümmerfrauen*) often worked under unregulated conditions. In the Western zones of occupation, the removal of rubble was a temporary measure allowing women's participation,[34] though their involvement has been interpreted as more or less voluntary. Employment meant larger rations, but this did not necessarily outweigh the time and energy expended during the working day, which many women could have utilised more efficiently in the illicit economy or in other activities outside the labour market. Other incentives were more popular. In Darmstadt a self-help scheme encouraged women and men to work on rebuilding the housing stock after normal working hours or at weekends. They were rewarded with the right to rent a flat for a guaranteed ten years as well as payment at construction work rates which could be converted into a rent reduction.[35] Other rubble women were conscripted on the grounds of being either related to former members of the Nazi party, or former members themselves. In Berlin, where the numbers of rubble women were much higher than in the Western zones, employment exchanges were instructed by the Allied authorities to allocate former active Nazis to the least desirable work.[36] Overall, however, the Nazi policy of relegating women to the sidelines of the regime benefited women after the war and they encountered less hostility from the occupying forces than did men.[37]

Women's work in the rubble has been misinterpreted, in that most accounts and pictures show women removing rubble, that is clearing away the destruction caused by the war. It is rarely suggested that women were also involved in rebuilding and reconstructing Germany.[38] This interpretation thus reduces women to the standard role of cleaning and tidying up. Recollections of the rubble women also served a further purpose. Heineman states that in West Germany they were a symbol of reconstruction and the achievements of the new Federal Republic.[39] Rubble women have indeed been glorified in some historical accounts, but it was the contrast between their hard labour and women's domesticity in the 1950s that marked the achievements of the 'economic miracle'.

It signified the lack of acceptance of women's involvement in the labour market, which is also evident in the lack of interest in and coverage of women's activities in other spheres. Women had been pivotal in keeping up production in agriculture and in the running of the railway services, too, as can be seen from the extent to which female unemployment became an issue in these sectors.

Women were particularly important in agriculture because their share in the overall volume of work (*Gesamtarbeitsleistung*) amounted to 56 per cent – compared to 21 per cent in industry and trades, 30 per cent in trade and transport, 39 per cent in public services and 99 per cent in domestic service. Moreover, the proportion of women in the sector's labour force increased from 45 per cent in 1946 to 54 per cent in 1949. It must be mentioned, however, that the majority (82 per cent) of these female agricultural workers were relatives of farmers or landowners.[40] In the aftermath of the currency reform, many farmers could no longer afford to pay wages and female workers in particular were often made redundant.[41] In the long term, this led to the ousting of female workers from agriculture, where the woman's role came more to resemble that of a rural housewife. This is in contrast to the East, where women held a variety of qualifications and occupations in the agricultural sector.[42] Despite, or possibly because of, the importance of family businesses in agriculture, it soon became difficult for women to continue in any regular employment in the sector. In 1955 seasonal unemployment was reported, especially amongst female workers, partly because employment would be terminated in wintertime and partly because the increase in technology on farms reduced the need for female workers.[43] As women in the sector faced either domesticity or redundancy, agriculture ceased to be a full employment option.

A further example of women's initial importance in and subsequent ousting from the labour market was the national railway, although the total number of women working in the transport sector was less significant. On 31 December 1946 there were 127,700 women working for the *Reichsbahn*,[44] whilst in the latter years of the war up to 20 per cent of staff in field and operational services (*Außen- und Betriebsdienst*) were women. As early as 1946 women working in these areas were being released, which in some regions was publicised in the press. The *Hamburger Allgemeine Zeitung* reported that in the Hamburg directorate of the *Reichsbahn* all female staff were withdrawn (*herausgezogen*) and replaced by invalids injured in the war or in other accidents (*Schwerkriegsbeschädigte* and *Unfallbeschädigte*).[45] The terminology employed here does not make clear what became of these women. They may have been released or redeployed to other departments. German SPD documents show, however, that the party was concerned at the number of female *Reichsbahn* workers who were being made redundant in the British zone. The SPD were interested in these redundancies because they saw them as a potential recruitment ground for party members. The Women's Office of the party suggested that regional SPD groups should hold meetings with the women who had been made redundant and asked the rail trade union for a statement on their situation.[46] The only response which it has proved possible to find is a reply from the union promising to rule out such unilateral measures in future,[47] though one may doubt how much influence this would have had on redundancy procedures. The *Reichsbahn* is thus an example of the way in which certain occupations or areas of employment were systematically closed off to women. Similar patterns emerged in a whole range of sectors and occupations. Women faced considerable intensification of their problems in the labour market, despite the fact that they were often experienced and able workers and, in comparison to invalids or repatriated POWs, possibly even physically and mentally stronger. Yet individual and social ambiguities towards women in the labour market set in train developments that would ultimately result in German women being identified with the role of '*Hausfrau*'.

The increase in female unemployment

Despite the overall increase in female employment mentioned above, the late 1940s saw a parallel increase in unemployment: between June 1948 and September 1949, for example, this rose by 300,000.[48] In 1951 it was reported that female unemployment had increased so sharply since the currency reform that women now made up a third of all those who were unemployed, compared to around a fifth of the total figure even during periods of high unemployment in the former Reich.[49] This resulted in a decrease in the number of male chief subsidy recipients (*Hauptunterstützungsempfänger*) and an increase of female recipients.[50] With regard to annual averages of total unemployment, women's proportion increased steadily between 1950 and 1952 (29 per cent, 32 per cent, 34 per cent) and fell only slightly in 1953 (to 33 per cent).[51] By 1956 the proportion of unemployed women was higher than that of unemployed men (55 per cent to 45 per cent).[52] It appears that those regions that absorbed most refugees, namely, Bavaria, Lower Saxony and Schleswig-Holstein, were hardest hit by unemployment. In these three *Länder* 70 per cent of the unemployed were refugees.[53] The situation seems to have improved in the early 1950s, when unemployment levels in these three *Länder* fell more rapidly than in other regions, but at the same time female unemployment was increasing nationally (especially in Hesse, Württemberg-Baden and North Rhine-Westphalia).[54] Amongst unemployed females, older women, i.e. those over the age of forty-five, were especially hard hit. Moreover, 93 per cent of unemployed women were single, widowed or divorced and were thus obliged to support themselves.[55] They were therefore in a very precarious position.

Female unemployment was in part triggered by concern about the dual-earner household, with the resultant shortcomings in childcare and the double burden that working mothers and housewives had to contend with. The Bavarian Ministry of Education, for example, started systematically to release female married teachers as early as 1948,[56] on the assumption that they were the second earners in their households. In addition, mismatching resulted in unemployment even in the immediate post-war period. In 1946 in Hamburg, for example, 3,000 women were registered as unemployed whilst at the same time a need was reported for around 10,000 female workers, mainly in the domestic sphere, in commerce, as highly qualified employees and as correspondence clerks with a knowledge of languages.[57] Berlin reported 22,000 unemployed domestic workers, whereas the labour exchange in the American-occupied part of Württemberg registered about 7,000 openings in this area.[58] In the first years after the war there were even complaints that Britain and Sweden were attempting to recruit German women to work in their domestic, agricultural and textile sectors when labour exchanges were already struggling to fill such positions in Germany.[59]

By 1952, there were indications that even qualified women, hairdressers, seamstresses, childminders and nurses, were unemployed or prepared to work in factories because they could not find employment elsewhere.[60] The currency reform of 1948 was a turning-point after which wages rose – as did unemployment, especially amongst women. Pfeiffer states that in Stuttgart alone 10,600 women registered with the labour exchange following 20 June 1948, and quotes one of these women as saying: 'we thought that, when things became "serious", the state would enable us to take up our rights.'[61] The emerging Federal Republic did not, however, provide employment for women but on the contrary was to discourage them from working. At the same time, the currency reform constituted a cut-off point after which women required more legitimate openings as their skills in the illicit economy became useless. Moreover, from 1952 onwards post-war exceptions were revoked and women were again excluded from working in industries such as construction.[62] Women's attempts to claim unemployment benefit were often frustrated by the fact that in previous years they had not registered or claimed exemption from employment. Women's refusal to form the reserve labour pool during the 'crisis years' was now used to deny them equal rights.[63] They were once again forced to become a latent labour reserve that would not represent a drain on the state but would be able to respond to the demands of the economy.[64]

Possible solutions

Despite this bleak situation, some attempts were made to cater for the unemployed. Considerable funds and effort were channelled into providing them with suitable employment and training. The city of Hamburg alone announced the allocation of 20,000,000 Deutschmark for these purposes,[65] and also created some training courses specifically for women. These included training in the use of tools, wood- and metal-working, as well as familiarisation with larger enterprises.[66] The *Arbeitslosenbildungswerk* (a training centre for the unemployed) in Hamburg hosted around 2,000 unemployed each week and also offered women's sessions which were very popular amongst unemployed women.[67] In addition to free training, the centre put on social and cultural events. This variety of activities is noteworthy, especially as training still seems to have been geared to activities that would have been considered more suitable for men. The recorded interest in these courses therefore indicates that there were considerable numbers of women who were not happy to give up on achievements and changes dating from the war and post-war years.

Such endeavours, however, were usually small-scale, and unemployed women in particular received little help from organisations or institutions. Trade unions, for example, were weak because of their twelve-year absence.[68] The Potsdam agreement permitted workers' organisations and the military governments actively encouraged them in the hope that they would contribute to building a new democratic Germany. Yet when it became apparent that unions were forming too slowly to be of service in building the new Germany, there was a relaxation of military governments' insistence on unionisation 'from the bottom up'.[69] Although the unions could not secure economic improvements for their members, they did get involved in political affairs and did have some influence. For example, the women's committee of the relevant union in the British zone proposed that women should be trained to fill the labour shortage in construction,[70] though with little result. SPD and trade union opposition led to the abandonment of the idea of introducing a compulsory year of domestic service for girls, to be completed before an apprenticeship or paid employment could commence.[71] In the long term, however, trade unions were not able to exert a positive influence on the position of women in either the labour market or in politics.

The re-established political structure, in the form of authorities such as the labour exchanges or labour inspectorates, was important in ousting women from the labour market, e.g. by enforcing previously ignored regulations.[72] Grounds for making women redundant were not always given, but included the claim that certain work was 'unsuitable for women', that women could be morally endangered by the work ('*sittliche Gefahren*'), and that there was a social duty to employ male breadwinners rather than female 'additional earners' (*Zusatzverdiener*). Employers also voiced concerns over having to allow women extra days off to do their housework. These *Hausarbeitstage* (domestic days) were introduced as a result of KPD initiatives in Bremen, Hamburg, Lower Saxony and North Rhine-Westphalia.[73] The regulations were, however, phased out in 1962 and part-time work became central to the West German 'solution', though in the GDR the *Hausarbeitstag* remained popular. Overall, the attempts to oust women from the labour market were also politically driven in that policy-makers aimed at establishing a clear contrast with developments in the Soviet zone. Thus, despite their considerable contribution to the reconstruction of Germany, women derived no lasting benefits.[74] In the absence of support from any powerful institution, individual convictions and social as well as policy pressures were too strong to enable a fundamental change in the gender order to be brought about.

Conclusions

In the immediate aftermath of the Second World War, German women played a significant role in the survival and, subsequently, development of the population and country as a whole. They looked after their families, providing them with scarce shelter, food and clothing and, in so doing, took on the roles of heads of the household in addition to their positions as mothers and housewives. For a short period, there was a significant change in the gender order. In part, this was due to the fact that men did not necessarily return from the war immediately, some POWs not being released until the 1950s. Women's activities were thus seen as a necessary but temporary stopgap. Yet individual women often changed more than they themselves realised, and some were unwilling to return to dependence and marriage. Although the rubble women have been turned into heroines of German post-war reconstruction, overall, women's place in society was not transformed. They ended up with little influence on the social conventions that governed the private lives of men and women. Economic prosperity, the end of shortages and a return to the established gender order, with women as a latent reserve army of labour, marked the end of the 'crisis years'. Women were now expected to return to their roles as mothers and housewives. But, as the present chapter has shown, behind these general tendencies a far greater degree of diversity is to be found.

The Germany of the post-war period was ambiguous in regard both to women's employment and motherhood. The Nazis, in their day, had pursued contrasting aims of increasing female employment whilst also glorifying the role of the housewife and mother. This dichotomy continued after the war, when, in addition to the struggle to survive, women were needed for the reconstruction of Germany. This double burden meant that many women – though by no means all – were glad to be able to withdraw from employment as soon as this became possible. Yet there was also a large group of women who wished or were obliged to continue to be self-sufficient. In part, this was due to the demographic shift which had created cohorts of women who would never marry or who had been widowed at an early age. Some married women, too, continued to head their households because of the effect the war had had on their husbands. However, it should not be forgotten that, during these years, women had been employed across a range of both typically female and male jobs, had experienced independence and seen what they were capable of. The importance of the social and political pressures exerted on women to make them conform to certain stereotypes should, on the other hand, not be underestimated. Women's employment, especially in male occupations, was seen as temporary, though, given the demand for labour, this sent out a very mixed message to women. The resultant ambiguity allowed policy-makers to permit the employment of women as a stopgap measure, only then to return them to the role of housewife and mother. These fluctuations resulted, amongst other things, in extensive female unemployment. This was recognised as a problem at the time but is not usually taken into consideration as a factor in determining the future of the Federal Republic.

Women's work in the immediate post-war period was fundamental to the rebuilding of the country. Yet women were subjected to all the distress caused by unemployment and the lack of basic financial security. Instead of use being made of the experiences and resources that women could have provided there was, ultimately, a return to traditional family values and expectations. The establishment of the Federal Republic marked the end of a brief period which could have heralded a new beginning for women. Despite the fact that the war-time generation of lone women was significant in size and, potentially, in impact, they were regarded as outsiders in the early Federal Republic. The Allied occupiers also had an impact on the position of women, in that they projected their own ideals on to post-war society. However, policies in the early years of the Federal Republic continued to evince ambiguities; most (male) policy-makers were in favour of a complete return to the established gender order but, in view of the actually prevailing gender imbalance, could not justify the ousting of all women from the labour market. There were thus always women in employment, and during the lifetime of the West German state they were to become increasingly active in the workforce.

Notes

1 The help of the Archiv der deutschen Frauenbewegung (AdF) in Kassel and of the Forschungsstelle für Zeitgeschichte in Hamburg (FZH) who gave access to materials, as well as of the Baufachfrau Berlin e.V., is gratefully acknowledged. The author would like to thank Alan Felstead, Henrietta O'Connor, Irmgard Weyrather, Georg Herrmann and Jörn Janssen for their time and comments.

2 See Jane Humphries, 'The "emancipation" of women in the 1970s and 1980s: From the latent to the floating', in *Capital and Class*, 20 (1983), 6–28.

3 Irene Bruegel, 'Women as a reserve army of labour: a note on recent British experience', *Feminist Review*, 3 (1979), 12.

4 Doris Schubert, *Frauen in der deutschen Nachkriegszeit, Band 1: Frauenarbeit 1945–1949* (Düsseldorf, 1984), 65.

5 Eva Kolinsky, *Women in Contemporary Germany* (Oxford, 1989), 25.

6 Irmgard Weyrather, 'Erfreuliche Bilder deutschen Neuaufbaus – Frauenarbeit in "Männerberufen" nach 1945', in H. König, B. von Greiff and H. Schauer (eds), *Sozialphilosophie der industriellen Arbeit* (Opladen, 1990), 135.

7 Rosemarie Nave-Herz, *Die Geschichte der Frauenbewegung in Deutschland* (Bonn, 1993), 58.

8 See Chapters 2, 6, 10, 14 by McDougall, Barker, Fenemore, and Pritchard in this book.

9 Schubert, *Frauen*, 33.

10 Kolinsky, *Women*, 27.

11 Elizabeth Heineman, *What Difference does a Husband Make? Women and Marital Status in Nazi and Postwar Germany* (Berkeley, CA, 1999), 121ff.

12 See Lisbet Pfeiffer, 'Keine Almosen: Arbeitsmöglichkeiten', *Die Welt der Frau*, 3:5–6 (1948), 26–7.

13 Schubert, *Frauen*, 45.

14 See Alfred Grosser, *Geschichte Deutschlands seit 1945* (Munich, 1991), 279.

15 Bruegel, 'Women as a reserve army', 19.

16 FZH Archiv, *Der Volkswirt* (Frankfurt/Main) (1 September 1956), 'Die Frau als Arbeitskraft: Umfang, Bedeutung und Probleme der Frauenarbeit'.

17 Petra Goedde, *GIs and Germans: Culture, Gender and Foreign Relations 1945–1949* (New Haven, CN, 2003), 89.

18 Schubert, *Frauen*, 16.

19 Carola Sachse, 'Frauenarbeit im Kalten Krieg', *Sozialwissenschaftliche Information*, 28:1 (1999), 14.

20 Gunilla-Friederike Budde, 'Einleitung: Zwei Welten? Frauenerwerbsarbeit im deutsch-deutschen Vergleich', in Gunilla-Friederike Budde (ed.), *Frauen arbeiten: weibliche Erbwerbstätigkeit in Ost- und Westdeutschland nach 1945* (Göttingen, 1997), 11.

21 Elizabeth Heineman, 'Gender, public policy and memory: waiting wives and war widows in the post-war Germanys', in Alon Confino and Peter Fritzsche (eds), *The Work of Memory* (Urbana, IL, 2002).

22 Heineman, *What Difference does a Husband Make?*, 87.

23 Claudia Born, 'Das Ei vor Kolumbus: Frauen und Beruf in der Bundesrepublik Deutschland', in Gunilla-Friederike Budde, *Frauen arbeiten*, 47.

24 Gabriele Strecker, 'Die Unruhe der Frauen', *Die Welt der Frau*, 4:8 (1950), 1–2.

25 Volker Berghahn, *Modern Germany: Society, Economy and Politics in the Twentieth Century* (Cambridge, 1987), 181.

26 M. Amann, 'Die Entwicklung der Frauenarbeit', *Zentralblatt für Arbeitswissenschaft*, 4 (1947), 74ff., quoted in Weyrather, 'Erfreuliche Bilder', 138.

27 Heineman, *What Difference does a Husband Make?*, 90, 159.

28 AdF Archiv, *Die Welt der Frau*, 1:8–9 (1947), 44–5, 'Was sollen sie werden?'

29 FZH Archiv, *Hamburger Allgemeine Zeitung* (27 January 1950), '"Sie können ja heiraten . . ." Trübe Aussichten für schulentlassene Mädchen – Frauenarbeit nicht gefragt'.

30 FZH Archiv, *Hamburger Echo* (8 March 1950), 'Die Frau im Erwerbsleben'.

31 FZH Archiv, *Hamburger Freie Presse* (17 November 1950), 'Frauenarbeitslosigkeit'.

32 FZH Archiv, *Rhein Neckar Zeitung* (Heidelberg) (29 September 1949), 'Frauenarbeit wenig begehrt? Steigende Beschäftigungslosigkeit weiblicher Arbeitskräfte'.

33 Irmgard Weyrather, 'Was Männer zerstören, bauen Frauen wieder auf', in R.A. Klönne, H. Reese, Irmgard Weyrather and B. Schütt (eds), *Hand in Hand: Bauarbeit und Gewerkschaften – Eine Sozialgeschichte* (Frankfurt/Main, 1989), 282ff. and 'Trümmerfrauen und Maurerinnen', in *Frauen in Bau- und Ausbauberufen, Entwerfen – Planen – Bauen* (Berlin, 1990), 19.

34 Jörn Janssen, 'Female labour in the German construction trades at the beginning of the Cold War', in L. Clarke, E. Frydendal Pedersen, E. Michielsens, B. Susman and C. Wall (eds), *Women in Construction* (Amsterdam, 2004).

35 AdF Archiv, *Die Welt der Frau*, 3:9 (1949), 22, 'Selbsthilfe'.

36 Weyrather, 'Trümmerfrauen und Maurerinnen', 18–19.

37 Goedde, *GIs and Germans*, 104.

38 Weyrather, 'Erfreuliche Bilder', 136.

39 Heineman, *What Difference does a Husband Make?*, 92.

40 FZH Archiv, *VWD* (Frankfurt am Main), Landwirtschaft No. 107 (6 March 1952), '82.1 Prozent familieneigne weibliche Arbeitskräfte'.

41 Kolinsky, *Women*, 34.

42 H. Albers, 'Hin zur "weiblichen Berufung": Bäuerinnen in Westdeutschland', in Budde (ed.), *Frauen arbeiten*, 166.

43 FZH Archiv, *VWD* (Frankfurt/Main), Landwirtschaft No. 4 (5 January 1955), 'Landwirtschaft entlässt weibliche Arbeitskräfte'.

44 FZH Archiv, *Wirtschafts Zeitung* (Stuttgart) (19 December 1947), 'Frauenüberschuß und Frauenarbeit, Ziffern aus der britischen Zone'.

45 FZH Archiv, *Hamburger Allgemeine Zeitung* (14 June 1946), 'Reichsbahn ohne Frauen'.

46 AdF Archiv, NL-P-11 Nachlaß von Elisabeth Selbert 00020M04, Rundschreiben Nr. 1/49 des Frauenbüros der SPD, Hanover, 5 January 1949.

47 AdF Archiv, NL-P-11 Nachlaß von Elisabeth Selbert 00020M04, Rundschreiben Nr. 2/49 des Frauenbüros der SPD, Hanover, 24 January 1949.

48 FZH Archiv, *Hamburger Echo* (8 March 1950), 'Die Frau im Erwerbsleben'.

49 FZH Archiv, *Die Welt* (Hamburg) (26 June 1951), 'Ein Drittel sind Frauen, beängstigender Umfang der Frauenarbeitslosigkeit'.

50 *Ibid.*

51 FZH Archiv, *Bulletin* (Bonn) (19 January 1955), 'Die Frau im Erwerbsleben: Die Zahl an weiblichen Arbeitnehmern stieg von 1939 bis 1953 um fast 41 v.H.'.

52 FZH Archiv, *Der Volkswirt* (Frankfurt/Main), (1 September 1956), 'Die Frau als Arbeitskraft: Umfang, Bedeutung und Probleme der Frauenarbeit'.

53 FZH Archiv, *Hamburger Freie Presse* (17 November 1950), 'Frauenarbeitslosigkeit'.

54 FZH Archiv, *Frankfurter Allgemeine Zeitung* (18 May 1951), 'Notiz'.

55 FZH Archiv, *Die Welt* (Hamburg) (8 September 1955), 'Frauen gingen leer aus. Das Schicksal der weiblichen Arbeitslosen'.

56 AdF Archiv, NL-P-11 Nachlaß von Elisabeth Selbert 00020M03, Rundschreiben Nr. 7 des Frauenbüros der SPD, Hanover, 17 March 1948.

57 FZH Archiv, *Hamburger Echo* (26 June 1946), 'Ein Drittel der Erwerbstätigen sind Frauen'.

58 AdF Archiv, *Die Welt der Frau*, 1:1 (1946), 15–16, 'Frauenberufe, die Zukunft haben: Warum gibt es keine Hausgehilfinnen'.

59 AdF Archiv, *Die Welt der Frau*, 3:1 (1948), editorial.

60 FZH Archiv, *Die Welt* (Hamburg) (16 October 1952), 'Erholung vom Fließband – Anregung für arbeitende Frauen'.

61 Pfeiffer, 'Keine Almosen', 27.

62 Weyrather, 'Was Männer zerstören', 284.

63 Heineman, *What Difference does a Husband Make?*, 93.

64 Humphries, 'The "emancipation" of women', 14.

65 FZH Archiv, *Hamburger Echo* (11 December 1953), 'Rund 20 Mill. DM für Dauerarbeitsplätze'.

66 FZH Archiv, *Handelsblatt* (Düsseldorf) (30 January 1956), 'Werkstattkurse für arbeitslose Frauen'.

67 FZH Archiv, Ordner 554-6-5 Gewerkschaften Hamburg/Nordmark Frauen 1945–1951, Bestand des DGB: Invitation and Report on the 'Arbeitslosenbildungswerk', Hamburg, of 20 September 1951 and 9 October 1951.

68 John Perkins, 'Restoration and renewal? West Germany since 1945', *Contemporary European History*, 8:3 (1999), 491.

69 Matthew Kelly, 'The reconstitution of the German trade union movement', *Political Science Quarterly*, 64:1 (1949), 32.
70 Weyrather, 'Was Männer zerstören', 292.
71 Kolinsky, *Women*, 33.
72 Weyrather, 'Trümmerfrauen und Maurerinnen', 25.
73 Carola Sachse, 'Ein "heißes Eisen": Ost- und westdeutsche Debatten um den Hausarbeitstag', in Budde (ed.), *Frauen arbeiten*, 257.
74 Kolinsky, *Women*, 33.

14

Women and the Left in post-war East Germany

Gareth Pritchard

Between 1945 and 1948, the primary tool by means of which the East German Communists attempted to steer political developments in the Soviet zone of occupation was the *Volksfront* (Popular Front), the purpose of which was to mobilise the population around a series of progressive measures, such as de-nazification, land reform, nationalisation, legal reform, education reform and reform of the civil service. These measures were intended to be radical enough to satisfy the aspirations of the traditional working-class constituency of the Communists, without being so revolutionary that they would scare off the rest of the population. It was in part on the basis of this seemingly reformist programme that the KPD engineered a merger with the SPD in April 1946 to form a new, united workers' party in the Soviet zone, the *Sozialistische Einheitspartei Deutschlands* (Socialist Unity Party – SED).[1]

Integral to the Popular Front strategy of the KPD/SED was the concept of the democratic, 'German' (as opposed to the revolutionary Soviet) road to socialism. Apparently eschewing their radical traditions, the Communists argued in the early post-war period that conditions in Germany would not permit the proletariat to seize power for itself. Instead, it was the task of the working class, under the leadership of the Communists, and in alliance with the peasantry and the progressive bourgeoisie, to construct in Germany a parliamentary democracy in which civil and property rights would be guaranteed.[2] From the point of view of the Communists and their Soviet masters, there were sound reasons for this ostensible conversion to the principles of what they had once derided as 'bourgeois democracy'. Throughout Western and much of East-Central Europe, Communist parties appeared to be in the ascendant. The German Communists had high hopes that they would be able to play the electoral game as successfully as their French or Italian comrades.

From the very beginning of the Soviet occupation, it was recognised by the Soviet Military Administration (SMAD) and the KPD leadership that women were vital to the success or otherwise of this electoral strategy.[3] With millions of German men having been killed during the war, and millions more still incarcerated in the POW camps, women now made up the bulk of the population. In 1946, the ratio of women to men amongst the indigenous population of the Soviet zone was 133:100, whilst amongst refugees it was 142:100.[4] If the Communists failed to win the votes of women, they would fail to win at all.

This chapter will explore the various aspects of the Communist campaign to secure the political and electoral support of women, the reasons for its failure and the far-reaching consequences of this failure for the political history of East Germany.

Women and the East German labour movement

Throughout the whole of the Weimar period, the KPD, SPD and trade unions had been, in essence, organisations of men. Women had made up only about one-fifth of the membership of the SPD and less than one-fifth of that of the KPD, whilst the number of women in positions of leadership had been vanishingly small.[5] Given the gender structure of the population in post-war East Germany, it would never be possible for the KPD or SED to become truly mass parties unless they broke out of their masculine political ghetto by recruiting women in large numbers. As Wilhelm Koenen, a leading light in the KPD in Saxony, told a meeting of party functionaries in Leipzig in March 1946: 'What I see sitting here before me today is essentially an organisation of men . . . If we have an organisation of men before us here, then we are not yet an organisation of the people.'[6]

A further pressing reason for the desire of the Communist leadership to build bridges to women stemmed from their understanding of the recent past. Amongst Socialist and Communist circles in post-war East Germany, it was an unchallenged axiom that the political ignorance of women before 1933 had made it easy for the Nazis to manipulate them, that women had voted for the Nazis in disproportionate numbers and that, after 1933, women had been the most ardent supporters of the Hitler regime.[7] In their speeches, leaflets, pamphlets and newspaper articles, Communist functionaries drove home the message that women could 'no longer be left devoid of ideas',[8] and that, unless they could be won over to progressive politics, women would continue to provide fertile soil for the forces of reaction. 'It is our task', proclaimed the main speaker at a women's meeting in Crimmitschau in March 1945, 'to school the mass of women intellectually and politically so that they never again become the victims of political criminals'.[9]

To this end, all the organisations of the East German labour movement after 1945 consistently stressed the importance of recruiting women. Prior to party and public meetings, speakers were instructed to place particular emphasis on 'women's issues', and to tread carefully when dealing with matters such as religion where it was felt that the sensitivities of women might easily be offended.[10] At party and trade union meetings, and in internal party literature, activists were continually exhorted to see the recruitment of women as a priority, and to regard women as absolute equals and comrades. As one KPD circular of January 1946 put it: 'Work amongst women is the task of the whole party. The party knows no women and men, only comrades.'[11]

Party and trade union managers, meanwhile, were instructed to pay particular attention to the political education (*Schulung*) of those women who had become active in the labour movement, and to ensure that as many women as possible were promoted to responsible positions.[12] 'An administrative apparatus without women can no longer be imagined', proclaimed one speaker to a women's meeting in the vicinity of Chemnitz in 1945; 'Up till now women have been too much preoccupied with the cooking-pot, but that must change.'[13] Wilhelm Koenen even went so far as to argue that, in order to reflect the gender structure of the population, no fewer than two-thirds of all offices in the party, even at the very highest level, should be held by women.[14]

The Communists also attempted to champion issues that they thought might attract the votes of women. For example, the SED argued for a liberalisation of Paragraph 218 of Germany's anti-abortion law and, in 1947, the law was duly changed to permit abortion on medical, social or ethical grounds.[15] Attempts were made by the SED to alleviate the lot of working wives and mothers by granting them one or more days off per month in order to attend to household chores, though, due to financial difficulties, at no stage in the immediate post-war period were such schemes fully implemented.[16] The SED also intervened with the Soviet military authorities to secure higher rations for housewives from the autumn of 1947.[17] In its propaganda, particularly in the run-up to elections, the SED produced vast quantities of leaflets and pamphlets that were aimed at a female audience, as well as staging innumerable public meetings for women.[18]

As a result of the strenuous efforts of the KPD/SED leadership, large numbers of women were indeed recruited to the left-wing parties and the trade unions. In absolute terms, more East German women became active in the labour movement than ever before. In 1919, for example, the SPD had claimed only 200,000 women members in the whole of Germany. By December 1948, there were over 400,000 female members of the SED in the much more limited territory of the Soviet zone, accounting for 24.1 per cent of the total membership.[19] Some at least of these women attained positions of power and responsibility. By 1947, there were 180 female *Bürgermeister* in the Soviet zone, 2,127 women in senior posts in local government and the state apparatus and 107 women representatives in the various regional parliaments. The vast majority of these women were members of the SED.[20] It should also be noted that women made up a significantly larger proportion of the SED than of the SPD in West Germany. In 1948, the SPD in the three western zones of occupation had approximately 150,000 female members, accounting for just 19.2 per cent of the total membership.[21]

For some of the women activists who made up these statistics, the early post-war years were an exciting period when, for the first time in their lives, a wider world of politics and public responsibilities opened before them. According to a female functionary from Chemnitz, writing about her experiences of those years: 'Women who had only attended elementary school took up posts . . . entailing great responsibility, to which they proved equal and which they mastered, mastered because they set about . . . their tasks with intelligence and enthusiasm.'[22] In a similar vein, a female Social Democrat, also from Chemnitz, related how, for the first time since joining the labour movement in 1918, she began to study the socialist classics and to speak at party meetings. With evident pride she recalled how, at a mass meeting held in November 1945, and attended by the eminent functionaries Hermann Matern and Otto Buchwitz, she 'overcame [her] inhibitions, and, for the first time, spoke in the discussion before such a large forum'.[23] For some women, at least, the new opportunities for public and political engagement were emancipatory.

But one should not exaggerate the degree to which women in the Soviet zone were politicised or won over to socialist politics. The proportion of women in the SED never came close to matching the proportion of women in the population as a whole. Upon its foundation in April 1946, just over one in five members of the SED were women and, by the end of 1947, this figure had increased slightly to just under one in four.[24] In June 1946, by contrast, no fewer than 44 per cent of members of the *Christlich-Demokratische Union* (Christian Democratic Union – CDU) in the Soviet zone were women.[25] By the early 1950s, moreover, the numbers of women in the SED were actually decreasing, in both absolute and relative terms.[26] The situation was just as bad in the trade unions. In 1947, for example, women accounted for 45 per cent of the workforce in Thuringia but only 31 per cent of the trade union membership.[27] At the Zeiss factory in Jena, just seventeen of the 1,100 females employees were members of a trade union.[28]

The higher one went up the party and trade union apparatus, the worse the imbalance became. In 1948, women accounted for just 3 per cent of the SED's leading cadre.[29] In the trade union elections of 1949, 17,105 women were elected as trade union officials, accounting for 21 per cent of the total, even though women made up 34 per cent of the trade union membership. Of these, a mere 150 became chairpersons of their workplace trade union organisations.[30]

Not only did women remain in a minority in the labour movement, but the evidence suggests that they were also much less likely than men to give the parties of the Left their passive or electoral support. In the local elections of September 1946 in Leipzig, for example, women and men cast their votes in separate ballot boxes in three of the city's wards. Ward 8 was primarily middle class, Ward 109 was mixed and Ward 309 was overwhelmingly working class. As one would have expected, the SED did much better in the working-class ward, and much worse in the middle-class ward. In all three wards, however, there were significant differences in the voting patterns of men and women. Though male and female voters were equally likely to vote LDPD (*Liberal-*

Demokratische Partei Deutschlands – Liberal Democratic Party), women voters were less likely than men to vote SED, and much more likely to vote CDU.[31]

Male and female voting patterns in Leipzig, September 1946

Ward	Sex	Votes cast	SED	LDPD	CDU	Other
8	M	418	110 (26.3%)	186 (44.5%)	110 (26.3%)	12 (2.9%)
	F	681	120 (16.6%)	293 (43.0%)	237 (34.8%)	31 (4.6%)
109	M	460	242 (52.6%)	129 (28.0%)	83 (18.0%)	6 (1.3%)
	F	732	325 (44.4%)	213 (29.1%)	175 (23.9%)	19 (2.6%)
309	M	526	348 (66.2%)	122 (23.2%)	46 (8.7%)	10 (1.9%)
	F	811	466 (57.5%)	204 (25.2%)	125 (15.4%)	16 (2.0%)

The picture in Dresden in the autumn of 1946 was very similar. Though 64 per cent of the voters were female, only 57 per cent of SED voters were women, compared to 64 per cent of LDPD voters and 69 per cent of CDU voters.[32] In Thuringia during the same period, women were estimated to have voted three to one against the SED.[33] In the trade union elections at the end of 1948, the SED did best amongst workers in the coal industry (79.3 per cent), the vast majority of whom were men, and worst amongst the clothing and textile workers (14.2 per cent), who were overwhelmingly female.[34] Such disappointing results necessarily called into question the viability of the whole electoral strategy of the Communists, and undermined those in the party who wanted to achieve socialism through democratic means rather than through *Diktat*.[35]

Social and welfare organisations involving women

In addition to trying to recruit as many women as possible directly into the labour movement, the Communists also endorsed or established a number of social and welfare organisations, the purpose of which was to address the pressing social problems of post-war East Germany at the same time as building a bridge to the mass of 'apolitical' women (i.e. women who had little interest in politics as defined by the Communists, and who were unlikely to join the KPD or SED in the foreseeable future).

In the immediate aftermath of the war, for example, women activists began, on their own initiative, to form 'anti-fascist women's committees' (*Antifaschistische Frauenausschüsse*). These committees engaged in a range of political and humanitarian activities, such as arranging public meetings on themes of interest to women, setting up warming halls and sewing rooms (*Nähstuben*), and providing childcare facilities for the benefit of working mothers. In the Western zones of occupation, such women's committees were regarded with hostility and suspicion by the military governments.[36] The Soviets, by contrast, not only tolerated the women's committees, but decreed in the autumn of 1945 that, where such committees did not yet exist, the political parties and local authorities should immediately set about establishing them.[37] By the beginning of 1947, there were some 7,451 women's committees in the Soviet zone, with a combined membership of 250,000.[38]

By a Soviet decree of November 1947, the women's committees were incorporated into a new, centralised women's organisation, the so-called *Demokratischer Frauenbund Deutschlands* (Democratic Women's Association of Germany – DFD) which, within a few months of its foundation, could boast a membership of around 300,000.[39] Also deserving of mention is the *Volkssolidarität* (People's Solidarity), a charitable organisation that, from its foundation in October 1945, was largely dependent on the efforts of female volunteers.

In purely practical terms, organisations such as the women's committees, the DFD and the *Volkssolidarität* made a substantial contribution to alleviating the terrible material problems that beset the population. In Thuringia alone, the women's committees had, by the end of 1946, established 274 sewing rooms, forty-eight residential homes (including ten homes for the elderly), thirty-two warming halls, twenty-four public kitchens, ninety advice centres for refugees, fifty-five advice centres for people with marriage or sexual problems and 1,200 advice centres for women.[40] In Chemnitz, the women's committees and *Volkssolidarität* set up twenty-four-hour stalls where returning POWs and refugees could find a hot meal, something to drink and advice about accommodation.[41] In Plauen, a report of December 1945 noted that the Christmas festivals organised throughout the town by the local *Volkssolidarität* were well attended and well organised, and in general could be regarded as a 'complete success'.[42] In the district of Saalfeld, the local women's committee not only arranged parties and days out for children and collected food for the needy, but also established a particularly successful sewing room which, in November 1946 alone, produced sixty-eight coats, seventy-five pairs of trousers, eighty-four vests, fifty-four jackets, 210 pairs of gloves, 145 caps and many other items of clothing.[43] In these and a thousand other ways, the women's committees, *Volkssolidarität* and the DFD were crucial in alleviating need, as well as enabling thousands of ordinary East German women to play an important public role.

From the point of view of the KPD and SED, the various organisations staffed mainly or entirely by women also went some way towards achieving the political goals they had been set. The *Volkssolidarität*, in particular, was genuinely popular, and the favourable impression its activities created did something at least to soften the hostility with which most women regarded the new regime. Otherwise 'apolitical' women were attracted into the women's committees or *Volkssolidarität* because they saw the practical good sense of many of their activities. This created a valuable political link between the party activists who ran these organisations and the ordinary women who constituted the bulk of the membership. In the sewing rooms and warming halls, for example, party speakers would often give short lectures, sometimes on entirely practical topics such as cooking, nutrition or domestic hygiene, and sometimes on political themes that were considered to be of interest to women, such as school reform or the refugee question.[44] The overall political significance of all this should not be exaggerated, for the majority of women never lost their distaste for the new order. Nonetheless, in so far as the regime made any headway with the female section of the population, it was largely due to the activities of the women's committees and *Volkssolidarität*.

One further organisation that should be mentioned at this point is the system of house and street deputies (*Haus- und Strassenbeauftragten*) which was set up throughout the Soviet zone in the late summer of 1945.[45] In every tenement building, one person would be elected in a residents' meeting, or appointed by the local authorities, to undertake the post of 'house deputy'. Overseeing the activities of all the house deputies in a particular road was a 'street deputy', who in turn answered to a functionary of local government called a district leader (*Distriktleiter*). This system does not seem to have been established with the intention of mobilising women,[46] but it was soon realised that it could provide an excellent means of drawing them into public life and political activity.[47] Given the fact that being appointed as a deputy resulted in a higher rations allocation, the campaign to recruit women as house or street deputies was rather successful. By the spring of 1946, for example, 54 per cent of deputies in Leipzig were women.[48]

The primary function of the deputies was to assist the local authorities in numerous practical tasks. They distributed ration cards amongst residents and put up official announcements and posters in the stairwells of communal buildings. They kept a close eye on former Nazis, and passed on information to the housing department about any living space that became available. If a resident fell ill with an infectious disease, it was the responsibility of the house deputy to inform the appropriate authority. Given the desperate material circumstances, these unpaid agents of local government made a real difference. Without their aid, it would have been much more difficult for the newly constituted, overstretched and often inexperienced authorities to cope with the enormous problems imposed on them by the post-war situation.[49]

The house and street deputies also had a clear political role. On the one hand, they could be used to exert leverage on public opinion, enabling the KPD/SED to make its presence felt in every street and every block of flats. For this reason, considerable efforts were made to give the deputies some measure of political schooling – or, better still, persuade them to become party members. On the other hand, the authorities were clear that the system of deputies was to be no re-creation of the Nazi system of 'block wardens', who had acted as spies and instruments of intimidation. Not only were the house deputies to function as 'the basic organ of the anti-fascist municipal administration', they were also expected to assume a representative role, passing on the complaints, suggestions and views of the population to the authorities.[50] In short, the house and street deputies were intended to act as a bridge between the workers' parties and local government on the one side, and the population on the other, creating thereby a new sort of municipal apparatus in which popular participation played a much greater role.

The motives of the KPD and Soviets in setting up this system were far from pure, and had much more to do with manipulating women than allowing them a more active role in local government. Moreover, most women seem to have become deputies for personal or practical reasons, rather than political ones.[51] Nonetheless, the system did provide a mechanism through which thousands of ordinary women could actively participate in public life to a greater degree than ever before.

Obstacles to the political mobilisation of women

Despite the qualified success of bodies such as *Volkssolidarität* and the system of house and street deputies, the policy of the new regime towards women must in general be regarded as a dismal failure. By the time the Soviet occupation came to an end in 1949, the Communists were no closer to winning the hearts and minds of women than they had been in 1945. Indeed, in many ways the relationship between the regime and the bulk of the female population was actually deteriorating.

There were many reasons why the new authorities found it difficult to secure the support of women, the most obvious of which was the close association of the German Left with the Russians, whose depredations could neither be forgiven nor forgotten by the thousands of women whom they had attacked and raped. A leftist German journalist, Walter Killian, wrote at the time that: 'The German Communist Party would have achieved great success if the Russian soldier had behaved differently.'[52] According to an SED field organiser in January 1947: 'Even if attacks and harassment occur only occasionally, fear and worry spread among all women and cripple all our work, not only in the women's committees but in the unions and the party.' The CDU, by contrast, 'could appeal unreservedly to women's sense of injury'.[53]

A second obstacle to the political mobilisation of women was the fact that the terrible material shortages that afflicted post-war Germany bore down even more heavily on women than on men. It was generally the woman who somehow had to find a way to feed her family, who had to stand for hours in queues and who had to travel out to the countryside to barter valuables for food with local farmers.[54] Often the woman suffered the 'double burden' of having to hold down a job at the same time as caring for dependents, amongst whom could be counted not just children and elderly parents but often a sick, disabled or traumatised husband.[55] Internal party reports from the period continually complained about the 'negative' attitudes of women, who were largely influenced by their daily concerns and problems and hence readily inclined to take a critical view of the new authorities.[56]

What made the antipathy of many women towards the Left even more intense was the fact that housewives received such a meagre rations allowance.

Here, the policy of the regime would seem to have backfired badly. Rather than encouraging housewives to go out to work, their pitiful rations merely alienated them still further from the new dispensation.[57] Similarly, the conscription of female labour seems to have produced 'strong ill-feeling' amongst those women who were compelled against their wishes to enter paid employment.[58]

But perhaps the most significant impediment to the implementation of the regime's policies towards women was the deeply rooted 'proletarian misogyny' of the rank-and-file and lower ranking functionaries of the labour movement itself. Amongst male Communists, Social Democrats and trade unionists, there was a widespread belief that women were incapable of rational thought. Typical is the male speaker at a women's meeting in September 1945 who argued that 'women are by nature credulous. They believe first and act afterwards.'[59] In Plauen, the KPD district leadership ascribed its lack of success in winning over women to the 'primitive style of thinking' of the female, which allegedly made it difficult for her to see beyond her day-to-day problems.[60]

Traditional prejudices about women were further intensified by the view that 'it was precisely the women who, on account of their mentality, fell prey to Hitler's ideology and promises'.[61] Here, again, the regime seems to have scored something of an own goal. The official line was that the Nazis had exploited the political ignorance of women to make them the most ardent supporters of the Third Reich. It was a very short journey, however, from believing that women had been manipulated into voting for the Nazis to holding that women were *to blame* for the Nazis. At the founding meeting of the KPD in Reichenbach, one of the speakers asserted that women had voted for the Nazis because of their fetish for uniforms.[62] In Chemnitz, the demand was even raised by Social Democrats that female voters should be disenfranchised because: 'Women are to blame for the Nazis!' (*An den Nazis sind die Weiber Schuld!*)[63]

Such views were both common and persistent, and, as the authorities were well aware, their frequent public expression was hardly likely to improve relations between women and the new order. Leading functionaries continually warned their underlings not to fall into the trap of blaming women.[64] For all their exhortations, however, the authorities never tackled the problem head on, which is probably why it proved so difficult to resolve. Rather than attacking the myth that women had been more sympathetic to Nazism than men, the authorities simply argued that, although women had indeed been more susceptible to the Nazi poison, they should not be blamed for their ignorance and gullibility.[65]

Misogynistic attitudes amongst male activists and functionaries were intensified still further by the disorderly social circumstances of post-war Germany. There was a widespread fear amongst many men that the war had undermined family bonds and traditional moral values, as a result of which women had become sexually promiscuous and obsessed with physical gratification. The substantial increase in the divorce rate, coupled with an explosion in the incidence of venereal disease, exacerbated these concerns and led to manifestations of some viciously misogynistic attitudes.[66] Some Communists suggested setting up brothels for Soviet soldiers, staffed by middle-class women who were all 'prostitutes anyway'.[67] In Leipzig, the authorities established police patrols in order to curb the activities of what they saw as 'love-starved women who could not wait until their husbands came home'.[68] In Potsdam, an isolation camp was opened for women with sexually transmitted diseases, many of whom were no more than fifteen or sixteen years old. Some of the girls were not infected at all, but were placed in the camp for alleged 'licentious behaviour and frequent changing of partners'.[69]

Given the pervasiveness of traditional prejudices in the labour movement, and the bitter twist given to these attitudes by the perception of women as both reactionary and sexually corrupt, it is hardly surprising that the campaign to mobilise women politically met with staunch resistance on the part of the rank-and-file. In internal party documents of the period, one can find innumerable examples of local activists refusing to accept that women merited a role in politics,[70] or attempting to frustrate the drive to promote women in the party and trade unions. According to a report from Weimar of August 1946: 'In principle the female comrades are very ready for action, but are constantly being prevented from and/or hampered in their work by the stupid behaviour of the district committees and/or comrades.'[71] A similar report from Altenburg noted that 'female comrades often have a great deal of interest in their work, but unfortunately their eagerness to work is very often frustrated by our male comrades'.[72] In August 1946, a group of SED women from the small Thuringian town of Menteroda complained that the local *Bürgermeister* always worked against them, and had refused to put any women on the SED election ticket.[73] It was a similar story in Trassdorf, also in Thuringia, where relations between the *Bürgermeister* and the women's political organiser were so bad that it had not been possible to arrange a public meeting for women.[74] At the IKA and Hart-metall plants in Ruhla, where 60 per cent of the workers were female, there 'prevailed a view that as few women as possible should be let into posts as functionaries'. As a result, not one single woman was elected as a trade union official in either plant in the elections of spring 1950.[75]

Those few women who did manage to overcome these obstacles to become functionaries were often perceived by their male comrades as cold and somehow unfeminine. In his autobiography, Herbert Prauss, who at that time was a high-ranking SED official, often comments upon the antipathy which he and many of his co-workers felt towards 'good female Communists', whom they regarded as cynical, 'relentless' – or, worse still, as shrill and dogmatic feminists. In a passage which throws a revealing light on the attitudes of Prauss and his colleagues, he criticises a female functionary of his acquaintance who 'had turned herself into such an advocate of women's rights that it was impossible to converse with her for half an hour without her bringing up the emancipation of women. She got on other comrades' nerves too with this twaddle.'[76]

Even where male functionaries and party members were prepared at least to tolerate the presence of women in the labour movement, they tended to have a very circumscribed vision of the sorts of political activities that would be appropriate for them. Women who became party functionaries or who attained positions in the state apparatus were almost invariably given jobs in fields such as education and public health. At party meetings, the very same speakers who demanded complete and unconditional equality for women within the labour movement also habitually talked of 'natural' women's spheres, without apparently being aware of the contradiction.[77] Hermann Matern, for instance, at the very same time as arguing that women should be incorporated fully into public life, also asserted that they should be given responsibilities 'suited to women, such as the school office, the youth office, welfare provision, the care of mother and child etc.'.[78] According to the speaker at a women's public meeting in Freiberg: 'The female belongs alongside the male in politics. Political leaders can very well be women . . . [But] their first and most sacred task must be to bring up children in the ways of peace.'[79]

For exactly the same reason, organisations such as the women's committees, *Volkssolidarität* and the DFD cannot be seen as constituting a major step towards the political mobilisation of women in East Germany. None of these organisations strayed very far from the traditional gamut of 'women's issues', such as food, clothes, children and health. Moreover, in some ways the social and welfare organisations that were staffed by women actually served as a barrier to the politicisation of women. Female members of the KPD, SPD or SED were often directed into the women's committees or *Volkssolidarität* in order to provide these organisations with reliable political leadership. As a result, female activists were diverted from general political activity towards the more restricted and 'feminine' world inhabited by these social and welfare organisations.[80]

For female activists in the labour movement, the indifference, condescension or outright hostility of their male colleagues was a source of great frustration. Female activists faced considerable public opposition to the new-fangled idea that women did not, in fact, belong in the kitchen. They had been given the mammoth task of changing these deeply rooted prejudices at the same time as shouldering their numerous and onerous practical responsibilities. But, as far as most female activists were concerned, they had not been given the corresponding resources or support. The reports they submitted to their superiors constantly complained about the shortage of petrol, cars, offices, paper and typewriters, the lack of attention given to women's issues by the party press and the low priority accorded to women's work by most of their male comrades.[81] Despite everything, they struggled on with the tasks that they had been given, often in the face of considerable private and domestic problems.[82]

Unsurprisingly, the frustration of such women frequently bubbled to the surface, leaving numerous traces in the archival record. Typical is the complaint of a female Communist at a meeting held in Leipzig in August 1945 that women in the party were always being told that they were the equals of the men. Yet women were not made 'to feel that we are their comrades, that, like them, we are seen as complete political equals'.[83] At a district conference of the KPD in Erfurt in April 1946, another female Communist lamented the fact that, at every conference or meeting, lip-service was paid to the principle of mobilising women. 'Male comrades', she noted with evident bitterness, 'seem to find it amusing when a woman stands here and speaks on the women's question. I believe, comrades, that this whole question is not being taken seriously, although the issue is indeed very serious.'[84] At a meeting in Eisenach, a female SED functionary decried the fact 'that there are comrades who present themselves as speakers at women's meetings, and who with their speeches achieve exactly the opposite of what we as female functionaries want and are attempting'.[85]

A telling little incident is recorded in the minutes of a KPD meeting in the Saxon town of Waldheim in March 1946. As so often happened, a female comrade stood up to complain about the low numbers of women in the party and especially in leading positions: 'Men still have for us a superior, sardonic smile and they leave us to muddle through, without granting us the rights and the posts due to us by virtue of our superior numbers and the necessity of our struggle for existence.' When she had finished her comments, a leading male bigwig in the local KPD addressed the floor and sternly rebuked the previous speaker for misleading the audience. In a remark that speaks volumes for male attitudes, he pointed out that women had great opportunities in the Soviet zone, for example in cultural and welfare matters, whilst in some areas, such as the provision of school meals and the sewing rooms, women had been granted sole responsibility! In a rare departure from normal practice, the minute taker, presumably a woman, added her own personal comment to her account of the proceedings. 'As was to be expected', she noted laconically, 'the *masculine* section of those assembled in particular applauded loudly'.[86]

Conclusion

By 1948, which in many ways was a watershed year in the history of the Soviet zone,[87] it was apparent that the Communists' Popular Front strategy was failing badly. All sections of the population – youth,[88] peasants,[89] the middle classes[90] and even the industrial working class[91] – were becoming increasingly disillusioned with the SED regime. There were many reasons for this, such as anger at the Soviet blockade of Berlin, irritation with the ongoing Soviet policy on reparations and frustration at the failure of the authorities to deliver the promised economic recovery. What added to the ire of ordinary East Germans was their awareness that, across the zonal border in West Germany, the currency reform and the arrival of Marshall Aid were leading to a marked improvement in the economic situation.[92]

One of the most important reasons for the collapse by 1948 of the Popular Front strategy was the failure of the regime's policy towards women. There were many reasons why the new order in East Germany was unattractive to women, some of which, such as the behaviour of Russian troops and the poor economic situation, were largely beyond the control of the Communists. But one fundamental cause of the failure of KPD/SED policy towards women was the fact that the male functionaries and activists who were responsible for implementing it were, at best, indifferent, and at worst actively hostile to the political mobilisation of women.

The bankruptcy of the SED's electoral strategy had important consequences, one of the most obvious of which was the abandonment, in September 1948, of the doctrine of the democratic 'German road to socialism'. Previously, the German Communists had claimed to be aiming for the creation in Germany of a parliamentary democracy in which civil and property rights would be respected. From 1948 onwards, all talk of 'bourgeois democracy' was abandoned, to be replaced by slogans about 'learning from the Soviet Union'. What this meant in practice, of course, was a ruthless shift on the part of the SED regime towards harder-line policies. The apparatus of the state was centralised and subordinated to SED control and Soviet-style economic planning was gradually introduced. The SED was purged of Social Democratic elements and transformed into a 'party of a new type', modelled closely on the Communist Party of the Soviet Union. Above all, the SED state became ever more repressive, and all forms of open political debate, and genuine multi-party pluralism, were closed down. The German Communists' brief flirtation with democracy was over.

These developments were in part driven by the foreign policy interests of the USSR. Given the escalating tensions with the Western powers, and in the light of the heresy of Tito and the Yugoslav Communists, Stalin had evidently decided that the time had come to haul the line back in on his eastern European satellites. There were also, however, important *domestic* and *social* factors at work in East Germany, and these have not, perhaps, been given the attention they deserve in the traditional historiography.

More specifically, the comprehensive failure of the Popular Front strategy meant that the only tool the SED could use to retain its political pre-eminence was dictatorship. In 1945, the Communists had been confident that they could do well even in a relatively open political system, where people had the right, within limits set by the Soviet occupiers, to speak their minds, to join the party of their choice and to vote. By 1948, it was blindingly obvious that if East Germans were allowed these rights, they would use their freedom of expression to lambast the SED, their freedom of political association to join one of the SED's rivals and their right to vote to get rid of the SED regime altogether.

In other words, given the increasing unpopularity of the SED regime by 1948 and the unwillingness of the Communists to relinquish power voluntarily, a transition to harder-line policies would have been highly likely even had there been no escalation in the Cold War or conflict with Yugoslavia. The turn to Stalinism from 1948 was the result not just of diplomatic factors, but also of the internal dynamic of East German politics.

In this process of mutual alienation between the Communist authorities and the masses, women played a crucial role, for the simple reason that they constituted the majority of the population. With so many men either dead or absent, the failure to win the hearts, minds, and votes of women, contributed substantially to the collapse of the Communists' whole political strategy and their swift recourse to dictatorship.

Notes

1 On these early post-war developments, see, for example: Horst Laschitza, *Kämpferische Demokratie gegen Faschismus* (East Berlin, 1969); Henry Krisch, *German Politics under Soviet Occupation* (New York, 1974), 37–56; Andreas Malycha, *Partei von Stalins Gnaden?* (Berlin, 1996), 54–69; Gareth Pritchard, *The Making of the GDR, 1945–53: From Antifascism to Stalinism* (Manchester, 2000), Chapters 1 and 3.

2 Anton Ackermann, 'Gibt es einen besonderen deutschen Weg zum Sozialismus?', *Einheit*, Heft 1 (1946).

3 Donna Harsch, 'Approach/avoidance: Communists and women in East Germany, 1945–49', *Social History*, 25:2 (2000), 156–8.

4 Donna Harsch, 'The dilemmas and evolution of women's policy', in Patrick Major and Jonathan Osmond (eds), *The Workers' and Peasants' State* (Manchester, 2002), 153.

5 Richard Hunt, *German Social Democracy 1918–1933* (Chicago, 1964), 127. Ben Fowkes, *Communism in Germany under the Weimar Republic* (London, 1984), 182–3.

6 Sächsisches Staatsarchiv (SStA) Leipzig, Bezirksparteiarchiv Leipzig, I/3/02, 151–4.

7 See, for example: SStA Chemnitz, Bezirksparteiarchiv Karl-Marx-Stadt, I-4/17, Bl.32, 35–6, and I-4/23, 4; Thüringisches Hauptstaatsarchiv (ThHStA) Weimar, Bezirksparteiarchiv Erfurt II/1-001, 'Wie kommen wir zur sozialistischen Einheit der deutschen Arbeiterklasse?', and AIV/2/17–193, 'Die Frau im neuen Deutschland'; SStA Leipzig, Bezirksparteiarchiv Leipzig, I/3/14, circular KPD Frauenabteilung, 'Warum Wärmestuben – warum Nähstuben'.

8 SStA Chemnitz, Bezirksparteiarchiv Karl-Marx-Stadt, I-4/17, 36.

9 SStA Chemnitz, Bezirksparteiarchiv Karl-Marx-Stadt, II-3/09, 86.

10 See, for example, SStA Leipzig, Bezirksparteiarchiv Leipzig, I-3/14, circulars from the KPD Kreisleitung Leipzig, 12 and 19 December 1945 and SStA Leipzig, Bezirksparteiarchiv Leipzig, IV/BV/04, 135.

11 SStA Chemnitz, Bezirksparteiarchiv Karl-Marx-Stadt, I-4/34, 22.

12 See, for example, SStA Leipzig, Bezirksparteiarchiv Leipzig, IV/BV/01, 80, and Hans Jendretzky, *Neue deutsche Gewerkschaftspolitik* (Berlin, 1948), 122.

13 SStA Chemnitz, Bezirksparteiarchiv Karl-Marx-Stadt, I-4/17, 34.

14 SStA Leipzig, Bezirksparteiarchiv Leipzig, I-3/02, 151-61.

15 Harsch, 'The dilemmas and evolution of women's policy', 153–4.

16 See, for example: Norman Naimark, *The Russians in Germany* (Cambridge, MA, 1995), 130; Stiftung Archiv der Parteien und Massenorganisationen der DDR im Bundesarchiv (SAPMO-BArch), DY/30 IV 2/17/12, 371; Kreisarchiv Aue, Rat der Stadt (RdS) Aue, 27, circular from the Landesverwaltung Sachsen, 20 March 1946.

17 Harsch, 'The dilemmas and evolution of women's policy', 154.

18 See, for example, SStA Chemnitz, Bezirksparteiarchiv Karl-Marx-Stadt, I-4/17, 27–33, 34–6, 37, and SStA Chemnitz, Bezirksparteiarchiv Karl-Marx-Stadt, I-4/34, 19, 21–3.

19 Jutta Menschik and Evelyn Leopold, *Gretchens rote Schwestern* (Frankfurt/Main, 1974), 17–18.

20 ThHStA Weimar, Bezirksparteiarchiv Erfurt, AIV/2/17–193, 'Die Frau im neuen Deutschland'.

21 Menschik and Leopold, *Gretchens rote Schwestern*, 17–18.

22 SStA Chemnitz, Bezirksparteiarchiv Karl-Marx-Stadt, V/5/165, 4.

23 SStA Chemnitz, Bezirksparteiarchiv Karl-Marx-Stadt, V/5/135, 3.

24 Hermann Weber, *Geschichte der DDR* (Munich, 1985), 177.

25 Harsch, 'Approach/avoidance', 161.

26 Menschik and Leopold, *Gretchens rote Schwestern*, 17–18.

27 ThHStA Weimar, Bezirksparteiarchiv Erfurt, AIV/2/17–193, 'Über die Bedeutung der gewerkschaftlichen Frauenarbeit'.

28 ThHStA Weimar, Bezirksparteiarchiv Erfurt, AIV/2/17–193, 'Frauen IDFF'.

29 Naimark, *The Russians in Germany*, 131.

30 SAPMO-BArch, DY/30 IV 2/17/54, 368–77.

31 *Leipziger Volkszeitung* (6 September 1946), 4.

32 Harsch, 'Approach/avoidance', 166.

33 Naimark, *The Russians in Germany*, 121.

34 ThHStA Weimar, Bezirksparteiarchiv Erfurt, IV/L/2/1–009, 72.

35 Malycha, *Partei von Stalins Gnaden?*, 74–81.

36 Warming halls were heated rooms made available to the public in periods of acute fuel shortage. See Florence Hervé and Ingeborg Nödinger, 'Aus der Vergangenheit gelernt? 1945–1949', in Florence Hervé (ed.), *Geschichte der deutschen Frauenbewegung* (Cologne, 1990), 191.

37 SStA Chemnitz, Bezirksparteiarchiv Karl-Marx-Stadt, I-4/34, 21–22.

38 Friedel Schubert, *Die Frau in der DDR* (Opladen, 1980), 40.

39 Menschik and Leopold, *Gretchens rote Schwestern*, 14.

40 SAPMO-BArch, DY/30 IV 2/17/53, 164.

41 *Ibid.*, 164.

42 SStA Chemnitz, Bezirksparteiarchiv Karl-Marx-Stadt, I-4/25, 341.

43 SAPMO-BArch, DY/30 IV 2/17/53, 164.

44 See, for example, SStA Chemnitz, Bezirksparteiarchiv Karl-Marx-Stadt, 19.

45 See, for example: Ursula Oehme (ed.), *Alltag in Ruinen: Leipzig, 1945–49* (Dresden, 1995), 45–6; Artur Schellbach, 'Die antifaschistisch-demokratische Umwälzung in Halle', in Erwin Könnemann *et al.* (eds), *Halle: Geschichte der Stadt in Wort und Bild* (East Berlin, 1983), 101; SStA Leipzig, Kreisverwaltung Leipzig, 161, 'Arbeitsanweisung', 13 July 1945; SStA Leipzig, Bezirksparteiarchiv Leipzig, I/3/03, 'Über die Hausbeauftragten'.

46 Oehme, *Alltag in Ruinen*, 45–6.

47 SStA Leipzig, Bezirksparteiarchiv Leipzig, I/3/14, circular from the KPD Unterbezirksleitung Leipzig, 2 August 1945.

48 SStA Leipzig, Bezirksparteiarchiv Leipzig, I/3/03, 'Über die Hausbeauftragten'.

49 SStA Leipzig, Bezirksparteiarchiv Leipzig, I/3/03, 'Schwer war der Weg', 9.

50 See SStA Leipzig, Kreisverwaltung Leipzig, 158, 2–8, and Oehme, *Alltag in Ruinen*, 45–6.

51 SStA Leipzig, Bezirksparteiarchiv Leipzig, I/3/03, 'Über die Hausbeauftragten'.

52 Quoted in Naimark, *The Russians in Germany*, 120.

53 Harsch, 'Approach/avoidance', 163–4.

54 Ute Frevert, *Women in German History* (Oxford, 1988), 257–9.

55 Elizabeth Heineman, *What Difference does a Husband Make? Women and Marital Status in Nazi and Post-war Germany* (Berkeley, CA, 1999), Chapters 4, 5.

56 See, for example: SStA Chemnitz, Bezirksparteiarchiv Karl-Marx-Stadt, I-4/25, 271; SStA Chemnitz, Bezirksparteiarchiv Karl-Marx-Stadt, I-4/33, 49; Kreisarchiv Aue, RdS Aue, 27, 'Monatsbericht der Frauenausschuß', 18 April 1946.

57 See, for example, SStA Chemnitz, Bezirksparteiarchiv Karl-Marx-Stadt, I-4/27, 'Bericht, Plauen, 12.45', and SStA Leipzig, Bezirksparteiarchiv Leipzig, I/3/29, 'Stimmungsbericht, Waldheim, 12.10.45'.

58 *Leipziger Volkszeitung* (7 September 1946), 3.

59 SStA Chemnitz, Bezirksparteiarchiv Karl-Marx-Stadt, I-4/17, 32.

60 SStA Chemnitz, Bezirksparteiarchiv Karl-Marx-Stadt, I-4/33, 23.

61 SStA Leipzig, Bezirksparteiarchiv Leipzig, I/3/23, 'Vorbereitung einer Frauenversammlung im Stadtteil Gohlis'.

62 SStA Chemnitz, Bezirksparteiarchiv Karl-Marx-Stadt, I-4/17, 19.

63 Beatrix Bouvier and Hans Schulz, '. . . *die SPD aber aufgehört hat zu existieren*' (Bonn, 1991), 254.

64 See, for example, SAPMO-BArch, DY/30 IV 2/17/53, 'Funktionär-Konferenz, Sondershausen', August 1946, and SAPMO-BArch, DY/30 IV 2/17/6, 8.

65 See, for example, SStA Leipzig, Bezirksparteiarchiv Leipzig, I/3/23, 'Vorbereitung einer Frauenversammlung im Stadtteil Gohlis'.

66 See, for example: Harsch, 'The dilemmas and evolution of women's policy', 153; Naimark, *The Russians in Germany*, 126, 130–1; ThHStA Weimar, Bezirksparteiarchiv Erfurt, II/1–001, 'Wie kommen wir zur sozialistischen Einheit der deutschen Arbeiterklasse?', 11–12; ThHStA Weimar, Bezirksparteiarchiv Erfurt, AIV/2/17–193, 'Die Frau im neuen Deutschland', 14.

67 Naimark, *The Russians in Germany*, 119.

68 SStA Leipzig, Bezirksparteiarchiv Leipzig, I/3/24, 'XII. Siedlung. Tätigkeitsbericht 2'.

69 Naimark, *The Russians in Germany*, 100.

70 See, for example, SAPMO-BArch, DY/30 IV 2/17/54, 'Aus der Mitgliederversammlung der SED-Ortsgruppe Schkortitz, 25.8.47'.

71 SAPMO-BArch, DY/30 IV 2/17/53, 84.

72 *Ibid.*, 113.

73 *Ibid.*, 71, 76.

74 SAPMO-BArch, DY/30 IV 2/17/54, 115–24.

75 ThHStA Weimar, Bezirksparteiarchiv Erfurt, AIV/L/2/1–011, 26–7, 43.

76 Herbert Prauss, *Doch es war nicht die Wahrheit* (West Berlin, 1960), 53–4, 62–3, 109.

77 See, for example, SStA Chemnitz, Bezirksparteiarchiv Karl-Marx-Stadt, I-4/34, 19.

78 SStA Chemnitz, Bezirksparteiarchiv Karl-Marx-Stadt, I-4/25, 7.

79 SStA Chemnitz, Bezirksparteiarchiv Karl-Marx-Stadt, I-4/17, 30. For further examples, see *Leipziger Volkszeitung* (11 January 1950), 3, and SAPMO-BArch, DY/30 IV 2/17/54, 31.

80 See, for example, SAPMO-BArch, DY/30 IV 2/17/10, 44 and SAPMO-BArch, DY/30 IV 2/17/54, 299–306.

81 See, for example: SStA Leipzig, Bezirksparteiarchiv Leipzig, I/3/02, 68–71; SStA Leipzig, Bezirksparteiarchiv Leipzig, IV/BV/04, 95; SAPMO-BArch, DY/30 IV 2/17/54, 220–1.

82 See, for example: SAPMO-BArch, DY/30 IV 2/17/54, 160 and 220–1; SAPMO-BArch, DY/30 IV 2/17/12, 261–65; SAPMO-BArch, DY/30 IV 2/17/53, 138–9, 236.

83 SStA Leipzig, Bezirksparteiarchiv Leipzig, I/3/01, 86.

84 ThHStA Weimar, Bezirksparteiarchiv Erfurt, I/1–001, 'Bezirksparteitag der KPD am 6.4.46'.

85 SAPMO-BArch, DY/30 IV 2/17/53, 121.

86 SStA Leipzig, Bezirksparteiarchiv Leipzig, I/3/23, 'Generalversammlung am 14. März 1946 im Kino'. The emphasis is in the original.

87 See Dierk Hoffmann and Hermann Wentker, *Das Letzte Jahr der SBZ* (Munich, 2000).

88 Gareth Pritchard, 'Young people and youth movements in the Soviet zone of occupied Germany', in Robert Pynsent, *The Phoney Peace* (London, 2000), 157–60.

89 Arnd Bauerkämper, 'Auf dem Wege zum "Sozialismus auf dem Lande": Die Politik der SED 1948/49 und die Reaktionen in dörflich-agrarischen Milieus', in Hoffmann and Wentker (eds), *Das Letzte Jahr der SBZ*.

90 See Theresia Bauer, 'Krise und Wandel der Blockpolitik und Parteigründungen 1948' and Rüdiger Schmidt, 'Der gewerbliche Mittelstand in der Sowjetischen Besatzungszone Deutschlands', in Hoffmann and Wentker (eds), *Das Letzte Jahr der SBZ*.

91 Pritchard, *The Making of the GDR*, Chapter 6.

92 *Ibid.*, 156–7, 161–2.

15

Gender and abortion after the Second World War: the Austrian case in a comparative perspective

Maria Mesner

I have chosen the issue of abortion as the lens through which I propose to scrutinise some aspects of gender relations and to highlight the relevant major developments and trends in post-war Austria. Why abortion? I start from the premise that norms relating to human reproduction touch on the core of gender relations. Norms pertaining to the power of decision-making on reproductive issues are crucial to the specific historical context of gender relations and their hierarchical structure. Who is to be able to make legitimate decisions on who is to have children, when and under what conditions is a basic question of social power relations. In the debates of the 1960s and 1970s, conflicts on abortion laws and regulations were therefore (correctly) described as conflicts concerning legitimate interpretations of society.[1] The basis of this analysis is Joseph Gusfield's concept of 'symbolic crusades'.[2] Abortion and abortion laws can (at least in specific historical situations) be interpreted as a 'symbolic issue': In a situation where the social status of certain groups or specific power relations are challenged by social change, endangered groups gather around a symbolic issue to uphold the legitimacy of their world views and their status. Laws concerning abortion are well suited to serve as a symbolic issue because they are connected to social reproduction and gender relations, which are fundamental in every modern society. Hence, negotiating abortion (be it in terms of relevant laws, regulations or actual access to medical services) is negotiating the social definition of gender roles and gender relations; in other words, the gender hierarchy is at stake. I wish to ask here whether this concept can also help us to understand post-war gender relations by looking into public discourses on abortion. My analysis will focus chiefly on the Austrian example. By also taking into account the German situation, I shall seek to provide a broader view of post-National Socialist societies.

As abortion laws touch on questions regarding the continuation and growth of society, the relevant discourses, policies and practices can be considered as especially significant at times when survival is literally at stake. During the post-war era, Central European societies were made up of people who had individually experienced deadly threats from war. These societies tried to (re-)build state structures, entities which had also come under attack from National Socialism before or during the Second World War, and were facing a very uncertain future. Unpredictable global power relations at the macro-level and unknown, possibly or actually menacing, occupation forces at the more local level made the reproduction of nation and society a crucial question of heavy symbolic weight.

It is generally agreed among gender and women's historians that the Second World War caused a serious crisis in gender relations which led, for example, to an increase in divorce rates after the war, reaching a peak in 1948, at least in the Austrian case. On this statistical level, the fact of falling birth-rates might also be seen as the result of a universal social crisis, of which the crisis in gender relations was a substantial part. The word 'de-masculinisation' ('*Entmännlichung*'),[3] a term coined in the post-war era, shows how contemporaries experienced that shift in gender relations. The female gain in responsibility and the power of (and need for) decision-making in post-war families was experienced by many of those concerned as a 'compulsory autonomy'. Women and wives were not eager to seize the situation as an opportunity for the active appropriation of space for their own self-determined activity. This applies to many aspects of social power relations: political representation, status in paid labour/work, access to resources and access to decision-making power in matters concerning reproduction.

The overall crisis in and shock to gender relations affected the abortion issue in various ways. I wish to scrutinise two of these aspects here: firstly, the topic of 'war-related pregnancies' ('*kriegsbedingte Schwangerschaften*' in contemporary language), secondly, the debate on the reform of the abortion laws, which had entered the public domain by the spring of 1946. Finally, I will include some evidence on related developments in Germany. I shall end by drawing a few conclusions concerning the state of gender relations in the post-war era.

I shall start by explaining the term 'war-related pregnancies'. This term was used in official language to refer to the fact that rapes of women belonging to the defeated population became common when the Allied forces entered former Austrian territory. In order to disguise these acts of violence and their results (which, besides inflicting physical and psychological injuries, also caused some women to become pregnant), the term 'war-related pregnancies' was coined; it entered the language of bureaucracy as a way of sheltering the Austrian public from the harsh reality, and avoiding giving offence to the liberating and occupying forces by over-explicitness.

It is important to note that the discourse on 'war-related pregnancies' was closely linked to anti-Soviet and/or anti-Russian codes, was rooted in National Socialist as well as Cold War terminology from the start and has largely remained the same ever since. I must stress that my analysis of 'war-related pregnancies' does not seek to obscure the cruelties perpetrated by soldiers of the Third Reich during their conquest of Eastern Europe or any other area. Nor do I wish to equate Soviet post-Second World War actions with Nazi aggression and thus try to make the latter look more tolerable. My research into 'war-related pregnancies' does not aim to join the chorus of those who try and have tried to turn the population of the Third Reich into victims in order to disguise the fact that many Germans – and, for that matter, Austrians – participated in the Nazi regime, whether actively, voluntarily or more passively. By comparing and relating the relevant events to each other and to their historical context I hope to contribute to a deeper understanding of specific societies and their gender relations. I do not wish to impugn the memory of those who were exposed to mortal danger, rape, death and suffering anywhere, whether on this or the other side of the Iron Curtain that was yet to fall.

In contrast to the German cases, no comprehensive research on rape by Allied soldiers during the liberation/occupation of the area called Ostmark/ Austria has yet been conducted. In terms of the bare numbers, there is evidence that rape was less frequent here than, for example, in Eastern Germany.[4] Marianne Baumgartner estimates that in a specific district in Lower Austria, namely, Melk, 5.8 per cent of all women between fifteen und sixty years of age fell victim to rape between May and December of 1945;[5] whereas Barbara Johr gives a figure of 7.1 per cent for Berlin,[6] other estimates speak of one in three women in Berlin being raped at the end of the war.[7] These numbers, again, should not be used to obscure individual suffering, mutilation and violence. Nor should one be misled by their apparent precision. Estimates in Germany vary wildly, from 20,000 to almost 1 million women raped, some repeatedly.[8] Austrian figures rely on a small empirical basis. Furthermore, nobody has ever scrutinised the history of the last days of the Second World War, the advance of the Allied forces and how this is related to attacks on the population. There is some fragmentary evidence, for example, that the Soviet troops acted most aggressively upon entering former Austrian territory, becoming more disciplined when they reached Vienna, at least according to what can be drawn from still existing sporadic reports by local authorities in areas south of Vienna. It seems very likely, however, that there were no 'mass rapes' comparable with those reported from Berlin.

What is important about these numbers, however inaccurate they may be, is that they clearly contradict the popular version, still reflected even in academic texts, which has 100 per cent of women being raped in some villages.[9] I do not want to pursue the reasons for this gap between public perception and estimates based on statistical evidence, which could include German racist and anti-Soviet propaganda, older anti-Slavic prejudices and patriarchal themes of women as property and the threat posed to this property by military defeat. Moreover, stories about Austrian victims fitted into post-war policies, which were eager to support and confirm the notion of Austria as a victim, first of Nazi aggression in 1938, then suffering innocently under German warfare and finally being exposed to Soviet rage, driven by the pursuit of retribution. The narrative of vast numbers of raped women stressed Austria's chosen post-war role as victim and was aimed at obscuring the participation of numerous Austrians in Nazi crimes. Finally, it strengthened anti-Communist arguments during the Cold War.

The focus of this chapter, however, is the question as to how the Austrian administration and bureaucracy, in comparison with their German counterparts, dealt with one of the consequences of these rapes, i.e. largely unwanted pregnancies. It is important to keep in mind that discourses and practices concerning 'war-related pregnancies' related almost exclusively to Soviet perpetrators, implying that these problems did not exist in those parts of Austria which were liberated and occupied by Western soldiers. But rapes and other acts of violence by members of Allied forces were of course also part of the liberation and occupation of Western Austria. It can be assumed that soldiers arriving there did not feel the same need for revenge as Soviet soldiers, though. Nazi warfare in the West was brutal, as modern wars inherently are, but it did not have the same atrocious quality as the war against the *Untermenschen* (subhumans) in Eastern Europe. Furthermore, Western, and especially American, soldiers came from a far richer society than those from the Soviet Union, and the line between rape and bribery for sex was perhaps sometimes blurred. A provision issued with the consent of the US military government by the highest health official of the province of Upper Austria, the *Landessanitätsdirektor*, referred explicitly to rapes in the American zone. It contained guidelines on how to deal with women who had become pregnant after rapes by US soldiers. They were to be examined by a public health officer, who had to supply a certificate, on the basis of which the woman could apply for public welfare for her child or relinquish him or her to a state institution.[10]

In general, the Austrian pre-war abortion law, reintroduced after the Second World War, failed to make provision for the ending of pregnancies legally on ethical or criminal grounds. Only if a doctor decided that a pregnancy threatened the very life of a woman could it be terminated. The strong influence of the Catholic Church on Austrian politics had prevented the liberalisation of the strict abortion laws which Social Democrat and Communist women had campaigned for intensively during the First Austrian Republic; even so, more liberal feminist ideas were not unknown to the Austrian public. It became clear after the Second World War, however, that the authoritarian *Ständestaat* (corporate state) and the Third Reich had made inroads on these traditions.

National Socialism had also provided and made hegemonic a selective approach to human reproduction. While one part of the population, the 'Aryans', were encouraged and indeed pressured to procreate, the birth of non-Aryan or 'unfit' life was prevented. As early as 1940 the Nazi Minister of the Interior issued a secret memorandum instructing local health authorities to consider 'voluntary' abortions in cases of rape and prospective undesirable racial mixtures in offspring.[11] Thus, the instructions issued by the Nazi Ministry of the Interior on 14 March 1945 only took up older deliberations, as the approaching front line made the matter urgent. The instructions laid down procedures for abortions for women who had been raped by Soviet soldiers.[12]

During my intensive search in the Austrian archives I was not able to find any evidence that these instructions, which were kept strictly secret, had reached hospitals and physicians in the area of today's Austria. This would not be very surprising; the war ended soon after the instructions were issued, hostilities ceasing as early as the start of April 1945 in most parts of Eastern and Southern Austria. Austrian officials asserted time and again, publicly and in communications among themselves, that all the relevant Nazi regulations had become void with the defeat of the Third Reich.[13]

It is astonishing to note, however, that the procedures which the Austrian authorities adopted for dealing with 'war-related pregnancies' were quite similar to those laid down in the Nazi regulations. Before coming to these regulations, a short digression concerning historical sources is called for: it seems very remarkable to me that nearly all the relevant files in the Austrian public archives have, amazingly, disappeared. Files with subject headings such as 'war-related pregnancies, their termination, legal regulations', are listed in the indices, but have vanished almost completely, without anybody in the archives now knowing where they have gone. The residual evidence is therefore very fragmented, consisting mainly of leftovers hidden in annexes and enclosures in documents concerning other topics. Oral history interviews provide some insight into medical practice in hospitals and doctors' offices, but do not say anything about debates and decision-making processes in political bodies and the state administration.

From this very fragmentary and random material it may be concluded that it appears unlikely that the Nazi regulations remained the formal basis for abortions resulting from rapes by Soviet soldiers after the liberation. Thus the situation in Austria differed slightly from that in Germany, where in the Soviet zone of occupation, as well as in the Western zones of occupation, abortions were performed on the strength of these regulations.[14] On the other hand, 'war-related pregnancies' became a political issue in Austria as well as in Germany. Perhaps the similarity between Nazi and post-war procedures can be explained by the fact that, in the minds of those who had to deal with these pregnancies within the general and public health administration, the memory of the Nazi regulations issued earlier remained and became the pattern for the post-war procedures in Eastern Austria too; women who had become pregnant after being raped by Soviet soldiers and who consulted their doctor were to be referred to hospitals. There an abortion was performed without much question. My search for the legal basis of this practice produced only minutes of meetings between clinic directors and public officials, mainly from provincial bodies, references to unspecified and untraceable instructions and announcements by one official body or another, reports from doctors in rural areas who described how they dealt with women asking them for help with their unwanted pregnancies, etc. In these reports references to unspecified, presumably still effective, German laws are frequently to be found. This applies, however, not only to abortion laws, but also for example to marriage laws, labour laws, etc. A widespread uncertainty about the legal situation can be observed among Austrian officials, and even in their highest ranks, during the first post-war months. To judge, for example, by Kirsten Poutrus's research on abortion politics in post-war Germany, a similar situation can be assumed to have existed in both Germanies-to-be.[15] The uncertainty is due at least in part to the lack of clarity in the demarcation of the spheres of jurisdiction of local German or Austrian administrations, on the one hand, and military authorities, on the other.

An indication of the continuity between the Nazi state and the new Austrian administration is afforded by the fact that women who wanted to terminate a pregnancy resulting from rape were in some parts of Austria referred to the *Ärztekammer*, the official chamber of physicians, which then decided whether an abortion would be permitted – this was clearly Nazi procedure, but could also be linked to former *Ständestaat* guidelines.[16] Under a 1937 law called the *Bundesgesetz zum Schutz des menschlichen Lebens*[17] (Federal Law for the Protection of Human Life), commissions were established at county level, headed by the *Amtsarzt* (county health officer), who was assisted by two other senior physicians. This committee had the task of deciding whether a pregnancy would really threaten a woman's life if allowed to go to full term or whether therapies other than an abortion could be applied. In contrast to Nazi regulations, the purpose of these commissions was strictly pro-natalist, without any selective bias. After the end of the war, a debate emerged as to whether the *Bundesgesetz* of 1937 was still effective.

Whilst some desired to deal with the problem in a way which at least appeared to accord with legal provisions, certain semi-informal groups also concerned themselves with the question during the transition period of 1945–46: Viennese public health officials met with senior gynaecologists and hospital directors in order to discuss how these doctors dealt with the situation, and what procedures they applied in the handling of the problem they called 'war-related pregnancies'. In July 1945, a group consisting of state and Viennese city functionaries, clinic directors and representatives of medical associations agreed that doctors should continue performing abortions in public hospitals. State officials recommended only that a thorough physical examination be carried out. For at least a year – until mid-1946 – abortions were performed mainly, but not solely, in Eastern Austria on a very informal basis, in clear disregard of existing laws, but with the consent of an influential though very small political, legal, medical – and, as some evidence shows, also clerical – elite. It is very unlikely that these procedures were made public.

These findings as to the secrecy apparent in all the surviving archival sources is contradicted by the version furnished by Irene Bandhauer-Schöffmann and Ela Hornung, who conducted oral history interviews on the topic of post-war Vienna.[18] One interviewee remembered having seen posters in the city announcing the possibility of obtaining an abortion after a rape. This poster cannot, however, be found in any archives. The appeal for strict confidentiality runs through all the relevant archival sources. When, for example, the *Landesgericht für Strafsachen Wien* (Viennese local court for criminal law) asked the *Volksgesund-heitsamt* (State Department for Public Health) about guidelines, the *Volksge-sundheitsamt* replied that physicians should carry out abortions, but only after a thorough physical examination. The letter closes with a request for it not to be placed on file, and for the guidelines not to be mentioned in open court. This concern for secrecy would make no sense at all if at the same time the availability of abortions was being announced publicly. Perhaps the recollection cited by Bandhauer-Schöffmann and Hornung refers to events before the collapse of Nazi Germany, namely the forecasts in Nazi propaganda, as the front line approached, of frequent and large-scale rape by Soviet troops.[19]

The situation in Germany in respect to regulations concerning abortion basically differed little from the Austrian situation, although fundamental differences in Allied policies towards Germany and Austria and their impact on political decision-making bodies and state structures must not be neglected. In Austria, where the *Bundesländer* (provinces) had already been less independent in legislative matters before 1934–38, legislative powers continued to be concentrated in the hands of the state after 1945. Nazi regulations such as the *Erbgesundheitsgesetz* (Law on Hereditary Health) were repealed at national level, while the situation in Germany differed according to occupation zones and *Länder*.[20] What was similar was the fact that existing laws did not cover the termination of 'war-related pregnancies'. The authorities were forced to improvise, in Germany chiefly, and more openly, on the basis of the Nazi regulation of 14 March 1945. Furthermore, the situation differed between the Soviet Zone and the Western zones: In the Soviet zone the mass rapes were jeopardising the moral basis of the claim of the Soviet Union to be *the* anti-fascist liberator. Hence, and also in order to stifle public discussion, members of SMAD opted for liberal abortion policies and/or a temporary repeal of the abortion laws. Basically, everywhere in Germany provisional and temporary arrangements were introduced to provide abortions on ethical grounds.

The climate which made abortions relatively easy to obtain started changing in late 1945. During the first half of 1946 physicians in Austria began to be accused of carrying out illegal abortions. A public discussion on abortion law reform arose, led on the one hand by conservative politicians and members of the Catholic hierarchy, who sought the re-establishment of the strict ban on abortion required by Catholic doctrine, and on the other hand by Social Democrat and Communist politicians who – reverting to inter-war republican traditions – started to campaign for a liberalisation of the strict laws which were still in place. The alternatives under consideration ranged from simply deleting abortion from the penal code to the inclusion of social considerations among the possible legal grounds for abortion.

Before turning to the political debate, I want to draw a few conclusions from the story of 'war-related pregnancies': What did the way the issue was handled by the authorities and medical experts mean for gender relations and politics? Obviously the ruling elites everywhere were confronted with a set of problems which forced them to improvise. The sometimes inconsistent nature of their behaviour and the regulations they issued was probably due to the conflicting aims and norms which conditioned their actions; Christian tenets about an absolute right to life clashed with racist and selectionist National Socialist ideas, though it would not have seemed very wise to give voice to the latter too loudly, and tactical considerations *vis-à-vis* the liberating and occupying powers prevented the use of openly racist or xenophobic language. On the other hand, local officials and doctors were confronted with the urgent problems of the pregnant victims of rape. It is remarkable that in Germany as well as in Austria abortions on ethical grounds became a 'public' problem, an issue to be tackled politically. In neither of the countries discussed here had that been the case during the pre-Nazi era. The fact that a pregnancy had been caused by rape and the victim wanted it terminated had never been considered a reason for a legal abortion. At the end of the Second World War the situation was obviously different; public officials in the defeated societies considered the unwanted pregnancies a problem appropriately solved by what would have been illegal abortions according to the letter of existing laws.

What were the reasons for this change of attitude – or, in other words, what was it about the situation after the Second World War that caused abortions to be considered appropriate when they had been absolutely illegal some years earlier? Of course, any answer can be only a speculative one, though it seems worthwhile at least to formulate a few thoughts. Firstly, the collapse of the Third Reich confronted populations and authorities with an incomparably higher number of rapes, rape victims and women who found themselves pregnant as a result. Thus, the problem was not perceived as one to be dealt with case by case, but almost immediately became a public issue. Oral history interviews conducted in both Germany[21] and Austria[22] show that women talked quite openly among themselves about what had happened to them. The situation was not the 'normal' one, where the victims of rape were often confronted with misogynistic prejudice, which tended to apportion some of the blame to the victims. At least in the case of Austria, the rape victims were also a symbol for Austria's general role as victim. Secondly, the rapes and the pregnancies were the outward and visible sign of military defeat, which was not generally perceived as liberation, either in Germany or in Austria. Hence, getting rid of possible offspring also meant not being constantly confronted with enduring reminders of that defeat in the shape of children. Thirdly, there is some evidence, not only from oral history interviews but also from the contemporary public debate, that the decision to make abortions more easily obtainable in the months following the end of the Second World War was further reinforced by concerns about the poor supply situation, in other words, the idea that in times of dearth and hunger the avoidance of further offspring was at least understandable, possibly even excusable, perhaps formed part of a 'moral economy' which was not always congruent with existing laws or religious beliefs. But all this could be said of Austria and Germany generally, not merely of areas liberated and occupied by Soviet troops (and to a smaller degree by black French troops in Western Germany), although admittedly the food supply situation was worse in Eastern Austria than in the rest of the country. Although I believe that all the aspects mentioned above are relevant, it seems clear that racist, anti-Soviet considerations formed the single most decisive factor in the post-war change of attitudes towards the termination of pregnancies.

In respect to social gender arrangements and gender hierarchies it seems obvious that the (temporary) relaxation of the abortion ban was not about changing gender roles. Context and procedures only confirmed existing ideas and mind-sets. Women were again put into the situation of helpless victims, who had very little decision-making power in regard to their bodies and their lives. Gender had a clear gate-keeping function in relation to the problem; it was only male members of the political, medical and administrative elites who were involved in the decision-making process. The female side of the equation consisted of those who were most directly affected by the decisions finally arrived at, but who had absolutely no voice in the negotiating process. The fact that the regulations left the decision as to whether an abortion could be legally sanctioned to doctors and other officials deprived the women concerned of virtually all room for making their own choices. They were, however, no longer forced to carry their pregnancies to full term, and this represents a highly important contrast to Nazi policies. On the other hand, the victims were not accorded the right to make up their own minds and reach their own decisions. They were kept dependent on the will of the physicians and on their specialist knowledge, which gave the latter power, not only in a medical sense. It can therefore be said that the temporary relaxation of the abortion ban did not increase the potential for emancipation and did not provide opportunities for the enlargement of the space for self-determination of action and decision-making for women in relation to their reproductive capacities.

The history of the public debate on reform of the abortion laws merely supports this assertion. In the Austrian case, it is not insignificant for post-war gendered power relations that in May 1945 the strict Austrian abortion law, which was heavily influenced by Catholic norms, was restored. It looks very much as if no debate or further consideration, which might have left traces in the historical record, took place. Hence, the legal status quo, which was reinstated in 1945, did not reflect the passionate debate on abortion laws which took place in the lifetime of the First Austrian Republic.

It was the Archbishop of Vienna, Theodor Innitzer, who re-started the debate in late 1945 by demanding absolute protection for unborn life. In justifying his demands he referred, though in veiled terms, to the abortions performed on rape victims. Innitzer thus initiated a debate which was characterised by the familiar irreconcilable gulf between those who called for a liberalisation of the law on social grounds, mainly Social Democrat women, and those who objected to any liberalisation, mainly on religious grounds. In the statements made by Catholic–conservative voices in a debate which was heating up in spring 1946, opposing abortion became a symbolic component in the defence of the 'old', that is, good, order in the post-war turmoil. The ban on abortion became a dyke or bulwark against the threats posed by the contemporary world. The Catholic argument linked the partial lifting of the ban on abortion to the alleged universal threat to marriage, to forced sterilisation and euthanasia, to Nazi concentration camps, and finally to the Second World War. In this reasoning, adherence to a strict ban on abortions became the symbol of Christian Western civilisation. And it was this Christian culture of the Occident which was allegedly being defended by the insistence on the abortion ban. (Incidentally, although there is no direct evidence for this, the likelihood of a connection between the Catholic campaign against abortions and the fact that more and more physicians and hospitals began to change their post-war attitudes and refuse to perform abortions cannot be overlooked.)

It was not only Catholic–conservative opinion, however, which sought to exert an influence; arguments were also put forward in favour of more liberal legislation. Picking up the threads from the 1920s and early 1930s, chiefly Social Democrat, but also some Communist functionaries tried to start a renewed campaign for a liberalisation of the laws. Because of Cold War dynamics which also affected the political balance of power in the Austrian party system, the Communists soon became marginalised, and in effect lost any influence they might have had immediately after the war. The likelihood of their succeeding in getting any of their proposals accepted dwindled away.

But those Social Democrat women, too, who were loudest in their demand for a liberal reform of the abortion laws were to find that they could not even count on their own party's support. After some internal, and no public, resistance they soon bowed to the party leadership's guidelines. This defeat of initially dissenting politicians and their adjustment to it may be illustrated at this point by just two quotations. In 1946 Marianne Pollak, a Social Democrat member of parliament, declared during a parliamentary debate: 'To me the adherence to Article 144 [the article of the Austrian penal code which prohibited abortions] is an assault upon gender equality . . . Humanity demands that the female population, that is to say, Austria's female citizens, should receive justice and that a woman's fate should be decided by that woman herself. Every person's body is that person's property!'[23] Ten years later that very same Marianne Pollak said at a conference of the Social Democrat women's department: 'Let us at long last move on from the negative struggle against Article 144 to giving positive support to all mothers!'[24]

The Social Democrat elite had sacrificed the long-held goal of liberal abortion law reform for the sake of other post-war priorities, namely, participation in a grand coalition with the Catholic–conservative party and engagement in a consensual political agenda of economic reconstruction – or, more correctly, construction; I prefer this term because the process I refer to cannot be adequately described as a return to any past society, but should rather be seen as the emergence of a historically new social formation. It goes without saying

261

that, had the Social Democrat women continued to insist on abortion law reform, this would have disrupted the fragile harmony within the coalition.

Though differing in social and political detail, developments in Germany were not very dissimilar in outcome. All over Germany a heated debate on abortion law reform started soon after the war and lasted well into the 1950s. In the Western zones, KPD politicians and members of the SPD *Frauenbüro* (department of women's affairs), taking up Weimar traditions, led the campaign for more liberal abortion laws. They demanded at least the inclusion of a social factor in the legal grounds for abortion.[25] Like their Austrian comrades, the *Frauenbüro* did not gain the support of party leaders, who felt that reforming Paragraph 218 would not be popular with the electorate and were afraid of losing ground to the conservative CDU if they insisted on their long-held tenet. When the West German *Grundrechte* (basic laws) were enacted, the legislators did not object to the opinion voiced by the CDU and other groups that the constitutional protection of human life included that of the foetus. This was a strategic decision of great significance, as none of the permitted political parties sought abortion law reform until the late 1960s, in deference to the resistance of a very resolute Catholic Church and the political strength of the CDU.

It has already been mentioned that the mass rapes posed a special problem in the Soviet zone of occupation, where concern for the political legitimacy of the ruling elites caused representatives of SMAD to take a pro-liberalisation stand. In 1946, SED representatives finally took the lead in reforming Paragraph 218, arguing for a temporary liberalisation, which would be withdrawn when the social situation had improved. In 1947–48 most *Land* legislatures in the Soviet zone passed laws allowing abortions on social and ethical grounds. At the same time, commissions consisting of physicians and social workers were established to decide upon individual applications. All these laws were, however, repealed in 1950 by the Law on the Protection of Mother and Child and on Women's Rights (*Gesetz über den Mutter- und Kindschutz und die Rechte der Frau*), which was passed by the GDR *Volkskammer* (People's Chamber). The law permitted abortions on medical and eugenic grounds only, and in effect reinstated the old Paragraph 218 in the new GDR.[26] As a result, GDR population policies became aligned with a trend also to be observed in other post-war, though 'capitalist', societies, thus resembling not only Austrian, but also Western German developments. This is astonishing, especially because, whilst in Western societies the Catholic Church can be seen as a powerful player in national and transnational scenarios, insisting on upholding strict abortion bans in law as well as in practice, in the GDR, by contrast, the churches were quite systematically stripped of political power.

This may suggest that, apart from party politics, another factor may be important in explaining post-war gender politics – namely, that a family model with clearly defined gender roles underpinned the post-war (re-)construction process. Irrespective of differing social realities, in publicly debated norms and representations the woman figured primarily as mother and housewife. In both the Austrian and the Western German cases this meant that the man was thought of as the head of this archetypal family, working outside it as the bread-winner, whereas, in the GDR example, wage earning was seen as a public value also in respect to women. This did not, however, greatly alter the fundamental reproductive arrangements of the post-war era, which ascribed reproductive functions exclusively to women. This, entirely secular, process finally resulted in the establishment during the late 1950s and the 1960s of a nuclear family model as the only accepted way of life. Political goals which were emancipatory in the sense of the inter-war women's movement did not fit into this process, but were replaced by pro-natalist family policies and gendered, essentialised and hierarchical role models. As a result, abortions fitted into the picture only when they were needed to erase the signs of military defeat and occupation, as an exception in exceptional circumstances, and had to be forgotten about during the post-war establishment of a new normality.

Returning to my first question, as to whether the concept of 'symbolic crusades' which has been applied to abortion debates can also be used to help us understand post-war gender relations, the answer is not a straightforward one. In particular, representatives of churches and confessional political parties used the abortion laws as a symbol for their world views and social norms. In our 'Western' case studies they can be seen to have succeeded in upholding their world view as hegemonic. As regards policy outcomes, the situation was not very different in the case of the GDR, where reproductive policies were shaped within the framework of the demands posed by the building of a social-ist state and society. Neither in the GDR, nor in Austria or West Germany, was the post-war debate on abortion laws part of an argument about gender equal-ity, nor was it framed in terms of women's rights, at least as far as the more pow-erful actors were concerned.

Notes

1 Gertrude Edlinger and Irmtraut Goessler, '"Die Frauen sind nun einmal geschaffen, daß sie die Kinder bekommen": Eine Analyse der Zeitungsberichterstattung zur Frage der Abtreibungsgesetzgebung in Österreich', in Heinz Steinert (ed.), *Der Prozeß der Kriminalisierung: Untersuchungen zur Kriminalsoziologie* (Munich, 1973), 66–80. See also Maria Mesner, *Frauensache? Zur Auseinandersetzung um den Schwangerschaftsab-bruch in Österreich* (Vienna, 1994). Faye Ginsburg, in her analysis of a local abortion debate in North Dakota, suggests a similar interpretation, as does Linda Gordon in her comprehensive analysis of the US birth control movement. See Faye Ginsburg, *Contested Lives: The Abortion Debate in an American Community* (Berkeley, CA, 1990); Linda Gordon, *Woman's Body, Woman's Right: Birth Control in America* (New York, 1990).
2 Joseph Gusfield, *Symbolic Crusade* (Urbana, IL, 1963).
3 Anton Burghardt, 'Anmerkungen zur Bevölkerungspolitik', *Die österreichische Furche*, 2:29 (1946), 5.

4 Barbara Johr, 'Die Ereignisse in Zahlen', in Helke Sander and Barbara Johr (eds), *Befreier und Befreite: Krieg, Vergewaltigung, Kinder* (Munich, 1992), 52.

5 Marianne Baumgartner, '*Jo, des waren halt schlechte Zeiten . . .': Das Kriegsende und die unmittelbare Nachkriegszeit in den lebensgeschichtlichen Erzählungen von Frauen aus dem Mostviertel* (Frankfurt/Main, 1994), 96.

6 Johr, 'Die Ereignisse in Zahlen', 54–5.

7 Atina Grossmann, 'A question of silence: the rape of German women by occupation soldiers', in Robert G. Moeller (ed.), *West Germany under Construction: Politics, Society, and Culture in the Adenauer Era* (Ann Arbor, 1997), 33–52.

8 *Ibid.*

9 See for example Norman Naimark, *The Russians in Germany: A History of the Soviet Zone of Occupation, 1945–1949* (Cambridge, MA, 1995), 72.

10 *Oberösterreichisches Amtsblatt* (5 October 1945), 100.

11 Grossmann, 'A question of silence', 41.

12 Bb 1067/18/8.III. German Federal Archives, BA-NS 6/vorl. 353, facsimile in Sander and Johr (eds), *Befreier*, 38.

13 Mesner, *Frauensache?*, 37.

14 Kirsten Poutrus, 'Ein fixiertes Trauma – Massenvergewaltigungen bei Kriegsende in Berlin', *Feministische Studien*, 13:2 (1995), 124.

15 Kirsten Poutrus, '"Ein Staat, der seine Kinder nicht ernähren kann, hat nicht das Recht, ihre Geburt zu fordern": Abtreibungen in der Nachkriegszeit 1945 bis 1950', in *Unter anderen Umständen: Zur Geschichte der Abtreibung* (Dresden, 1993) (Catalogue of the exhibition of the same title in the Deutsches Hygienemuseum, Dresden, 1 July–31 December 1993), 78ff.

16 Mesner, *Frauensache*, 37–8.

17 *Bundesgesetzblatt* Nr. 203/37.

18 Irene Bandhauer-Schöffmann and Ela Hornung, 'Von Mythen und Trümmern: Oral History-Interviews mit Frauen zum Alltag im Nachkriegs-Wien', in Irene Bandhauer-Schöffmann and Ela Hornung (eds), *Wiederaufbau weiblich: Dokumentation der Tagung 'Frauen in der österreichischen und deutschen Nachkriegszeit'* (Vienna, 1992), 44.

19 Grossmann, 'A question of silence', 39.

20 See Michael Gante, *§218 in Diskussion. Meinungs- und Willensbildung 1945–1976* (Düsseldorf, 1991), 29ff.

21 Atina Grossmann, 'Eine Frage des Schweigens: Die Vergewaltigung deutscher Frauen durch Besatzungssoldaten. Zum historischen Hintergrund von Helke Sanders Film *Befreier und Befreite*', *Frauen und Film*, 54/55 (1994), 15–28.

22 I am grateful to Christiane Holler for letting me have the transcripts of the interviews she conducted for the book, Severin Berger and Christiane Holler, *Trümmerfrauen: Alltag zwischen Hamstern und Hoffen* (Vienna, 1994).

23 'Ich empfinde die Aufrechterhaltung des §144 als einen Faustschlag gegen die Gleichberechtigung der Geschlechter . . . Die Menschlichkeit fordert, daß auch der weiblichen Öffentlichkeit, das heißt, den weiblichen Bürgern Österreichs, Gerechtigkeit wird und daß das Schicksal der Frau von der Frau selbst bestimmt wird. Jeder Menschenkörper ist Eigentum dieses Menschen selbst!' Minutes of the Austrian *Nationalrat*, V. GP, 17th session, 23 May 1945, 309–10.

24 'Gehen wir endlich vom negativen Kampf gegen den Paragraphen 144 über zur positiven Hilfe für alle Mütter!' Marianne Pollak, *Frauenschicksal und Frauenaufgaben in unserer Zeit* (Vienna, 1957) (series 'Die Frau' 12), 9.

25 Michael Gante, 'Das 20. Jahrhundert (II). Rechtspolitik und Rechtswirklichkeit 1927–1976', in Robert Jütte (ed.), *Geschichte der Abtreibung: Von der Antike bis zur Gegenwart* (Munich, 1993), 173.
26 Poutrus, 'Ein Staat, der seine Kinder nicht ernähren kann', 83.

16

Hungarian women in politics, 1945–51[1]

Andrea Pető

The topic of Hungarian women in politics, as part of the broader spectrum of social movements, constitutes a forgotten area of Hungary's post-1945 history. This chapter tells the hidden story of what was happening within the fascinating world of Hungarian women's associations and women politicians between 1945 and 1951. Their story illustrates the process of political transition – from the pre-war situation to a one-party system – at the level of civil society. It also traces the process by which women were mobilised, demobilised and remobilised for political action by other political forces after the Second World War.

The research on which this chapter is based was begun with a view to filling the gap that exists in the history of women's participation in politics. At the beginning of the 1990s, in a wave of scholarly and journalistic articles, attempts were made to analyse the reason for the dramatic decrease in women's participation in politics after the collapse of Communism. The historical approach of this research acted as a spur: while the explanations given merely referred to the legacy of 'state socialism', the present writer's interest was in the roots of this system. As no previous studies had been written on this topic, the search for historical sources on women's political activism began in the various archives. The project was launched at a particularly opportune moment – after the fall of the Berlin Wall the files, records and correspondence of various associations that had been banned in 1945 were moved from the classified section of the archives of the Ministry of the Interior (the Police Archives) to the National Archives, where they were accessible to the public. As the research progressed, it gradually became possible to piece together the forgotten world of the Hungarian women's associations. The references found in the material on women's associations led to further information regarding the political parties. The present chapter contains analyses of the major political parties active in post-1945 Hungary.

The Iron Curtain represented a dividing line in many different ways. In the countries of the Soviet bloc, those involved in women's politics – referred to in the literature as 'statist feminism' – called, in the name of 'equality', for higher numbers of women in the workplace. In Hungary, following an evaluation of policy on women in 1951, the dominant family model was seen as one that included two breadwinners. Thus, after 1989, when Western feminists began to talk of the real absence of women's consciousness, they met with fierce contradiction from their counterparts in the East – a contradiction that had historical origins. At first, those involved in feminist studies in both the East and the West came from precisely the same social groups, that is, they were intellectuals and university scholars. The difference between them lay in the strength of civil society in the West, and in the extensive network of associations and organisations that not only protected individual women scholars but also acted as pressure groups. In Eastern Europe, the abolition of women's associations and the '*Gleichschaltung*' (assimilation) of the women's movement between 1945 and 1951 not only put an end to institutional political pressure in furtherance of the interests of women, but also prevented the emergence of female politicians who could have represented women's interests in other spheres.[2] The political assimilation of women was carried out through the Democratic Alliance of Hungarian Women (*Magyar Nők Demokratikus Szövetsége*, hereafter MNDSZ), in contrast to efforts made by male politicians to maintain and renew their own – male – power. The present chapter aims to highlight the consequences of eliminating the rich network of women's associations for the present democratisation process in Hungary.

Research into the history of Hungarian women in politics demands years of initial investigations in order to identify the missing pieces of the story, while relying on the methodological and contextual achievements of feminist theory. Our efforts point not only towards the uncovering of this hidden area of women's history (hidden not just for political reasons but because power relations have remained essentially unchanged despite the collapse of Communism) but also to the recovery of a common history for all.[3]

Hungarian women in associations and parties after 1945

'I generally believe that if women played a bigger role in today's world there would be greater order.' This was how Mihály Farkas, a man not famous for his feminist sympathies, ended his speech at the Budapest Women's Congress in 1947.[4] Why was it that the so-called 'women's question' became central after 1945? The phrase does not fully convey the prominence that Hungarian women enjoyed after the Second World War. This prominence can be explained with reference to the general European demographic situation: as a result of the war there was a higher proportion of women in the population. However, the 'female surplus', the 'matriarchy born of need' that emerged during the war, was not merely a question of numbers. Since women's economic activity had also increased during the war, it was a factor that had economic as well as political implications.

In Hungary, women's political weight was ensured by general suffrage for women, which was achieved in 1945, and which proved to be the single most important factor in changing the situation of women. Between 1945 and 1947 the Hungarian legislature passed, in unprecedented numbers, the very laws and regulations that the liberal feminist and Social Democrat women's movements had called for in the early years of the twentieth century. Unrestricted access to the universities, family law reform, pension reform, the regulation of childcare benefits and the abolition of sex discrimination in various professions – including the police force, where women were badly needed – had all been demanded by earlier women's movements. These post-war legal provisions created new opportunities for women.

Until now, the history of women's movements after 1945 has been approached with a degree of scepticism and via a number of stereotypes. Sceptics have questioned the very existence of this historical phenomenon, while women's traditionally apolitical role has given rise to a variety of stereotypes. Charles Tilly's belief that a movement suppressed without bloodshed is bound to fall out of historical memory is particularly well founded in the case of the Hungarian women's organisations. A women-only project, such as the creation of a women's association in order to start up a nursery, can justifiably be viewed as part of the women's movement. Participation in voluntary organisations, whether aimed at providing care for abandoned babies or fighting against unequal pay for women, represents conscious social protest. However, in order to give a more comprehensive picture, it is important to know who established a particular organisation, and why. We need to know why people joined existing organisations, how they drew up their programmes, what their aims were, what kind of relationships they had with the authorities and what their lived experience within these organisations was. Answers to such questions will help us to understand the world of women's movements and of women's politics. These are the questions which will be addressed in the following discussion of the period between 1945 and 1951.

However, if one is to analyse organisations with an exclusively female membership one cannot restrict the investigation to social movements. The formation of an organisation on the basis of gender does not explain precisely why the people concerned thought it so important to declare their demands publicly at a given time. In general, men are more ready than women to believe that the female role is socially constructed, yet it is not men who form the backbone of the women's movement. The fact that an organisation consists of women only does not make it any more democratic than one made up exclusively of men. However, when it turns out that the professionals within the women's organisations – such as the public notaries and lawyers who played key roles in mediating between society and the women's organisations formed to defend women's interests – were exclusively men, then it is clearly our task to analyse the given power relations within that society.

The organisations created by women were not completely independent but were often part of other social movements. Women who joined religious organisations or movements formed within the national framework also formulated objectives connected to their female identity, though these objectives admittedly took the shape of demands for the recognition of the importance of motherhood and the family. Similarly, it would be misleading to measure women's political participation and influence by the same yardstick as that used for men. 'Politics' has always meant different things for women than for men. Women were completely excluded from party politics in Hungary until the first introduction of partial suffrage in 1918. Universal suffrage was achieved only in 1945, so that it would be illusory to talk of women exerting any kind of direct parliamentary political pressure before that date. Instead of politics, we should think in terms of 'political opportunities', of occasions when women's organisations figured in the public arena.

The size of the women's organisations varied from small to truly massive. However, they cannot be judged merely on the basis of numerical size: a small group of female doctors, for example, could, in certain situations, have a greater influence than the mass membership of the Communist women's organisation.

In the literature on social movements, the establishment of women's organisations in the nineteenth century is seen as the unlooked-for result of modernisation. An upper and a middle class came into existence that had sufficient material wealth and leisure time to found women's organisations. The first organisations were ameliorative – that is, they were formed by women who wanted to improve conditions for the poor, the elderly, or children. Next came revolutionary organisations, which can also be seen as a product of modernisation, urbanisation and industrialisation. The mass involvement of women in paid employment and the inequalities experienced in the workplace then resulted in the creation of Social Democrat feminist women's organisations at the end of the nineteenth century.[5] Social and economic processes played an important role in the recognition of the female identity during the second wave of feminism. The example set by the first women's movements and the importance of personal continuity deserve attention in this respect.

The first women's organisations in Hungary were created before the reform age in the early nineteenth century and thus involved aristocratic women. The charitable organisations or 'women's clubs' started by these women also served as examples to the lower strata of society. The aims of these charitable societies were formulated in a 'maternal framework', stressing women's role as the preservers of the family. At the same time, their role was connected with the social welfare of the nation, since the nation was depicted as a great family. The connection between the maternal framework and the national framework ensured that the women's societies were favourably received in the influential strata of society.

Formed in parallel with these societies were women's religious organisations. Their aims were also formulated in the context of the 'maternal framework', with the addition of missionary goals. Of particular importance among the religious societies for women were the Jewish women's associations, which played a major role in the history of Hungary's Jewish population.[6]

269

By the end of the nineteenth century, a certain prestige attached to participation in women's organisations among the upper strata of Hungarian society.
However, a change was brought about in this situation with the creation of the
'revolutionary' women's organisations, such as trade unions, and the acceptance of women as equal members of men's Social Democrat organisations.
With the creation of the Female Civil Servants' Association (*Nőtisztviselők*), and
later of the Feminists' Association (*Feminista Egyesület*), intellectual middle-
class women's groups were established which, up until the First World War,
voiced their demands alongside the progressive political forces within Hungary.
Their aim was the elimination of laws discriminating against women, and their
main focus was the struggle for women's suffrage. The presence of women in
the professional sphere brought with it demands for 'equality for difference'.
These demands were formulated by women's organisations established by the
female representatives of the various professions.

The history of women's suffrage in Hungary after the First World War is itself
an example of how a demand within the 'framework of equality' manifested
itself as part of the 'national framework'. The period following the First World
War brought changes to women's organisations on many fronts.[7] The achievement of partial women's suffrage meant that women were able to enter politics
for the first time as members of parliament. General demands for a revision of
the Treaty of Trianon – which had imposed new borders on Hungary in 1920,
drastically reducing the country's territory – meant that the 'national framework' became the only framework acceptable at the public level. Attempts to
realise a programme drawn up according to the 'maternal framework' could
thus take place only within the national context. At the same time, the 'revolutionary' organisations survived, although their membership decreased and
they became invisible in public discourse. The activities of both the Communist
and feminist organisations after 1919 were typically carried out in the context
of these 'submerged networks'. Many previously large and influential organisations were reduced in size and significance. Their membership decreased to just
a chosen few, while at the same time a centralised organisational structure
became necessary to ensure their survival. The activities pursued by the 'submerged network' were narrowed down primarily to cultural events, which
allowed the most dedicated members to maintain a double identity. The similarity in world-view of the feminists and Communists in their joint but separate
cultural activities became clear. Good and tight-knit personal relations were
typical among their memberships.

After the First World War, with the women's organisations now able to formulate their aims in terms of the 'national framework', the women's question
was discovered by national conservatism. National loyalty and the revisionist
struggle brought about the first women's mass movement within the 'maternal
framework' that also achieved popularity within the national framework.
A further change was the appearance of the 'party framework'. Attempts to
renew the National Unity Party (*Nemzeti Egység Pártja*) and the Christian

Women's Camp (*Keresztény Női Tábor*) led to the mobilisation of women.[8] As a result of the major economic crisis, the role of the state increased in the sphere of social welfare. This brought with it a reduction in the role of civil and religious charitable societies, although the activities of such societies were not made entirely redundant.

During the Second World War, women's organisations became polarised according to the extent of their identification with the 'national framework'. The Social Democrats joined the organisations of the 'submerged network' after the German invasion of Hungary in 1944, as did religious and other civil organisations .

The picture after 1945 would at first sight appear simple: the Second World War had brought about the eradication of the previous network of women's organisations, and a mass movement in the shape of the MNDSZ was established that mobilised women in a manner accordant with Communist ideals.

The year 1945 was one of new beginnings and of rebuilding. This was the golden age of the 'submerged network'. The tried and tested members of the Communist women's movements, reinforced by those returning home from emigration in Moscow or Western Europe, immediately drew up a programme and established an organisation. The 'revolutionary-equality framework' that had previously been pushed so hard was transformed after the 1945 elections, and elements of the 'maternal framework' appeared, particularly in the campaigns for the repatriation of prisoners-of-war.

The Social Democrats, who were traditionally the representatives of workers' radicalism, also joined the 'revolutionary framework'. With their organisational and theoretical experience and their well-established operational structure, they tried to carve out a niche for themselves in the 'revolutionary-equality framework'. However, in political practice they were careful to refer neither to the 'maternal' nor to the 'national' framework. It was vital for each of the organisations to get its members into well-paid positions, but the Social Democrats were increasingly unable to do so and, as a result, failed to retain the support of their younger members.

In the case of the feminists, the tactics of the 'submerged network', which had worked so well between the wars, did not prove so effective after the Second World War. The general democratisation of the country and the achievement of general suffrage for women in 1945 meant that the feminists lost ground. Inter-generational conflicts and the class struggle made it difficult for the Feminists' Association and the MNDSZ to co-operate: the average age of Feminists' Association members was much higher than that of members of the MNDSZ, and the fact that the leadership and membership of the two organisations came from different social backgrounds only added to the tensions. The mission of those involved in the 'submerged network' had been to keep ideas alive in order to be able to strike when the time was right. However, the struggle was no longer theirs. No one needed the feminists' experience, yet the centralised structure of their organisation, its identity as an accepted element of the

women organisations run parallel to communists ideas (handwritten margin note)

'submerged network' and the cultural values it upheld, meant that the Feminists' Association continued to survive for some time.

Women's organisations operating within the 'maternal–national' framework were banned in the wake of the Armistice of 1945. The activities of organisations within the 'maternal framework' were reduced since the membership no longer had either the time or the means to continue its charitable work. The social prestige of ameliorative work was reduced to a minimum as the MNDSZ, supported by the MKP, assumed control in this area. As a result of the Communist take-over, the middle and upper middle class as well as any institutional networks that had previously been independent of the state – including schools, hospitals and public libraries – ceased to exist.

As for the members of these organisations, those who had belonged to 'national framework' movements were left powerless and would have had no public role even if they had remained in the country rather than opting for emigration. Nor were 'maternal framework' organisations able to attract new members either: those who wished to be active turned towards the MNDSZ, which had dynamic policies and influential supporters. If one looks at the leadership of the various women's associations in the immediate post-war period it becomes obvious that it was largely made up of members of the middle and older generation. This was the generation that had lived through revolutionary changes in women's lives – changes such as the increase in the number of opportunities for employment and education. However, these women were now somewhat out of touch with political life. Meanwhile, the religious associations, including their female membership, took up the fight in the '*Kulturkampf*' against the 'revolutionary' Communist–Social Democrat coalition, but without success.

With the dominance of the 'revolutionary-equality' framework, the rich political experience of Hungarian women was deemed irrelevant, indeed detrimental. Neither formulating new objectives nor resorting to previous tactics was now of any avail. Women's identity was given a new content.

Women's enfranchisement in Hungary took place without the active participation of either women's organisations or female politicians. The political elite executed the requirements of the Yalta agreement. There is no evidence in the documents of the women's secretariats of the various parties to suggest that they exerted any political pressure for the presence of female politicians in parliament. Even so, by the time the Provisional Government was established in 1944, the number of female politicians had risen from one or two to twelve, and after the 1945 elections this figure rose to fourteen. After the 1947 elections there were twenty-two female politicians, and by 1949 there were seventy-one, some 17 per cent of all MPs. In 1953 only fifty-two women sat in the by then completely powerless parliament, representing 17 per cent of the total.

The claim that male politicians introduced female enfranchisement only as part of the general democratisation and transformation programme in order to take the wind out of their sails is borne out by the words of Mihály Farkas, which illustrate why the present writer does not regard him as a champion of feminism in Hungary: 'The women's camp is still the Achilles heel of Hungarian democracy.' What did he mean by the term 'women's camp'? We know that women made up more than half the population. Furthermore, we know that the 1945 elections were the first, and the last, in which voting preferences were indicated by gender (the colour of the ballot papers being different for the two sexes). The results were unambiguous – the Communist Party came last in the competition for women's votes. Of the votes cast by women alone, the MKP received 15 per cent, the MSZDP 17 per cent, the National Peasant Party 6 per cent and the Smallholders 60 per cent in the first democratic general election.[9] Until the elections of 1947, Hungarian women were stigmatised by an increasingly powerful Communist Party as politically backward and as riding on a reactionary bandwagon. Beyond mere stigmatisation, which was led by the highly politically conscious female activists within the Communist Party, such as the elegant Mrs Révai (one of this group of women and the wife of a powerful Communist party ideologist), who, in her disappointment that women had not rushed to embrace the one true way, even went so far as to call the intellectual capacities of Hungarian women generally inferior. Mátyás Rákosi's sober political calculations went yet further, and from 1945 the Communist Party was highly successful in mobilising women in the various strata of Hungarian society. The results of this mobilisation cannot, of course, be measured precisely since election data broken down according to gender do not exist. However, this mobilisation, which was concurrently taking place in neighbouring countries, served as an important contributing factor in the formation of the Communist system.

In order to mobilise women, the first requirement was the creation of passivity – that is, the establishment of control over the activities of the Hungarian women's organisations. This was achieved by means of the MNDSZ, which infiltrated the women's organisations and then disbanded them. On the basis of data from 1946, excluding the big national women's movements, there were, according to the present writer's calculations, several women's organisations with over 1,600 members that were in the process of applying to re-form. Law No. I of 1946 recognised the incontrovertible right of citizens to assemble, although at the same time another law placed responsibility for all organisations in the hands of the Minister of the Interior. The Ministry of the Interior was controlled by the Communist Party, and the minister used his power, and the help of an increasingly influential police force, steadily and gradually to ban these organisations. Law No. XLIII, which came into effect on 26 November 1948, granted equal rights to women. By the time the Constitution of 1949 had recognised the right of all workers to freedom of association, all women's organisations – including the most significant one, the women's division of the Social Democratic Party – had officially merged with the MNDSZ.

The other method of winning over the 'women's camp' was through active politics. This role, too, was fulfilled by the MNDSZ, which, although it claimed to

[handwritten margin note: communist party began control organi]

be independent from party politics, was in fact directed and influenced by the Communist Party. Those legal political parties that had existed before 1945 continued their political activities on behalf of women from where they had left off in March 1944. However, as a new party, the case of the MKP was different. By operating its own women's section it, too, formally fulfilled the requirements, but it was under the direction of this highly efficient party that the only women's organisation founded after 1945, the MNDSZ, operated. At the beginning of 1945 the MKP experimented by establishing a united women's and youth movement, but this was opposed by both the Social Democrats and the Smallholders and met with initial failure.[10] In contrast to other women's organisations, the MNDSZ did not have to contend with financial or legal problems. The mobilisation of the 'women's camp' led not only to various charitable and training projects; the MNDSZ emerged as an organisation that mobilised women and brought them out into the streets to campaign for political goals. On 6 December 1946, for example, there was a protest by housewives against rising prices.

The Hungarian women's associations did not provide women with any help in breaking out from the private domain into the public sphere. In fact, they actually preserved this dichotomy between the public and the private by clearly defining the scope of women's activities. This trap might have been avoided in two possible ways: either by joining an already existing political party or by creating a new movement. The latter course had been pursued by the Feminists' Association since 1904, with some limited success. After 1945, however, the leaders of the newly founded MNDSZ did not have a particularly favourable opinion of their 'sisters'. They considered them old-fashioned and regarded their aims as outdated. However, the MNDSZ tried to show that they cared about women's role in society and also that they were bringing something new to the political arena. This was probably true in the case of their attitude towards women's work. Nevertheless, in reality their view of the role of women in society remained as traditional as that of any other political party.

From the beginning of 1948 the main issue was the creation of women's unity, and this resulted in a purge within the MNDSZ leadership. However, inter-generational conflicts plagued the MNDSZ as it had its predecessor organisations. Prior to 1949 it had been members of the middle-aged generation who were involved in social projects, most of them having gained experience in women's associations abroad during their time in exile (mainly in Germany or Austria, then in France and the Soviet Union). After 1949, new cadres emerged who were younger – mainly under twenty-five. These women generally lacked experience and education and came mostly from rural areas. This younger generation pushed out the older, mainly intellectual middle-class women from the women's organisations. By the end of 1949 the MNDSZ leadership had been completely transformed and hardly any intellectuals remained. The new cadres reshaped their organisation along Soviet lines. The fact that women really did now play an incomparably greater role in daily life was of little importance: order did not improve. Mihály Farkas was wrong even in this regard.

Theoretical issues of women's participation in
post-1945 politics in Hungary

This chapter has sought to shed light on a previously unknown area of Hungarian women's history, namely, the policies on women of the main political parties in Hungary after 1945, which have until now been at the periphery of political history. The opening up of the relevant archives made possible research into the period between 1945 and 1951. From two points of view, the year 1951 marks the end of an era; it was then that the last women's association representing civil society ceased its operations, and it was then that the MDP adopted the guiding principles of its new policy on women. This Stalinist policy on women lasted for only a short time in Hungary, but it had an enormous effect on society. The periodisation of women's history does not always correspond with the generally accepted periodisation, which is based on important political events – as Joan Kelly, in her pioneering essay on the Renaissance, has shown.[11] The present study, based on hitherto unexplored archival sources from the much-debated era of 1945–51, attempts to enrich our knowledge in this area.

After 1945, the extent of women's political representation became the measure of democracy. In earlier years, democracy had been the privilege of the few, and limited suffrage meant that it worked 'selectively'. The democratisation that took place after 1945 brought with it 'elected' democracy. One characteristic of 'selective' democracy was that the social groups excluded from the political parties tried to exert pressure on 'selectively' chosen political decision-makers by forming associations and other organisations in the civil sphere. However, when it comes to 'elected' political representation, the pressure exerted by these civil groups, and their supervisory role, necessarily decreases and can exert itself once again only in a political crisis.

The post-war political system in Hungary shifted from 'selective' political representation to 'elected' representation. Thus it would have been entirely natural for the network of civil organisations to become weaker, even if the Communist-run Ministry of the Interior had not forced this process by every legal and illegal means available. At the same time, the electoral roll, which was drawn up according to political criteria, reduced the number of eligible voters. Meanwhile, the elimination and banning of political parties homogenised the political representation of different social groups.

We shall now sum up the theoretical issues relating to women's political representation and attempt to analyse these as they apply to the period between 1945 and 1951.

One of the basic theoretical issues in connection with women's political representation is the relationship between formal political parties and informal civil organisations. Many have taken the view that formal party politics is a man's world and it is illusory to try to achieve women's representation within it, unlike in civil organisations, where women can achieve more authentic representation.

However, we must agree with Ruth Lister's argument that 'the value of informal politics does not provide an alibi for the continued under-representation of women and minority groups in the formal structures of power'.[12] Women should have political representation in both spheres and, in addition, the two structures should be such as to strengthen and support one another effectively.

In post-1945 Hungary, as the present chapter has sought to show, the existing network of women's associations was liquidated by a system based on representational democracy – partly for political reasons, and partly because a quasi-civil organisation, the MNDSZ, was established, which promised to mobilise women at the non-party political level. At the same time, there was no constructive contact between the political parties and the parties' female membership; female politicians did not become 'women's politicians'.

The other important question with respect to women's political representation concerns the 'multi-layeredness' of political power. According to Joni Lovenduski, 'the representation of a group's interests has two dimensions: the presence of its members in decision-making arenas and the consideration of its interests in the decision-making process'.[13] Thus in the first form of representation the proportion of women and men requires to be reflected in parliament – in other words, half the representatives should be women. Anthony Birch believes that the endeavour to cause more women to take part in the activity of political institutions is in fact characteristic of a multi-faceted type of political representation – the representative body itself consists of many social groups, the political interests of which it undertakes to promote.[14] However, this approach questions the basis on which these interest groups are formed by asking what it is that qualifies the representatives of society as a whole: ethnic origin, gender, occupation, or membership of a religious or linguistic minority? Anne Phillips believes that this type of thinking represents a *'reductio ad absurdum'*, since it is not clear how far one can follow this proportional principle.[15] Representational democracy cannot totally reflect social reality; only direct democracy, parliament as a body elected by all citizens, can ensure this.

The number of women politicians in the 1945 parliament and later parliaments in Hungary was very far removed from the social reality, in that, as a result of the war, women represented the electoral majority. I would emphasise, in analysing political life in Hungary, that in parliamentary decision-making their party loyalty was of primary importance. At the same time, the real decisions were not made in the parliamentary parties but in the narrow leading circles of the parties where, with the exception of Anna Kéthly, there were no women, or at the coalition negotiation meetings, to which the parties did not send female delegates.

From the second part of Lovenduski's definition it follows that, theoretically, it is not only women who can represent women's interests; men can do so as well. At the same time, social experience proves that women make more effective representatives of women's interests. This is what Anne Phillips calls 'the politics of presence', pointing out that 'women's perspectives need to be articulated directly in political debate and decision making'.[16]

A further theoretical question arises in regard to women's political representation: In decision-making institutions, should we regard women as a separate interest group? Do women have separate common interests that need to be represented? Anne Phillips believes that women do have separate interests, since they 'occupy a materially different position in society' than their male counterparts.[17] Lister maintains that these interests 'potentially conflict with those of men',[18] which is why there is a need for direct women's representation in order that women can represent their own interests in decision-making governmental bodies rather than entrusting them to men. Policy on women after 1945 was characterised by the fact that the decisive initiating and supervisory role belonged to the men. The women's departments or sections of individual political parties, without exception, ranked lower in the party hierarchy. Women politicians did not even have the autonomy to determine the issues that were important to them and that were ripe for solution. Approval always had to come from above – as, for example, in the case of the campaigns on behalf of the POWs. The low level of realisation of women's interests also had to do with women's lack of political experience. Although the various political parties had trained female politicians in varying numbers, a deliberate policy of cadre training was typical only of the MNDSZ, though its purpose in developing women's identity and autonomy was not without a certain amount of ambiguity.

The notion of political representation is related to the question of responsibility and of the independence of representatives. How should political representatives act? Should they represent their electors, or the public good in a broader sense? This duality is referred to in the literature as 'the paradox of representation'.[19] Both types can be effective and acceptable in various situations, as Birch points out: 'What establishes their status as representatives is that they have been appointed by a certain process of election.'[20] In the case of women, issues of responsibility and autonomy are even more closely linked. Should an elected woman primarily represent the interests of women? Can votes won by a woman representative as a woman be separated from those won by her as a party politician representing a certain political viewpoint?

In Hungarian political life after 1945 it was the Smallholders in 1945 and the Communists in 1947 who targeted women's votes by deliberately including a high proportion of women candidates on their lists, or at least by stressing women's rhetoric in their electoral campaigns. This conscious policy can be seen to have borne fruit in the shape of the high numbers of votes, primarily women's votes, that they received.

Women could obtain political power only through the political parties. Phillips believes that 'within representative democracy it is the political parties that provide the vehicle for representation',[21] and hence they offer a means by which women can enter the inner circles of political life. In democratic countries political parties have a defining role in the formation of the electorate's behaviour, in the selection of representatives and in the definition of the government agenda. Women in political parties often do not understand, or move with difficulty among, regulations that are strange to them, but this is the only way in which to realise women's interests. Given that, for the time being, women politicians are in a minority in parliament, women representing women's interests often find themselves facing the risk of marginalisation even within their own political party. This is the case particularly when the representation of women's interests is not supported by the whole of society. We must not forget the general stereotype of politics as something in which women should not indulge. Those women who become representatives have to be careful not to admit openly their representation of women's matters, since by doing so they reinforce their own second-class status.[22]

After 1945, the historically unique situation in Hungary meant that women's suffrage was broadened in the framework of the general democratisation of the country. The nature of political parties, the mechanisms of political power and the lack of high-calibre women politicians prevented the 'matriarchy born of need' from being transformed into political fact, even though in the 1945 and 1947 elections the electorate were able to choose from among political alternatives, albeit to an ever lesser extent. The 1949 elections differed from the previous two in that by then there were no political alternatives. The policy on women adopted in 1951 began to denote a 'conservative revolution' in women's politics.[23]

Notes

1 This chapter is based on Andrea Pető, 'Women's associations in Hungary: Mobilisation and demobilisation, 1945–1951', in Claire Duchen and Irene Bandhauer-Schöffmann (eds), *When the War was Over: Women, War and Peace in Europe, 1940–1956* (Leicester, 2000), 132–46 and Andrea Pető, 'Hungarian women in politics', in Joan Scott, Cora Kaplan and Debra Keats (eds), *Transitions, Environments, Translations: The Meanings of Feminism in Contemporary Politics* (New York, 1997), 153–61.

2 Andrea Pető, *Nőhistóriak. A politizáló nők történetéből, 1945–1951* (Budapest, 1998), 183; Andrea Pető, 'Writing women's history', *Open Society News* (Fall 1994), 10–11; Andrea Pető, *Hungarian Women in Politics 1945–51* (New York, 2003).

3 Joan Scott, 'Gender as a tool of historical analysis', in Joan Scott (ed.), *Feminism and History* (Oxford, 1996), 152–83.

4 Politikatörténeti Intézet Levéltára (Institute of Political History Archive, hereafter PIA), speech by Mihály Farkas on 10 November 1947 at the Budapest Women's Congress: 276.19.3, 113. Mihály Farkas (1904–65) was a printer and a member of the underground Communist movement in Czechoslovakia before 1945. After 1945 he was a member of the Party's Political Committee. Between 1948 and 1953 he was Minister of Defence and was responsible for political purges in Hungary.

5 Judit Szapor, 'Les associations féministes en Hongrie, XIXe–XXe siècle', in *Penelope pour l'histoire des femmes*, 11 (1984), 169–74; Susan Zimmermann, 'Frauenbestrebungen und Frauenbewegungen in Ungarn: Zur Organisationsgeschichte der Jahre

1848–1918', in Bea Nagy and Margit S. Sárdi (eds), *Szerep és alkotás* (Debrecen, 1997), 171–205; Andrea Pető, 'A missing piece? How women in the Communist nomenclature are not remembering', *East European Politics and Society*, 16:3 (2003), 948–58.

6 See also, Andrea Pető, 'Ungarszkie jevreiki mezsdu Holokauszta i sztalinizma, Organizacii na ungarszki jevreiki v Ungarija cled Vtorota svetovna voina 1945–1951', in Kracimira Daskalova and Raina Gavrilova (eds), *Granicci na grazsdansztvoto: evropeiski zseni mezsdu tradicijata i modernocta* (Sofia, 2001), 302–18; Andrea Pető, 'Continuity and change: Hungarian women's organisations', in Helena Flamm (ed.), *Pink, Purple, Green: Women's Religious, Environmental and Gay–Lesbian Movements in Central Europe Today* (New York, 2001), 47–57; Andrea Pető, 'The history of the women's movement in Hungary', in Rosi Braidotti and Gabriele Griffin (eds), *Thinking Differently: A Reader in European Women's Studies* (London, 2002), 361–72.

7 Andrea Pető, 'Kontinuität und Wandel in der ungarischen Frauenbewegung der Zwischenkriegsperiode', in Ute Gerhard (ed.), *Feminismus und Demokratie: Europäische Frauenbewegung der 1920er Jahre* (Königstein, 2001), 138–59.

8 József Vonyó, 'Női szerepek a Nemzeti Egység Pártjában (1932–1939)', in Nagy and Sárdi (eds), *Szerep és alkotás*, 279–90.

9 Sándor Balogh, *Választások Magyarországon. 1945: A fővárosi törvényhatósági és a nemzetgyulési választások* (Budapest, 1984), 157.

10 Sándor Balogh, *Parlamenti és pártharcok Magyarországon 1945–47* (Budapest, 1975), 57.

11 Joan Kelly, 'Did women have a renaissance?', reprinted in Joan Kelly, *Women, history and theory. The essays of Joan Kelly* (Chicago, 1984), 19–50.

12 Ruth Lister, *Citizenship: Feminist Perspectives* (London, 1997), 155.

13 Joni Lovenduski, 'Introduction: the dynamics of gender and party', in Joni Lovenduski and Pippa Norris (eds), *Gender and Party Politics* (Thousand Oaks, CA, 1993), 2.

14 Anthony H. Birch, *The Concepts and Theories of Modern Democracy* (London, 1993), 72.

15 Anne Phillips, *Engendering Democracy* (Cambridge, 1991), 65.

16 *Ibid.*, 155.

17 *Ibid.*, 70. See also Elisabeth Fox-Genovese, *Feminism without Illusions* (London, 1991), 56.

18 Lister, *Citizenship*, 155.

19 Birch, *The Concepts and Theories of Modern Democracy*, 70.

20 *Ibid.*.

21 Phillips, *Engendering Democracy*, 77.

22 Lister, *Citizenship*, 157.

23 For more on this point see: Andrea Pető, 'Lebensumstände der Arbeiter in einem Grosswerk in den 1950er Jahren', in *Acta Historica Academiae Scientiarum Hungaricae* (Budapest), 35 (1989), 251–65; Andrea Pető, 'As he saw her: Gender politics in secret party reports in Hungary during the 1950s', in *CEU History Department Working Paper Series* no. 11994, 107–21; Andrea Pető, 'Family life and the social position of women in the 1950s', in Judit Forrai (ed.), *Civilization, Sexuality and Social Life in Hidden Context – Hidden Faces of Urban Life* (Budapest, 1996), 181–90; Chris Corrin, *Magyar Women: Hungarian Women's Lives, 1960–1990s* (New York, 1994).

Index